The First Amendment
and LGBT Equality

The First Amendment and LGBT Equality

A Contentious History

Carlos A. Ball

Harvard University Press

Cambridge, Massachusetts
London, England
2017

Second printing

Library of Congress Cataloging-in-Publication Data

Names: Ball, Carlos A., author.
Title: The First Amendment and LGBT equality : a contentious history / Carlos
   A. Ball.
Description: Cambridge, Massachusetts : Harvard University Press, 2017. |
   Includes bibliographical references and index.
Identifiers: LCCN 2016043742 | ISBN 9780674972193
Subjects: LCSH: Sexual minorities—Legal status, laws, etc.—United
   States—History—20th century. | Gay rights—United States—History—20th
   century. | Freedom of expression—United States—History—20th century. |
   Discrimination—Law and legislation—United States—History—20th century.
   | United States. Constitution. 1st Amendment.
Classification: LCC KF4754.5 .B35 2017 | DDC 342.7308/7—dc23
LC record available at https://lccn.loc.gov/2016043742

To my tía Annette and my tío Rafael,
and to my tío Tony and my tía Katia

Contents

The First Amendment
and LGBT Equality

Introduction

SUPPORTERS of the lesbian, gay, bisexual, and transgender (LGBT) rights movement have for several decades emphasized claims to equality and privacy, viewing them as the bases for the greater acceptance of sexual minorities in our society.[1] During that time, considerations of equality and privacy have displaced earlier reliance on the First Amendment as a source of protection for sexual minorities. To the extent that contemporary LGBT rights supporters give much consideration to the First Amendment, they tend to view it as an impediment to, rather than a facilitator of, the attainment of movement objectives. This is because, for several years now, it has been LGBT rights *opponents* who have regularly raised free speech, free association, and religious liberty claims to try to limit the government's ability to promote LGBT equality.

In many ways, the LGBT movement's recent failure to prioritize First Amendment rights is understandable given that, unlike in previous decades, government officials today rarely try to limit the expressive and associational rights of sexual minorities. Nonetheless, an exclusive focus on the equality and privacy implications of contemporary LGBT rights disputes occludes the crucial role that the First Amendment has played in creating the political, social, and legal conditions that have permitted sexuality-based identities and communities to form and thrive while allowing the LGBT movement to achieve many of its objectives. Protections related to free speech and association have allowed LGBT individuals to better understand their sexuality, to find each other and form identity-based bonds, to highlight and criticize discriminatory government policies and social norms, and to organize politically in order to provide sexual minorities with many of the legal rights and protections long available to heterosexuals. Even though the LGBT movement today largely takes First Amendment protections for granted, the story of how those rights were initially claimed and enforced, making possible the free and diverse forms of expression and association currently enjoyed by sexual minorities in the United States, merits greater exploration.[2] There has also been insufficient recognition of how the First Amendment successes of the earlier LGBT movement made possible the more recent equality and privacy gains, including the abolition of sodomy laws, the enactment of antidiscrimination laws, and the attainment of marriage equality. One of this book's objectives is to give the First Amendment the credit it deserves for making possible many of the LGBT movement's successes.

But, as the book also explores, the relationship between the LGBT movement and the First Amendment does not move only in one direction; the amendment, to put it simply, does not only give to the movement—it also takes. That is, the amendment, and its corresponding principles and values, not only have made it possible for the movement to attain some of its most important objectives, it has also to some extent limited the ability of the government to promote LGBT equality. Social and religious conservatives have grounded much of their recent opposition to LGBT rights measures, most prominently the recognition of same-sex marriages, in the claim that considerations related to free speech, association, and the free exercise of religion place significant limits on the government's authority to promote LGBT equality. As this book seeks to show, in order to fully understand the relationship between the First Amendment and LGBT rights, it is necessary to explore how the amendment has been used by *both* sides to achieve their legal and political objectives.

The book is divided into two parts. Part I, "From the First Amendment to LGBT Equality," explores how the early LGBT movement, at a time when sexual minorities had few legal rights of any kind, was able to gain crucial First Amendment protections that permitted LGBT people to start speaking about and associating around shared experiences, oppressions, and objectives. Part II, "From LGBT Equality to the First Amendment," explores how social and religious conservatives have turned to First Amendment principles and values to try to counteract and slow down the nation's growing embrace of equal rights for sexual minorities.[3]

The book begins with the use by government officials of obscenity laws in the 1950s and 1960s to censor gay publications, efforts that led the Supreme Court for the first time to rule in cases involving the interests of LGBT people.[4] The book ends with the push by LGBT rights opponents, more than fifty years later, to gain religious exemptions from LGBT equality measures for religious organizations, small business owners, and government employees. These two sets of controversies, as well as the many other disputes explored in the book that took place during the intervening decades, reveal the interplay between the First Amendment and LGBT equality. As the book makes clear, it is impossible, both as a descriptive and normative matter, to understand the role that First Amendment rights have played in the context of LGBT issues without continuously grappling with questions of equality, including the rights of sexual minorities to equal treatment, the obligations that those rights impose on the state, and the constitutional and statutory limits on the ability of the state to promote equality. To put it differently, First Amendment issues, on the one hand, and questions of whether, how, and to what extent the state should guarantee equality to sexual minorities, on the other hand, have been inextricably linked since the early days of the LGBT movement in the United States.

The objective of Part I is to explain how the exercise of First Amendment rights made it possible for the LGBT movement, first, to begin articulating equality claims and, second, to start gaining meaningful equality protections for sexual minorities. The book's first three chapters explore the historical contexts, and explain the social, political, and legal consequences, of LGBT activists' exercise of First Amendment rights during the movement's early decades in three areas: the publication of political and erotic gay magazines (Chapter 1); the formation of LGBT organizations (Chapter 2); and the coming out by LGBT individuals (Chapter 3). Constitutional litigation played a crucial role in all three of these settings as activists challenged, usually successfully, government efforts to restrict the ability of sexual minorities to express themselves and to associate with each other. The judicial recognition of sexual minorities' First Amendment rights during the early days of the LGBT rights movement contributed to the upsurge in lesbian and gay publications in the 1960s and 1970s; to the explosive growth of LGBT organizations of every kind (including political, social, artistic, and religious) in the 1970s and the 1980s; and to the growing number of LGBT individuals throughout this period who made the personal and political decision to come out of the closet. One of the most striking aspects of this history is the extent to which LGBT people were able to gain First Amendment protections at a time when neither constitutional nor statutory law provided sexual minorities with any meaningful protection from public or private discrimination. This history shows the ways in which the exercise of First Amendment rights can contribute to identity formation by stigmatized minorities while laying the groundwork for the initial articulation of equality claims and the later attainment of equality objectives.[5]

The focus of Chapter 1 is on the law of obscenity, its deployment against sexual minorities, and how the Supreme Court, several years before Stonewall, sided with gay claimants in two important, but now largely forgotten, obscenity cases. Although the two cases constitute the first LGBT rights victories before the Court, their outcome had little to do with the rights of LGBT people as such and much to do with the process of moral displacement within obscenity law that had been taking place for several years. By "moral displacement," I mean the courts' growing skepticism that the government's interest in promoting public morality granted it virtually untrammeled discretion to regulate books, magazines, and other materials that contained sexual ideas, themes, and depictions.

The changes in obscenity law contributed to the growing availability of same-sex political and erotic materials during the 1960s, and therefore to the formation and strengthening of LGBT identities and communities. The moral displacement within obscenity law also helped sexual minorities advocate on behalf of a new understanding of sexual morality and to begin articulating claims for equal treatment and full citizenship.

Chapter 2 focuses on the role that the exercise of the right of association by LGBT activists played in the movement's early period. The years leading up to Stonewall saw an increased resistance by gay activists to government campaigns of harassment and intimidation targeted at sexual minorities who dared to come together in public, particularly in bars. The resistance led a handful of courts to recognize that sexual minorities had the right to congregate in public. The resistance also reflected the beginning of a new phenomenon in American life: the willingness of a growing number of LGBT people to band together to form organizations aimed at protecting themselves from government intimidation and discrimination.

The chapter explores how early activists were able to gain court victories in some jurisdictions that limited the ability of government officials to close down bars and other public establishments simply because they allowed LGBT people to congregate. In addition, Chapter 2 explains how harassment by police departments and liquor license investigators of sexual minorities who congregated in lesbian and gay bars sparked political organizing and mobilizing by LGBT people. In turn, in the years leading up to Stonewall, it became clear that this organizing and mobilizing, in response to government harassment, was protected by the First Amendment.

In the 1970s, growing numbers of sexual minorities pursued common objectives by creating a wide variety of LGBT organizations. As also explored in Chapter 2, some government officials tried to place roadblocks in the new groups' paths in order to minimize their effectiveness and diminish their visibility. This was particularly reflected in the refusal by administrators at some public universities to recognize LGBT student groups and in the efforts by officials to prevent LGBT groups from enjoying the benefits of incorporation and of participation in public forums. But the courts consistently ruled that such efforts were unconstitutional under the First Amendment. At a time when sexual minorities as a class enjoyed few other constitutional rights, they won almost every time they relied on the First Amendment to challenge government actions aimed at making it more difficult for them to find mutual support, and pursue common goals, by coming together in groups.

By the late 1970s, hundreds of LGBT organizations had sprung up throughout the country, groups that constituted the movement's backbone. The organizations served as vehicles through which sexual minorities, in a variety of contexts and ways, amplified their individual voices in challenging how society understood and regulated sexual minorities, their relationships, and their sexual conduct.

Chapter 3 explores a new category of LGBT employment discrimination cases involving public sector employees that surfaced in the 1970s. While most of the cases before Stonewall involved firings that followed the arrest of gay civil servants (usually for engaging in same-sex sexual solicitation or conduct), most of the post-Stonewall dismissals followed the employees' voluntary disclosure of their sexual orientation (that is, their coming out of the closet). The fact that government agencies moved to terminate employees after they *voluntarily* revealed their sexual orientation made it possible, for the first time, to start using the First Amendment to provide some protection from discrimination to LGBT government workers. Although the LGBT litigants did not always succeed in these cases, some prevailed, demonstrating that the First Amendment could play an important role in protecting the rights of sexual minorities to self-identify. And when courts ruled against the LGBT plaintiffs, they did so in generally strained, convoluted, and unpersuasive ways that failed to afford sexual minorities the same kinds of speech protections enjoyed by heterosexuals.

After discussing free speech cases involving gay employees, Chapter 3 explores the historical intersection of free speech and self-identification in two other contexts. First, it discusses how LGBT activists in California in the 1970s exercised their First Amendment rights to defeat a ballot box initiative aimed at keeping lesbian, gay, and bisexual public school teachers in the closet. Second, it explores an important First Amendment challenge brought by a male teenager in Rhode Island in 1980 after his high school prohibited him from bringing a male date to his senior prom.

The courts' repeated willingness to recognize and enforce the First Amendment rights of sexual minorities contributed to the fact that by the 1980s, government officials rarely attempted to directly interfere with the ability of LGBT individuals to express themselves and to join collectively to pursue common objectives. There was, however, one important and troubling exception to this governmental restraint: the military's policy excluding lesbian, gay, and bisexual service members, in particular the Don't Ask, Don't Tell (DADT) version of the policy first implemented in 1993. The DADT policy purported to allow sexual minorities to serve in the armed forces (the "don't ask" part), while simultaneously requiring them to remain silent about their sexual orientation (the "don't tell" part). As detailed in the first section of Chapter 4, DADT raised serious First Amendment concerns, both because it greatly limited the ability of sexual minorities in the armed forces to participate in public discourse and because it interfered with their rights to autonomy and self-determination. Unfortunately, most courts in the military context were unwilling to do what many courts had done in the civilian context: strike down state action that interfered with the ability of sexual minorities to be open about their sexuality.

Although the courts forewent their role as guardians of free speech rights in the DADT context, it is important to keep in mind that LGBT rights activism has never been limited to the filing of constitutional lawsuits. Indeed, if we were to focus only on constitutional litigation, we would reach the conclusion that (outside of the military arena) by the 1980s, the First Amendment began playing a relatively minor role in the pursuit of LGBT rights objectives. This is because (again, outside of the military context) government officials by that time rarely took direct steps to interfere with the ability of LGBT individuals to express themselves and form organizations. But, as explored in the rest of Chapter 4, the absence of First Amendment *litigation* did not reflect a diminishment in the importance of the *exercise* of First Amendment rights. In fact, in order to fully understand the equality successes of the LGBT movement, it is necessary to explore not only how advocates have protected their First Amendment rights through litigation, but also how they have exercised those rights outside of the courts. For that reason, the chapter focuses on three important examples of such advocacy: on behalf of the elimination of sodomy laws following the Supreme Court's 1986 decision upholding their constitutionality in *Bowers v. Hardwick*;[6] on behalf of people with AIDS in the late 1980s and early 1990s; and on behalf of marriage rights for lesbians, gay men, and bisexuals after the turn of the century. This advocacy history shows that significant equality gains remained unobtainable until LGBT rights proponents were able to begin changing social and moral understandings of sexual minorities through the exercise of First Amendment rights. Or to put it more simply, free speech came first and equality came second.

It bears noting that this book provides historically based analyses of First Amendment issues implicating LGBT equality over the course of fifty years. In doing so, the book explores how First Amendment claims were pursued, why they succeeded or failed, and their impact on questions of LGBT equality. At times, the book addresses important issues of theory. For example, the end of Chapter 2 includes a brief discussion of the difference between free speech and equality claims as they relate to governmental neutrality. In addition, the beginning of Chapter 3 provides a brief account of the competing "public discourse" and "human autonomy" understandings of free speech protections and how they both call for the constitutional protection of self-identification by sexual minorities. However, the book's objective is not to provide a comprehensive theoretical construct for how to understand the intersection of free speech and LGBT rights (that is the subject of another book). Instead,

the book's objective is to provide a wide-ranging and systematic historical exploration of the role that the First Amendment has played in LGBT
rights disputes over the decades.

Part I ends as the LGBT movement was on its way to attaining significant reforms, including the enactment of sexual orientation antidiscrimination laws by a growing number of jurisdictions; the legislative repeal or
judicial invalidation of sodomy laws; and the recognition by some states
of same-sex marriages. As the scope of LGBT rights measures expanded,
social and religious conservatives began sounding the alarm about what
that expansion meant for those opposed to legally mandated LGBT
equality. In particular, many conservatives started claiming, as explored
in Part II, that LGBT equality measures threatened the rights to speech,
association, and the free exercise of religion of those who questioned
the moral acceptability of same-sex relationships and conduct. In other
words, as the need for LGBT advocates to challenge government measures
under the First Amendment decreased, their political opponents felt an
increased need to challenge state action under the same amendment, and
its corresponding principles and values, with the objective of slowing
down or carving exceptions to laws and policies aimed at promoting the
equality rights of sexual minorities. Interestingly, the reliance by social
and religious conservatives on the First Amendment has become as central to their pursuit of political and legal objectives in matters related to
sexual orientation as it was for the LGBT movement in earlier decades.

Chapter 5 explains that contemporary disputes about the rights of
individuals who dissent from LGBT equality are only the latest iterations
of ongoing debates in American law and policy over the extent to which
liberty considerations should limit the government's pursuit of equality
objectives. The chapter explores some of the most important debates in
American history pitting the government's interest in promoting equality through antidiscrimination laws against the liberty interests of those
who have dissented from that objective. Those debates date back to the
Civil Rights Act of 1875 and extend through the enactment of the Civil
Rights Act of 1964 and the controversy, in the early 1980s, over whether
Bob Jones University and other nonprofit religious educational institutions were entitled to beneficial treatment under the federal tax code
despite their racially discriminatory policies. Similar debates took place
during the 1980s and 1990s as courts grappled with the application of
gender antidiscrimination laws to all-male organizations, and during the

last forty years as courts have developed and implemented the ministerial exception to antidiscrimination laws, a doctrine that constitutionally protects the ability of religious organizations to choose their ministers free from the application of antidiscrimination regulations. The chapter canvasses these earlier controversies over the enactment and enforcement of race and gender antidiscrimination laws with the purpose of gleaning insights and lessons that can help us better understand and assess similar contemporary disputes over the scope of the government's authority to promote equality in the context of LGBT rights.

Two overarching themes emerge from the history explored in Chapter 5. First, that the clash between equality and liberty is a recurring one in the application of American antidiscrimination law, rendering the ongoing debates over LGBT equality neither exceptional nor surprising. Second, that it has been possible in the past to reach workable and reasonable compromises between the pursuit of equality for marginalized groups and the protection of important liberty interests of opponents of that equality. There is every reason to believe that similar compromises can be reached in the context of LGBT rights.

Chapter 6 explores three legal controversies involving the intersection of sexual orientation antidiscrimination regulations and the First Amendment that reached the Supreme Court between 1995 and 2010. In those cases, the dissenters from LGBT equality were, respectively, the organizers of the Boston St. Patrick's Day Parade, the national leaders of the Boy Scouts of America, and a conservative religious student group at a California public law school.[7] Although there were important differences among the cases, the fundamental issue raised by all of them was whether the Constitution granted the entities in question the right to exclude sexual minorities in ways that trumped the application of antidiscrimination laws and policies.

In exploring the three cases, the chapter focuses on the dual nature of the First Amendment that both helps to create the conditions for greater equality and limits the ability of the state to promote equality. The kind of state neutrality that the First Amendment demands vis-à-vis private expression on matters of sexuality, which was so helpful to the early LGBT rights movement, prohibits the state from promoting equality by requiring organizations to admit LGBT individuals when doing so conveys a message that is inconsistent with the organizations' values and views. As we will see, the balancing of free speech/association and equality considerations sometimes requires the making of difficult assessments regarding the impact of forced inclusion of sexual minorities on the ability of organizations to express themselves as they wish on issues related to sex and sexuality.

Chapter 7 addresses the question of religious exemptions from LGBT equality measures, an issue that has lately received an immense amount of political, media, legal, and scholarly attention. The expansion of marriage equality and of laws protecting LGBT people from discrimination has led many social and religious conservatives to complain that LGBT equality measures threaten the religious freedom of those who have moral objections to same-sex sexual conduct and relationships. The argument, in a nutshell, is that the government should not have the power to enforce LGBT antidiscrimination laws in ways that require, for example, government clerks who object to same-sex marriage on religious grounds to issue marriage licenses to same-sex couples, or that require businesses operated by religious owners opposed to same-sex marriage to provide their goods and services at gay weddings.

The chapter explains why it is that, as a legal matter, the question of whether those who object to marriages by same-sex couples on religious grounds are entitled to exemptions from antidiscrimination obligations is largely one of legislative discretion rather than constitutional obligation. The chapter also explores when, how, and why issues of religious freedom became part of marriage equality debates in the United States. The chapter ends by arguing that, in accommodating religious dissenters from marriage equality, it is neither necessary nor appropriate to depart significantly from the established ways in which American antidiscrimination law for decades has accommodated the views of those who dissent from the pursuit of equality objectives on religious grounds.

There is nothing particularly new or distinctive about the clash between equality goals and liberty norms that our nation is currently working through in the context of LGBT rights. The country since the Civil War has repeatedly grappled with how to balance the pursuit of antidiscrimination objectives and the protection of liberty interests. Although it is certainly possible to criticize particular policy outcomes arising from that balancing, there is no reason to craft new exemptions from antidiscrimination measures as applied to LGBT people that depart significantly from the framework already in place to address racial and gender discrimination. In short, there is no need for LGBT rights exceptionalism when determining how religious liberty considerations should limit the scope and application of antidiscrimination laws.

Well-established exemptions, such as the constitutionally based ministerial exemption to antidiscrimination laws and the religious exemption contained in Title VII of the Civil Rights Act of 1964, have provided important protections to religious organizations by allowing them to pursue their religious missions without having to abide by antidiscrimination obligations applicable to other entities. At the same time, the well-established religious exemptions have not interfered in any significant way with the ability of antidiscrimination law to achieve its equality objectives. The ways in which our country through the decades has balanced the pursuit of equality for marginalized groups against the liberty interests of equality opponents, including those associated with religious freedom, constitute time-tested, workable, and reasonable compromises that decision-makers and citizens should use as guides in addressing contemporary disputes arising from the tension between the attainment of LGBT equality and the protection of religious freedom.

The relationship between the First Amendment and LGBT equality has been a dynamic and complex one that resists easy characterizations and generalizations. As this book shows, First Amendment principles and the pursuit of LGBT equality have intersected in many different contexts and ways over the last sixty years. As such, the amendment has served as both a foundation for the attainment of LGBT equality and as a limitation on the state's authority to promote that equality.

Overall, however, the First Amendment has "given" significantly more to the LGBT movement than it has "taken." It is fair to say that the amendment has been a great friend to the movement, a fact that may be easy to miss in the ongoing and heated debates over the ways in which First Amendment values and principles should limit the government's authority to promote LGBT equality. Although a narrow focus on contemporary LGBT rights disputes, especially those related to religious exemptions, may make it seem as if the First Amendment is more of a hindrance than a contributor to LGBT equality, my hope is that the historically based perspectives provided in this book demonstrate that the amendment's protections contributed in crucial ways to the initiation and expansion of LGBT equality in the United States. It was precisely because of the significant equality gains made possible by the exercise of First Amendment rights by early LGBT rights advocates that our country has more recently turned to the question of how First Amendment values and principles should limit the state's authority to promote LGBT equality. At the end of the day, if it were not for the protections afforded by the First Amendment to those who have advocated for LGBT rights though the decades, there would be little LGBT equality to speak of. It seems particularly important to keep this point in mind as the nation continues to grapple with how to protect sexual minorities from discrimination while respecting the First Amendment rights of those who object to laws and judicial rulings aimed at promoting LGBT equality.

From the First Amendment to LGBT Equality

CHAPTER ONE

Moral Displacement and Obscenity Law

I
N 1954, post office officials in Los Angeles seized several hundred copies of *ONE*, the second gay magazine published in the United States.[1] About a year earlier, FBI agents had begun reading each issue of *ONE* looking for possible obscene or subversive materials. Also in 1953, the Post Office had seized one of the publication's issues while officials in Washington determined whether it contained obscene materials. Although the Post Office a few weeks later agreed to distribute that particular issue, officials refused to dispatch the 1954 issue through the mails on the ground that it violated the federal obscenity statute.

Congress enacted the obscenity statute in 1873, making it a federal crime to use the mails to distribute "obscene, lewd, or lascivious" publications. In addition to criminalizing the distribution of obscene materials via the mails, the act authorized the Post Office to refuse to mail obscene materials.[2] According to the Post Office, the 1954 issue of *ONE* was obscene because it contained a short story about a lesbian relationship, a poem that alluded to sexual relationships between men, and an advertisement for a gay European magazine that officials claimed was itself obscene.[3]

A few years later, prosecutors charged Henry Womack, a gay businessman who published erotic gay magazines, with multiple violations of the federal obscenity statute for selling photographs of naked men to customers via the mails. After a federal judge found Womack guilty and sentenced him to serve one to three years in prison, post office officials seized more than four hundred copies of Womack's so-called physique magazines because they contained pictures of half-naked men.

The publishers of *ONE* and Womack challenged the government's seizures of their magazines in the federal courts, contending that the Post Office had violated their rights to free speech. After losing resoundingly in the lower courts, they succeeded—*ONE* in 1958 and Womack in 1962—before the Supreme Court.[4] Although these two cases, decided years before the Stonewall riots, have been largely forgotten today, they are historically important because they were the first two LGBT victories before the Supreme Court.

This chapter explores the background and impact of the two cases. In doing so, the chapter seeks to understand why the Supreme Court sided with the gay claimants in both instances at a time when (1) society strongly condemned same-sex relationships and conduct on moral grounds, and (2) the law refused to recognize that sexual minorities had any rights to equality or privacy. I argue that the cases' outcomes had little to do with the rights of LGBT people as such and much to do with the process of moral displacement within obscenity law that had been taking place for several decades. By "moral displacement," I mean the courts' growing skepticism that the state's interest in promoting public morality granted it almost complete discretion to regulate books, magazines, and other materials that contained sexual ideas, themes, and depictions.

The promotion of public morality through law was grounded in the notion that it was appropriate for the state to discourage individuals from engaging in conduct that society deemed to be morally wrong.[5] This chapter traces the development of obscenity law in the United States with an emphasis on the use of public morality as a regulatory justification. Although courts in the nineteenth and early twentieth centuries embraced public morality as the normative basis for obscenity law, around the 1930s a growing number of judges began to express skepticism of the notion that public morality granted the government virtually untrammeled discretion to regulate obscenity. Indeed, by the time the Supreme Court decided the two cases involving gay publications, considerations of public morality were playing a reduced role in obscenity law.

The chapter makes two other main points about the displacement of morality within obscenity law that allowed the LGBT litigants in the two cases to prevail with their free speech claims. First, the displacement contributed to the growing availability of same-sex political and erotic materials during the 1960s, and therefore to the formation and strengthening of LGBT identities and communities. Viewed more broadly, the displacement helped sexual minorities, as further explored in Chapters 2 through 4, begin to advocate on behalf of a new understanding of sexual morality and articulate claims to equal treatment and full citizenship.

Second, the moral displacement within obscenity law that led to the gay publications' victories before the Supreme Court in the pre-Stonewall years presaged the moral displacement that took place decades later in the Court's equal protection and privacy jurisprudence involving issues of sexual orientation. As such, the moral displacement in the context of obscenity law was the start of a pattern (also explored in Chapters 2 through 4) that would repeat itself in the decades to come: LGBT advocates winning First Amendment victories that preceded, and set the stage for, equality and privacy gains.

The Obscenity Case against a Gay Political Magazine

The national mobilization engendered by World War II helped to create the conditions that allowed for the emergence of the homophile movement, as the early LGBT rights movement called itself. The war brought together millions of men and women in single-sex environments, leading some to realize that they were not alone in experiencing same-sex attraction.[6] After the war, many of these individuals chose not to return to their places of origin, and instead relocated to large urban areas where others with similar sexual and romantic interests lived.

The publication of Alfred Kinsey's books on the sexual practices of Americans also contributed to the formation of the homophile movement. The empirical findings in *Sexual Behavior in the American Male* (1948) and in *Sexual Behavior in the American Female* (1953), based on interviews with more than ten thousand individuals, suggested that there was much greater diversity in the sexual practices and proclivities of Americans than might first appear given the conservative sexual mores prevalent at the time. Kinsey found that not only were his subjects engaging in large amounts of premarital and extramarital heterosexual intercourse, but also a surprisingly large percentage of them reported same-sex sexual attraction and experiences.[7] The Kinsey books, which were best sellers and received an immense amount of media attention, contributed to the growing sense by many lesbians and gay men that they were not alone and that they belonged to a distinct group of individuals who shared sexual and romantic interests in others of the same sex.

The postwar years were also characterized by repression of sexual non-conformity. This repression was most clearly reflected in the so-called Lavender Scare of the 1950s in which the federal government sought to purge from its ranks those whom it suspected of being gay or lesbian, viewing them, as it did suspected communists, as threats to national security.[8] The government witch-hunts aimed at sexual minorities began in earnest in 1950 after a committee of the U.S. Senate issued a report titled *Employment of Homosexuals and Other Sex Perverts in Government* that deemed "sex perverts" to constitute security threats, accused lesbians and gay men of moral perversion, and urged government agencies to enforce the civil service's long-standing policy against "immoral conduct."[9] The report was followed three years later by an executive order issued by President Dwight Eisenhower listing "sexual perversion" as an automatic reason for firing federal employees.[10] In the sixteen months following the order's issuance, the federal government dismissed an average of forty civil servants a month, not counting those who were permitted to resign quietly, on "perversion grounds."[11] At around the same time, the military intensified its efforts to search for lesbians and gay men in the armed services in order to expel them.

The repression of sexual nonconformity was also reflected in the targeting of gay men through sexual psychopath laws; in the growing number of arrests of men for soliciting other men to have sex; and in the repeated police raids across the country of lesbian and gay bars (as explored in Chapter 2).[12]

Although the repression caused much suffering, it also encouraged a band of brave LGBT activists to come together to do what they could to protect their communities and themselves from government coercion and harassment. The first homophile organization, the Mattachine Society, was formed in Los Angeles in 1951 by a handful of men, most of whom were former members of the Communist Party.

The early years of the Mattachine Society were characterized by considerable infighting and a penchant for secrecy. This led a group of dissatisfied members, both men and women, to create a new organization with the goal of publishing a magazine that would advocate for gay equality more openly.[13] The purpose of the magazine, as expressed in the articles of incorporation of the nonprofit entity that published it, was to address "homosexuality from the scientific, historical and critical point of view, and to aid in the social integration and rehabilitation of the sexual variant."[14] The founders called their magazine *ONE* (letters capitalized) based on the nineteenth-century Scottish writer Thomas Carlyle's declaration that "a mystic bond of brotherhood makes all men one."

The first issue of *ONE*, published in January 1953, included an account by Dale Jennings, a cofounder of both the Mattachine Society and *ONE*, of his arrest and trial in Los Angeles for allegedly soliciting a male undercover vice-squad police officer to commit a sexual act.[15] Early issues also included poetry, fiction, and news clippings on topics of interest to gay people. In addition, several of *ONE*'s articles decried the treatment of lesbians and gay men by police authorities and called for an end to the entrapment tactics of vice squads.[16]

At first, newsstand operators refused to carry the magazine, but after sales in gay bars in Los Angeles proved there was a market for the publication, some newsstands agreed to sell it.[17] As for those who subscribed, most paid extra to have the magazine sent to them first class, in sealed envelopes without a return address.

By July 1953, the magazine's paid circulation had reached two thousand, with a readership that was considerably larger given that copies were frequently circulated among friends. Letters to the editor indicated that the magazine was being read across the country. The fear of being identified as gay or lesbian meant that the letters were often published without accompanying names, sometimes with the only identifying information being "m" for male and "f" for female, in addition to the name of the town and state where the writer lived.[18]

Despite the rather quick growth in *ONE's* circulation, the magazine remained a shoestring operation. Only one staff member, the business manager, was put on a salary, and even he was paid only when enough money remained after covering production and mailing costs, which was not very often. Most staff writers used pen names, both to hide their identities and to make it seem as if the number of contributors was larger than it truly was.

Although staff members did not know it at the time, three months after the magazine was first published, FBI agents in Los Angeles began reading it in search of obscene or subversive material. In July 1953, the FBI opened a formal investigation of the magazine, which included mailing each issue to FBI headquarters in Washington for further review.[19] A few weeks later, local postal authorities seized copies of *ONE's* August issue pending review by officials in Washington to determine whether it was mailable under the federal obscenity statute. That particular issue, with a cover titled "Homosexual Marriage?," included the first article published in a gay American magazine discussing whether the law should allow same-sex couples to marry.[20] Only after officials in Washington determined that the issue was mailable did the Post Office distribute the copies, three weeks after it had seized them.

The magazine's perseverance in the face of threatened censorship led its editors to proclaim on the next issue's cover that "we have been pronounced respectable. The Post Office found that *ONE* is obscene in no way. . . . Never before has a government agency of this size admitted that homosexuals not only have legal rights but might have respectable motives as well." At the same time, the editors expressed anger at the fact that authorities continued to harass and intimidate lesbians and gay men across the country:

> As we sit around quietly like nice little ladies and gentlemen gradually educating the public and the courts at our leisure, thousands of homosexuals are being unjustly arrested, blackmailed, fined, jailed, intimidated, beaten, ruined, and murdered. *ONE*'s victory might seem big and historic as you read of it in the comfort of your home (locked in the bathroom? hidden under a stack of other magazines? sealed first class?). But the deviate hearing of our late August issue through jail bars will not be overly impressed.[21]

The brush with government censors led the magazine's editors to ask Eric Julber, their unpaid attorney who had graduated from law school only a few years before, to read everything scheduled for publication to make sure there were no violations of obscenity laws. As a result of one of his recommendations, the editors went so far as to remove passages from Walt Whitman's poetry from an article exploring whether the poet was gay.[22]

In response to complaints from some readers that the magazine was too tame, the editors also asked Julber to write an essay, published in the October 1954 issue—the same issue that postal officials later seized after deeming it obscene—detailing how the magazine determined what it could publish in order to steer clear of obscenity laws. Julber opined that *ONE* did not run afoul of obscenity statutes as long as it published materials limited to "the discussion of the social, economic, personal and legal problems of homosexuals, for the purpose of better understanding of and by society." But the magazine had to stay away from materials that "appealed to the lusts or salacity or sexual appetites . . . of *ONE*'s readers. . . . *ONE*, in other words can appeal to the heads, but not the sexual desires, of its readers." Julber then proceeded to list the kinds of contributions that could not be published, including "lonely hearts ads, . . . 'cheesecake' art or photos, . . . descriptions of experiences [that are] too explicit, . . . descriptions of homosexuality as a practice which the author encourages in others, or waxes too enthusiastic about [and] fiction with too much physical contact between the characters."[23]

Ironically, postal authorities refused to mail the approximately six hundred copies of the issue—sardonically titled "You can't print it!"—containing Julber's explanations of *ONE*'s obscenity prevention policies.[24] In justifying its conclusion that the issue was "nonmailable" under the federal obscenity statute, postal authorities pointed to three of its contents: a short story, a poem, and an advertisement. The short story, titled "Sapho Remembered," was about a "helplessly young" woman of twenty who turns down her boyfriend's proposal of marriage in order to stay with the older woman whom she loves. The story contained several references to physical contact between the two women, including the pressing of knees together while sitting in the back of a car and the caressing, by the older woman, of the younger woman's "child-like temple."[25]

The poem, titled "Lord Samuel and Lord Montagu," poked fun at a recent newspaper article by a British lord complaining "that the vices of Sodom and Gomorrah [are] rife among us." The poem also told of another British lord who was imprisoned for a year for having sex with "Scouts" and "airmen" and of a member of Parliament who was fined for "importuning." The poem, furthermore, made references to men looking to have sex with other men in some of London's public bathrooms.[26] In addition to the short story and the poem, postal officials claimed that the *ONE* issue was not mailable because of an advertisement placed by the gay Swiss magazine *Der Kreis* (*The Circle*), a publication that the government contended was itself obscene.

Several months after the Post Office seized their issue, *ONE*'s editors authorized Julber to file a lawsuit in federal court challenging the government's action. (Julber asked the American Civil Liberties Union for assistance, but the organization turned down the request because the magazine was a gay one.)[27] After the trial court ruled in the government's favor, Julber appealed. But a federal appellate court rejected his claim that the government had violated the Free Speech Clause in refusing to mail the gay magazine. In doing so, it explained that whether material was obscene under the federal obscenity statute could only be determined "by some discussion of the moral sense of the public." Recognizing that "morals are not static," the judges believed it was necessary to define the statutory terms "in the light of today's moral dictionary." According to the court, the story "Sapho Remembered" was obscene because its main character, after struggling between lesbianism and "a normal married life," chose the former. In the court's view, the story was "nothing more than cheap pornography calculated to promote lesbianism." Similarly, the poem about the same-sex sexual interests of some members of the British aristocracy, and the searching for sexual partners in London's public bathrooms, "pertains to sexual matters of such a vulgar and indecent nature that it tends to arouse a feeling of disgust and revulsion. It is dirty, vulgar and offensive to the moral senses." Finally, the Court of Appeals concluded that the advertisement for *Der Kreis* rendered the issue of *ONE* nonmailable because the judges' examination of the Swiss publication "clearly reveals that it contains obscene and filthy matter which is offensive to the moral senses, morally depraving and debasing, and that it is designed for persons having lecherous and salacious proclivities."[28]

ONE responded to the Court of Appeals' decision with an angry and pugnacious editorial explaining that the magazine saw itself as fighting for the free speech rights of all Americans and that, in some ways, the Post Office had done it a favor by raising the issue of its rights under the First Amendment: "Events may prove that in no other way could the rights of homosexual American citizens be adequately and finally tested, and the legal and social problems of the homosexual be thoroughly and publicly aired." The editorial also complained that lesbians and gay men were permitted few outlets of expression and that whenever someone wrote realistically about "homosexual attachment—the specter of Obscenity stands ready with fangs bared." The editorial ended with a promise: "*ONE* intends to fight to . . . insure for homosexuals the right to speak for themselves, to publish and disseminate literature wherein the homosexual may answer the prejudice and false charges against him with facts and forthright statements. In simple words, *ONE* rightfully demands the 'Freedom of the Press.'"[29]

ONE ended up fulfilling its promise by succeeding in its appeal to the Supreme Court. But before we explore how and why it prevailed before the nation's highest court, it is necessary to discuss another federal obscenity case that reached the Court at around the same time. The subject of the government's censorship efforts in that case was not a gay magazine that advocated on behalf of the political, social, and legal rights of sexual minorities. Instead, the government in the second case chose to target gay erotic publications known as "physique magazines."

Government Censorship and Gay Erotic Magazines

Physique magazines, featuring photographs of muscular men and emphasizing the importance of physical fitness, first appeared in the United States at the end of the nineteenth century.[30] The historian David Johnson notes that the "magazines were an outgrowth of the turn-of-the-century physical culture movement, which many historians have seen as the result of a crisis in masculinity in a rapidly urbanizing and industrializing America."[31] By the 1930s, a growing number of gay men were buying and sharing the magazines, a phenomenon that made their publishers uneasy. When those publishers a few years later refused to carry advertisements for the selling of "photographs of barely clad men, often in erotic but ambiguous scenarios such as wrestling matches," gay entrepreneurs began publishing their own physique magazines specifically aimed at gay audiences.[32]

One of those entrepreneurs was Henry Womack. Womack, who had a Ph.D. in philosophy, taught at George Washington University and at Mary Washington College. In 1952, he left academia after buying two printing companies in Washington, D.C., with the hope of becoming a magazine publisher. At around this time, Womack, who had been married twice and had a daughter, acknowledged to himself that he was gay.[33]

Womack was one of the first businessmen in the country to recognize the money-making potential of selling gay erotica. Under the corporate heading of Manual Enterprises, Inc., Womack quickly built a large male erotica business by publishing magazines with titles such as *MANual* and *Manorama*. Although the publications billed themselves as traditional physique magazines, it was readily apparent that they aimed to appeal to readers who appreciated male physical beauty rather than physical fitness as such. The photographs almost always depicted men in titillating positions wearing few garments, implying sexual awareness and availability.[34]

Womack also operated a separate business that sold pictures of naked men directly to customers via the mails. As described by a federal district court, "the subjects of the photographs were represented in lascivious and suggestive poses, with the camera obviously being focused so as to emphasize the private organs."[35] In early 1960, federal authorities arrested Womack and charged him under the federal obscenity statute for distributing the photographs. A few months later, a judge convicted him on twenty-nine obscenity counts and sentenced him to serve between one and three years in prison.[36]

Womack was not the only publisher of gay physique magazines who was the victim of government prosecution. As Johnson notes, "almost all of the publishers and photographers connected with physique magazines were arrested by the police and tried in court at some point in their careers."[37] It was also not uncommon for buyers of the magazines to be arrested for possessing obscene materials.[38]

In Womack's case, government officials were not satisfied with the criminal convictions relating to the nude pictures. They also wanted to stop his distribution of gay physique magazines. Four days after the judge found him guilty, the Post Office refused to mail 405 copies of Womack's magazines, claiming they were nonmailable under the federal obscenity statute. A few weeks later, a hearing was held before the Post Office's judicial officer to determine whether the magazines could be distributed under federal law.

Although Womack claimed that his publications were aimed at readers interested in body building, the government at the hearing set out to establish that their purpose was instead to sexually arouse gay men. To prove this point, the government called on a psychiatrist who treated "homosexual patients." At the hearing, the expert testified at length about how the magazines' photographs, many of which showed models wearing, for example, G-strings or loincloths, sexually aroused gay men. According to the psychiatrist, gay men were attracted to the erotic male photographs to compensate for their sense of weakness and inferiority. He also expressed particular concern about the magazine's impact on young men "who we might classify as borderline sexual cases where they haven't had intercourse with women" and who "have always tried to fight back homosexual tendencies." A second expert, a clinical psychologist, testified that the magazines had no literary, scientific, or educational value and that they would lead male adolescents to "react primarily with instinctual arousal, sexual arousal which would take the form of fantasies, immoral and sexual thoughts," masturbation, and sexual behavior with other males.[39]

The judicial officer ruled that the publications were obscene and therefore not mailable. Agreeing with the government, the officer concluded that the magazines threatened to lure men and adolescents "into the abnormal paths of the homosexual," a ruling that was upheld by a district court and a federal appellate court.[40]

The Supreme Court would end up reversing the lower courts' rulings in both the case involving *ONE* and that involving Womack's magazines. The Court's decisions did not reflect changing social or judicial views of homosexuality; same-sex sexual relationships and conduct remained highly controversial and stigmatized throughout American society. Instead, the rulings reflected the courts' growing skepticism of the government's assertion that it enjoyed almost unlimited power to promote public morality through the enforcement of obscenity laws.

Obscenity and Public Morality in the Courts

During approximately the first 120 years of obscenity prosecutions in the United States (that is, roughly between the 1810s until the 1930s), courts frequently, and without much controversy or disagreement, pointed to the promotion of public morality as the main objective behind obscenity laws. As the twentieth century progressed, however, courts began to focus on considerations beyond public morality such as the social and artistic value of the materials in question. The Supreme Court in the late 1950s, at around the same time it decided the cases involving *ONE* and Womack's magazines, issued two opinions, *Roth v. United States* and *Kingsley International Pictures v. Regents of the University of the State of New York*, that contributed to the moral displacement within obscenity law.[41]

The Primacy of Public Morals in Early Obscenity Cases

The first reported obscenity conviction in the United States took place in Philadelphia in 1815. The defendants in *Commonwealth v. Sharpless* were charged under the common-law crime of public indecency for allowing members of the public, after paying a fee, to enter "a certain house" in order to observe a painting "representing a man in an obscene, impudent and indecent posture with a woman." In upholding the convictions, the Pennsylvania Supreme Court explained that "what tended to corrupt society, was . . . a breach of the peace and punishable by indictment. The courts are guardians of the public morals. . . . Hence, it follows, that an offence may be punishable, if in its nature and by its example, it tends to the corruption of morals."[42]

The same concern about public morals was behind the first reported obscenity prosecution in the United States for the publishing of a book. The book in question was *Memoirs of a Woman of Pleasure*, more commonly known as *Fanny Hill*, which, in telling the story of a young girl who worked at a London brothel in the eighteenth century, provides readers with extensive and detailed accounts of its characters' sexual experiences.[43] The indictment of the book's publisher, upheld by the Massachusetts Supreme Judicial Court in 1821, alleged that the defendant, "a scandalous and evil-disposed person," aimed to "debauch and corrupt" the morals of citizens and youth.[44]

The understanding of the state's power to regulate obscenity as arising from its authority to protect public morals was further strengthened by the Court of Queen's Bench's ruling in *Regina v. Hicklin* in 1868. The British court in that case adopted a definition of obscenity that greatly influenced American judges for decades to come. According to the court, the "test of obscenity is . . . whether the tendency of the matter charged as obscenity is to deprave and corrupt those whose minds are open to such immoral influences, and into whose hands a publication of this sort may fall."[45]

The element of the *Hicklin* test that eventually received the most attention, and led to the greatest controversy, was its use of the most vulnerable members of society, such as children, as the proper subjects for determining which materials were obscene. But more important for our purposes is the aspect of the test that was entirely taken for granted and was assumed for decades to be entirely appropriate, namely, the issue of whether the publication in question had "*immoral* influences" on its readers. Under *Hicklin*, materials were obscene if they had "the immediate tendency of demoralizing the public mind" regardless of whether the defendant intended that result.[46]

In 1879, a federal appellate court adopted the *Hicklin* test in *United States v. Bennett*, a case involving the mailing of a pamphlet promoting the view that individuals had the right to engage in sex outside of marriage. The *Bennett* court followed its British counterpart in *Hicklin* by holding that the defendant's intent was irrelevant as long as the publication had the tendency to corrupt public morals.[47] A few years later, the U.S. Supreme Court embraced the *Hicklin* test.[48] It is clear, therefore, that courts throughout the nineteenth century both understood the primary objective behind the legal regulation of obscenity to be the protection of public morality and refused to place any meaningful limits on the government's ability to use obscenity law to promote that morality.

The same focus on morality continued well into the twentieth century. For example, in 1928, the publisher Donald Friede was charged under New York's obscenity statute for publishing the lesbian novel *The Well of Loneliness*.[49] That novel, which had been deemed obscene in England, tells the story of a woman who initially struggles with her sexual attraction to women only to later understand and accept her sexual orientation.[50]

In rejecting the defendant's motion to have the criminal charge dismissed, the magistrate judge reasoned that "the novel is not only anti-social and offensive to public morals and decency," but also written in a way that "attract[ed] and focus[ed] attention upon perverted ideas and unnatural vices and [was] strongly calculated to corrupt and debase those members of the community who would be susceptible to its immoral influence."[51] The magistrate was particularly concerned with the novel's moral impact on those who might find same-sex sexual conduct appealing. In response to the publisher's argument that the *Hicklin* test inappropriately relied on the susceptibilities of society's "dullest-witted and most fallible members" to determine what was obscene, the judge noted that this particular novel, which was literary and well-written, was problematic precisely because it aimed to corrupt "those of mature age and of high intellectual development and professional attainment."[52]

In upholding the obscenity prosecution, the magistrate embraced the notion of "thematic obscenity," that is, the idea that a publication was obscene if it presented intimate relationships outside of heterosexual marriage as morally acceptable, even in the absence of explicit depictions of sexual acts.[53] The judge expressed particular concern about the novel's portrayal of "unnatural and depraved" (that is, same-sex) relationships as ones that were to be "idealized and extolled." Rather than criticizing these relationships, the book presented the characters "who indulge in these vices . . . in attractive terms, and it is maintained throughout that they be accepted on the same plane as persons normally constituted, and that their perverse and inverted love is as worthy as the affection between normal beings and should be considered just as sacred by society."[54] According to the magistrate, the mere portrayal of same-sex relationships in positive (or presumably even neutral) ways violated the state's obscenity statute. Under this view, the book was obscene independently of the degree of explicitness of its descriptions of sexual conduct.

Although a three-judge panel eventually refused to deem *The Well of Loneliness* obscene, obscenity foes in New York City at around the same time succeeded in closing down a series of plays with lesbian and gay themes.[55] And in 1927, the New York legislature enacted a law authorizing the police to padlock for a year any theater that contributed "to the corruption of youth or others" by showing plays that depicted or dealt with "sex degeneracy or perversion."[56] That statute was prompted by the Broadway production of a play called *The Captive*, a work exploring the attraction of a married woman for another woman.[57] An appellate court, in refusing to grant the holder of the rights to the play an injunction seeking to force the owner of the theater to continue the production after the district attorney threatened to bring obscenity charges, concluded that "it cannot be said dogmatically that the morals of youth, or even of adults, would not be affected by presenting a theme of the character here exhibited with the action and dialogue which accompany it."[58]

In short, for more than a century after the first obscenity prosecution in the United States, there was a wide consensus among courts that the state had an almost unlimited authority to regulate obscenity in order to protect or promote public morality. Eventually, that consensus began to break down, a phenomenon driven initially by increasing judicial agitation against the *Hicklin* test.

The Demise of *Hicklin* and the Search for Provable Effects

The undermining of *Hicklin* began with a judicial opinion penned by Judge Learned Hand in 1913 in which he questioned whether materials should be deemed obscene simply because they contained a few references that might corrupt the minds of those who were particularly vulnerable "to such immoral influences." Morals, Hand noted, were not static, but changed with the times. As a result, although the *Hicklin* test might have been "consonant . . . with mid-Victorian morals, [it did] not seem . . . to answer to the understanding and morality of the present time, as conveyed by the words 'obscene, lewd, or lascivious' as used in the federal obscenity statute."[59]

Although Learned Hand, as a district court judge, could do little to modify the legal definition of obscenity, the same was not true of appellate courts. The U.S. Court of Appeals for the Second Circuit did precisely that in two rulings issued in the early 1930s. The first case, *United States v. Dennett*, involved the federal government's prosecution of Mary Dennett, a feminist and birth control advocate, for using the mails to distribute a sex education pamphlet. In overturning Dennett's conviction, Judge Augustus Hand emphasized the pamphlet's educational objective. The fact that a discussion relating to sex might arouse lust in some readers was not enough to render the material obscene, especially because the alternative was to leave the young uninformed about the mechanics and consequences of sexual intimacy.[60]

In the second case, Judge Hand, again writing for the Second Circuit, rejected the federal government's effort to ban the importation of James Joyce's novel *Ulysses* on the ground that it was obscene. As in *Dennett*, Hand focused on the primary purpose of the writings. Although *Ulysses* contained sexually explicit scenes, they were "relevant to the purpose of depicting the thoughts of the characters and are introduced to give meaning to the whole, rather than to promote lust or portray filth for its own sake." According to Hand, the scenes describing sexual acts and desires were part of a greater effort to convey the full life of the characters rather than to promote or incite lust.[61]

The Second Circuit in *Ulysses* explicitly refused to follow the *Hicklin* test. If all that was required before a book could be deemed obscene was that it contain a handful of passages that might sexually arouse the most susceptible of readers, then "much of the great works of literature" were legally obscene, a result that Congress could not have intended.[62] One of the consequences of rulings like *Ulysses* was that they shifted the legal focus from conclusions based on the (im)morality of the material as determined by the (in)decency of its content to an assessment of whether "the likelihood that the work will so much arouse the salacity of the reader to whom it is sent . . . outweigh[s] any literary, scientific or other merits it may have in that reader's hands."[63]

Dennett and *Ulysses* represent a crucial shift in the judicial understanding of obscenity in the United States. The federal appellate court in both instances was unwilling to assume, as earlier courts had done, that sexually explicit materials harmed society because they morally corrupted their readers or observers. Instead, the court reasoned that the educational value of the pamphlet in *Dennett* and the literary value of the novel in *Ulysses* greatly outweighed whatever speculative moral harms might result from the fact that they could engender sexual urges and desires in some readers. The court's reasoning showed that it was willing to limit the government's ability to promote public morality through the enforcement of obscenity laws.

Critics of obscenity statutes, emboldened by the Second Circuit rulings, started demanding that the government produce evidence of social harm arising from the distribution and consumption of sexual materials. In particular, they asked that obscenity regulations be justified through empirical evidence showing a link between the consumption of sexually explicit materials and specific social harms such as an increase in juvenile delinquency.[64]

This demand for evidence of cause and effect is reflected in two opinions issued by the Second Circuit in *United States v. Roth*, the case eventually used by the Supreme Court to delineate the constitutional limitations of obscenity laws. The trial judge had sentenced Roth to five years in prison after a jury convicted him of mailing obscene books, pamphlets, and photographs. Roth appealed his conviction by challenging the constitutionality of the federal obscenity statute. In writing for the appellate court, Judge Charles Clark reasoned that because courts had been upholding convictions under the statute for decades, only the Supreme Court could render it unconstitutional. But Clark also noted that judges had to be careful before striking down the statute given "our own lack of knowledge of the social bearing of this problem [of selling obscenity], or consequences of such an act; and we are hardly justified in rejecting out of hand the strongly held views of those with competence in the premises as to the very direct connection of this traffic with the development of juvenile delinquency."[65]

Judge Clark was willing to defer to the government's claim that there was a link between the consumption of obscenity and juvenile delinquency. But what is important for our purposes is the extent to which his opinion, despite its deferential posture toward the government, deemed the prevention of provable social harms, rather than a generalized need to protect public morals, to be the statute's principal objective.

Judge Jerome Frank, in a concurring opinion in *Roth*, went even further: Not only did he demand evidence of a link between obscene materials and social harms, he also would have squarely placed the burden of establishing that connection on the government. The government could not, consistently with the Free Speech Clause, paternalistically try to prevent individuals from having certain thoughts unless those thoughts led to *behaviors* that caused social harm. As Frank rhetorically asked, "if the government possesses the power to censor publications which arouse sexual thoughts, regardless of whether those thoughts tend probably to transform themselves into anti-social behavior, why may not the government censor political and religious publications regardless of any causal relation to probable dangerous deeds?"[66]

The Second Circuit's opinions in *Roth* reflected a new perspective in obscenity law, one that focused on the need to establish a causal connection between obscenity and social harm, a requirement that arose explicitly from the First Amendment. The Supreme Court took the opportunity to weigh in on the constitutional scope of obscenity law when, a few months later, it agreed to hear the *Roth* case.

The Supreme Court Weighs In on the Question of Obscenity

The Supreme Court's ruling in *Roth* marked the beginning of an intense constitutionalization of obscenity law in the United States. It was rare, prior to *Roth*, for courts in obscenity cases to grapple directly with the regulatory limitations imposed on the state by the First Amendment. Although, as we have seen, courts had for decades been struggling with the proper definition of obscenity, they had done so generally without accounting for constitutional principles of free speech. It was not until later opinions, such as Judge Frank's concurring opinion in *Roth*, that judges began to weave extended discussions of constitutional doctrine into their obscenity analysis. Prior to the 1950s, the prevailing assumption among judges was that the First Amendment did not limit the authority of the state to regulate obscenity.[67]

The government in *Roth* argued that obscenity laws served the public interest through "the preservation of public morality."[68] In contrast, the accused contended that the First Amendment required the government to show that obscene materials caused social harm, a burden that it could not meet merely by raising generalized or speculative concerns about the need to protect public morality. Roth further claimed in his brief to the Court that "there is no reliable evidence that obscene publications or pictures have any appreciable effect on the conduct of human beings."[69]

Despite the arguments raised by the parties, the Supreme Court refused to address the question of whether the protection of public morality was a sufficient justification for obscenity regulations or, alternatively, whether the government had to show proof of a causal connection between the reading or viewing of obscene materials and antisocial conduct. Instead, the Court in *Roth*, speaking through Justice William Brennan, made two other points. First, it held that whether materials were obscene, and therefore not constitutionally protected by the First Amendment, depended on whether they had some social value. According to Brennan, "implicit in the history of the First Amendment is the rejection of obscenity as utterly without redeeming social importance."[70]

Second, the Court emphasized that sex did not equal obscenity. The mere portrayal or depiction of sexual acts was not enough to render materials obscene, and therefore constitutionally unprotected. Focusing once again on the question of the publications' social value, Brennan explained that sex is one of the great mysteries of life and, as such, "one of the vital problems of human interest and public concern." As a result, it was crucial to distinguish between the artistic, literary, and scientific (that is, socially valuable) portrayals of sex and depictions that treated it "in a manner appealing to prurient interest[s]."[71] Only publications with dominant themes that appealed to such interests were obscene, and it was therefore only those materials that were constitutionally unprotected.

By focusing on the artistic, literary, and scientific value of at least some sexually explicit material, the Court in *Roth* refused to assume, as courts had done consistently in prior decades, that society was inevitably harmed by the distribution of publications that incited sexual desires. Rather than understanding such materials as ones that uniformly represented threats to society because they "corrupted morals," the Court in *Roth* took the position that sexually explicit materials sometimes had social value. The Court's failure to mention, much less grapple with, the question of state objectives (whether moral or otherwise) behind obscenity regulations meant that its ruling was consistent with the recent judicial trend of limiting the state's ability to rely on public morality to defend exceedingly broad understandings of the government's authority to regulate obscenity.

I acknowledge that my contention that *Roth* reflected the judiciary's growing skepticism of granting the government almost unlimited authority to promote public morality through obscenity laws may strike obscenity scholars and others as odd because *Roth* is generally understood as having approved of the link between obscenity law and morality. This widely held view is grounded in the fact that the obscenity test adopted by the Court required a determination of whether the materials in question appealed to the "prurient interests" of readers according to "contemporary community standards." It is often assumed that the Court, by referencing such standards, sought to encourage lower courts and juries to incorporate notions of morality into the obscenity analysis.

However, in order to fully understand the reasoning and implications of *Roth*, it is necessary to place it in its proper historical context. Most explorations of contemporary obscenity law start with *Roth*, which is in some ways understandable because the case marks the beginning of the Court's intense constitutionalization of obscenity law. But the Court decided *Roth after more than one hundred years* of obscenity prosecutions in the United States. If we view *Roth* in that historical context, it becomes clear that it reflected a partial move toward limiting the ability of the government to rely on public morality as a justification for obscenity prosecutions.

Lower courts, prior to *Roth*, had for some time been pushing for the "community standards" test as an alternative to the *Hicklin* test; the former was increasingly appealing precisely because it was *narrower*. It was less likely that materials would be found obscene if the assessment was based on broad community standards, rather than on the sensitivities of society's most vulnerable members. In choosing the narrower definition of obscenity, without referring to the state's interest in promoting public morality, the Court partially restricted the ability of the government to rely on public morality to justify expansive obscenity prosecutions.

Admittedly, the limits that *Roth* placed on the government's use of public morality in enforcing obscenity laws could have been both more explicit and extensive. In particular, the Court could have held that the First Amendment did not allow the state to ban publications solely on the basis of public morality, requiring instead the showing of a causal link between the materials and harmful behaviors. What the Court did instead was to focus on the purported social value of the materials in question, a focus that indirectly limited the ability of the government to rely on public morality considerations to regulate obscenity. The crucial analytical point after *Roth* was not whether the state had legitimate interests (moral or otherwise) for adopting obscenity regulations, but whether the materials in question had some social value. The Court's focus, in other words, was not on the government's interests behind the regulations, but on the nature and content of the materials themselves. Whatever difficulties inhered in distinguishing between publications that had some social value from those that did not—difficulties clearly reflected in the rash of fractured Supreme Court obscenity cases that followed *Roth* and in Justice Potter Stewart's famous claim that, while it might not be possible to come up with a clear definition of obscenity, he knew hard-core pornography when he saw it—the judicial review of obscenity regulations after *Roth* was less firmly rooted in the types of public morality considerations that had completely dominated the legal analysis in decades past.

It bears noting that *Roth*'s impact on obscenity prosecutions of materials with gay content was immediate. A few weeks before the Court issued its ruling, authorities in San Francisco had arrested and charged Lawrence Ferlinghetti, the owner of the City Lights bookstore and the publisher of Allen Ginsberg's *Howl and Other Poems*, with violating the state's obscenity law. The government contended that *Howl*'s raw and frank depiction of sex, including that between men, was immoral and obscene.[72]

Three months later, a bench trial was held in which the defense called several expert witnesses to testify about the poem's literary merits. In his ruling following the trial, Judge Clayton Horn noted that the Supreme Court in *Roth* had explicitly rejected the notion that descriptions of sexual acts were always obscene. Even more importantly, the crucial question for the judge, following *Roth*, was whether the material "has the slightest redeeming social importance." Because Judge Horn concluded that the poems had such value, he found the defendant not guilty.[73]

The Question of Thematic Obscenity

The Supreme Court in *Butler v. Michigan*, decided the same year as *Roth*, closed the book on whatever remained of the original *Hicklin* test by holding that the government could not deem as obscene materials available to adults on the ground that they might have deleterious effects on minors.[74] Two years later, the Court in *Kingsley International Pictures v.*

Regents of the University of the State of New York rejected the idea of thematic obscenity, that is, the notion that some materials are obscene because of their immoral sexual themes or messages, independently of the degree of explicitness of the materials' depictions of sexual acts.[75] Such a rejection by the Court had significant consequences for publishers of gay publications given the widespread belief at the time that same-sex relationships and conduct were immoral.

The lawsuit in *Kingsley Pictures* arose after New York state denied a license for the showing of the movie *Lady Chatterley's Lover*. Based on the 1928 novel by D. H. Lawrence of the same name, the film told the story of a young woman who, after her husband is paralyzed while fighting in World War I, has a deeply satisfying sexual relationship with a man whom she plans to marry after divorcing her husband. Although the movie version was significantly less sexually explicit than the book, the New York Court of Appeals had nonetheless upheld the license denial because the movie exalted an adulterous relationship and presented it as morally acceptable. The government had the constitutional authority, the state court concluded, to ban materials that were "clearly approbatory" of sexual immorality and had a "corrosive effect" on public morality even if they lacked explicit depictions of sexual conduct.[76]

If the Supreme Court in *Kingsley Pictures* had endorsed the state court's embrace of thematic obscenity, it would have provided the government with the constitutional authority to regulate a broad array of materials with same-sex sexual themes given that prevailing social mores clearly deemed same-sex sexual relationships and conduct, like adultery, to be morally unacceptable. Instead, the Supreme Court rejected out of hand the notion that materials could be constitutionally banned solely because they encouraged individuals to enter into sexual relationships that society deemed immoral. In writing for the Court, Justice Stewart reasoned that refusing to license a movie because of its approbatory treatment of adultery was essentially to refuse the license because of its advocacy of an idea, something the government could not do without violating the Free Speech Clause's core purpose. Stewart explained that the proposition that the government could deny a license to a movie based on the need to protect public morals "misconceives what it is that the Constitution protects. Its guarantee is not confined to the expression of ideas that are conventional or shared by a majority. It protects advocacy of the opinion that adultery may sometimes be proper, no less than advocacy of socialism or the single tax. And in the realm of ideas it protects expression which is eloquent no less than that which is unconvincing."[77]

Whereas *Roth*'s contribution to the displacement of morality within obscenity law was implicit—by focusing on the social value of the materials in question rather than on the state's interest in promoting public morality—*Kingsley Pictures*'s contribution was direct: The Court explicitly held that the government could not constitutionally regulate the distribution of materials on the ground that they promoted sexual immorality. As two leading commentators on obscenity law noted in 1960, "the main thrust of the opinion in *Kingsley Pictures* is a strong declaration of the constitutional right to advocate unconventional ideas and behavior 'immoral' by current standards, and to do so in effective and dramatic ways."[78]

It is clear, therefore, that when the Court decided its first two cases involving LGBT issues, it was in the process of contributing in crucial ways to the ongoing displacement of morality within obscenity law. It did this by either paying little attention to the sufficiency of the government's interest in protecting public morality (*Roth*), or by holding, in the context of materials that lacked explicit depictions of sexual acts but that the government believed promoted sexually immoral relationships, that the interest was insufficient to trump free speech considerations (*Kingsley Pictures*).[79]

The First Two LGBT Cases before the Supreme Court

ONE's challenge of the government's effort to censor it became the first case directly implicating the interests of lesbians and gay men to reach the Supreme Court. Four years later, the justices agreed to hear Womack's contention that the government's attempt to suppress his gay physique magazines violated the First Amendment. Unlike questions related to discrimination against African Americans, the Court had had no exposure to, or expressed any interest in, issues related to sexual orientation. As we have seen, however, the justices were developing a growing interest in the scope of obscenity regulations. It was from that perspective that the Court approached the first two LGBT rights cases, as we would characterize them today, to reach it.

One v. Olesen

The Supreme Court granted the certiorari petition in *One v. Olesen*, but rather than asking for briefs and scheduling oral arguments, it instead summarily reversed the Court of Appeals in a one-sentence, unanimous, and per curiam (unsigned) opinion that cited to *Roth*.[80] It was not surprising that the Supreme Court, in reversing the lower court's ruling, cited *Roth*, its most important obscenity decision to date, issued several months after the federal appellate decision in *One* and several weeks before *ONE* filed its certiorari petition. Clearly, the Supreme Court did not believe that the October 1954 issue of the gay magazine was obscene under *Roth*. The question that remains unanswered—and will likely never be definitively answered given its summary reversal in *One*—is precisely *why* the Court so believed.

Despite the unavoidable uncertainty that accompanies one-sentence rulings, it is possible, in looking at *One* and *Roth* together, to reach reasonable conclusions about the Court's prevailing views on obscenity as they applied to a gay publication. First, the Court likely concluded, after presumably analyzing the magazine's content, that it did not sufficiently appeal to prurient interests to qualify as obscene under *Roth*. The Court, it is reasonable to believe, concluded that the magazine lacked the minimum degree of *explicit* sexual content required to support a finding that its primary objective was to appeal to the prurient interests of its readers.

At the same time, however, the magazine did have *some* sexual content. The issue in question, after all, included a story about a romantic relationship between two women; a sardonic poem about the same-sex interests of some British peers and the visit to public bathrooms by men looking for sex with other men; and an advertisement by a Swiss magazine that, in addition to publishing political and sociological articles, contained erotic pictures.[81] But, as we have seen, the Court had made clear in *Roth* that "sex and obscenity are not synonymous."[82] What distinguished permissible from impermissible depictions and references to sex under *Roth* was the extent of the material's social value. The second reasonable conclusion that we can reach when interposing the two cases, therefore, is that the gay magazine's content, to use Judge Horn's phrase, manifested, at the very least, "the slightest redeeming social importance."

It is in many ways astounding that the Supreme Court *in 1958* was willing to recognize that a magazine dedicated to the needs and interests of lesbians and gay men had sufficient social importance—despite containing some sexual content—to reverse the lower court's finding of obscenity. In thinking about what the Court did in *One*, it is essential to keep in mind the prevailing social consensus that same-sex sexual relationships and conduct were immoral and deviant. As the two leading commentators on obscenity law noted at the time, "it could scarcely be said that *One, The Homosexual Magazine* enjoys any substantial degree of public acceptance in the nation or that it comports with contemporary standards of the average or majority of the national community."[83]

The outcome in *One* strongly suggests the Court believed that, for purposes of determining the scope of free speech protections, the assessment of the social value of publications deemed by the government to be obscene had to be conducted independently of majoritarian judgments about the morality of the sexual relationships and conduct depicted therein. Indeed, *One* reflects the extent to which the Supreme Court by the late 1950s had embraced the idea that majoritarian moral objections to certain kinds of sexual relationships and acts should be kept separate from the determination of whether particular materials were legally obscene. If the Court in *One* had accepted the federal appellate court's reasoning that the morality of the sexual relationships in question, as determined by contemporary social standards, was a crucial factor in assessing whether the materials were legally obscene, it is highly unlikely that it would have protected the gay magazine under the First Amendment.

One constituted another instance in which the government invited the Court to link the state's authority to regulate obscenity to the preservation of public morals. Its unwillingness to do so foreshadowed its holding the following year in *Kingsley Pictures* that the government could not constitutionally prevent the distribution of materials on the ground that they promoted immoral relationships.

After *One*, it became clear that the government could not censor a publication dedicated to exploring the place of sexual minorities in society, even if most Americans deemed same-sex sexual relationships and conduct to be morally unacceptable. What was not so clear was whether the First Amendment provided protection to publications that, for their era, had significant same-sex erotic content. It was that question which the Court addressed in the second LGBT case to reach it.

Manual Enterprises v. Day

As it had done in *One,* the Supreme Court concluded that the materials at issue in *Manual Enterprises* were not obscene. Justice John Marshall Harlan II, in announcing the Court's judgment, explained that the photographs in question were not obscene because they did not satisfy an element of obscenity that was as essential as the "appeal to prurient interests" element adopted in *Roth,* namely, that the materials be "so offensive on their face as to affront current community standards of decency."[84] This requirement meant that the government had the burden of showing that the materials were "patently offensive."

Harlan explained that the government had to satisfy the patently offensive standard because otherwise it would be able to censor "many worth-while works in literature, science, or art" on the ground that their dominant theme appealed to the prurient interests of readers or observers. To conclude that the federal obscenity statute required nothing more than the inciting of "impure desires relating to sex" would run afoul of the First Amendment because it would render obscene large swaths of materials that, while appealing to prurient interests, were not patently offensive.[85]

Interestingly, Justice Harlan effectively accepted the government's morality-based view of gay men; in his ruling, Harlan described gay men as "unfortunate persons" and "sexual deviates."[86] Crucially, however, he nonetheless concluded that Womack's magazines were not obscene. In doing so, Harlan rejected the government's position that erotic pictures of partially naked men aimed at a gay audience were obscene because they violated moral community standards in ways that female pinup photos aimed at male heterosexuals did not. As Harlan explained, "our own independent examination of the magazines leads us to conclude that the most that can be said of them is that they are dismally unpleasant, uncouth, and tawdry. But this is not enough to make them 'obscene.' Divorced from their 'prurient interest' appeal to the unfortunate persons whose patronage they were aimed at capturing (*a separate issue*), these portrayals of the male nude cannot fairly be regarded as more objectionable than many portrayals of the female nude that society tolerates."[87]

Harlan made clear that, in determining whether gay materials were obscene, it was necessary to put aside the perceived deviancy of those who purchased the materials and instead focus on whether the publications were patently offensive. *That inquiry had nothing to do with moral judgments about gay men and same-sex sexual acts.* The fact that gay men were "unfortunate persons" was, for Harlan, "a separate issue." In establishing whether the magazines' photographs met the "patently offensive" standard, courts had to stick to their four corners, so to speak. As Harlan explained, "it is only material whose indecency is *self-demonstrating*" and that can "be deemed so offensive on [its] *face*" that can constitutionally be considered obscene.[88] In short, Harlan's analysis in *Manual Enterprises* is notable because it separated questions of moral judgments about same-sex sexuality from the issue of whether gay erotic materials were patently offensive and therefore obscene.

The extent to which Justice Harlan's ruling in *Manual Enterprises* separated society's (and his own) moral condemnation of gay men from the legal question of what constituted obscenity is striking. As had occurred in *One*, the distinction between, on the one hand, the moral condemnation of same-sex relationships and, on the other hand, the government's authority to regulate obscenity was crucial in accounting for the LGBT rights victory before the Supreme Court.

It is important to note that the Court's ruling in *Manual Enterprises* was the *first time* that *any court* in the United States had ever suggested that there was an equivalence of sorts between heterosexuality and homosexuality. In concluding that gay physique magazines were not obscene because they were no different from "many portrayals of the female nude that society tolerates," the Court rejected the government's contention that erotica aimed at gay men was, due to that fact alone, more problematic than erotica directed at heterosexuals. The Court's analogy between gay and straight erotica provided same-sex sexuality with a modicum of judicially approved legitimacy, grounded in considerations of rough equivalence with different-sex sexuality, that it had never enjoyed before.

At the same time, it bears emphasizing that the protection afforded by the Supreme Court to gay materials, several years before Stonewall, was not the result of the justices' embrace of a more tolerant understanding of LGBT people. Justice Harlan's negative references to sexual minorities in *Manual Enterprises* make that clear. The source of the protection was instead internal to obscenity law and the ways in which courts by the 1950s and 1960s were more likely, in the face of free speech challenges, to scrutinize government claims that the objective of promoting or protecting public morality was enough to justify expansive applications of obscenity statutes.

The Impact of the Two Judicial Victories

It is important to point out that obscenity prosecutions based on the publication or distribution of gay materials did not cease altogether as a result of the Supreme Court's rulings in *One* and *Manual Enterprises*.[89] Sexually explicit gay materials involving full nudity or depictions of sexual acts were still vulnerable to government censorship.[90] What the two rulings accomplished was to end the enforcement of obscenity laws against publications, such as *ONE*, that addressed political, social, and legal issues while presenting gay people in a positive light, as well as erotic magazines, like physique magazines, that fell short of depicting full nudity.[91]

If the government had prevailed in *One*, it would have made it much more difficult for gay publications, through fictional and nonfictional accounts of the lives of lesbian and gay individuals, to challenge prevailing moral understandings of sexual minorities by presenting same-sex sexuality as not being different than heterosexuality in morally significant ways. The partial displacement of morality within obscenity law, in other words, allowed for the beginning of a process of moral replacement, as early gay and lesbian advocates began to challenge the prevailing moral opprobrium of sexual minorities.

ONE's legal victory allowed for the continuation and expansion of a phenomenon that had never before taken place in American history: lesbians and gay men sharing their views in print about both their sexuality and their place in society. This expression took place not only through the publication of homophile magazines such as *ONE*, the *Mattachine Review* (published by the Mattachine Society), and the *Ladder* (published by the Daughters of Bilitis), but also through other printed forms, such as the growing number of novels being published with gay and lesbian themes. During the late 1950s and early 1960s, for example, there was an explosion in the publication of lesbian pulp novels, many of which contained positive, and increasingly erotic, portrayals of female same-sex sexual relationships.[92] If the Court in *One* had affirmed the government's victory in the lower courts, it would have made it possible for prosecutors and other law enforcement officials to prevent the distribution of books and magazines simply on the basis that they contained lesbian and gay themes. The fact that the government after *One* could no longer justify its regulation of publications aimed at presenting same-sex sexual relationships and conduct in a positive light on the ground that they violated society's moral strictures provided constitutional protection for publishers, writers, and advocates who questioned those strictures. The judicial victory encouraged the publication of books and magazines that helped to render lesbians and gay men more visible, and to do so on terms set by them rather than by a hostile society.

Although the mainstream press in the 1950s and 1960s was paying increasing attention to lesbians and gay men, it did so almost exclusively through articles written with contemptuous themes and in derisive tones. In 1966, for example, *Time* magazine published an article vilifying homosexuality, warning that "it deserves no encouragement, no glamorization, no rationalization, no fake status as minority martyrdom, no sophistry about simple differences in taste—and, above all, no pretense that it is anything but a pernicious sickness."[93] Similarly, a *New York Times* article published three years earlier claimed that "the absence of any legal ties, plus the basic emotional instability that is inherent in many homosexuals, cause [them] to founder on the jealousies and personality clashes that a heterosexual union would survive."[94]

Gay publications allowed lesbians and gay men to present and describe their lives and aspirations in ways that directly contradicted such outlandish claims. As the journalism professor Rodger Streitmatter notes, homophile magazines in particular "created a national venue for homosexuals, forming an arena in which lesbians and gay men could, for the first time, speak above a whisper about issues fundamental to their lives."[95] Indeed, the magazines contained some of the first manifestations of lesbian and gay *pride*, that is, the notion that despite society's harsh disapproval, the lives and relationships of lesbians and gay men were worthy of acknowledgment, celebration, and ultimately, moral respect.

This public discourse helped to forge links of identity and community among those with same-sex sexual orientations. Unlike racial and religious minorities, whose communities and identities were usually formed at a young age within their own families, sexual minorities had to construct their identities and communities as adults without assistance from their families and communities of origin. The availability of magazines that described the few joys and many challenges of being gay in America helped to create a common language and a sense of solidarity and mutual support among sexual minorities. As the historian John D'Emilio notes, the homophile magazines "played a part in creating a common vocabulary. In evolving a shared language to articulate their experiences, gay men and women came a step closer to emerging as a self-conscious minority."[96]

It was not just access to homophile publications and novels with positive portrayals of lesbians and gay men that helped to form identity and community links among those with same-sex sexual orientations. Also contributing to this process were publications, constitutionally protected after *Manual Enterprises*, which focused more explicitly on the eroticism of same-sex sexuality.

The physique magazines reached a much greater number of readers than did homophile publications. The monthly circulation of Womack's publications alone was forty thousand, and the combined circulation of all gay physique magazines was in the hundreds of thousands. In contrast, the circulation of *ONE* never reached above five thousand.

Physique magazines, like homophile publications, played important roles in forming gay identities and communities. As David Johnson notes, "countless men who came of age in cold war America vividly remember their first encounter with physique magazines as part of their journey to self-identification as homosexual."[97] By unashamedly celebrating the beauty of the male body, the magazines helped gay men feel less conflicted about their sexual orientation. As another commentator notes, "physique magazines told homosexuals they were not alone, that they had a distinct shared culture."[98]

The Court's ruling in *Manual Enterprises* allowed not only the continued publication of physique magazine, but also the publication of new types of magazines that combined political/social commentary *and* erotic content. These new magazines, which proved to be highly popular among gay men, promoted and reinforced the notion that the sexual was political.

One of the new publications was *Drum*, a magazine first published by the Janus Society, a Philadelphia homophile organization, in 1964. Like *ONE*, *Drum* published news and advocacy articles aimed at a gay audience. And like Womack's publications, it also contained male erotica. This combination proved to be immensely popular. By 1966, *Drum*'s circulation had reached more than ten thousand, a huge number for a homophile publication. As Rodger Streitmatter and John Watson note, "after this success, virtually every editor who founded a publication aimed at gay readers incorporated homoerotic images into his editorial mix."[99] The publishing strategy of combining political and erotic materials led to an explosion of publications like *Drum*; by the end of the decade, there were about 150 such publications with a combined circulation of more than 250,000.[100]

The response by some of the more traditional homophile organizations to *Drum* and other magazines that sought to merge the political with the sexual was highly critical.[101] For older homophile activists, an emphasis on sex and eroticism undermined the movement's political objectives. But younger activists, in the throes of the sexual revolution of the 1960s, were increasingly emphasizing the liberationist potential of sexuality while criticizing what they saw as the assimilationist tendencies of the older generation of activists. At the same time, many in the LGBT community by the late 1960s came to dismiss magazines like *ONE*, which had seemed so radical a decade earlier, as conservative and timid. As a result, lesbian and gay publications that were more politically confrontational grew in size and influence. Similarly, on the erotic side, there was growing demand for more sexually explicit publications, including ones that showed individuals engaging in same-sex sexual acts.

But the fact that the magazines at issue in the two Supreme Court cases were eventually supplanted by more politically forceful and sexually explicit publications only magnifies the importance of the two judicial victories. Those victories helped to create the necessary legal and social conditions that contributed to the blossoming of lesbian and gay publications during the 1960s.[102] Those publications, in turn, played important roles in challenging the terms of public debates over LGBT people, their relationships, and their sexual conduct. As D'Emilio explains, the two Supreme Court rulings removed "legal barriers to the presentation of homoeroticism in print and in visual media" and, in the process, led to "a bewildering variety of images and viewpoints about homosexuality. . . . This barrage of information made it easier for people to come to a self-definition as homosexual or lesbian, strengthened the institutions of the subculture, and gave activists more opportunity for action."[103]

Of course, the United States by the end of the 1960s was, politically and culturally, a very different country than it had been when the two gay obscenity cases reached the Supreme Court only a few years before. By the time of the Stonewall riots and other manifestations of the sexual and political revolutions that were convulsing the nation by the decade's end, postal investigators and other government officials were paying little attention to gay publications that were, by then, considered rather tame. But whether any given publication is deemed tame or radical (or somewhere in between) depends on prevailing social norms. What is ultimately most fascinating, and important as a legal matter, about *One* and *Manual Enterprises* is that the Supreme Court was able to assess the extent to which the publications at issue were obscene *independently* of the pervasive moral condemnation of same-sex relationships and conduct that prevailed throughout society at the time. That separation between law and public morality contributed in crucial ways to the first two LGBT rights victories before the Supreme Court. The separation also foreshadowed the Court's unwillingness to allow majoritarian morality to determine LGBT individuals' constitutional rights to equality and privacy in its later, and much more famous, cases involving sodomy and marriage laws.

Later Moral Displacement

One and *Manual Enterprises* showed that the Court, very early in the history of the LGBT rights movement, was willing and able to separate majoritarian judgments about the relationships and intimacies of LGBT individuals from questions related to their free speech rights. The Court's approach to the intersection of morality and free speech in LGBT cases stood in marked contrast to how it understood the role of morality in the context of substantive due process and the right to privacy decades later in *Bowers v. Hardwick*, a case involving the arrest of a gay man in his Atlanta home for having consensual sex with another man. Georgia defended the constitutionality of its sodomy law by claiming that homosexuality was at odds with "traditional Judeo-Christian values," as reflected in its having been condemned for centuries in Europe and the United States. As far as the state was concerned, "homosexual sodomy" was nothing more than "sexual deviancy. . . . It is purely an unnatural means of satisfying an unnatural lust, which has been declared by Georgia to be morally wrong." From the state's perspective, it was entirely appropriate for the legislature to codify the majority of Georgians' moral values into the sodomy proscription: "In Georgia, it is the very act of homosexual sodomy that epitomizes moral delinquency. Th[e] . . . choice [to criminalize the conduct] has been made by the representatives of the people of this State, based upon the traditional moral values of society."[104]

The Court in *Bowers* embraced the state's understanding of the proper role of morality in accounting for both the government's authority to regulate sexual relationships and the lack of privacy rights for LGBT people in matters related to sexuality. In explaining that the Constitution did not recognize a fundamental right to engage in "homosexual sodomy," the Court pointed to the sodomy statutes' "ancient roots" and to the fact that all of the original thirteen states had them at the time they ratified the Bill of Rights. To argue, in the face of such long standing condemnation of same-sex sexual conduct, that there was a fundamental right at issue was, "at best, facetious."[105]

In addition, the Court rejected the contention that morality constituted an impermissible basis upon which to legislate by explaining that "the law . . . is constantly based on notions of morality, and if all laws representing essentially moral choices are to be invalidated under the Due Process Clause, the courts will be very busy indeed."[106] For his part, Chief Justice Warren Burger wrote a concurring opinion emphasizing the point made by the majority: that sodomy had been denounced "throughout the history of Western civilization" and that the "condemnation of those practices is firmly rooted in Judeao-Christian moral and ethical standards."[107] Both of these opinions stood in marked contrast to how the Court, decades earlier in *One* and *Manual Enterprises*, had rejected the moral condemnation of same-sex sexuality as a justification for censoring gay publications.

It was not until the Court revisited the constitutionality of sodomy laws in 2003 that it rejected government arguments justifying the proscription of same-sex sexual conduct (as opposed to speech) on public morality grounds. In striking down sodomy laws in *Lawrence v. Texas*, the Court rejected *Bowers*'s holding that moral objections and disapproval of same-sex sexual conduct sufficed to uphold the constitutionality of those statutes. As the Court had done in *One* and *Manual Enterprises*, a majority of the justices in *Lawrence* concluded that their obligation was to determine the constitutional rights enjoyed by all without relying on their own, or society's, moral code.[108]

The same kind of moral displacement in its constitutional reasoning, decades after *One* and *Manual Enterprises*, is also found in the Court's LGBT equal protection rulings. In *Romer v. Evans*, the Court struck down a 1992 Colorado constitutional amendment that sought to prevent lesbians, gay men, and bisexuals, but no others, from receiving antidiscrimination protections under state and local laws. The *Romer* Court found the state measure to be unconstitutional because it was the result of animus grounded in the moral disapproval of sexual minorities.[109]

The Court returned to the question of whether a statute enacted in order to express moral disapproval of a class of individuals could survive constitutional scrutiny in 2013 when it considered the constitutionality of the Defense of Marriage Act (DOMA) in *United States v. Windsor*, a case decided under both the liberty and equality protections afforded by the Fifth Amendment.[110] In striking down the DOMA provision that prohibited the federal government from recognizing state-sanctioned marriages by same-sex couples, the Court emphasized that the statute's purpose and effect was to express disapproval of same-sex couples. The majority quoted from a House Committee report explicitly stating that DOMA was intended to express "both moral disapproval of homosexuality, and a moral conviction that heterosexuality better comports with traditional (especially Judeo–Christian) morality."[111] As the Court explained, the statute's very purpose, according to the report itself, was to promote an "interest in protecting the traditional moral teachings reflected in heterosexual-only marriage laws."[112] This meant that the DOMA provision was unconstitutional because it sought to use federal law to demean same-sex couples by relegating their state-approved marriages to second-class status.

The Court in both *Romer* and *Windsor* made clear that moral disapproval of same-sex sexual relationships and conduct does not constitute a constitutionally valid justification for the differential treatment of lesbians, gay men, and bisexuals under the Equal Protection Clause. As such, the two rulings are consistent with the Court's holding in *Lawrence* that moral disapproval constitutes an insufficient basis upon which to regulate the sexual intimacy choices of sexual minorities under the Due Process Clause.

The chronology of moral displacement in constitutional law as it has impacted sexual minorities—with free speech coming first and privacy/equality second—is one that, on reflection, makes sense. The question of whether same-sex sexual *conduct* could be regulated based on moral grounds was a highly disputed one for decades, in part because of the intuitive point that much of what the criminal law prohibits—murder, rape, and theft, among other acts—is morally wrong conduct. But the constitutional questions raised in *One* and *Manual Enterprises* were about *speech* rather than conduct.

As we have seen, starting around the 1930s, courts became increasingly skeptical of the proposition that sexually explicit materials inevitably harmed society because they undermined public morals. Furthermore, as the Supreme Court explicitly recognized in *Kingsley Pictures*, the notion that the government could censor speech on the ground that what was being advocated, portrayed, or discussed violated majoritarian moral norms was deeply inconsistent with free speech principles. Under such reasoning, there were no limits to the viewpoints that the government could squelch (socialist ideas, the appropriateness of legalizing marijuana, the defense of polygamy) based on the notion that they were morally offensive to the majority of the population.

It is not surprising that it took the Court longer to conclude that majoritarian morality was also an impermissible basis upon which to justify both the regulation of consensual same-sex sexual conduct (the due process question) and the differential treatment of individuals based on their sexual orientation (the equal protection question). As a general matter, the government is on firmer ground when it regulates conduct than when it regulates speech. As the Court has explained, "the Constitution presumes that attempts to regulate speech are more dangerous than attempts to regulate conduct. That presumption accords with the essential role that the free flow of information plays in a democratic society."[113]

The Court did eventually conclude, primarily under the doctrine of substantive due process, that engaging in certain conduct (such as having an abortion or using contraceptives) is constitutionally protected.[114] And when it did so in the context of same-sex sexual conduct, it reached the same conclusion it had reached in the gay obscenity cases of several decades earlier: that the promotion and protection of public morality is an insufficient justification for state action that impacts on the constitutional rights of individuals.

The moral displacement within due process and equal protection doctrine in the context of sexuality that took place as a result of rulings such as *Lawrence*, *Romer*, and *Windsor* occurred alongside large shifts in social and moral understandings of LGBT individuals and their relationships, shifts that were made possible—as explored in Chapters 2, 3, and 4—by the freedom of sexual minorities to speak on, advocate for, and associate around issues that were important to them. The deep changes in social mores that came about as a result of these constitutionally protected modes of expression contributed to the Court's rejection of the constitutional sufficiency of moral condemnation of same-sex sexuality as a basis for government policy under due process and equal protection analyses, and also to its recognizing the dignity that inheres in LGBT individuals and their relationships.[115]

Although the Court's more recent skepticism of moral disapproval as a constitutionally valid justification for the differential treatment of sexual minorities parallels changing social views toward those minorities, the same cannot be said about *One* and *Manual Enterprises*. Rather than reflecting changed understandings of LGBT individuals and their relationships, the outcomes in those two cases were instead the consequence of the Court's growing skepticism, under free speech principles, of the notion that the government's interest in promoting public morality granted it virtually untrammeled discretion to regulate books, magazines, and other materials that contained sexual ideas, themes, and depictions. To put it another way, the Court's skepticism of broad public morality justifications for obscenity regulations as they impacted gay publications took place *before* society began to change its views about sexual minorities. In contrast, the Court's rejection of moral justifications for the regulation of consensual same-sex sexual conduct took place *alongside* changing understandings of LGBT people and their relationships.

It is, once again, not surprising that the moral displacement first took place in the context of speech. The essential purpose of the Free Speech Clause is to afford protection to those who express views that differ from majoritarian perspectives and preferences. It was only after the Court protected the ability of sexual minorities to express themselves despite society's deep moral disapproval that it also concluded, decades later, that moral disapproval constituted a constitutionally invalid justification for regulating same-sex sexual conduct and for classifying individuals according to their sexual orientation.

CHAPTER TWO

Coming Together and Free Expression

THE ABILITY of sexual minorities to start demanding equal treatment and full citizenship rights depended not only on the freedom to publish and distribute magazines and other publications, but also on the ability to come together in groups and organizations to pursue common interests and objectives. Most gay groups in the 1950s and 1960s consisted of small, politically driven homophile organizations. In contrast, the 1970s saw an explosion in the number and variety of LGBT organizations, spanning the gamut from political to cultural to educational to social to artistic to professional to religious groups.

The First Amendment played a crucial role in making it possible for sexual minorities to come together. Initially, the efforts by LGBT people to associate with each other were not explicitly political, as sexual minorities in urban areas during the first decades of the twentieth century sought simply to find friendship and support in public spaces, most particularly bars. Local officials across the country responded to the growing gatherings of "deviants" and "inverts" (as sexual minorities were called at the time) in public establishments by unleashing campaigns of harassment and intimidation, most prominently through aggressive police raids and, after Prohibition ended, relentless liquor license investigations. Although these government campaigns caused grave harms to their targets through countless arrests, public humiliations, the shutting down of businesses, and physical injuries resulting from police violence, they had two unintended and positive consequences: first, they led to the recognition by some courts that sexual minorities had the right to congregate in public without being subjected to government harassment; and second, they encouraged LGBT people to band together to form organizations aimed at protecting themselves from government intimidation and discrimination.

As this chapter explains, sexual minorities, in forming their own organizations, benefited greatly from Supreme Court First Amendment rulings that protected the ability of civil rights organizations and activists during the 1950s and 1960s to agitate for political and legal reforms aimed at promoting racial equality. Among other things, that case law established that the First Amendment protects the right of association, a right that generally prohibits the government from interfering with the ability of individuals to band together to pursue common objectives. Interestingly and ironically, it would be this same right, as we will see in Chapter 6, that opponents of LGBT equality later turned to in order to try to limit the state's authority to promote equality for sexual minorities.

The chapter also explores how early activists succeeded in getting courts in some jurisdictions to limit the government's authority to penalize bars and other public establishments simply because they allowed LGBT people to congregate. In addition, the chapter explains how harassment by police departments and liquor license investigators of sexual minorities who congregated in lesbian and gay bars sparked political mobilizing and organizing by LGBT people. In turn, in the years leading up to Stonewall, it became clear that the First Amendment protected this mobilizing and organizing.[1]

In the 1970s, growing numbers of sexual minorities pursued common objectives by creating a wide variety of LGBT organizations. As also explored in this chapter, some government officials tried to place roadblocks in the new groups' paths in order to minimize their effectiveness and diminish their visibility. This was particularly reflected in the refusal by some public university administrators to recognize LGBT student groups and in the efforts by officials to prevent LGBT groups from enjoying the benefits of incorporation and from speaking and participating in public forums. But the courts consistently ruled that such efforts were unconstitutional under the First Amendment. At a time when sexual minorities, as a class, enjoyed few other constitutional rights, they won almost every time they relied on the First Amendment to challenge government actions aimed at making it more difficult for them to find mutual support, and pursue common goals, by coming together in groups.

As the chapter explains, the hundreds of LGBT organizations that existed throughout the country by the late 1970s constituted the backbone of the LGBT movement. The groups served as vehicles through which sexual minorities, in a variety of contexts and ways, amplified their individual voices in challenging how society understood and regulated LGBT people, their relationships, and their sexual conduct. In doing so, LGBT organizations contributed in crucial ways to the process of moral replacement through which growing segments of the American society shifted from viewing homosexuality as immoral and perverse to seeing sexual orientation as a morally benign trait and sexual orientation discrimination as a moral wrong.

The consistency with which gay organizations won free speech cases during the 1970s is remarkable. These victories stood in stark contrast to the general inability of lesbian, gay, and bisexual litigants to prevail in constitutional challenges under the Equal Protection and Due Process Clauses. At the end of the chapter, I identify four reasons why LGBT litigants, during the early days of the LGBT rights movement, generally succeeded in their free speech claims at a time when they consistently lost equality and privacy cases.

The First Amendment, Ideological Silencing, and Group Exclusion

The Supreme Court began to engage with the First Amendment in earnest during, and in the aftermath of, World War I. Before then, the law that generated the most controversy because of its impact on speech in the United States was the Sedition Act of 1798, the constitutionality of which the Supreme Court did not address. The Sedition Act, enacted by the Federalist-controlled Congress and signed into law by President John Adams as the young nation seemed to be on the brink of war with France, essentially prohibited criticism of the federal government. More than a dozen Republicans, including newspaper editors and a Congressman, were prosecuted under the law, and some were sent to prison. The much-reviled statute expired of its own accord in 1801.[2]

A little more than a century later, shortly after the United States entered World War I, Congress enacted the Espionage Act of 1917, which, among other things, prohibited interference with military operations and recruitment. Although the statute was not directed at expression as such, federal prosecutors during the war, and the politically unsettled years that followed, used it to charge thousands of individuals whom they believed were essentially enemies of the state. Officials claimed that large numbers of pacifists, anarchists, communists, and socialists (including Eugene Debs, who ran for president several times as the Socialist Party's candidate and received around one million votes in 1912 and then again in 1920 *after* he was jailed for giving an antiwar speech) were undermining the government's ability to defend the nation by criticizing the war, the military draft, and the country's foreign policies. Several of those prosecuted challenged the statute (as well as a related provision, known as the Sedition Act of 1918, which directly targeted expression by prohibiting the "use of any language intended to bring . . . contempt, scorn, . . . or disrepute" upon the government) under the First Amendment. These challenges required the Supreme Court, for the first time, to grapple extensively with the amendment's free speech protections.[3] The Court, uniformly and disappointingly, upheld the constitutionality of the prosecutions, largely accepting the government's contention that criticism of its foreign and military policies imperiled national security.[4] In hindsight, the only redeeming aspect of these rulings was that some were accompanied by concurring and dissenting opinions by justices Oliver Wendell Holmes Jr. and Louis Brandeis that crucially distinguished between criticism of the government and the inciting of others to commit unlawful acts. Although it would take several decades, the Court eventually adopted the Holmes/Brandeis view that the Free Speech Clause protects the ability of citizens to forcefully and vehemently criticize government policies, both foreign and domestic, and that such speech can only be criminalized when the expression is imminently likely to lead to significant and grave harm.[5]

Government campaigns to squelch free speech following the nation's entry into World War I, which continued for several years after the end of hostilities, were aimed at those whom officials believed to be the nation's ideological enemies. Although the prosecutions themselves were based on alleged efforts to obstruct the draft and, after the war, to overthrow the government, it is clear that officials targeted anarchists, socialists, and syndicalists not only because they perceived the defendants to have misplaced national loyalties—initially, in favor of Germany, and upon the war's end, the Soviet Union—but also because of the targets' political and economic ideas. The government at this time aimed its censorship efforts almost exclusively at vehement critics of the capitalist economic system as strongly supported by the nation's political and corporate leaders. All of this meant that the Supreme Court, in addressing the scope of constitutional free speech protections during in the late 1910s and into the 1920s, was in essence confronted with instances of ideological exclusion as the government sought to silence many of its most radical critics.

The 1930s saw fewer overt efforts by the federal government to target radical critics, as the nation turned more inward and focused on addressing the many economic and social ills caused by the Great Depression. But in 1940, after Stalin and Hitler signed a nonaggression pact and war returned to Europe, Congress thought it necessary to deal once again with perceived domestic threats to national security by enacting the Alien Registration Act. That law, commonly known as the Smith Act, required all resident aliens to register with the government and made it a crime to advocate the violent overthrow of the government. Ten years later, Congress enacted the McCarran Internal Security Act, which required all communists to register with the government and denied those who registered the ability to work for the government, military, or unions. And in 1954, Congress passed the Communist Control Act, which stripped the Communist party of "all rights, privileges, and immunities."[6]

The Supreme Court did little to remedy these laws' clear abridgement of free speech rights. In 1952, the Court, in *Dennis v. United States*, upheld the convictions of twelve senior leaders of the Communist Party under the Smith Act, concluding that prosecutors had met their constitutional obligation to show that the defendants' speech advocating communism created a "clear and present danger" to the federal government.[7] After *Dennis*, prosecutors charged dozens of other communists under the Smith Act.[8] These prosecutions took place alongside congressional witch-hunts and other government investigations, led most prominently by Senator Joseph McCarthy, aimed at uncovering the purportedly large number of communists and their sympathizers working for the federal civil service, the military, and the movie industry.[9]

But it was not only communists who were perceived to be threats to national security; so were lesbians and gay men. In responding to Senator McCarthy's accusation in 1950 that the State Department was teeming with communists, the Deputy Undersecretary of State attempted to reassure Congress by explaining that while there were no Communists working for the department, the agency had recently expelled a large number of employees believed to constitute security threats, including ninety-one "homosexuals." This revelation, far from calming the waters, led incensed congressmen and newspaper editorialists to ask why there were so many "homosexuals" working for the government to begin with and to demand that those who remained be rooted out. As a result, over the next several years, hundreds of lesbians and gay men lost their government jobs, and hundreds more were denied civil service employment to begin with.[10]

Although the motivations and fears behind the Red Scare and the Lavender Scare had much in common, there was an important difference: the prosecution of Communists and their sympathizers was driven by the targets' ideological views; in contrast, the persecution of lesbian and gay civil servants was driven not by what they believed, but by *who they were*. The witch-hunts aimed at sexual minorities, therefore, raised questions not of ideological silencing but of group exclusion.

The lesbian and gay victims of the 1950s government witch-hunts were not in a position to challenge them constitutionally, much less politically or legislatively. But there was another group that, by the end of the 1950s, was in a better position to challenge government efforts to exclude and silence them: African Americans. By then civil rights activists, empowered by the Supreme Court's ruling in *Brown v. Board of Education* and by the gradual, and much belated, recognition by a growing number of white Americans of the suffering and injustice inflicted by racial segregation, were starting to turn increasingly to the First Amendment for protection. And the Supreme Court, which had been entirely unmoved by the government's ideological silencing of communists and their sympathizers, started showing little tolerance for government efforts to silence civil rights activists. Eventually, in the years following Stonewall, LGBT rights activists were able to build on the First Amendment cases from the civil rights era to begin the process of gaining basic civil rights for sexual minorities.

The Civil Rights Movement and the First Amendment

During the 1950s and 1960s, the Supreme Court decided a series of First Amendment cases involving civil rights organizations and protestors that played a crucial role in helping the civil rights movement end de jure racial segregation. Although the equal protection case of *Brown v. Board of Education* understandably symbolizes the movement's legal gains during this period, the Court also decided important, albeit less well-known, First Amendment cases rendering unconstitutional efforts by Southern officials to use state authority to intimidate, harass, and ultimately silence African Americans.

One of the most important of those cases was *NAACP v. Alabama*, decided in 1958. The case arose after the NAACP challenged the authority of Alabama officials to force it to reveal the names and addresses of its members living in the state. The push to have the NAACP release its member rolls in Alabama was a transparent attempt to intimidate it into ceasing its agitation in favor of equal rights for African Americans. The Court, in holding that the organization had a constitutional right to withhold its membership list from the state, for the first time found a government action unconstitutional based on the right of association. As the Court explained, the "freedom to engage in association for the advancement of beliefs and ideas is an inseparable aspect of the 'liberty' assured by the Due Process Clause of the Fourteenth Amendment, which embraces freedom of speech." After holding that state action which has "the effect of curtailing the freedom to associate is subject to the closest scrutiny," the Court concluded that Alabama did not have a compelling interest in forcing the NAACP to make public its membership rolls given that doing so would significantly impact the ability of its members to advocate collectively in favor of their political positions.[11]

In the years that followed, the Supreme Court repeatedly struck down efforts by state and local governments to interfere with the NAACP's ability to pursue its civil rights objectives. The Court in those cases made clear that the right of association allowed organizations, like the NAACP, not only to withhold its membership lists from the state, but also to use litigation to pursue political objectives.[12] In addition, the Court held that the First Amendment prevented the government from forcing public school teachers to reveal the organizations to which they belonged.[13] (In Arkansas, officials tried to use such a law to pressure and silence black teachers who belonged to the NAACP.) Prior to the Court's intervention in these cases, harassment and intimidation by both government officials and private citizens had led to a dramatic fall in NAACP membership rolls in the South—from 128,000 in 1955 to 80,000 in 1957—and the closing of 250 local chapters.[14] As one commentator puts it, "the NAACP could not have survived in the South, and the civil rights movement would have been set back for years, without the Court's new freedom of association protections."[15]

In another First Amendment case from the civil rights era, *New York Times v. Sullivan*, the court addressed a question of fundamental import that had been left unresolved since the Sedition Act of 1798: Was it possible to defame the government, or its representatives, through criticism? The Court, in a case involving a libel lawsuit brought by an Alabama official against the *New York Times* for publishing an advertisement paid for by a civil rights organization critical of his policies, answered no. As the Court explained, the First Amendment stood for "a profound national commitment to the principle that debate on public issues should be uninhibited, robust, and wide-open, and that it may well include vehement, caustic, and sometimes unpleasantly sharp attacks on government and public officials."[16] It was not until the *New York Times* case—decided 166 years after the first Sedition Act's enactment—that the Court made clear that the "central meaning" of the Amendment was to protect vigorous criticism of the government, a form of protection, as a leading First Amendment commentator put it at the time, "without which democracy cannot function."[17]

In addition, the Court during the civil rights years came to the aid of those who took to the streets to demand equal treatment on the basis of race. As many Americans were seeing for themselves on the evening news, these protestors were often at the mercy of Southern law enforcement officials who consistently used and abused their authority in order to harass, intimidate, and silence them. In one case from 1963, the Court overturned the breach of the peace convictions of almost two hundred African-American high school and college students who were protesting peacefully against segregation on the grounds of the South Carolina State House.[18] Two years later, the Court overturned the conviction of an African-American minister who had been sentenced to serve almost two years in prison for leading a peaceful demonstration by two thousand African-American college students—protesting the arrests of other students for picketing stores that maintained segregated lunch counters—near the courthouse in downtown Baton Rouge, Louisiana.[19]

The NAACP cases, as well as those involving civil rights street protests, raised the fundamental question of whether organizations and individuals advocating for certain reforms and ideals were entitled to constitutional protection from laws and enforcement actions that were intended to discourage political mobilization and agitation. The reason why the affirmative answer to that question seems so obvious to us today is due largely to the collective holdings of the Court's free speech cases from the civil rights era.

It was not the case, however, that the Court in the early 1960s was deeply committed to protecting political advocacy and association from state repression in all circumstances. Indeed, the Court at around this time continued to uphold the constitutionality of state efforts to squelch whatever remnants of the Communist Party still existed in the United States.[20] Part of what explains the different outcomes between the "red" and the "black" First Amendment cases is undoubtedly the fact that a majority of the justices into the 1960s were still willing to defer to Congress's judgment that the U.S. Communist Party, despite having few members, little money, and no influence to speak of, somehow was capable of overthrowing the American government. But it is also the case that the "black" cases, as a practical (if not a doctrinal) matter, were not just about free speech—they were also about equality. To put it simply, the civil rights activists who were repeatedly filing First Amendment challenges were trying to bring to fruition the lofty equality ideals that stood behind the Court's rejection of racial segregation in *Brown v. Board of Education.*

That monumental ruling by the Court infuriated many white Southerners who viewed integration as an existential threat to their communities and lifestyles, leading large numbers of Southern government officials to do everything they could—including enacting laws aimed at getting around *Brown*'s mandate and supporting police efforts to harass and intimidate civil rights demonstrators—to protect the Jim Crow regime from what they took to be outside (that is, Northern and federal) intervention. The reactionary and intransigent resistance by many Southern whites to racial integration meant that the constitutional claims to free speech and association raised by civil rights advocates, in challenging that resistance, became inextricably linked to the attainment of equality objectives. To rule against the advocates' free speech claims was to make it significantly less likely that meaningful equality for African Americans would be achieved in the foreseeable future. Similarly, the First Amendment challenges brought by LGBT individuals and organizations, starting in the 1970s, were also closely linked to the growing efforts by the LGBT rights movement to promote equality for sexual minorities.

Policing Sexuality through Anti-Association Measures

The enforcement of obscenity laws, as we saw in the last chapter, was one way in which the government sought to keep lesbians, gay men, and bisexuals both silent and invisible. Another way of doing so was through measures aimed at making it difficult for sexual minorities to find each other and come together by socializing and organizing. As they had done with obscenity laws, early gay activists challenged, under the First Amendment, government anti-association measures aimed at sexual minorities.

As law professor William Eskridge has noted, although "Americans had seen feminized men and . . . women [who passed as men] before and during the Civil War," what changed after the war was the growing number of such individuals who seemed to be coming together in public places in many of the nation's cities, in particular in bars (or saloons, as they were called back then).[21] By the 1880s, for example, there were several saloons in New York City's Bowery and San Francisco's Presidio neighborhoods that showcased female impersonators and where men cruised other men for sex.[22] But meeting places for socializing and cruising were not limited to bars. As the sexologist Havelock Ellis noted in 1915, "the world of sexual inverts is, indeed, a large one in any American city, and it is a community distinctly organized—words, customs, traditions of its own; and every city has its numerous meeting-places: certain churches where inverts congregate; certain cafes well known for the inverted character of their patrons; certain streets where, at night, every fifth man is an invert. The inverts [even] have their own 'clubs,' with nightly meetings."[23]

During this era of increased urbanization, government officials and civic leaders began to sound the alarm about both prostitution and so-called sexual degeneracy. As Eskridge documents, government officials around the turn of the twentieth century began persecuting "degenerates" and "inverts" at rates not seen before in American history. The persecution of those who engaged in same-sex sexual conduct was carried out by enforcing sodomy laws more aggressively and by applying laws originally aimed at curtailing prostitution, including vagrancy, loitering, indecent exposure, public lewdness, and solicitation statutes. Some states, like New York and California, went even further by enacting laws specifically used to "arrest or detain cruising or parading inverts: in New York, the offense was 'disorderly conduct—degeneracy'; in San Francisco and Los Angeles, it was the state misdemeanor 'lewd vagrancy.'"[24]

By the 1920s, several large city police departments had created vice squads whose main responsibilities were to investigate female heterosexual prostitution and target LGBT people for prosecution. Although many of the vice squads' arrests of LGBT people were made on city streets and in public parks, usually by enticing men to solicit sex from undercover male officers (entrapment), establishments that catered to gender-variant individuals were also tempting targets for law enforcement officials. By raiding bars, dancing halls, bathhouses, and other establishments where LGBT people congregated—venues that were often the subject of complaints by morality-promoting civic associations such as the New York's Society for the Prevention of Vice—officials could arrest and prosecute large numbers of "degenerates" and "inverts" in one fell swoop.

As George Chauncey and other historians of gay and lesbian life in large American cities before World War II have shown, the ability to come together in public meeting places—to drink, dance, find lovers, or simply talk—was a growing feature of the development of gay and lesbian subcultures.[25] At this point, few individuals were thinking of associating to pursue explicitly political objectives. (The short-lived Society for Human Rights, the nation's first organization formed to advance the interests of sexual minorities, was an exception before it fell victim to a Chicago police raid in 1924.)[26] Instead, the goal was to find camaraderie, entertainment, support, and sexual release in a society that otherwise denied such opportunities to gender-variant individuals.

The state was able to discourage LGBT people from associating with one another through the enforcement of criminal laws and also, following the end of Prohibition in 1933, through the regulation of liquor licenses. After Prohibition, most states enacted laws authorizing the revocation of licenses if establishment owners allowed disorderly or immoral conduct to take place on their premises.[27] State liquor officials in cities across the country relied on these laws either to revoke the liquor licenses of restaurants and bars that permitted lesbians and gay men to congregate or to force them to exclude LGBT people under the threat of revocation. The loss of licenses, for the vast majority of establishments, led to a severe drop in revenue and, eventually, to closure.

Officials frequently combined aggressive police raids with liquor license investigations to harass gender-variant individuals and to discourage them from congregating in public view. For example, officials in New York City, while "cleaning up" the city in preparation for the 1939 World Fair, used police raids and license revocations to close several gay bars.[28] In 1943, a joint task force in San Francisco composed of local police officers, liquor license investigators, and military officials targeted gay bars in order "to protect" servicemen from gay men. At one of the bars, the

Rickshaw in Chinatown, a raid led to a small riot and the beating by police officers of two lesbians.[29] By the time the task force closed shop, it had arrested fifty individuals and suspended the licenses of several bars.[30]

The national mobilization created by World War II led to a dramatic increase in the numbers of lesbians and gay men who flocked to the nation's cities. This migration, in turn, led to a significant increase in the number of public establishments that catered to sexual minorities. But the accompanying greater public visibility of lesbians and gay men soon clashed with postwar conservative sexual mores and with the outright paranoia aimed at those who were different, leading to a ratcheting up of state efforts to harass and intimidate sexual minorities. As a result, the number of police raids of lesbian and gay establishments, along with the number of arrests of their patrons, grew considerably after the war. For example, the Chicago police in 1949 raided the Windup, a popular gay bar, and arrested eighty-seven of its male patrons.[31] In 1953, police officers in New Orleans arrested sixty-four women at a lesbian bar in the French Quarter.[32] That same year, the Director of the Crime Commission of Greater Miami called for a crack-down on gay establishments after claiming that "there is a connection between the open operation of [gay] bars and nightclubs with reported cases of child molestation."[33] In 1954, the mayor of Miami threatened to fire the police chief and city manager unless they closed down all the gay bars in town. Shortly thereafter, police officers repeatedly visited all known gay bars in the city, leading customers to stay away and some to close.[34] In 1955, the police in Baltimore raided a gay bar called the Pepper Hill Club, arresting 162 customers, forcing them to either pay the costs of their being booked for "disorderly conduct" or spend the night in jail. The charges were dismissed against all but five persons who were convicted and fined $50.[35] A year later, the police in Lawrence, Massachusetts, arrested five bartenders for operating "gathering places for sex perverts." One of the bartenders was sentenced to serve four months in jail.[36] Also in 1956, the Board of Police Commissioners of Los Angeles revoked the operating license of a bathhouse on the grounds that its owners "suffered and permitted its premises to be used not only as a gathering place for homosexuals and sexual perverts but as a place where they openly solicited partners and actually engaged in homosexual practices and sex perversion."[37] In 1959, Philadelphia police officers raided a coffeehouse after undercover agents observed men dancing and hugging. The police arrested eighteen patrons and fined them $10 each.[38]

These are only a handful of the hundreds of government enforcement actions during the years following World War II aimed at making sexual minorities, alongside the businesses that catered to them, pay for having the temerity of congregating in public. These campaigns of harassment and intimidation created much anxiety and pain among their victims. But the campaigns, entirely unintentionally, also stirred some of the first manifestations of collective resistance to government oppression by LGBT people in the United States.

A Turn to the Courts

In the late 1940s, a handful of establishment owners who catered to lesbians and gay men began challenging the authority of state liquor officials to revoke their licenses, usually by asserting that investigators did not have sufficient evidence to support the claim that the owners were allowing disorderly or immoral conduct to take place on their premises. The courts uniformly sided with state liquor authorities in these cases until the California Supreme Court in 1951 issued a ruling involving the Black Cat bar in San Francisco. Government officials in that case claimed, based on the reports of undercover agents, that the bar was serving alcohol to "persons of known homosexual tendencies" and operating a "hangout for homosexuals."[39]

The owner of the Black Cat was Sol Stoumen, a heterosexual Holocaust survivor. Stoumen hired lawyer Morris Lowenthal to represent him. In challenging the suspension of the liquor license, Lowenthal became the first attorney in the United States to argue—several years before the United States Supreme Court recognized a constitutional right of association in *NAACP v. Alabama*—that lesbians and gay men had a constitutional right to congregate in bars and restaurants. Two lower California courts rejected Stoumen's challenge, concluding that "for a proprietor of a restaurant knowingly to permit his premises to be regularly used as a meeting place by [homosexuals] with all of the potentialities for evil and immorality drawing out of such meetings" justified the license suspension.[40] But the California Supreme Court reversed, holding that the mere presence of lesbians and gay men at a public establishment did not constitute a sufficient ground upon which to suspend its liquor license.[41]

The impact of the state supreme court's ruling in *Stoumen v. Reilly* was limited because it did not explicitly ground its ruling in constitutional protections. The court also left state officials with significant enforcement discretion by concluding that they could revoke liquor licenses when patrons committed "illegal or immoral acts" on the premises. Nonetheless, the *Stoumen* decision is historically significant because it constituted the first ruling by an American court granting lesbians and gay men the right to meet in public without state interference (as long as they did not engage in "illegal or immoral acts").

The *Stoumen* court was also the first to distinguish between the status of being gay or lesbian and the conduct that accompanies that status. The status/conduct distinction later became a crucial one in LGBT constitutional law following the Supreme Court's 1986 ruling in *Bowers v. Hardwick*.[42] After the Court concluded in *Bowers* that the government could constitutionally criminalize consensual same-sex sexual conduct, LGBT legal advocates emphasized the aspects of antigay laws and policies that targeted status rather than conduct. Although this emphasis made a certain amount of strategic sense given the Court's ruling in *Bowers*, the distinction between being lesbian, gay, or bisexual and engaging in same-sex sexual conduct is largely artificial because most individuals who identify as such engage in the conduct in question.[43]

Despite the difficulties that inhere in distinguishing between status and conduct, scholars have paid insufficient attention to the ways in which the distinction consistently helped litigants in early LGBT First Amendment cases. It was in many ways understandable for the early courts to focus on the distinction because there was something particularly troubling, as the *Stoumen* court recognized, about the exercise of punitive state authority—in this instance through the suspension of a liquor license—based on the *mere presence* of lesbians and gay men in a public establishment. By emphasizing status rather than conduct, it was possible for courts to begin questioning state action that negatively impacted sexual minorities without getting into what, at the time, were thornier legal and social issues associated with the public expression of same-sex sexual intimacy and affection. From this small kernel of protection, as limited as it was, much would grow in the years and decades to come.

When early courts, like the *Stoumen* court, were able to separate status from conduct, they were more likely to provide some limited recognition of the right of LGBT people to congregate in public. The separation of status from conduct allowed some early courts to see past society's disdain and contempt for gay people, and permitted them to start recognizing the rights of sexual minorities as "human beings," which was the term used by the *Stoumen* court to refer to the Black Cat's gay patrons.[44]

In contrast, when courts equated status with conduct, their legal analysis quickly degenerated into little more than rank homophobia. One of the ways in which this homophobia manifested itself was in an understanding of gay people's public association as constituting an extension of their supposedly perverted sexual urges. As the California Court of Appeal put it in upholding a gay bar's liquor license revocation following *Stoumen* based on the testimony of investigators who observed same-sex couples (both male and female) kissing and dancing at the establishment, the bar's patrons were "persons who are prone to and do engage in aberrant sexual conduct . . . and . . . use this public place as a haunt or gathering place for mutual stimulation of their sexually aberrant urges and a place of assignation for the renewal of old and the making of new associations looking toward the consummation of those urges."[45]

It appears that, in the years following *Stoumen*, California liquor officials, especially in San Francisco, tempered their harassment campaigns aimed at gay establishments.[46] But in 1955, the California legislature responded to *Stoumen* by unanimously enacting a statute explicitly authorizing the revocation of an establishment's liquor license when the premises were used as "a resort for . . . sexual perverts" (or for "prostitutes, pimps, [or] panderers)."[47] Armed with this new statutory authority, liquor investigators soon began targeting lesbian and gay bars with renewed vigor, often in cooperation with law enforcement agencies. A few days after Valentine's Day in 1956, thirty-five agents representing the state liquor authority, county sheriff deputies, military police, and the California Highway patrol descended on a gay bar located just south of San Francisco called Hazel's. The agents rounded almost three hundred patrons, of which ninety were arrested—seventy-seven men, ten women, and three minors—on vagrancy grounds after undercover agents identified them as being regular customers. Although most of the criminal charges were eventually dismissed, the authorities revoked the establishment's liquor license.[48]

Liquor authorities also targeted the First and Last Chance Bar, an Oakland establishment catering primarily to lesbians. After visiting the bar on an almost daily basis for nine months to gather evidence showing that it served as a place where sexual minorities congregated, the liquor authorities used the new law to revoke its license. The government argued that "while it may all be very legal for one homosexual to take a drink, it is harmful to the public interest for homosexuals to gather or associate in a bar."[49] After the bar's owners challenged the new law, the California Supreme Court, in *Vallerga v. Department of Alcoholic Beverage Control*, struck it down as unconstitutional on the ground that it authorized the revocation of licenses based not on conduct, but on an establishment's reputation for allowing certain classes of people to congregate. Once again, the court refused to allow government officials to target establishments simply because sexual minorities congregated in them.[50]

It bears emphasizing, however, that the protection provided by *Stoumen* and *Vallerga* was quite limited. The court in both cases made clear that same-sex conduct, including same-sex dancing and kissing, constituted sufficient grounds for license revocation. This made it easy for government officials to continue to revoke licenses based on the testimony of undercover officers who observed patrons of the same sex dancing or holding hands.[51] At the same time, the court established an important principle: the mere gathering of gay people in an establishment open to the public did not justify punitive state action.

Although the court in *Vallerga*, unlike in *Stoumen*, made clear that its holding was grounded in constitutional law, its discussion of the constitutional principles at stake was unhelpful and opaque. But when the New Jersey Supreme Court in 1967, in *One Eleven Wines & Liquors v. Division of Alcoholic Beverage Control*, entertained an appeal by the owners of several gay bars challenging the decision of state liquor officials to suspend or revoke their licenses, it more fully addressed the constitutional issues. The New Jersey liquor control agency, like its California counterpart, claimed that the mere presence of gay people at an establishment justified the revocation or suspension of its liquor license. (The agency in *One Eleven Wines & Liquors* claimed that it knew gay men patronized the bars in question because the customers spoke "in a lisping tone of voice . . . used limp-wrist movements . . . . [and] when they drank their drinks, they extended their pinkies in a very dainty manner.")[52] But the New Jersey Supreme Court, relying on federal constitutional principles, thought otherwise.

The court first noted that "though in our culture homosexuals are indeed unfortunates, their status does not make them criminals or outlaws."[53] In support of the latter proposition, the New Jersey court cited to *Robinson v. California*, a case in which the U.S. Supreme Court had held that the government cannot criminalize the status of being addicted to illegal drugs, only their actual use.[54] Second, the court pointed to the right of association under the federal constitution, recognized by the Supreme Court in *NAACP v. Alabama*, to support its conclusion that sexual minorities enjoyed a constitutional right to associate with others in public.

Although rulings like *One Eleven Wines & Liquors* helped curb some of the most egregious forms of government harassment of places of public accommodation that catered to lesbians, gay men, and bisexuals, their status-based reasoning, when coupled with the limited number of rulings, meant that police raids and liquor license revocations of gay establishments continued in many cities throughout the 1960s, as the infamous police raid of New York City's Stonewall Inn in 1969 showed. The legal victories, however, demonstrated that it was possible to get at least some courts to recognize the important principle that there were limits to the state's authority to prevent or discourage sexual minorities from gathering in public.

A Turn to Organizing

Before the 1970s, many establishments that catered to lesbians and gay men were owned by heterosexual businessmen, including, in some places, by individuals with ties to organized crime syndicates, who cared little about LGBT people or their issues. However, in San Francisco, lesbians and gay men in the 1950s began operating a growing number of bars.[55] In 1962, a group of gay bar owners and employees came together to form the Tavern Guild of San Francisco, the nation's first gay business association. One of the organization's main objectives was to help owners and bartenders deal with harassment by government officials. Toward that objective, the Tavern Guild instituted a phone-banking system to keep members informed of police and liquor license investigations, set up a fund to assist bar employees who lost their jobs after police raids led to the closing of their establishments, and worked to dispel rumors of police actions that had in fact not taken place.[56] (On this last point, one historian has noted that "because the rumor of a bust could be as financially crippling as a license revocation, bar owners used Tavern Guild meetings to reassure one another that they were still operating.")[57] In addition, the organization retained a lawyer and a bail bondsman to assist customers arrested in or near gay bars.[58]

The Tavern Guild also organized social events—including an annual Halloween drag ball (the Beaux Arts Ball) that quickly became popular among transgender women and gay men—meant to bring LGBT people together and to raise money for organizations like the Mattachine Society and the Daughters of Bilitis. In 1965, the Guild started hosting political events at which candidates interested in the gay vote could speak to members of the increasingly visible gay community in San Francisco.[59]

One of the Tavern Guild's main objectives was to protect the ability of LGBT people to associate in public. The opportunity to congregate freely in public settings was simultaneously the source of continued profits for bar owners and of political empowerment for sexual minorities. The historian Nan Alamilla Boyd notes that as the Tavern Guild "developed more social and political power, the group positioned the right of public association as the cornerstone of a gay and lesbian civil rights agenda, and it applied this right to any and all communities in the public space of gay bars and taverns."[60]

One of the Tavern Guild's founders was José Sarria, a waiter and drag performer who had started working at Stoumen's Black Cat bar in 1947. (Sarria had wanted to be a teacher, a career path that became impossible to pursue after he was arrested in a police sting operation in a public bathroom at the St. Francis hotel.)[61] Sarria's drag shows mixed the humorous with the political as he exhorted his gay audiences to live openly and to resist police repression.[62] In 1961, Sarria cofounded an organization called the League for Civil Education, which, as his *New York Times* obituary put it decades later, "was dedicated to overturning laws that prohibited serving alcohol to gay people."[63] The organization published a newsletter informing readers which gay bars were open for business, where police actions had taken place, and how to avoid entrapment. It also worked on voter registration and encouraged political participation by sexual minorities.[64]

At around this time, the state alcohol control agency revoked, or was in the process of revoking, the licenses of twenty-seven of the city's thirty gay bars.[65] The police department in 1961 also conducted its biggest raid yet of a gay establishment—the Tay-Bush Inn—arresting around 100 "suspected sex deviates," herding them onto seven patrol wagons, and whisking them to the city's jail.[66] The continued police harassment of gay bars and their patrons led Sarria to run for a seat on San Francisco's Board of Supervisors. To the surprise of everyone, Sarria gathered more than five thousand votes, finishing ninth in a field of thirty candidates for five seats. Sarria's campaign for public office, the first by an openly gay person in the United States, showed the growing political clout of the gay and lesbian community in San Francisco. Candidates for elected city offices noticed and, for the first time, some began seeking the votes of sexual minorities.

Despite the growing visibility of the LGBT community in San Francisco, government-led repression of gay establishments continued. In 1963, for example, the Black Cat finally closed, the victim of a relentless fifteen-year harassment campaign by the police department and the liquor license authority.[67] The following year, gay activists in San Francisco formed a new organization, the Society for Individual Rights (SIR), composed not only of bar owners and employees, but also of other members of the gay community. As the organization's president wrote in the inaugural issue of its monthly magazine Vector, "by trying to give the individual a sense of dignity before himself and within his Society, SIR is dedicated to [the] belief in the worth of the homosexual and adheres to the principle that the individual has a right to his own sexual orientation."[68] The organization also aimed, as an editorial in Vector explained, "to present the homosexual as he is—by far and large a responsible and moral member of his community and one seeking only the equal protections of the laws guaranteed by the 14th Amendment to the Constitution of the United States."[69]

The new group held voter registration drives, hosted increasingly popular candidate forums, and organized dances in venues other than bars—and away from the prying eyes of police officers and liquor investigators. It also distributed a pocket-sized publication—titled the "Pocket Lawyer"—informing gay men of their rights if the police harassed or arrested them. As Boyd points out, unlike earlier homophile groups like the Mattachine Society, SIR "projected a bold language of social activism that was more in sync with civil rights organizations."[70] By 1968, the group's outreach to broad sectors of the LGBT community, when combined with its democratic structure, led it to become the biggest gay group in San Francisco—and the nation—with a membership of almost a thousand.[71]

Although government agents in San Francisco in the early 1960s continued to harass lesbian/gay bars and their patrons, there was little officials could do, in the face of the First Amendment, to stop the growing political organizing and mobilizing by members of the gay community fueled by the government's relentless harassment and intimidation campaigns. The right to join organizations like the Tavern Guild, the League for Civil Education, and SIR was clearly protected by the recent Supreme Court's decisions in freedom of association cases involving state efforts to silence the NAACP. In addition, the right to vigorously criticize government officials for their treatment of sexual minorities, and to advocate for their basic civil rights, was protected by the Court's ruling in *New York Times v. Sullivan*. Finally, the right to publish and distribute publications, as LGBT organizations of all kinds were increasingly doing in the 1960s, was protected by the Court's decisions in *One v. Olesen* and *Manual Enterprises v. Day*. As a result, although police officers and liquor license investigators could conduct raids of gay bars in order to intimidate and harass their patrons, there was little that officials could do to stop activists from organizing and mobilizing in order to denounce those raids.

The growing political mobilization and clout of San Francisco's gay community meant that government harassment of gay establishments in the city largely ended by 1966.[72] Although that progress came about as a result of political activism rather than constitutional litigation, the organizing and mobilizing took place within a constitutional construct that made it increasingly clear that officials lacked the authority to restrict the free speech and association rights of lesbians and gay men. If there was any doubt about this limitation on governmental authority, it was dispelled by a series of cases first litigated in the early 1970s, and discussed in the following pages, involving the rights of lesbian, gay, and bisexual students to form organizations at public universities and colleges.

At the time, lesbians and gay men in San Francisco and elsewhere could be arrested for a wide range of crimes (from sodomy to public lewdness to sex solicitation to disorderly conduct), could be fired at will from government and private sector jobs, could be denied entry to the country (if they were immigrants) and access to their children (if they were parents), and of course, could be denied the right to marry. The one thing that the government could not constitutionally do was deny them the right to come together in order to advocate for the rights of sexual minorities.

The Explosion of LGBT Organizations

The riots that followed the New York City police's raid of the Stonewall Inn in 1969 ushered a new era for the movement. The fact that a motley crew of gay men, drag queens, and lesbians fought back in the face of yet another outrageous instance of police harassment and violence sent a powerful message that some LGBT people, at least, were not going to take it anymore. Stonewall galvanized many around the country who were starting to question society's cruel and unjust treatment of LGBT people—for them, the Stonewall riots were a stark and inspiring example of how sexual minorities, like African Americans and women, could publicly and, when necessary, defiantly assert their rights to equal rights and dignity.

There were many complex social and political forces that accounted for the rise of the gay liberation movement following Stonewall, including the breaking down of traditional mores engendered by the sexual revolution of the late 1960s and 1970s, the growing radicalization of American youth brought about by the Vietnam War, and the critique of patriarchal and sexist laws and norms voiced by an increasingly powerful feminist movement. But whatever the precise reasons for the emergence of the gay liberation movement, there can be little doubt that it represented a larger, more vibrant, and more outspoken political force pushing for gay equality and visibility than had existed in the years leading up to Stonewall.

This shift toward more assertive and visible activism was evident in many ways, including in the push by sexual minorities to form organizations of all kinds. In the twenty years of homophile politics preceding Stonewall, fewer than fifty lesbian and gay groups had been created (including local chapters of groups like the Mattachine Society). By 1973, there were more than eight hundred such organizations across the country.[73] The focus of the new organizations ran the gamut from political to cultural to educational to social to artistic to professional to religious matters. In Chicago, for example, LGBT political activists founded three organizations: Gay Liberation of Chicago, the Chicago Gay Alliance, and the Illinois Gay and Lesbian Task Force. Gays of color also started their own groups, including one called the Third World Gay Revolutionaries. In 1971, a gay community center opened in Chicago, and another in 1974. As in San Francisco a decade earlier, owners of gay bars in Chicago formed a Tavern Guild. The nation's first lesbian rock band, Family of Woman, was also formed in Chicago in the early 1970s. And as in many cities across the country, Chicago saw the creation of numerous gay religious organizations, including the Metropolitan Community Church (originally founded by the Reverend Troy Perry in Los Angeles in 1968),

Dignity/Chicago for Catholics, and the Congregation Or Chadash for Jews. Several lesbian and gay sports associations were created, as well as a support group for the parents of lesbian and gay children, originally called Parents of Gays, from which the national organization Parents, Family, and Friends of Lesbians and Gay Men (PFLAG) later emerged.[74]

In Los Angeles, a few months after the Stonewall riots, activists formed the L.A. Gay Liberation Front (LAGLF), which organized protests at the offices of media outlets for peddling homophobic representations of gay people, picketed restaurants and bars that excluded sexual minorities, and organized the city's first gay pride parade in June 1970. Although the LAGLF disbanded a little more than a year later, lesbian and gay activists formed other organizations around the same time, including the Los Angeles Gay Community Services Center (the first gay entity granted nonprofit status by the IRS); the Feminist Women's Health Center; and a lesbian artists organization called the Women's Building, which promoted female artists and owned a building containing galleries, studios, a bookstore, and a theater.[75]

A similar upsurge in the number of LGBT organizations took place in other cities around the country. Many of those groups focused on the needs and interests of lesbians. Although most homophile organizations founded in the 1950s and 1960s—with the notable exception of the Daughters of Bilitis—had been dominated by men, the 1970s saw an explosion of lesbian groups throughout the country. These organizations included lesbian feminist groups, such as Radicalesbians in New York City and the Furies Collective in Washington, D.C.; regional groups that provided support and opportunities for political activism, like the Atlanta Lesbian Feminist Alliance and the Central Ohio Lesbians; lesbian mothers groups, such as the Lesbian Mothers National Defense Fund in Seattle, and Dykes and Tykes in New York City; and black lesbians groups, such as Sapphire Saphos in Washington, D.C., and the Combahee River Collective in Boston.[76]

Like the marked increase in the number and variety of gay publications that blossomed a decade earlier following the Supreme Court's rulings in *One* and *Manual Enterprises*, the surge in the number and variety of LGBT organizations in the 1970s served as vehicles through which sexual minorities increased their visibility in society, formed and strengthened bonds of identity and community, and began to make claims for the equality rights of LGBT individuals, especially through the more politically oriented organizations. As was true of gay magazine publishers, those who came together to form LGBT organizations were protected by the First Amendment. Largely as a result of the Supreme Court's free speech and association cases from the civil rights era, there was little that government officials could directly do to censor or shut down these new organizations.[77]

However, it was still possible for officials who decried the growing visibility of sexual minorities to try to withhold benefits from gay groups, in particular those associated with official government recognition. These efforts were evident in two contexts in particular: the application by gay organizations for incorporation status and by college gay groups for recognition by their institutions. In both of these contexts, courts generally interpreted the First Amendment in ways that prevented the government from withholding official recognition as a means of silencing sexual minorities.

A Return to the Courts, Part I: The Question of Incorporation

The first gay political organization formed in New York City in the wake of Stonewall was the Gay Liberation Front (GLF). The GLF had a decidedly radical bent—the group not only demanded equal rights for lesbians and gay men, but also, unlike earlier homophile organizations, waded into other social and political controversies by, for example, vociferously opposing the Vietnam War and participating in Black Panther Party rallies.[78] The organization's radicalism, as well as its purposeful lack of structure, frustrated some of its members who wanted to focus on promoting specific civil reforms that would protect gay people from discrimination and harassment. In December 1969, a group of GLF dissidents peeled off to form the Gay Activists Alliance (GAA) with the purpose of agitating exclusively on behalf of gay equality. Activists in other cities, including Chicago, Philadelphia, San Francisco, and Los Angeles, soon opened chapters of both organizations.

The GAA quickly became famous in New York City for organizing direct action protests (called "zaps") at which activists, for example, descended on the headquarters of magazines to protest homophobic articles, showed up at the marriage license bureau to insist boisterously that licenses be issued to same-sex couples, and staged sit-ins at the offices of the governor and mayor to demand their support for civil rights legislation for sexual minorities. The GAA also mobilized a large demonstration to protest the death of a man who jumped from a second story window during a police raid of a gay bar in Manhattan in 1970. That same year, GAA organized a march that eventually became the city's annual gay pride parade.[79] The organization's logo, the Greek letter lambda, became the symbol of the gay rights movement until it was replaced by the pink triangle later in the decade.

In 1970, the GAA filed a petition with the New York Secretary of State seeking to incorporate as a nonprofit corporation. It is common for organizations, especially as they grow, to seek incorporation, a legal status that provides them with considerable advantages, including tax benefits for the entities and liability limits for their officers. The Secretary of State objected to GAA's application on two grounds: first, the Secretary deemed the name of the proposed corporation, which contained the word "gay," to be unacceptable; second, he claimed that the group's purposes, which included protecting gay people from discrimination and working to repeal criminal laws regulating sexual conduct between consenting adults, were inconsistent with the state's public policies.

The GAA sued the Secretary of State for turning down its incorporation request, but a trial judge upheld the government action. The judge, after noting that a recent revision of the state's criminal laws had left the provision prohibiting consensual sodomy in place, concluded that the GAA, by calling itself "a homosexual civil rights organization," demonstrated "a present or future intent to disobey a penal statute of the State of New York." The judge added that because a person, in order to claim to be gay, had to either engage or contemplate engaging in illegal acts, the state could properly deny the incorporation application on the ground that it did not want to give the "imprimatur of incorporation" to an organization composed of individuals who broke the law.[80]

The GAA immediately appealed the trial court's ruling, and a panel of the appellate division reversed. That court first noted that the word "gay" was neither vulgar nor obscene. In addition, the court emphasized that none of the organization's stated purposes were unlawful, including its seeking to repeal laws that targeted gay people. As the court explained, "it is well established that it is not unlawful for any individual or group of individuals to peaceably agitate for the repeal of any law."[81]

It bears noting that in many gay rights lawsuits from the 1970s until the Supreme Court's ruling in *Lawrence v. Texas* in 2003, the existence of sodomy laws, even when not directly at issue in the cases, colored the courts' legal analysis. For many judges from that era, the fact that the government deemed consensual same-sex sexual conduct a criminal offense justified the continued differential treatment of sexual minorities in matters as diverse as family law, employment opportunities, and immigration status. As a result, gay, lesbian, and bisexual parents could be denied custody of or visitation with their children; gay, lesbian, and bisexual applicants could be denied public sector jobs; and immigrants could be denied entry or citizenship on the ground that they engaged, or probably engaged in, sodomy.[82] The one consistent exception to the judicial indifference toward the government's discriminatory treatment of LGBT people was the category of cases in which government officials tried to discourage sexual minorities from leading open lives by impinging on their rights of free speech and association; in those instances, officials met significant judicial resistance.

For example, the New York appellate court in the GAA case rejected the view that the state's criminalization of sodomy meant that the government had the authority to limit the ability of the organization and its members to demand the sodomy law's repeal by exercising their free speech rights. The same kind of First Amendment exceptionalism, in the face of otherwise expansive understandings of state authority to regulate the lives of sexual minorities and to discourage same-sex sexual conduct and relationships, is also evident in a 1984 decision by a federal appellate court striking down an Oklahoma statute requiring school districts to fire teachers who advocated, encouraged, or promoted same-sex sexual conduct. After noting that the case did not turn on the authority of the government to proscribe same-sex sexual conduct, the court proceeded to hold the statute unconstitutional because it penalized teachers who, for example, advocated in their free time for the repeal of the state's sodomy law.[83] Similarly, another federal appellate court in 1997 relied on the Free Speech Clause to strike down an Alabama statute that prohibited the use of public funds or facilities by any university student group "that fosters or promotes a lifestyle or actions prohibited by the sodomy and sexual misconduct laws."[84] Once again, a court faced with a First Amendment challenge to a law or policy that negatively affected sexual minorities refused to hold that the state's ability to criminalize sodomy justified granting it authority to burden the expressive and associational rights of LGBT people.

The question of corporate status recognition was also at issue in the effort by the Lambda Legal Defense and Education Fund in 1972 to be recognized as a legal assistance corporation under New York law. In its application, the organization explained that it sought to provide free legal services in cases involving the rights of gay people; "to promote the availability of legal services to homosexuals by encouraging and attracting homosexuals into the legal profession; [and] to disseminate to homosexuals general information concerning their legal rights and obligations." An intermediate appellate court denied the group's application contending that it had failed to establish a demand for its services that could not be met by the private bar. The judges added that "we should not put our imprimatur upon any corporation which seeks approval to practice law for no more reason than that it claims to represent a minority."[85]

The state's highest court overturned the lower court's ruling.[86] A concurring opinion explained that the U.S. Supreme Court had deemed the right of association to be a fundamental one and that New York corporation law therefore could not be interpreted, as the lower court had done, in ways that interfered with the ability of a gay rights organization to agitate and litigate in order to attain its political objectives.[87]

There is one ruling from this period, issued by the Ohio Supreme Court in 1974, that did uphold the denial of a request by a gay organization (the Greater Cincinnati Gay Society) to incorporate. Without much explanation, the court simply stated that "it agree[d] with the Secretary of State that the promotion of homosexuality as a valid life style is contrary to the public policy of the state."[88] However, as a dissenting justice pointed out, not only was this conclusion inconsistent with the First Amendment, given that it protects advocacy except when it leads to imminent unlawful and harmful conduct, it was not clear which public policy the Secretary of State had relied on to deny the application, especially given that the Ohio legislature had recently repealed the state's sodomy law.[89] Despite its loss in the courts, the gay organization prevailed in the end: a few months after the Ohio Supreme Court's ruling, state officials allowed it to incorporate.[90]

A Return to the Courts, Part II: College Organizations

The government's policing of same-sex sexuality and conduct following World War II took place not only on the streets, in public workplaces, and in places of public accommodation (like bars and restaurants), but also on the nation's campuses. In the years after the war, officials at public universities and colleges, along with their counterparts at some private institutions, routinely investigated, interrogated, and expelled male students for allegedly having sex with other men or even for simply associating with those whom administrators suspected were gay. For example, officials at the University of Missouri in 1949 expelled several students arrested as part of a police raid of an off-campus party attended by gay men. (The university noted on the students' transcripts that they had been arrested for "homosexual activity.") Two years later, administrators at the University of Illinois expelled a student after they learned he had been arrested following a police raid of a gay bar in Chicago. For their part, investigators with the University of Wisconsin's police department in 1962 offered immunity from expulsion to male students who were suspected of having had sex with other men as long as they provided the names of others on campus whom they knew to be gay.[91]

Sometimes school officials, in lieu of expulsion, demanded that gay students seek psychological counseling. As Patrick Dilley notes, starting in the mid-1950s, on-campus psychological "treatment became a method of controlling students' concepts of how their sexuality was a part of their lives, as well as allowing administrators a closer locus of supervision over physical or social expressions of the students' sexuality."[92] For example, after seven Stanford male students were arrested in a police raid of "sex perverts" at a public bathroom in 1956, the university placed them on "medical leave," allowing them to return if they provided "satisfactory evidence of rehabilitation."[93]

Pre-Stonewall homophile organizations, like the Mattachine Society and the Daughters of Bilitis, expressed little interest in matters related to lesbian and gay youth. In fact, most homophile groups required members to be at least twenty-one years old, in part to avoid accusations that they sought to "recruit" young people.[94] Such a stance contributed to the fading relevance, within the movement, of homophile organizations as the 1960s progressed. During that time, large numbers of young Americans, especially college students, were becoming increasingly active politically, in particular around civil rights issues and the Vietnam War.[95] One of the ways in which this politicization among the young manifested itself was in the push by a growing number of lesbian and gay college students to form organizations aimed at promoting the political and social interests of sexual minorities.

The first such group was formed at Columbia in 1967, followed shortly by the creation of similar organizations at other private universities (such as Cornell and Stanford) as well as public ones (such as Penn State and Rutgers).[96] As the 1960s turned into the 1970s, and as that decade progressed, new student gay groups cropped up at a growing number of campuses, big and small, public and private, across the country. Although many lesbians and gay men around this time, as we have seen, were coming together to form groups of all kinds, the student organizations were distinctive in that they were embedded within larger institutions. Most LGBT organizations formed during the 1970s were "stand-alone" groups unaffiliated with heterosexual-dominated institutions; in contrast, LGBT students who formed gay college groups did so as members of larger, socially important, and influential institutions that had rarely paid any attention to the needs and interests of sexual minorities. As such, LGBT student groups were particularly well situated to increase the visibility of sexual minorities and gay rights issues both on campuses and in the wider society. By organizing social events for LGBT students, sponsoring lectures and conferences on sexual orientation and civil rights, demanding additions to curricula that addressed the existence and concerns of sexual minorities, and lobbying campus and local authorities to adopt sexual orientation antidiscrimination policies, LGBT student groups challenged prevailing moral and social understandings of sexual minorities, their relationships, and their sexual conduct. In short, the LGBT student groups played an important role in persuading growing segments of society, including many administrators and faculty in higher education, that sexual orientation was a benign human trait and that sexual orientation discrimination was morally wrong.

As LGBT college students formed the new groups, some universities, in a sign of the changing times brought about by the political and sexual convulsions of the 1960s, did not oppose them. However, other universities were not so tolerant. Some institutions refused to officially recognize the gay groups, rendering them ineligible for school funding and the use of school facilities and means of communication. Other universities grudgingly recognized the organizations, but then restricted their activities on campus. Both of these types of responses led gay student groups to bring legal challenges grounded in their members' rights to free speech and association.[97]

University administrators had for decades relied on the doctrine of in loco parentis (in the place of the parent) to justify much greater regulatory control over college students than government officials had over adults outside educational settings. Although college students had been chipping away at the doctrine since the mid-1960s—the most famous manifestation of this phenomenon was the Free Speech Movement at the University of California at Berkeley—the Supreme Court did not address the constitutional limits of the in loco parentis authority of public university administrators until 1972 in *Healey v. James*.[98] The Court in *Healy* held that a public college had violated students' rights to free speech and association when it refused to recognize a student chapter of the Students for a Democratic Society because of its radical left-wing views.

University administrators, in defending their decision either to not recognize gay student groups or to limit their activities on campus, generally relied on three claims. First, they contended that the existence of the student groups would result in greater illegal activity on campuses. Second, that official recognition would constitute an endorsement of the groups' views. And third, that universities had a responsibility to promote the values of the broader community, and that recognizing LGBT student groups undermined those values.

Between 1974 and 1978, three different federal courts of appeals rejected all of these claims after LGBT student groups filed First Amendment lawsuits. In the first of those cases, *Gay Students Organization of the University of New Hampshire v. Bonner*, the U.S. Court of Appeals for the First Circuit assessed the constitutionality of the University of New Hampshire's decision to prohibit a gay student group from holding social events on campus. The court held that the university had violated gay students' associational and free speech rights. In doing so, the court concluded that it was up to the organization, and not university officials, to decide how to attract "members and promote its point of view."[99] The purpose of the social events, the court explained, was to send a very specific message: "that homosexuals exist, that they feel repressed by existing laws and attitudes, that they wish to emerge from their isolation, and that public understanding of their attitudes and problems is desirable for society."[100] The university, which did not prohibit any other student group from holding social events, was targeting the gay student organization because of the message it wanted to convey, a targeting that violated the First Amendment. At the same time, because the university recognized so many different other student groups and allowed all of them to hold social events, there was no reason to believe that its equal treatment of the gay organization would be understood as an endorsement of its views.

The *Bonner* ruling is notable for four reasons. First, it constituted, at the time, the most extensive recognition by a federal appellate court of the First Amendment rights of gay people. Although the Supreme Court had by then already decided the two gay obscenity cases explored in Chapter 1, neither of those rulings included extensive discussions of why gay people sought to speak their minds and why that expression was entitled to constitutional protection.

Second, the case was decided at a time when gay people had few other constitutional protections. No appellate court, whether state or federal, had held that gay people had a constitutional right to privacy, and no court had held that discrimination on the basis of sexual orientation violated constitutional equality mandates. Despite the absence of other constitutional protections, the *Bonner* court vigorously and unambiguously protected the First Amendment rights of gay university students.

Third, the *Bonner* court dealt directly with the question of the state's authority to promote public morality in light of the First Amendment rights of sexual minorities. The appellate court opined that the LGBT student group "stands for sexual values in direct conflict with the deeply imbued moral standards of much of the community whose taxes support the university," values that according to the court were "far beyond the pale of the wider community's values"[101] However, like the Supreme Court in *One* and in *Manual Enterprises*, the appellate court refused to uphold the state action in question on the ground that it promoted public morality.

Not only did the *Bonner* court find public morality to be an impermissible basis for restricting the speech and associational rights of LGBT students, but it also concluded that *the university's moral claims evinced an intent to target* the gay group because of its views. The university claimed: (1) it had an "obligation and right to prevent activities which the people of New Hampshire find shocking and offensive"; (2) it had an "obligation to prevent activity which affronts the citizens of the University and the town"; and (3) the "ban on social functions [by the LGBT student group] reflects the distaste with which homosexual organizations are regarded in the State."[102] Rather than deferring to the university's moral condemnation of LGBT people, the court relied on that condemnation to conclude that administrators were treating the gay organization differently because of its message, a content-based restriction that violated the First Amendment.

Fourth, and finally, the court recognized the crucial link between the First Amendment rights at issue in the case and *the equality objectives* of the gay student group. As the court explained before citing to the Supreme Court's NAACP First Amendment cases, the gay student group's "efforts to organize the homosexual minority, 'educate' the public as to its plight, and obtain for it better treatment from individuals and from the government . . . represent but another example of the associational activity unequivocally singled out for protection in the very 'core' of association cases decided by the Supreme Court."[103] For the *Bonner* court, there was no constitutionally relevant distinction between what the gay student organization was trying to accomplish through its social events and what organizations like the NAACP had been trying to achieve through its civil rights work.

Although the *Bonner* court decided the case exclusively on First Amendment grounds, it acknowledged that the litigation also raised serious equal protection concerns because university officials had targeted the gay group, and no others, in limiting their ability to organize social events on campus.[104] The court's reasoning on this point illustrates the way in which the First Amendment issues in *Bonner*, at their core, were about group exclusion rather than ideological exclusion. It was clear, in other words, that the university had targeted gay students because of who they were; it was their status as openly lesbian, gay, and bisexual students that triggered the constitutionally impermissible restriction. In fact, it was highly unlikely that the university would have prohibited a politically progressive group of heterosexual students who supported gay rights from holding social events. This showed that the university was troubled by the presence of certain students (namely, openly gay ones) and the message that their presence sent, rather than students' positions favoring gay rights.

The university's targeting of LGBT students because of who they were was also evident from its effort, after it lost the federal case, to persuade state courts to uphold its refusal to allow the gay student organization to hold social events on campus on the ground that gay people were mentally ill. That effort failed when the state supreme court ruled that the university was barred from raising this new argument given that it could have raised it during the federal lawsuit.[105]

Unlike the *Bonner* court, the U.S. Court of Appeals for the Fourth Circuit in 1976 was faced with a First Amendment challenge arising from a university's outright refusal to recognize a gay student group. The court, in *Gay Alliance of Students v. Matthews*, addressed the contention by officials at Virginia Commonwealth University that withholding recognition was constitutionally proper because such recognition, if granted, would "increase the opportunity for homosexual contacts."[106] In rejecting that argument, the court—like the California Supreme Court in the gay bar cases from the 1950s—distinguished between status and conduct. The university had the constitutional authority to try to prevent students from engaging in illegal (that is, same-sex) sexual conduct. But the First Amendment limited the university's in loco parentis authority in the absence of evidence that the gay group "is an organization devoted to carrying out illegal, specifically proscribed sexual practices. While Virginia law proscribes the practice of certain forms of homosexuality, Virginia law does not make it a crime to be a homosexual. Indeed, a statute criminalizing such status and prescribing punishment . . . would be invalid."[107] The court added that although the university could exclude those who engaged in illegal conduct from student organizations, its effort to prevent that conduct by withholding recognition of the student group constituted an impermissibly overbroad regulation under the First Amendment because it significantly and detrimentally impacted the gay students' associational rights.

The *Gay Alliance of Students* court, like other courts that sided with lesbian, gay, and bisexual student groups around this time, emphasized the constitutional impermissibility of government policies that regulated on the basis of status, especially those that burdened rights to free speech and association. As already noted, when LGBT rights legal advocates later turned their attention to challenging conduct-based regulations (like sodomy statutes), they reasonably questioned the constitutional distinction between targeting gay people because of who they were and targeting them for the (consensual and intimate) conduct they engaged in. But whatever the merits of the status/conduct distinction in the context of later equality- and privacy-based challenges, the distinction was one that helped courts in early First Amendment cases recognize the deleterious impact on free speech and associational rights of policies that targeted sexual minorities and LGBT organizations. When the government regulates conduct, it does not usually run afoul of the First Amendment. But when the state targets individuals because of their status, it violates the First Amendment if the targeting makes it more difficult for them to express themselves and associate with each other, as the courts that heard the gay student group cases in the 1970s and 1980s consistently held.

Although Virginia Commonwealth University did not introduce evidence to support its contention that recognition of the gay student group would lead to more "homosexual activity," the University of Missouri, in defending its decision not to recognize a gay student group, called on two psychologists to testify that if the university were to recognize the group, sodomy rates on campus would increase.[108] But the U.S. Court of Appeals for the Eighth Circuit held in 1977 that such speculative testimony did not justify the university's decision to withhold recognition, a decision that constituted a prior restraint of speech and association. The court, in *Gay Lib v. University of Missouri*, explained that the Supreme Court's free speech case law required that the prior restraint "be justified only by a far greater showing of a likelihood of imminent lawless action than that presented here." In doing so, the federal appellate court pointed to the lack of any evidence that the gay student organization encouraged its members to engage in illegal conduct. In the end, the university was pursuing an impermissible status-based policy, one that attempted to "singularly ascribe evil connotations to the group simply because they are homosexuals."[109]

Although some universities, into the 1980s, continued to place obstacles in the way of gay student groups, those efforts, when challenged under the First Amendment, consistently failed to withstand judicial scrutiny.[110] The courts' vigorous enforcement of gay students' rights to free speech and association contributed to the remarkable growth in the number of LGBT student organizations across the country—from about a dozen at the beginning of the 1970s to approximately two hundred in 1978 to more than two thousand in 1996.[111] These groups brought a great deal of attention to LGBT issues on university campuses, and often in surrounding communities as well. The groups invited LGBT activists to campuses to inform students and faculty about issues of discrimination against sexual minorities, agitated for inclusion of LGBT issues into curricula, pushed for the enactment of antidiscrimination policies by universities and local governments, and organized social events that increased the visibility of sexual minorities on campuses and in the broader communities. In doing all of this, the student groups helped to create the social conditions that made a growing number of sexual minorities more comfortable with coming out of the closet; asserting their pride in being lesbian, gay, or bisexual; and making equality claims on behalf of LGBT people. As Brett Beemyn explains, the members of gay student organizations "helped make it possible for many more gay people to accept themselves and come out. In no small way, these efforts contributed to the development of a large-scale political movement."[112]

A Turn to the Courts, Part III: The Public Forum Cases

The First Amendment victories by gay organizations in the 1970s were not limited to those of student groups on college campuses. In 1975, several Rhode Island LGBT organizations, including the Metropolitan Community Church, Gay Community Services, Gay Women of Providence, and the Rhode Island College Gay Alliance, formed an umbrella group called Toward a Gayer Bicentennial Committee. The committee's objective was to disseminate information about "the legal, social, and political circumstances and aspirations of persons with a homosexual or bisexual preference, through the medium of events and activities related to the celebration of the bicentennial of the founding of this country."[113] The committee asked the Rhode Island Bicentennial Commission, the state agency responsible for planning public events commemorating the bicentennial, for permission to use the Old State House, a historical landmark in Providence designated by the commission as a site for bicentennial events, to hold a gathering called a "Congress of People with Gay Concerns." The gay umbrella organization also asked that its gay pride parade be listed in "the Commission's schedule of bicentennial events and, in general, to be a part of the total bicentennial celebration."[114] The commission denied the requests, leading the committee to file a federal lawsuit challenging the denials under the Free Speech Clause.

Like many of the universities and colleges that refused to recognize gay student groups, the commission defended itself from the First Amendment challenge on the ground that state law criminalized sodomy and that allowing the gay umbrella organization to participate in the bicentennial celebrations would constitute state endorsement of illegal conduct. But the district court sided with the LGBT group, holding that the government, in inviting a broad range of organizations to use the Old State House for bicentennial celebrations, had created a limited public forum under the Free Speech Clause. As such, the government could only enforce reasonable regulations that were not based on the speakers' viewpoints.

As a brief aside, there are three different kinds of public forums for purposes of the amendment. The government cannot regulate based on the subject matter of expression in "traditional public forums" (such as sidewalks and parks) or in "designated public forums" (public areas that officials have made available for expressive purposes even though those purposes are not traditionally part of their use).[115] The third type of forums are known as "limited public forums," that is, government-created forums that invite expression *on certain subjects*—such as those related to the bicentennial celebration. Although the Free Speech Clause allows the government to place subject-matter restrictions in limited public forums, the state may not do so on the basis of viewpoint.[116] For purposes of the 1976 celebrations, therefore, the government could limit the expression to matters related to the bicentennial, but could not, for example, welcome liberal speakers while rejecting conservative ones.

The federal court in the Rhode Island case concluded that the commission was violating the Free Speech Clause because it did not have clear standards in place to determine which organizations could participate in the bicentennial events. These standards were constitutionally required because, in their absence, the commission had unfettered discretion to decide which applications for participation to approve. As the court explained, "unbridled discretion by public officials over the use of a public forum is anathema to a free society, not to be condoned."[117] The court added that it could not "help but note the irony of the Bicentennial Commission expressing reluctance to provide a forum for the plaintiffs' exercise of their First Amendment rights because they might advocate conduct which is illegal. Does the Bicentennial Commission need reminding that, from the perspective of British loyalists, the Bicentennial celebrates one of history's greatest illegal events?"[118]

It is important to note that the use of public forum doctrine to protect LGBT speech and, in the process, advance LGBT equality constitutes another link between the LGBT rights movement's reliance on the First Amendment and that of the civil rights movement. As noted earlier in this chapter, the Supreme Court, a little more than a decade before the LGBT public forum cases, made clear that civil rights protestors had the right to access public forums in order to agitate in favor of equal treatment.[119]

The First Amendment's public forum doctrine aided another gay organization in 1976 when the mayor of Anchorage ordered that information about the Alaska Gay Coalition (an LGBT rights advocacy group) not be included in a city publication aimed at informing residents about the work of public agencies and private organizations. During the trial that followed the Coalition's lawsuit under the Free Speech Clause, "the Mayor admitted to a personal aversion to homosexuality [and] that he felt that state statutes against sodomy and incest made it improper for a government publication to include reference to a group such as the Coalition."[120]

The Alaska Supreme Court concluded that the city publication was a public forum. In doing so, the court explained that a public forum does not have to involve a physical space such as the Old State House in Providence; it can also entail a government program whose main purpose is to encourage the dissemination of information. The court then held that the mayor and city had violated the gay group's rights under the First Amendment because they denied it "access to a public forum based solely on the nature of its beliefs."[121]

The types of First Amendment protections, explored in this chapter, enjoyed by LGBT organizations contributed to the immense growth in their numbers. At the time of Stonewall, there were only a handful of such groups; by the end of the 1970s, there were hundreds of them across the country. These organizations helped to change the terms of the debate over the morality of same-sex sexual relationships and conduct. It was much easier to contend that gay people were perverted and morally compromised when they remained closeted and fearful of being "exposed." It was much less likely that such outlandish claims would go unaddressed after tens of thousands of LGBT people across the country—from all walks of life, socioeconomic classes, and racial and religious groups—started coming together to pursue common interests, share ideas and passions, and provide mutual support in socially active and visible organizations. Political, cultural, educational, social, artistic, professional, and religious organizations constituted the backbone of the LGBT movement. Working within their particular areas of interest, LGBT groups continuously strived to question stereotypes, bring greater visibility to sexual minorities, and agitate in favor of the equal treatment of LGBT people.

There was also a vital link between the ability of sexual minorities to form organizations and the willingness of a growing number of LGBT people to come out of the closet. That particular individuals revealed their sexual orientation was not by itself reason for media and public attention (with the exception, as we will see in the next chapter, of those in certain positions, such as teachers). But the fact, for example, that a group of owners of gay businesses was meeting with city officials to discuss their concerns about police actions, or that LGBT students at a nearby college were creating a group to bring attention to gay issues, or that a Catholic or Presbyterian gay organization was offering support for those who wanted to come out of the closet while remaining within their faith was likely to receive considerable media and public attention. The greater attention, of course, brought with it greater visibility, which in turn helped closeted gay people understand both that they were not alone and that the cause of LGBT rights was closely linked to the willingness of sexual minorities to come out of the closet. It was easier and safer for business owners, students, religious believers, and others to come out of the closet, and to understand the political implications of their doing so, knowing that there were LGBT organizations willing and able to provide support.

The consistency with which gay organizations won First Amendment cases during the 1970s is nothing less than astounding. These victories stood in stark contrast to the general inability of lesbian, gay, and bisexual litigants to prevail in constitutional challenges based on considerations of equal protection and substantive due process/privacy. The next, and last, section of the chapter explores some of the reasons for that difference.

Why Free Speech Victories and Equality/Privacy Defeats?

As I seek to make clear throughout Part I, early LGBT free speech cases were imbued with equality implications, making it possible for the movement to attain important equality objectives through the pursuit of free speech claims.[122] The question then arises, why did the movement prevail in many First Amendment cases at a time when it was consistently losing equality and privacy claims? I think there are four main reasons for that disparity.

First, and perhaps most simply, LGBT litigants benefited from the Supreme Court's case law, strongly protective of free speech rights, which resulted from Southern resistance to the civil rights movement's quest for racial equality. There was no corresponding equality or privacy case law that LGBT activists could harness with the same degree of effectiveness.

Second, LGBT free speech challenges were more likely to benefit from the status/conduct distinction than equal protection and due process claims brought by sexual minorities. That distinction was grounded in the reasoning of the Supreme Court's 1962 decision in *Robinson v. California*, in which the justices held that although the Constitution allowed the government to criminalize drug use (conduct), it prohibited the state from punishing individuals because they were drug users (status).[123]

LGBT rights challenges based on equality and privacy grounds tended to implicate same-sex sexual conduct in some form or another, making it easier for courts to defer to the government's contention that it could legitimately regulate conduct that it deemed harmful to society. The presumption in the equal protection and due process/privacy cases was that because the government could criminalize same-sex sexual conduct, it could also treat those who engaged in the conduct unfavorably in matters related, for example, to family law, employment, and immigration without offending the Constitution. But the cases explored in this chapter were not primarily about conduct. Instead, they were primarily about government efforts to penalize sexual minorities for who they were as reflected in what they said and with whom they associated. This made it possible for LGBT advocates to contend that speech restrictions imposed on sexual minorities targeted their status in constitutionally impermissible ways.

Third, courts were less likely to defer to the government's morality-based justifications for imposing burdens on sexual minorities in the free speech context than they were in equality and privacy cases. This phenomenon was reflected in the two Supreme Court gay obscenity cases discussed in Chapter 1 and in some of the litigation explored in this chapter. For example, public university administrators, in defending their refusal to recognize gay student groups, contended that they had a responsibility to promote the values of the broader community and that recognizing LGBT student groups undermined those values. These were the kinds of morality-based justifications that allowed the government to consistently prevail in LGBT equal protection and due process cases until rulings such as *Romer v. Evans* (striking down a state constitutional amendment that prohibited the government from protecting sexual minorities from discrimination under the Equal Protection Clause) and *Lawrence v.*

Texas (striking down sodomy laws under the Due Process Clause) made it increasingly difficult to justify anti-gay laws on morality grounds.[124] But in the First Amendment context, as illustrated by the LGBT student group cases, government efforts to defend regulations on those same grounds failed years earlier. It was one thing to say, for example, that the government's interest in promoting public morality justified regulating gay sex differently from straight sex. It was quite another to argue that sexual minorities had fewer rights to free speech and association because of society's moral disapproval of them. After all, the right to express opinions and perspectives, whether political, moral, or otherwise, in dissent from government-sanctioned views lies at the core of the protections afforded by the Free Speech Clause.

Finally, the free speech analysis, unlike the equal protection analysis, did not require that LGBT litigants be "similarly situated" to heterosexuals in order to qualify for constitutional protection. The understanding of equality, traceable all the way back to Aristotle's writings, that has dominated American law is that of formal equality, that is, the idea that the government should treat similarly those who are similarly situated.[125] As a constitutional law treatise explains, "equal protection is the guarantee that similar people will be dealt with in a similar manner and that people of different circumstances will not be treated as if they were the same."[126] Although some theorists, including many feminists and critical race theorists, have proposed alternative understandings of equality by emphasizing, for example, notions of structural inequality and subordination, it is the concept of formal equality that has dominated American law. As a result, courts in equal protection cases have traditionally asked whether the group asserting the equality claim is similarly situated to those who already enjoy the rights or benefits in question.

The unfortunate reality is that until relatively recently, most judges, like most Americans, did not generally believe that sexual minorities were "similarly situated" to heterosexuals in their abilities, character, and contributions to society, a phenomenon that contributed in crucial ways to the inability, also until relatively recently, of LGBT litigants to prevail in constitutional equality cases. The fact that LGBT litigants did not have to establish that they were "similarly situated" to heterosexuals in order to prevail in free speech cases made it more likely that they would succeed in that arena than in that of equal protection during the LGBT movement's early years.

It bears noting that the inapplicability of the "similarly situated" analysis to free speech claims reflects the different role that the concept of neutrality plays in the context of free speech than it does in that of equality. There is wide agreement, especially in the area of political speech (such as LGBT rights advocacy), that the Free Speech Clause requires the government to remain neutral regarding the substance of the views expressed through that speech. For example, the notion that free speech protections are required to protect a marketplace of ideas and the search for truth (or at least the search for the best policy solutions for social problems and challenges), which has served, at different times and to different degrees, as a normative foundation for the Supreme Court's free speech jurisprudence, is premised on the impermissibility of relying on the value or merits of private speech in deciding whether and how to regulate expression.[127] The principle of state neutrality is also deeply embedded in the well-established free speech doctrine prohibiting the government from favoring some viewpoints over others.[128] All of this means that courts, in assessing the free speech claims of sexual minorities, have not compared the substance (or viability or defensibility) of the views expressed by LGBT individuals with those expressed by heterosexuals.

But it is not possible to abide by the type of government neutrality demanded by the Free Speech Clause when the issue is whether the individuals raising equality claims are similarly situated to the individuals who already enjoy the benefits in question. As law professor Peter Westen argued several decades ago, the question of whether two classes of individuals are similarly situated (that is, the question that determines whether the principle of formal equality applies) cannot be answered by deploying the principle of equality itself. Westen explained that before it is possible to determine whether individuals *ought* to be treated alike, it is necessary to establish whether they *are* alike.[129] The norm of formal equality by itself does not tell us which traits are relevant in deciding which groups should be eligible for (or subject to) the equal distribution of particular benefits (or burdens). To answer *that* question, we must step outside the confines of equality, so to speak, unless we take the illogical (and unworkable) position that all individuals should be treated equally in all matters.

The crucial judgment in determining whether a particular class of individuals should be protected by formal equality principles, then, is whether they share relevant characteristics with those who are benefited or burdened by government policy. That assessment, as a conceptual matter, is antecedent to the question of whether equality principles require equal treatment. Formal equality, in other words, is not a "free-standing" concept, that is, one that is independent of antecedent normative judgments.[130]

The conceptual working of formal equality can be illustrated in the following way: *Before* courts and legislatures can conclude that the government should not, for example, take sexual orientation into account in allocating benefits and burdens, they must first make the prior judgment that sexual orientation differences are irrelevant for most or all purposes. To make that judgment, courts and legislators must grapple with normative questions regarding human sexuality and intimate relationships, questions that cannot be answered by the principle of formal equality itself. It is only after the judgment is reached that sexual orientation does not impact the abilities, character, or potential of human beings that it is possible to proceed, as a matter of morality and law, to implement equality principles by prohibiting discrimination on the basis of sexual orientation.

All of this means that free speech principles demand a greater degree of neutrality on the part of government decision-makers than do equality ones, a factor that contributed to the LGBT movement's early First Amendment victories. In deciding whether to recognize the types of free speech claims raised by LGBT litigants during the movement's early days, courts did not have to grapple with questions related to whether same-sex relationships and intimacy were similar, in crucial respects, to those of heterosexuals. Instead, as called for by the First Amendment, courts were generally able to assess the free speech claims from a neutral position regarding the underlying truthfulness or merits of the expression in question. To put it differently, in most of the free speech cases explored in this chapter, courts paid little attention to the question that would have been central to the analysis had the cases been explicitly grounded in equality considerations: whether important or relevant differences existed between heterosexuals and sexual minorities.

If free speech doctrine had required judges to grapple with that question, most LGBT rights claims grounded in the First Amendment during the movement's early days would have failed, as did most claims explicitly grounded in equality doctrine, because almost no judges at the time believed that LGBT people were similarly situated to the rest of the population. The fact that the question was irrelevant under the Free Speech Clause contributed to the general success of the LGBT First Amendment cases explored in this chapter.

CHAPTER THREE

Coming Out and Free Expression

THE SUPREME COURT has noted that "the essential thrust of the First Amendment is to prohibit improper restraints on the voluntary public expression of ideas; it shields the man [sic] who wants to speak ... when others wish him to be quiet."[1] As explored in this chapter, one of the most important questions of legal doctrine for the LGBT movement in its early days was whether the Free Speech Clause protected sexual minorities' assertions of identity (or to put it differently, their coming out of the closet) when government actors pressured them to remain silent about that identity.

During the middle decades of the twentieth century, the coming together of lesbian and gay people in large numbers—first in New York City and San Francisco, and then increasingly in a growing number of other cities as well—usually took place before their coming out. That is, most lesbians and gay men who associated with others did so while keeping their sexuality firmly hidden from their families of origin, employers, landlords, and for those who were married, their (opposite-sex) spouses and children. It was one thing for lesbians and gay men to be open about their same-sex sexuality while in the presence of other sexual minorities; it was another to acknowledge that sexuality while leading their daily lives in a society that was deeply homophobic. For most gay people, the consequences of coming out of the closet were terrifyingly severe, and could include the loss of employment, housing, friends, and family. Faced with these consequences, it was understandable and rational for most LGBT people to remain in the closet.

It was not until the 1970s that sexual minorities in the United States started to come out of the closet in significant numbers. There are several reasons that account for this phenomenon, including the growth in the number and visibility of LGBT organizations as detailed in the last chapter. The fact that a few courageous and politically active lesbians, gay men, and bisexuals were willing to form, or be associated with, these groups showed other LGBT people that it was possible, despite the many obstacles that society put in the way, to be open about their sexuality. Another reason for the growing number of LGBT people who began coming out of the closet was the loosening of traditional sexual mores across society, a loosening that went far beyond sexual minorities and their concerns. By the 1970s, an increasing number of heterosexuals were refusing to abide by traditional sexual mores that deemed sexual relationships outside of marriage to be immoral and sinful. Indeed, there was a growing sense among many Americans, first among young adults and then later among older people too, that questions of relationships and sex fell under the realm of individual autonomy and personal freedom rather than that of societal morality or religious doctrine. This changing social and moral environment made it easier for some lesbians, gay men, and bisexuals—especially those living in cities with visible LGBT communities—to come out of the closet. Finally, as a political matter, post-Stonewall LGBT activists repeatedly encouraged sexual minorities to come out as a means for resisting societal oppression. If the subordination of LGBT people was premised on their being forced to remain silent and invisible, then liberation and equality depended on their being open about their sexuality.

This chapter explores the link between self-identification by sexual minorities, claims to LGBT equality, and free speech protections. It begins with a brief discussion of free speech theory in order to explain why the concept of self-identification by sexual minorities, which has been such an important aspect of the quest for LGBT equality in the United States, is one that properly implicates free speech considerations. The chapter then explores the first group of legal disputes that grappled in significant ways with the free speech implications of LGBT self-identification: cases from the 1970s in which government employees were fired after they self-identified as gay. The fact that government agencies in these disputes terminated employees after they *voluntarily* revealed their same-sex sexual orientation made it possible, for the first time, to start using the First Amendment to try to protect LGBT people from employment discrimination.

After discussing the free speech cases involving gay employees, the chapter explores the historical intersection of free speech and the coming out of the closet in two other contexts. First, it discusses how LGBT activists in California in the late 1970s exercised their free speech rights to defeat a ballot box initiative aimed at keeping gay public school teachers in the closet. Second, it explores a little-known, but conceptually important, case involving a free speech challenge brought by a male teenager in Rhode Island in 1980 after his high school prohibited him from bringing a male date to the senior prom.

First Amendment Theory and LGBT Identity Speech

The Supreme Court has never provided a unified, conceptual understanding of the Free Speech Clause that accounts, as a normative matter, for both the scope and content of its free speech jurisprudence. Instead, the Court has developed that jurisprudence in a largely ad-hoc manner by demarcating different categories of speech, such as expression that may induce unlawful conduct, obscenity, and commercial advertising, and then applying relatively distinct analytical approaches to each. As a result, and perhaps not surprisingly, the task of developing holistic understandings of free speech values and doctrine has been taken up almost entirely by academic commentators.

The first American theorist to do so in a comprehensive way was the philosopher Alexander Meiklejohn in the 1940s. According to Meiklejohn, the essential purpose of the Free Speech Clause is to promote self-governance by the people. In order for individuals to participate meaningfully in their own self-governance, they must have unrestricted access to information and ideas. For Meiklejohn, "the principle of the freedom of speech [is] not the Law of Nature or of Reason in the abstract. It is a deduction from the basic American agreement that public issues shall be decided by universal suffrage."[2] From this perspective, freedom of speech does not have deontological value as an end in itself, but instead constitutes an instrumental means through which self-governance, and therefore American-style democracy, is pursued.

Following Meiklejohn's influential work, some legal scholars, such as Owen Fiss and Cass Sunstein, have emphasized the role that the First Amendment plays in promoting robust forms of public discourse and political deliberation.[3] Although there are important differences in their approaches, this group of academics normatively prioritizes the role that free speech protections play in making self-governance viable and vigorous. As Sunstein explains, the "government should be under a special burden of justification when it seeks to control speech intended and received as a contribution to public deliberation."[4] From this perspective, government regulations should be assessed under the Free Speech Clause in relation to their contribution to, or interference with, the degree, quality, and expansiveness of participation in public discourse.

The principal alternative to the public discourse model of free speech is grounded in considerations of self-development and self-realization. This model focuses, as a foundational matter, not on the systemic impact of regulations that burden expression, but on their impact on the ability of individuals to lead autonomous lives. In doing so, the model assigns deontological value to personal liberty; that liberty serves as a foundational norm that has value in itself, quite independently of the social effects of its exercise. From this perspective, freedom of speech has intrinsic value because the exercise of meaningful autonomy is impossible in its absence.

C. Edwin Baker, one of the leading defenders of the autonomy model of free speech, contended "that the free speech clause protects not a marketplace but rather an arena of individual liberty from certain types of governmental restrictions. Speech is protected not as a means to a collective good but because of the value of speech conduct to the individual. The liberty theory justifies protection because of the way the protected conduct fosters individual self-realization and self-determination without improperly interfering with the legitimate claims of others."[5]

As is clear from Baker's reasoning, the autonomy model (sometimes referred to as the self-realization or self-determination model) prioritizes the *capacity* of individuals to decide how to conduct their lives. That capacity is understood as a basic human capability that, as a moral matter, requires the government, before restricting it, to show the existence of compelling justifications. As David A. J. Richards, another prominent exponent of the autonomy model of free speech, explained, "the significance of free expression rests on the central human capacity to create and express symbolic systems, such as speech, writing, pictures, and music, intended to communicate in determinate, complex and subtle ways. Freedom of expression permits and encourages the exercise of these capacities: it supports a mature individual's sovereign autonomy in deciding how to communicate with others; it disfavors restrictions on communication imposed for the sake of the distorting rigidities of the orthodox and the established. In so doing, it nurtures and sustains the self-respect of the mature person."[6]

Although there are some free speech theorists who do not follow either of the two broad models summarized here and others who seek to bridge the gap between them, the "public deliberation vs. private self-realization" distinction constitutes a crucial divide among American theorists of free expression. For our purposes, it is important to note that the idea that self-identification by sexual minorities merits protection under the Free Speech Clause fits comfortably under *both* theoretical approaches.

At its most basic level, self-identifying speech (such as "I am a lesbian") communicates a fact to the world. But self-identification also plays a crucial role in the *construction* of identity. As legal scholar Nan Hunter notes, "identity cannot exist without [self-identification]. That is even more true when the distinguishing group characteristics are not visible, as is typically true of sexual orientation. Therefore, in the field of lesbian and gay civil rights, much more so than for most other equality claims, expression is a component of the very identity itself."[7]

To punish LGBT people for self-identifying as such is to prevent them from participating in the construction of their own identities. This prohibition implicates the Free Speech Clause both because the identification itself is intrinsically expressive in nature and because, to the extent the First Amendment concerns itself with protecting personal autonomy and integrity, the prohibition interferes with the self-determination interests of LGBT people. Commanding LGBT individuals to be silent about their sexuality prevents them from participating in the construction of their own identities and lives as they deem appropriate. Government policies that limit the ability of sexual minorities to self-identify restrict their ability to determine and control crucial aspects of their lives, including those related to personal relationships and family.

The command to be silent about having a same-sex sexual orientation, in a society that presumes everyone is heterosexual, as the American society pervasively and relentlessly did in the early days of the LGBT rights movement, also interferes with considerations of personal autonomy and integrity because remaining silent in this context is frequently understood as expressing a message of heterosexuality. The prevailing assumption in our society, even to this day, is that everyone is heterosexual unless there is reason to believe otherwise. Requiring sexual minorities to be silent about their sexual orientation, therefore, impermissibly requires them to send a message ("I am heterosexual") they do not wish to express. The forced command to send an unwanted message has clear implications for considerations of personal autonomy, integrity, and self-realization; the command essentially forces its subject to be (or to pretend to be) a person with identities, viewpoints, or preferences that are different from those that the individual actually holds. It can be argued that this is one of the reasons why the Supreme Court, in interpreting the Free Speech Clause, has been highly skeptical of efforts to use state authority to compel individuals to express messages that are inconsistent with their values and beliefs.[8]

The view that the First Amendment prohibits restrictions on the ability of sexual minorities to self-identify is supported not only by a conceptual understanding of free speech grounded in considerations of personal autonomy and self-realization, but also by theories of free speech that emphasize its role in fomenting robust forms of public deliberation. Commands that require sexual minorities to be silent about their sexual orientation deprive them of the ability to participate openly and honestly in public debates on issues that affect, or are implicated by, sexual orientation. This deprivation, by necessity, circumscribes the scope of the public discourse because it excludes from it voices and viewpoints that are, in part, determined and constructed by considerations of identity.

Legal scholar Tobias Barrington Wolff has noted the crucial link that can sometimes exist between identity and public discourse. As he explains, "citizens engage with politics from a position of personal experience and identity. Personal experience provides the font of information that nourishes the formation of political beliefs; identity offers a vernacular through which those beliefs can find expression. To single out and silence a group of speakers who possess a distinctive identity that is germane to an issue of public importance . . . is to distort the terms of political debate and call into question the legitimacy of the State's authority."[9]

State action that silences LGBT people, therefore, is problematic from the perspective of human flourishing and development, and also from that of democratic theory and processes. The harm caused by the forced silencing, in other words, is not borne solely by the individuals immediately affected; instead, when state action prevents classes of individuals from disclosing their identity, the polity as a whole is harmed because viewpoints and perspectives that emanate from that identity are necessarily excluded from public discourse and deliberations. As a result, both government officials and citizens are deprived of the opportunity to learn about ideas and experiences that can be relevant to the setting of policy. In the same way that denying certain categories of adult citizens the ability to vote undermines democratic values and processes, prohibiting distinct classes of individuals from self-identifying undercuts the polity's ability to govern itself.

With this brief summary of some of the conceptual issues raised by state action that limits the ability of LGBT people to self-identify, we can proceed to explore the first group of legal disputes that grappled in significant ways with the First Amendment implications of self-identification: gay civil-servant cases from the 1970s. It should be noted that cases challenging the military's Don't Ask, Don't Tell policy, which prohibited lesbian, gay, and bisexual service members from self-identifying, also raised crucial First Amendment issues. Those issues are discussed in the next chapter.

The Gay Civil Servant Cases from the 1970s: Victories and Defeats

For many LGBT people, including those who worked for the government, coming out of the closet, or having their sexuality revealed by others, could lead to the loss of employment. As already noted, the federal government, starting in the early 1950s, routinely fired lesbian and gay civil servants. The first gay person to legally challenge his dismissal was Charles Kameny, an astronomer with the Army Map Service, who was fired in 1957 after the police arrested him for soliciting sex from another man. Kameny lost his case, as did several other gay men who, in the years that followed, challenged their firings. Unlike the later cases (most of them from the 1970s) explored in this section, these early lawsuits did not involve instances of government employees who came out of the closet first and were fired second. Instead, the first lawsuits brought by gay government workers (all of the plaintiffs in these cases were men) involved civil servants who were fired after the police informed their superiors that they had been arrested, usually by undercover officers, on sex-related charges such as public lewdness and solicitation. For federal employees, any allegation of homosexuality was sufficient, under Civil Service Commission regulations, to trigger a dismissal.

The early challenges brought by gay civil servants were grounded in due process considerations involving allegations that the firings were arbitrary and capricious. At the time, courts were highly deferential toward the Civil Service Commission and its regulatory priorities; as a result, judges almost always rejected claims that the federal government violated the Constitution when firing employees on the basis of sexual orientation.[10] But in 1969, the U.S. Court of Appeals for the District of Columbia Circuit departed from the earlier rulings in *Norton v. Macy*. Two police officers with the Washington, D.C., Morals Squad had arrested Norton after they observed him pick up a man near Lafayette Square, drive around, and then drop him off. The man told the police that Norton had touched his leg and invited him back to Norton's apartment for a drink. The National Aeronautics and Space Administration (NASA), which employed Norton as a budget analyst, fired him because of the arrest. The appellate court concluded that the dismissal was improper, holding that government employees could not be fired simply because they were gay. Instead, the court ruled that the Due Process Clause required the government to demonstrate the existence of a "rational nexus" between the same-sex sexual orientation of employees and their ability to perform their jobs.[11]

The *Norton* ruling was helpful to gay civil servants for two reasons. First, under the court's reasoning, homosexuality was no longer a per se ground for dismissal. Second, the court placed the burden on the government to justify sexuality-based dismissals. Despite *Norton*'s gay-friendly reasoning, several post-*Norton* courts continued to defer to the government's judgment that gay employees—in particular, those arrested because of their sexual orientation—evinced characteristics that were unsuitable for government employment.[12]

Starting in the early 1970s, a new type of constitutional employment discrimination case began reaching the courts, one in which the government agency fired employees on the basis of sexual orientation as a result not of arrests, but because the employees revealed their orientation either to the employers or, more frequently, to others and the employers later learned of it. The fact that government agencies moved to terminate employees after they *voluntarily* revealed their same-sex sexual orientation made it possible, for the first time, to start using the Free Speech Clause to try to protect gay government workers from employment discrimination.

The firings, after all, usually took place only after the employees identified themselves as gay through speech.

It bears noting at the outset that the plaintiffs in the employment discrimination cases from the 1970s did not always prevail in their First Amendment claims. Indeed, the rate at which gay employees prevailed in their free speech challenges does not match, for example, gay student groups' perfect rate of success in their First Amendment lawsuits against public colleges and universities during the same period. There are several reasons for this difference. First, the student cases raised not only issues of free speech, but also of free association, thus providing the student plaintiffs an additional and powerful First Amendment basis for their claims. Second, courts were, on the whole, more willing to defer to the government in its role as employer than they were willing to defer to the government's in loco parentis claims in the context of college students. Arguments related to the need to maintain proper working environments and the public's trust in government agencies had more traction as justifications for the challenged government actions than did arguments, in the student cases, about the need to deter same-sex sexual conduct on the nation's campuses.

Nonetheless, several of the gay plaintiffs in the employment discrimination cases prevailed, demonstrating that the First Amendment could play an important role in protecting the ability of lesbians, gay men, and bisexuals to come out of the closet. And when courts ruled against the gay plaintiffs, they did so in generally strained, convoluted, and unpersuasive ways that failed to afford gay people the same kinds of speech protections enjoyed by heterosexuals.

It Started with Same-Sex Marriage

The first federal employment lawsuit involving a claim that the government discriminated against a gay person because he voluntarily revealed his sexual orientation followed from the first time that a same-sex couple in the United States sued after being denied a marriage license. In 1966, Jack Baker met Michael McConnell at a Halloween barn party near the University of Oklahoma, where McConnell was pursuing a degree in library sciences. Shortly after they met, Baker, who was an engineer and an Air Force veteran, took a civilian job at the Tinker Air Force Base in Oklahoma City, only to be quickly fired for being openly gay. After a few years together, the couple agreed they wanted to marry, by which they meant not just the entering into a committed relationship for life, but a legal one as well.[13]

In 1969, Baker moved to Minneapolis to start attending the University of Minnesota Law School. McConnell followed several months later after he was told by University of Minnesota librarians that he would be offered a position—as the Head of the Cataloguing Division of one of the university's libraries—after pro forma approval by the university's board of regents.

Shortly after arriving in Minneapolis, Baker joined the student group Fight Repression of Erotic Expression (FREE), Minnesota's first gay rights organization (then only three months old), quickly becoming its president. The group worked to increase the visibility of gay people on campus; held social events; lobbied the state's human rights commissioner for discrimination protections; and sent speakers to high schools, colleges, and churches throughout the area. The organization also agreed to help Baker and McConnell with their application for a marriage license.

FREE informed the media that two of its male members would apply for a marriage license and hold a press conference. After the press conference, Baker and McConnell walked with other FREE members to the Hennepin County courthouse in Minneapolis accompanied by a throng of reporters. A few minutes later, the two men stood together before the court clerk, raised their right hands, and swore to answer his questions truthfully. At that moment, a photographer with United Press International took a picture of the two clean-cut men wearing suits and ties; the photo appeared the following day in newspapers across the country. The clerk's office accepted the marriage application (and the $10 filing fee), only to deny it four days later because there were "sufficient legal impediment[s] . . . prohibiting the marriage of two male persons."[14]

When the Board of Regents of the University of Minnesota learned that McConnell had attempted to marry his male partner, it refused to approve the job offer "on the grounds that his personal conduct, as represented in the public and University news media, is not consistent with the best interest of the University."[15] In response, McConnell sued in federal court claiming that the university violated his constitutional rights to due process, equal protection, and free speech. As to the latter claim, McConnell pointed out that it was his decision to exercise his First Amendment rights by publicly disclosing his sexual orientation in seeking to marry another man, a disclosure that received considerable media attention, which had led the board not to approve the job offer. (It was the first time in more than a decade that the board had refused to authorize a job offer recommended by an academic department.)[16] In effect, McConnell argued that he was denied the job because he exercised his rights to free speech by publicly revealing his sexual orientation.

At the trial, the board's chairman defended the decision not to hire McConnell by claiming that his "professed homosexuality connotes to the public generally that he practices the acts of sodomy, a crime under Minnesota law"; that the university could reasonably believe that McConnell's attempt to get a license to marry another man meant that he intended to engage in sodomy; and that the university should not be required to condone the engaging in criminal acts by its employees.[17]

The trial court ruled in favor of McConnell, but the U.S. Court of Appeals for the Eighth Circuit reversed. In doing so, it refused to even address McConnell's First Amendment claim, deeming his decision to disclose his sexual orientation publicly by seeking to marry another man to be nothing more than an "antic."[18] The appellate court then rejected the due process and equal protection claims by contending that the case was not, in the end, about the plaintiff's job. Instead, it was "a case in which the prospective employee demands, as shown both by the allegations of the complaint and by the marriage license incident as well, the right to pursue an activist role in *implementing* his unconventional ideas concerning the societal status to be accorded homosexuals and, thereby, to foist tacit approval of this socially repugnant concept upon his employer, who is, in this instance, an institution of higher learning. We know of no constitutional fiat or binding principle of decisional law which requires an employer to accede to such extravagant demands."[19]

Interestingly, the court's very reasons for denying McConnell's due process and equal protection claims reflected the extent to which the case was imbued with free speech considerations. As the court acknowledged, it was the plaintiff's political activism, "his unconventional ideas," and his efforts to promote the "socially repugnant concept" of same-sex marriage that led the board to not approve his job offer.

The importance of the free speech claim to McConnell's legal challenge was also reflected in the fact that the board had not withheld the job offer simply because he was gay. Unlike the military, for example, the university did not have a policy prohibiting the hiring of gay people. Instead, the university had a problem with gay employees only when they made their sexual orientation publicly known, as McConnell had done in seeking to marry Baker.

If the court had been willing to recognize that the case, in fact, raised First Amendment issues, it should have looked to the Supreme Court's 1968 decision in *Pickering v. Board of Education* for guidance. In that case, a school district fired a teacher after he wrote a letter to the editor, published in a local newspaper, criticizing the school board's budgetary priorities. The Court in *Pickering* explained that when public employees raise free speech claims in challenging a negative employment decision made by their employers, it is necessary to balance the right of an employee to speak on issues of public concern against the public employer's legitimate interests in the proper functioning of its workplaces and in its ability to provide effective services to the public. The Court found the firing of the teacher to be unconstitutional because the letter to the editor did not undermine the ability of the school district to maintain discipline and harmony among its workers or to accomplish its mission of educating students.[20]

It seems clear that the gay plaintiff in *McConnell* would have prevailed had the court of appeals applied the *Pickering* test. By speaking to the press about his interest in marrying his male partner, McConnell addressed an issue of public concern: the way in which the law failed to provide same-sex couples with the opportunity to marry. It is difficult to see how McConnell's speech, including the disclosure of his sexual orientation, could have negatively affected his ability to serve as the Head of the Cataloguing Division of one of the university's libraries. Like the teacher's protected expression in *Pickering*, McConnell's public statements and conduct (namely, applying for the marriage license) were unrelated to his responsibilities as a librarian.

McConnell paid for exercising his free speech rights with the loss of a job offer that he otherwise would have received. Ironically, the court was so offended by the public and political messages that were part of McConnell's public disclosure of his sexual orientation that it did not even recognize, much less address, the free speech issue that was so clearly before it.[21]

A Gay Teacher Wins a Battle but Loses the War

In 1970, Joseph Acanfora, an education major at Penn State University in his junior year, helped to form the Homophile Organization of Penn

State (HOPS) and became the group's treasurer. The following year, HOPS applied to be recognized by the university, a request that administrators denied because "the chartering of [the] organization would create a substantial conflict with the counseling and psychiatric services the University provides to its students and . . . such conflict would be harmful to the best interests of the students of the University."[22] After school officials refused to recognize HOPS, Acanfora and three other students filed a First Amendment lawsuit. In speaking to the press about the suit, Acanfora acknowledged on several occasions that he was gay.[23] A state court eventually ordered the university to grant recognition to HOPS.

Three days after the filing of the lawsuit, the dean of the College of Education revoked Acanfora's assignment as a student-teacher at a local school, an assignment that was a prerequisite for receiving a teaching degree. After Acanfora sued again, claiming that the dean's action infringed on his First Amendment right of association because it penalized him for his activities with HOPS, the university reinstated his student-teacher privileges.

But Acanfora's problems with the university were not yet over. After he applied for a certificate to teach in Pennsylvania during his last year of college, the dean raised the issue of whether Acanfora's sexual orientation deprived him of the "good moral character" required to receive the certification. As a result, the university's Teacher Certification Council held a hearing in which six deans asked Acanfora highly intrusive questions about his sexuality and sexual relationships. The council eventually deadlocked on whether Acanfora possessed the requisite "good moral character" to be a teacher and referred the matter to the state's Secretary of Education.[24]

In the meantime, Acanfora got a job as an eighth-grade science teacher at a school in Montgomery County, Maryland. When he filled out the job application for the position, he failed to disclose, in response to a question asking him to list his extracurricular college activities, that he had been a member of HOPS. He later explained that he had omitted any mention of HOPS in applying for the job because he suspected that it would have rendered him ineligible for a teaching position, an assumption that Montgomery County school officials later acknowledged was correct.[25]

About a month after Acanfora started teaching in Maryland, the Pennsylvania Secretary of Education held a press conference announcing he had decided to grant him a teaching certificate. Several newspapers, including the *New York Times*, published stories about the granting of a teaching license to a gay man and mentioned that Acanfora was currently teaching at a junior high school in Montgomery County.[26] School officials, after learning of their employee's sexual orientation from the media, immediately moved him out of the classroom and assigned him to a clerical position. At the end of the school year, they refused to renew his contract.

The school district's decision to keep Acanfora away from students received a great deal of media attention. In the months following his removal from the classroom, Acanfora gave several television, radio, and newspaper interviews, including one on CBS's *60 Minutes*, in which he explained his situation and decried discrimination against gay people.

Acanfora filed a lawsuit in federal court arguing that the decision by school officials to remove him from the classroom violated his constitutional rights to due process, equal protection, and free speech. At the trial, the state's "expert witnesses" testified that there was a grave risk that having a teacher whom the students knew was gay might lead some to experiment with homosexuality.[27] After the trial, the district court ruled that school officials had violated Acanfora's constitutional right to privacy when they made a negative employment decision based on his sexual relationships. (The court's decision appears to be the first judicial opinion in the United States recognizing a right to privacy by a gay person grounded in the right to have intimate relationships with others.) But the court proceeded to rule that, despite the constitutional violation, Acanfora was not entitled to return to teaching because he had spoken at length to the media after school officials removed him from the classroom. According to the court, Acanfora's exchanges with the press were irresponsible and sensationalistic because they "sparked the controversy" and "were likely to incite or produce imminent effects deleterious to the educational process."[28]

The district court's reasoning in refusing to order school officials to return Acanfora to the classroom after concluding they had violated his constitutional right to privacy was perplexing because the interviews he gave to the press, about his case and the discrimination faced by gay people, were clearly protected by the First Amendment. The court, in effect, punished Acanfora for exercising his free speech rights. Such an odd outcome did not survive appellate review. The U.S. Court of Appeals for the Fourth Circuit held that school officials had violated Acanfora's

constitutional right to free speech (and not his right to privacy). The ruling is historically important because it was the first time that a federal
appellate court held that a public employee—in this case a teacher—had a
First Amendment right to speak openly about issues of importance to the
gay community without fearing for his job. As the court explained,

> the record discloses that press, radio, and television commentators con-
> sidered homosexuality in general, and Acanfora's plight in particular, to
> be a matter of public interest about which reasonable people could differ,
> and Acanfora responded to their inquiries in a rational manner. There
> is no evidence that the interviews disrupted the school, substantially
> impaired his capacity as a teacher, or gave the school officials reasonable
> grounds to forecast that these results would flow from what he said. We
> hold, therefore, that Acanfora's public statements were protected by the
> First Amendment and that they do not justify either the action taken by
> the school system or the dismissal of his suit.[29]

Despite the appellate court's recognition that the school violated
Acanfora's First Amendment rights, it refused to grant him the remedy
he sought, which was to return to the classroom. The court reasoned that
Acanfora's failure to disclose his membership in HOPS when he filled out
the job application constituted fraud, thus rendering him ineligible for
the judicial relief he sought. In the end, although Acanfora won judicial
recognition that the school district had violated his rights to free speech,
he was nonetheless unable to regain his teaching job.

The outcome of the *Acanfora* litigation exposed the bind that many
LGBT people found themselves in: If they came out of the closet publicly, they faced the likelihood of discrimination and harassment, often at
the hand of government officials, as Acanfora's experiences going back to
his college days clearly showed. At the same time, to remain in the closet
had its own costs, including the dissatisfaction and stress that came with
deceiving others (employers, fellow employees, family members, friends,
and so on) about one's personal life.

Acanfora's decision not to come out to his employer while applying for
the teaching job was an understandable one; if he had revealed his activities with HOPS (and therefore his sexual orientation) to school officials,
they would not have hired him. Such brazen discrimination by government
officials, of course, raised serious equal protection concerns. But for the
reasons explained at the end of Chapter 2, the courts in the 1970s, and for
some time afterwards, were not yet ready to take seriously equal protection

lawsuits brought by LGBT individuals challenging discriminatory state action. And although a handful of courts, relying on the government's due process obligation not to act in arbitrary and capricious ways, had been willing to condemn the firing of employees simply because they were gay, it was not particularly difficult for the government to prevail in due process cases when gay employees expressed their sexuality in any way. In 1976, for example, a federal appellate court, in *Singer v. U.S. Civil Service Commission*, upheld the firing by the Equal Employment Opportunity Commission (of all federal agencies!) of a gay clerical worker on the ground that he was too open about his sexual orientation. The agency complained, for instance, that he had kissed and embraced another man by the elevator in the building where he worked at a prior job and, several years earlier, had sought to marry another man.[30] According to the *Singer* court, the firing was justified because the plaintiff had engaged in "the open and public flaunting or advocacy of homosexual conduct."[31]

In this legal environment of limited constitutional protection for government employees who came out of the closet, the First Amendment had a crucial role to play. Although the *Acanfora* litigation's outcome was disappointing to LGBT rights activists because the gay plaintiff was unable to regain his teaching position, at least the court had made clear that the First Amendment protected the right of gay public employees to speak on gay issues that were of public concern. Several other courts, in the years that followed, built on this important principle to provide more substantial protection for government workers who acknowledged their same-sex sexual orientation while publicly speaking on gay issues.

Coming Out and Winning in Court

In 1972, Richard Aumiller arrived at the University of Delaware as a graduate student in theater. Two years later he became a faculty member in the theater department under a one-year contract that was then renewed for another year. As a student, Aumiller had joined the Gay Community, a student organization on campus. After Aumiller became a faculty member, students asked him to serve as faculty advisor to Gay Community, which Aumiller agreed to do. (It bears noting that the activities of gay college student groups were implicated in *McConnell*, *Acanfora*, and *Aumiller*, showing how the activism of such groups had political and legal repercussions that went far beyond university campuses.)

The existence of Gay Community, and its activities on campus, attracted the attention of local newspapers. Because Aumiller was the group's faculty advisor, reporters sought to interview him on issues of concern to LGBT people. A federal district court eventually summarized the articles as follows: "The clear emphasis in each article is on an examination of how homosexuals adapt to life in a predominately heterosexual society. Aumiller appears as one example of a homosexual and his statements are directed toward educating readers of the article to an acceptance of homosexuals as equals and to the demythologization of certain stereotypes commonly applied to homosexuals."[32]

In other words, Aumiller, like many of his contemporary LGBT activists, was speaking out in order to encourage society to replace the traditional social and moral understandings of sexual minorities, which viewed them skeptically and scornfully, with a new understanding that conceived of sexual orientation as a morally benign trait and of sexual orientation discrimination as a moral wrong. In doing so, individuals like Aumiller were subject to much criticism by those who defended the traditional understandings of LGBT people and their sexual intimacy. One of those individuals was the president of the University of Delaware, who contended that Aumiller had abused his faculty position by speaking to the media about sexual orientation issues. In particular, the president opined that while "I really don't care what Mr. Aumiller does in his bedroom, . . . I consider it an effront [sic] to the University and to me as an individual that he insists in making his bedroom activities public information and a point of evangelistic endeavor to recruit more gays to his supposed cause."[33] Contending that Aumiller's statements to the press showed that he was trying to convert "heterosexuals to homosexuality," the president ordered that his contract not be renewed for the following academic year. Aumiller responded by suing under the First Amendment, arguing that the university refused to renew his contract because he was speaking about gay issues and advocating in favor of gay rights positions.

After holding a four-day trial, a federal district court agreed with the gay plaintiff. In its decision, the court explained that Aumiller's statements to the press, contrary to the president's contention, were not about trying to convert "heterosexuals to homosexuality." Instead, the remarks were aimed at changing the social understanding of gay people and, as such, were protected by the First Amendment. While the court recognized that "homosexuality is an extremely emotional and controversial topic and that Aumiller's opinions on the subject quite likely represent a minority view," both of those facts counseled in favor of affording, rather than denying, free speech protections. In the end, the court ordered that the university renew Aumiller's contract, that it pay him damages for emotional distress, and that the president pay him punitive damages for what the court characterized as "a malicious or wanton disregard for Aumiller's constitutional rights."[34]

It is worth noting that the court rejected the president's contention that the nonrenewal of Aumiller's employment contract was justified because he improperly brought private matters ("what Mr. Aumiller does in his bedroom") into public view. During the course of the litigation, the university took the position that Aumiller's decision to raise publicly matters that were best left to the private sphere rendered the speech in question unprotected by the First Amendment. But the *Aumiller* court, like the *Acanfora* one, rejected the view that a person's disclosure of his same-sex sexual orientation was beyond the protection of the Free Speech Clause. In doing so, the court acknowledged that, as William Eskridge has put it, "for gays and lesbians, identity speech ('I am gay') was both personal and political."[35]

A few years after the court's ruling in *Aumiller*, the U.S. Court of Appeals for the Fifth Circuit also provided a gay public employee with robust protection under the First Amendment. The plaintiff in that case, Gary Van Ooteghem, was hired by the defendant Hartsell Gray, the treasurer of Harris County, Texas, to serve as assistant county treasurer. A few months later, the defendant became so pleased with the plaintiff's job performance that he allowed Van Ooteghem to set his own work schedule. However, the friendly relationship between the two men came to an abrupt end when Van Ooteghem informed Gray that he was gay and that he soon intended to address the county's legislative body on why laws should be enacted to prohibit discrimination against gay people.

Gray grew increasingly upset, not only because he had unknowingly hired a gay man, but also because his employee intended to speak out on behalf of equal treatment for sexual minorities. A few days later, Gray informed Van Ooteghem that he now had to be in the office during certain hours of the day, making it impossible for him to testify before the county legislature. Gray asked Van Ooteghem to agree in writing to this restriction, and when the latter refused, his boss fired him.

Van Ooteghem sued Gray, contending that his dismissal violated his free speech rights. After holding a trial, the federal district court concluded that the defendant impermissibly fired the plaintiff in an effort to prevent him from speaking out in favor of gay rights positions. The appellate court affirmed, concluding that the plaintiff's intended speech was protected by the First Amendment under the *Pickering* balancing test because it would not disrupt the workplace or impede his job obligations. As the court of appeals explained, "it may be true that some treasury workers, or Gray himself, found the prospect of an employee addressing the [county legislative body] on homosexual rights to be distressing. However, the ability of a member of a disfavored class to express his views on civil rights publicly and without hesitation—no matter how personally offensive to his employer or majority of his coemployees—lies at the core of the Free Speech Clause of the First Amendment."[36]

The 1970s free speech cases involving gay employees explored in this section encouraged courts to grapple with and, in at least some circumstances, remedy the unequal treatment of sexual minorities at a time when they enjoyed few equality protections, whether statutory or constitutional.[37] Indeed, the 1970s gay public employee free speech cases, like almost all the other LGBT free speech and free association cases discussed in Part I of this book, were imbued with equality implications. The victories in cases like *Aumiller* and *Van Ooteghem* were important because they made clear to the growing number of LGBT people who were coming out of the closet that advocacy on behalf of gay rights was constitutionally protected, a protection that was not diminished or weakened by the type of self-identification as lesbian, gay, or bisexual that almost always accompanied that advocacy. In affirming the constitutional protection, courts were recognizing that the exercise of free speech rights by sexual minorities was linked both to their identity as LGBT individuals and to their quest for equal rights. Or to put it differently, courts were acknowledging that efforts to silence sexual minorities were aimed at making their push for equal treatment and social inclusion more difficult. As the California Supreme Court stated in 1979, "the struggle of the homosexual community for equal rights, particularly in the field of employment, must be recognized as a political activity." The court added that "a principal barrier to homosexual equality is the common feeling that homosexuality is an affliction which the homosexual worker must conceal from his employer and his fellow workers. Consequently one important aspect of the struggle for equal rights is to induce homosexual individuals to 'come out of the closet,' acknowledge their sexual preferences, and to associate with others in working for equal rights."[38]

Although some courts, such as the California high court, understood the link between self-identification as gay, lesbian, or bisexual and free speech considerations, other courts resisted the connection. There were two main reasons for such resistance. First, there was the claim that self-identification speech by sexual minorities was, in effect, private speech of little public concern. This was the conclusion of the U.S. Circuit Court of Appeals in *Rowland v. Mad River Local School District* decided in 1984. The plaintiff in *Rowland* had been employed by an Ohio school district as a vocational counselor. After she told some of her colleagues that she was bisexual, her supervisors reassigned her to a position that did not involve contact with students and later refused to renew her contract. Rowland sued in federal court, alleging that school officials had violated her rights to free speech and equal protection. The federal appellate court rejected both positions, reasoning on the free speech claim that the plaintiff's revelation of her sexual orientation was a private matter and thus not subject to protection by the First Amendment.[39]

Although a majority of the Supreme Court did not believe it necessary to hear Rowland's appeal, Justice William Brennan, joined by Justice Thurgood Marshall, disagreed. For Brennan, Rowland's self-identification as a bisexual had a close relationship to the deliberation of issues of public concern and, therefore, was protected by the Free Speech Clause. As Brennan explained, "the fact of petitioner's bisexuality, once spoken, necessarily and ineluctably involved her in [the] debate [regarding the rights of LGBT people]. Speech that touches upon this explosive issue is no less deserving of constitutional attention than speech relating to more widely condemned forms of discrimination."[40]

It seems clear that Brennan had the better of the two arguments. The claim that Rowland's disclosure of her bisexual identity was a private matter was belied by the many ways in which government policies and social norms sought to regulate, ostracize, and subordinate sexual minorities based on their sexual orientation. From society's perspective, sexual orientation *mattered*—otherwise, the law would not have denied sexual minorities a broad panoply of rights and benefits based on their intimate relationships. In addition, lesbian, gay, and bisexual individuals in the 1970s and 1980s, as they do today, understood and experienced their sexual orientation based on their "standing and treatment in society."[41] Far from being a matter of private concern, sexuality in contemporary society is a subject of intense public interest, scrutiny, and regulation. Brennan was therefore correct when he concluded that Rowland's sexual orientation was no more a private matter than the race or gender of individuals who claim they have been discriminated against on the basis of race or gender.

If some courts refused to recognize the link between coming out as a sexual minority and constitutionally protected speech because the self-identification was purportedly a matter of private and not public concern, other courts provided a second reason, namely, that the constitutional claims ceased being about protected expression once the self-identification in question was carried out not just through pure speech, but through conduct as well. That was the conclusion of the court in *McConnell*, already discussed at some length, as well as by the court in *Singer*, involving the gay clerk who worked for the Equal Employment Opportunity Commission. In both cases, the plaintiffs' conduct, in particular their attempts to marry their same-sex partners, proved fatal to their constitutional claims because the courts agreed with the government that the gay-related conduct in question justified the negative employment decisions.

The readiness with which some courts were willing to put the First Amendment aside when LGBT people engaged in conduct, no matter how expressive or political, rendered particularly significant, as a conceptual matter, a 1980 decision by a federal district court recognizing the First Amendment right of a male student to attend his high school prom with another young man. That case proved conceptually important because it involved expressive conduct rather than pure speech. But before we explore the high school prom case, it is necessary to look outside the courts to understand how questions related to employment protections, coming out of the closet, and the exercise of free speech rights intersected in a California ballot initiative fight that took place in the late 1970s.

The Briggs Initiative

Around the mid-1970s, a few liberal municipalities, many of them college towns, enacted the first laws in the United States prohibiting discrimination on the basis of sexual orientation. After Miami-Dade County,

Florida, in 1977 became the first Southern municipality to adopt such an ordinance, a coalition of conservative political and religious groups gathered enough signatures to place a repeal measure before voters. The repeal campaign was led by Anita Bryant—a singer, former runner-up in the Miss America Pageant in the 1950s, and born-again Baptist—who founded an antigay organization called Save Our Children. As its name suggested, the group claimed that laws prohibiting discrimination on the basis of sexual orientation were not about civil rights but about the gay movement's purported interest in "recruiting" young people. "The recruitment of our children," Bryant's group explained in an ad it placed in the *Miami Herald*, "is absolutely necessary for the survival and growth of homosexuality—for since homosexuals cannot reproduce, they *must* recruit, *must* freshen their ranks." Another of the group's ads went even further by claiming that gay people engaged in "a hair-raising pattern of recruitment and outright seduction and molestation, a growing pattern that predictably will intensify if society approves laws bringing legitimacy to the sexually perverted."[42]

In June 1977, a week after Dade County residents voted overwhelmingly to repeal the antidiscrimination ordinance, California state Senator John Briggs, who represented conservative Orange County, introduced legislation that would require the firing of gay public school teachers throughout the state. Briggs, an ambitious politician who made no secret of his interest in running for governor or U.S. senator, took a page from Bryant's playbook by claiming that gay teachers should be fired because their presence in the state's classrooms made it more likely that children would become gay and be sexually molested. As Briggs starkly put it, the presence of gay teachers in schools was "about the right of parents to determine who will be teaching their children. We don't allow people who believe in practicing bestiality to teach our children. We don't let prostitutes teach our children. And the reason we don't is because it is illegal to be a prostitute. But it is not illegal to be a homosexual in California."[43]

After the state senate refused to take up his bill, Briggs worked with conservative groups to gather the necessary signatures to put his proposal before voters. That effort yielded roughly five hundred thousand signatures, about two hundred thousand more than were required.[44] The ballot measure, officially known as Proposition 6, but generally referred to as the Briggs Initiative, sought to codify into law a requirement that school districts refuse to employ teachers who engaged in "public homosexual activity" or "public homosexual conduct." The first category referred to same-sex sexual acts that were not "discreet," regardless of whether they constituted a crime. The measure defined the second category as "the advocating, soliciting, imposing, encouraging or promoting of private or public homosexual activity directed at, or likely to come to the attention of schoolchildren and/or other employees."[45] By its own terms, the second proscription was triggered whenever lesbian, gay, and bisexual teachers publicly disclosed their sexual orientation, as well as when teachers advocated, inside or outside the schools, on behalf of gay rights *regardless of their sexual orientation*.

This last point is important because, as law professor Nan Hunter has noted, the Briggs Initiative, by targeting not just gay people but also the expression of progay positions regardless of the speaker's sexual orientation, "marked the moment when American politics began to treat homosexuality as something more than deviance, conduct, or lifestyle; it marked the emergence of homosexuality as an openly political claim and as a viewpoint."[46] This shift had crucial First Amendment implications because it (along with litigation such as the gay student challenges discussed in the last chapter and the gay public employee cases explored in this chapter) led to an understanding of LGBT speech as the advocacy of ideas rather than advocacy of particular types of sexual conduct. This meant that, as Hunter puts it, "the once-bright boundary between sexual speech and political speech began to fade."[47]

The prohibition on the advocacy of progay viewpoints rendered the Briggs Initiative unconstitutional under the Free Speech Clause, as a federal court of appeals ruled several years later after the Oklahoma legislature enacted a statute that replicated the Briggs Initiative's language.[48] But it did not become necessary for LGBT activists to challenge the initiative in court under First Amendment principles because a broad coalition of LGBT organizations, exercising their First Amendment rights, led a successful political campaign to persuade voters to reject the measure at the polls.

In the fall of 1977, a group of political activists from Los Angeles and San Francisco created the Concerned Voters of California (CVC) to fight the Briggs Initiative. With the help of donors such as David Goodstein, the millionaire owner of the *Advocate*, CVC bought large amounts of media advertising urging voters to reject the initiative. The CVC worked closely with David Mixner and his partner Peter Scott, two experienced political consultants, who coordinated an outreach campaign aimed at elected officials and the media.[49] In September 1978, Mixner and Scott met with Governor Ronald Reagan and persuaded him to publicly oppose the initiative.[50]

The CVC pursued a political strategy that avoided discussions of sexuality and purposefully failed to raise gay people's visibility because of a fear that doing so would be politically counterproductive. Rather than addressing issues of sexuality and directly challenging the appropriateness of discrimination against LGBT individuals, CVC sought to paint the initiative as a threat to the human rights and civil liberties of *all* Californians.

But many LGBT activists, working with grassroots organizations at the local level, rejected this strategy, especially after it had failed to secure victory against Anita Bryant's forces in Florida.[51] (Activists grew even more concerned when, in the spring of 1978, voters in St. Paul, Minnesota; Wichita, Kansas; and Eugene, Oregon also voted to repeal ordinances prohibiting sexual orientation discrimination.)[52] These grassroots activists, who were more progressive in their political outlook than the CVC leaders, believed it necessary not just to object to the initiative on civil liberties grounds, but also to raise the visibility of sexual minorities in the state while explaining, time and again, that the Briggs Initiative was driven by invidious discrimination against LGBT people. As these activists saw it, Briggs and his allies would prevail at the ballot box unless straight Californians repeatedly heard from their lesbian, gay, and bisexual family members, neighbors, and coworkers about the impact that laws like the one proposed by the initiative had on their lives.[53]

The fact that the initiative was a clear manifestation of the moral condemnation of LGBT people and their forms of intimacy presented activists with an opportunity to challenge that condemnation by seeking to replace it with a different moral understanding of gay people. As Amber Hollibaugh, a lesbian community organizer who worked on the anti–Briggs Initiative campaign, explained in a 1979 interview, "one of the most profound things about the Briggs Initiative is that it forced people to have to deal with sexual issues in a society that actively represses non-oppressive forms of sexual searching. This society encourages things like sexual 'liberation' for a minority of the population but by and large does not encourage sexual debate on controversial issues. It doesn't do that around sexuality in general for women and it certainly doesn't do that around same-sex issues. The [anti-Briggs Initiative] campaign transformed that."[54]

As early as September 1977, fourteen months before the vote, three organizations based in Los Angeles (the Lesbian Feminists, Latinos Unidos, and the Coalition for Human Rights) organized a conference, attended by almost 150 activists from throughout the state, to plan a coordinated effort to defeat the initiative. The activists at that meeting agreed that the anti-Briggs Initiative campaign should prioritize encouraging gay people who were not politically active to come out of the closet and to speak against the measure.[55]

A month later, LGBT grassroots activists formed the Committee Against the Briggs Initiative, an umbrella organization with several chapters across the state, the biggest of which were in San Francisco and Los Angeles. The chapters organized demonstrations and rallies; sponsored debates; held fundraisers; and distributed "No on 6" fliers, bumper stickers, and buttons. The San Francisco chapter in particular reached out to differently focused organizations seeking, and in many cases receiving, the support of racial minority groups, women's groups, labor unions, and even the Young Republicans.[56]

Another anti-Briggs Initiative organization, the California Outreach Group, engaged in grassroots work in California's vast rural areas. Hollibaugh, who was a full-time organizer with the group, gave dozens of speeches in small towns all over the state urging listeners to reject the homophobic stereotypes and assumptions behind the initiative.[57] To also help reach voters throughout California, San Francisco Supervisor Harvey Milk followed Briggs around the state speaking against the initiative and responding to his wild accusations about the supposed threat that gay teachers represented to children. During those speeches, and during a televised debate with Briggs a few days before the election, the highly articulate Milk spoke passionately about the humanity of gay people—who loved, feared, and hurt like everyone else—and the need to protect the basic civil rights of sexual minorities, perspectives that most Americans had never heard before.

A key aspect of the political campaign against the Briggs Initiative was the encouraging of lesbians, gay men, and bisexuals to come out of the closet. Milk made the political implications of coming out a central theme of his speech at the 1978 Gay Freedom Day Parade in San Francisco. The parade, attended by an estimated 350,000 people—more than participated in the 1963 civil rights March on Washington—was the site of much anti-Proposition 6 activism. During the speech, Milk exhorted his

> gay brothers and sisters . . . [to] come out. Come out . . . to your parents.
> . . . I know that it is hard and will hurt them, but think about how they
> will hurt you in the voting booth! Come out to your relatives. . . . Come
> out to your friends . . . if they indeed . . . are your friends. Come out to your
> neighbors. . . . To your fellow workers. . . . To the people who work where
> you eat and shop. . . . Once and for all, break down the myths, destroy
> the lies and distortions. For your sake. For their sake. For the sake of the
> youngsters who are becoming scared by the votes from Dade to Eugene.[58]

Milk added, "we can defeat the Briggs Initiative if all the gay people come out," but "if they don't come out, then it will be a very tight race."[59]

One of the individuals who heeded the call to come out of the closet was Larry Berner, a thirty-eight-year-old second-grade public school teacher in the small Northern California town of Healdsburg (population 6,200). Berner placed his job at risk in order to campaign against the initiative. After a local newspaper identified Berner as a gay educator who opposed the initiative, Briggs began using him as an example of the kind of teacher who did not belong in the classroom. In addition, the president of the local school board asked that he be fired. As she starkly put it, "we want to protect our children from the rape of their minds before they're raped physically" by gay teachers.[60] She then added, "we don't allow necrophiliacs to be morticians. We've got to be crazy to allow homosexuals who have an affinity for young boys to teach our children. We're not here to say that homosexuals can't teach. We're saying that public homosexuality shouldn't be tolerated."[61]

For his part, Berner pointed out that his sexual orientation had been unknown in the community where he worked until he started doing political work against Proposition 6. As he explained, "my gayness was disclosed during political activity. I feel they're attacking my right to free speech."[62] Although parents removed fifteen children from his classroom, most of the school's parents, teachers, and students sided with Berner; hundreds of them showed up to support him at a school board hearing and at an event, held in Healdsburg two weeks before the vote, in which Berner debated Briggs himself.[63] Although the school board wanted to fire Berner, it decided it could not do so unless voters in the state first approved the initiative.[64] The board's position strikingly highlighted the importance of the upcoming vote for gay teachers and LGBT people across the state.

Berner was not the only teacher who campaigned against the initiative. Two San Francisco LGBT teachers organizations, the Gay Teachers and School Workers and the Lesbian School Workers, as well as the Gay Teachers of Los Angeles, held many fundraising events and successfully worked to persuade the teachers unions to oppose the initiative.[65] The LGBT teachers groups also engaged in educational campaigns to counteract the malicious stereotypes of gay and lesbian teachers promoted by the initiative's leading supporters. In doing so, the organizations sought to provide "living testimonies" of real lesbian and gay teachers as a way of persuading parents that they did not constitute a threat to their children. As one of the groups put it, "in the past others, both straight and gay gave presumed to speak for us; [now] we will speak for ourselves."[66]

For almost a year after Briggs first announced his intention to push for a law that would oust lesbian, gay, and bisexual public school teachers from their jobs, polls showed a majority of Californians supporting the initiative. A poll taken as late as August 1978, found that 61 percent of respondents intended to vote yes.[67] But by September, the year-long campaign by grassroots activists throughout the state started to have an impact as polls for the first time showed opponents in the lead. In the end, voters soundly defeated the initiative by a margin of 58 percent to 42 percent, with the No side winning by more than a million votes.

The Briggs Initiative was an explicit effort to silence sexual minorities and to keep them deep in the closet. Ironically, however, the initiative had the opposite effect: it showed to thousands of LGBT people across the state and the country, beyond the relatively small number of activists who were already working on LGBT issues, the importance of speaking up and the corresponding dangers of remaining silent. There was, of course, a price to pay for speaking up; sexual minorities who identified themselves were vulnerable to stigma, harassment, and discrimination. But the push by Briggs and his social conservative allies to fire gay teachers also showed LGBT people that there were risks and harms associated with remaining silent. Faced with this difficult choice, a growing number of LGBT individuals began exercising their free speech rights, first, by coming out of the closet, and second, by demanding equal rights.

Given that the Briggs Initiative targeted not just same-sex sexual conduct, but also gay rights advocacy, it represented a clear threat to the free speech rights of sexual minorities and their supporters. At the same time, it was the repeated and effective exercise of those rights, through speaking, debating, organizing, canvassing, and educating, that led to the initiative's defeat. In the case of the Briggs Initiative, First Amendment rights were protected through the exercise of those rights, rendering a judicial challenge in the courts unnecessary.

The Prom Case: Protecting LGBT Expressive Conduct

In the spring of 1980, Aaron Fricke, a senior at Cumberland High School in Rhode Island, decided to invite a male date to the prom. Aaron was gay, but it was not until he asked the school principal for permission to attend the prom with a male date that he came out of the closet at school. The principal denied Fricke's request because he was concerned that the prom might be disrupted by the presence of a same-sex couple and that some of the other students might physically assault Fricke and his date. The year before, another male student at Cumberland High School had been denied permission to take a male date to the prom, a fact that received considerable attention in the school and in the community, leading some students to taunt and, on one occasion, even to spit on the gay student.[68]

Fricke sued the school district in federal court, arguing that the principal's decision not to allow him to bring another young man to the prom violated his rights to free speech and equality. The lawsuit was the subject of stories in Rhode Island and Boston newspapers. A few days after the media stories appeared, a fellow student punched Fricke in the face, an attack that required five stitches under his right eye. After the violent incident, school officials provided Fricke with a protective escort as he moved from one class to the next.[69]

Fricke viewed his attending the prom with a male date as an opportunity to reject stereotypes about gay people, question society's disapproval of same-sex relationships, and assert a moral claim about his dignity as a human being. In many ways, Fricke's effort to attend the prom as an openly gay person aimed to replace society's moral rejection of LGBT people with a moral perspective that demanded equal treatment of and respect for sexual minorities. Fricke explained his objectives as follows:

I believed that those who had themselves faced discrimination or prejudice would immediately understand what I was doing and its implications for human rights. There would be others who may never have had direct experiences with prejudice but who would recognize my right to the date of my choice. These people may have been misled to believe that homosexuality is wrong, but they could still understand that my rights were being denied.

At the opposite end of the spectrum were the homophobics who might react violently. But the example I set would be perfect for everyone. We would be just one more happy couple. Our happiness together would be something kids could relate to. I would be showing that my dignity and value as a human being was not affected by my sexual preference.

I concluded that taking a guy to the prom would be a strong positive statement about the existence of gay people. Any opposition to my case (and I anticipated a good bit) would show the negative side of society—not of homosexuality.[70]

Fricke's First Amendment lawsuit was different from the others discussed in this chapter because, although it involved the coming out of a gay individual, it did not involve speech as such. Instead, Fricke's case implicated conduct (the attending of a high school prom with someone of the same sex) with considerable expressive meaning.

The Supreme Court in *United States v. O'Brien*, a 1968 ruling involving the criminal prosecution of an anti–Vietnam War protestor for burning his draft card, held that conduct can be protected by the Free Speech Clause if it is expressive in nature. (Although the Court in *O'Brien* concluded that the burning of the draft card was "speech" within the meaning of the First Amendment because of the message it conveyed, the Court upheld the conviction on the ground that the government had valid reasons, related to the administration of the draft, for punishing the defendant's destruction of the card.) The federal district court in *Fricke* concluded that the conduct in question—attending the prom with a date of the same sex—constituted protected speech under the First Amendment because it expressed a political message about the rights of gay people to equal treatment. As the court explained, "Aaron testified that he wants to go because he feels he has a right to attend and participate just like all the other students and that it would be dishonest to his own sexual identity to take a girl to the dance. He went on to acknowledge that he feels his attendance would have a certain political element and would be a statement for equal rights and human rights. . . . I believe Aaron's testimony that he is sincerely although perhaps not irrevocably committed to a homosexual orientation and that attending the dance with another young man would be a political statement."[71]

Although the court acknowledged that the school had legitimate concerns about possible disruptions at the prom because of the presence of a male couple, those concerns could be addressed by bolstering security rather than by prohibiting Fricke from attending the prom with his male date. The court explained that if it allowed security concerns to prevail, it would grant disruptive students a "heckler's veto" that would "completely subvert free speech."[72]

The high school prom lawsuit was a conceptually important case. In Chapter 2, we saw how courts in the 1950s and 1960s, when grappling with the First Amendment rights of sexual minorities, placed great emphasis on the distinction between status and conduct. From those courts' perspective, the protections offered by the First Amendment to sexual minorities were contingent on the absence of *any* conduct suggesting that the individuals in question were lesbian or gay. As we saw in exploring cases involving state efforts to revoke the liquor licenses of lesbian and gay bars, conduct as innocuous as dancing or holding hands with someone of the same sex was enough, in many instances, to deprive sexual minorities of their rights of association.

The 1970s public employment cases, explored earlier in this chapter, in which gay plaintiffs succeeded added an additional layer of protection because the courts in those instances recognized that self-identification as gay (that is, coming out of the closet) went hand-in-hand with publicly advocating in favor of gay rights. This recognition bolstered the view, promoted by the LGBT rights movement, that coming out of the closet was a personal decision with crucial political connotations and implications.

However, the gay employment litigants who successfully raised First Amendment claims came out while *speaking* on gay rights issues and advocating on behalf of greater social acceptance of LGBT people. Fricke, by attending the prom with someone of the same sex, was not "speaking" in the traditional meaning of that word. As a result, the court's reasoning in *Fricke* offered yet another potential layer of protection because it linked having a gay identity not with explicit spoken advocacy, but with the political and social consequences of simply being out of the closet in particular public settings. It was the combination of the high school student's (1) self-identification as a gay person and (2) the act of going to the prom with another male that imbued the conduct with political and social meaning and thus rendered it protected "speech" under the First Amendment. If the bar cases were about status to the exclusion of conduct, and the employment cases were about status (or identity) coupled with speech to the exclusion of conduct, *Fricke* was about the link between identity, conduct, and expression. In short, *Fricke* stood for the proposition that in a society which stigmatizes sexual minorities, the "mere" fact of coming out of the closet could be an intrinsically political act.

Although the court's reasoning in *Fricke* offered sexual minorities considerable First Amendment protection in the face of government efforts to keep them silent and inside the closet, it also planted the seeds, unintentionally and paradoxically, for some of the free speech and association claims that LGBT rights *opponents* would later raise. If the mere presence of openly lesbian, gay, and bisexual individuals in certain settings sent a political message in favor of social toleration of sexual minorities that was worthy of constitutional protection, then the First Amendment might also be implicated if the government mandated the inclusion of LGBT individuals over the ideological, moral, or religious objections of those who owned or controlled those settings. The same kind of political message conveyed by Fricke's "mere presence" at the prom with his male date might be sent, for example, by the "mere presence" of openly gay individuals in organizations, such as the Boy Scouts, that did not welcome LGBT people. Government mandates requiring the inclusion of lesbian, gay, and bisexual individuals, it was later argued, violated the free speech and associational rights of individuals and organizations that opposed LGBT rights positions. As we will see in Chapter 6, this type of reasoning constituted the basis for efforts to use the First Amendment to limit the scope of laws aimed at promoting sexual orientation equality. To put it simply, what the First Amendment gave to the LGBT movement with one hand, it might take away (or at least limit) with the other..

Starting in the 1980s, overt government efforts to restrict the rights of speech and association of LGBT individuals and groups became increasingly rare. As a result, the number of LGBT First Amendment cases dropped significantly. The absence of litigation, however, did not mean that the rights to speech and association became unimportant in promoting LGBT rights. In fact, the truth was just the opposite—the exercise of those rights, as I explore in the next chapter, contributed in fundamental ways to the movement's eventual equality and privacy gains.

CHAPTER FOUR

Activism in and out of the Courts

THE PROTECTIONS afforded by the First Amendment played piv-
otal roles in the early days of the LGBT rights movement: they contributed to the explosion of lesbian and gay publications in the 1960s and
1970s; to the large growth of LGBT organizations of every kind, including political, social, artistic, and religious, in the 1970s and 1980s; and to
the growing number of LGBT individuals during those two decades who
engaged in the personal and political act of coming out of the closet.

In these various and diverse contexts, government agencies and officials
had attempted to interfere with efforts by LGBT individuals to express themselves and to associate with each other. On several occasions, the affected
individuals turned to the courts seeking judicial recognition of their free
speech rights. As we have seen, the LGBT plaintiffs generally succeeded in
those efforts. In doing so, they helped to establish the principle that the
government lacked the constitutional authority to prevent the distribution
of gay-themed publications, interfere with the ability of LGBT individuals
to come together to form organizations that promoted the interests of sexual minorities, and penalize individuals for publicly acknowledging their
same-sex sexual orientation. The courts' repeated willingness to enforce
the First Amendment rights of sexual minorities meant that by the 1980s,
government officials rarely took direct steps to interfere with the ability of
LGBT individuals to express themselves and form organizations.

There was, however, one important and troubling exception to this
governmental restraint: the military's policy excluding lesbian, gay, and

bisexual service members, in particular the Don't Ask, Don't Tell version of the policy first implemented in 1993. The DADT policy purported to allow sexual minorities to serve in the armed forces (the "Don't Ask" part), while simultaneously requiring them to remain silent about their sexual orientation (the "Don't Tell" part). As detailed in the first section of the chapter, DADT raised serious First Amendment concerns, both because it greatly limited the ability of sexual minorities in the armed forces to participate in public discourse and because it interfered with their rights to autonomy and self-determination as related to matters of expression. Unfortunately, courts in the military context were unwilling to do what courts, as we saw in Chapter 3, had generally done in the civilian context: strike down state action that interfered with the ability of sexual minorities to be open about their sexuality. Indeed, although DADT had grave free speech implications, the lower courts did not begin to strike down the policy until after the Supreme Court made clear that the Constitution provided equality and privacy protections to sexual minorities. In this way, DADT is an exception to the general trend identified in Part I: In the military context, the recognition of LGBT rights to equality and privacy came before the recognition of free speech rights.

Although the courts forewent their role as guardians of free speech rights in the DADT context, it is important to keep in mind that LGBT rights activism has never been limited to the filing of constitutional lawsuits. Indeed, if we were to focus only on constitutional litigation, we would reach the conclusion that, outside of the military arena, the Free Speech Clause, by the 1980s, began playing a relatively minor role in the pursuit of LGBT rights objectives.[1] This is because, again outside of the military context, government officials, by that time, rarely took direct steps to interfere with the ability of LGBT individuals to express themselves and form organizations. But as explored in the remainder of the chapter, the absence of First Amendment *litigation* did not reflect a diminishment in the importance of the *exercise* of free speech rights. Indeed, the LGBT movement's exercise of those rights contributed in fundamental ways to its eventual attainment of many of its major victories.

After discussing the DADT policy, I focus on three important examples of LGBT advocacy that followed the movement's decreased reliance, outside of the military context, on free speech litigation: on behalf of the elimination of sodomy laws following the Supreme Court's 1986 decision upholding their constitutionality in *Bowers v. Hardwick*; on behalf of people with AIDS in the late 1980s and early 1990s; and on behalf of marriage rights for lesbians, gay men, and bisexuals after the turn of the century. This advocacy history shows that significant equality gains remained unobtainable until LGBT rights proponents were able to begin changing social and moral understandings of sexual minorities through the exercise of free speech rights. Or to put it more simply, free speech came first and equality came second.

It is not possible in one chapter to provide a full account of the many different manifestations and objectives of LGBT activism in the areas of sodomy, AIDS, and same-sex marriage. As a result, my objective here is a more modest one: to highlight some of the ways in which activities protected by the First Amendment—the speaking, associating, mobilizing, and organizing—around sodomy regulations, the AIDS epidemic, and marriage equality contributed in crucial ways to substantive equality gains over the long run.

The Silencing of Don't Ask, Don't Tell

The military enforced various policies excluding sexual minorities for most of the twentieth century. Bill Clinton, when he ran for president in 1992, promised to change that by allowing lesbians, gay men, and bisexuals to serve openly in the military. But after Congress refused to go along, a purported compromise was implemented under the name of "Don't Ask, Don't Tell." At the time, almost everyone involved in the debates over gays in the military acknowledged that sexual minorities had served in the armed forces for generations. But for the policy's proponents, the presence of *openly* lesbian, gay, and bisexual individuals in the services, in the words of the statute enacted by Congress, "create[d] an unacceptable risk to the armed forces' high standards of morale, good order, and discipline, and unit cohesion that are the essence of military capability." As a result, DADT ostensibly allowed sexual minorities to serve in the armed forces as long as they did not (1) engage in "homosexual acts" (broadly defined to include any physical contact, including holding hands and kissing, between two individuals that showed a "propensity" to engage in same-sex sexual conduct); (2) make any statements acknowledging or discussing their same-sexual orientation; and (3) seek to marry someone of the same sex.[2] It was the second of these prohibitions that most clearly implicated free speech considerations.

On the surface, DADT seemed less draconian than the categorical exclusionary policy it replaced because it seemed to allow sexual minorities to serve (as long as they did not engage in the prohibited conduct or speech). However, the reality was that the policy called for a degree of regulation and oversight of sexual minorities that can only be categorized as Orwellian. In practice, the policy's application led to a marked increase in the number of investigations by military officials of service members suspected of being lesbian, gay, or bisexual, resulting in a significant jump in the number of sexual minorities expelled from the military.[3]

Under DADT, military commanders repeatedly conducted investigations of, and instituted discharge proceedings against, lesbian, gay, and bisexual individuals simply on the basis of statements they had made to others. It is important to note that the scope of DADT's prohibition on expression applied well beyond the confines of the service members' official duties. In fact, (1) any statement (2) made at any time and (3) at any place (4) to anyone acknowledging or referencing that the speaker was lesbian, gay, or bisexual constituted grounds for expulsion. This meant that any assertion of having a same-sex sexual orientation (such as "I am a lesbian") was enough for dismissal. It also meant that any expressive statement or conduct that might be perceived as revealing the person's same-sex sexual orientation (such as placing the photograph of a same-sex partner on a work desk) could be used by the government as evidence in separation proceedings. The policy placed the burden on the service member charged with being lesbian, gay, or bisexual to prove that the expression in question did not show "a propensity to engage in . . . homosexual acts."[4] All of this meant that, as law professor Tobias Barrington Wolff explained, "DADT constitutes a total regulation of the speech of all gay men and lesbians connected with the military. The policy prohibits gay soldiers from identifying themselves as gay, talking about their sexual identities, or otherwise speaking honestly about the relationship between their sexuality and their emotional or spiritual lives, to anyone, under any circumstances, ever. Gay soldiers must erase their identities in civilian as well as military settings or else they will violate the terms of the policy."[5]

As noted in the last chapter, theorists have articulated two broad conceptual understandings of the Free Speech Clause. The first, and largely instrumental, approach focuses on promoting robust forms of public discourse necessary for effective self-governance. The second, and largely deontological, approach focuses on protecting human autonomy and self-development from government interference. The DADT policy raised serious issues under both of these understandings of why the Constitution protects free speech.

In terms of public discourse, the DADT policy prevented lesbian, gay, and bisexual service members from honestly participating in conversations regarding matters of public importance that addressed questions of sexuality. In this sense, the DADT policy was similar to the Briggs Initiative, as well as a law enacted by the Oklahoma legislature and struck down by a federal appellate court in 1984, which sought to keep LGBT teachers silent on issues related to sexuality as a condition for keeping their jobs.[6] More specifically, as Wolff notes, DADT prevented sexual minority service members from identifying themselves honestly to officials, both elected representatives and military leaders, responsible for the setting of policies, including those tasked with crafting military personnel policies.[7] It surely distorts public discourse when those who are the subject (or in the case of DADT, the target) of a regulation are prohibited by the same regulation from identifying themselves as such. Under the DADT strictures, policy-makers were prevented from hearing from the very individuals who were most directly affected by the policy in question.

In addition to its impact on the nature and extent of public discourse on matters related to sexuality, the DADT policy's *complete* prohibition on self-identification gravely implicated liberty and autonomy considerations as reflected in constitutional free speech protections. To see why this is the case it is helpful to compare the armed services' sexual orientation policy with another military personnel regulation challenged under the First Amendment only a few years before the adoption of DADT. In *Goldman v. Weinberger*, the Supreme Court upheld a military dress regulation that prevented the Jewish plaintiff, an Air Force captain, from wearing a yarmulke while on duty.[8] (The regulation in question prohibited the wearing of any headgear while on duty and indoors.) Although the regulation impacted the plaintiff's ability to decide how to express his Jewish identity, that impact was limited in two crucial ways. First, the regulation did not affect the plaintiff's ability to wear the yarmulke in civilian life. Second, and more broadly, the regulation did not restrict the many other ways in which the Air Force captain could identify as a Jewish person, such as by telling others, including fellow service members, about his faith and by attending Jewish religious services.

The dress regulation at issue in *Goldman* addressed (1) a particular way of expressing identity (through headgear) that applied (2) to all service members *regardless of their identities*. In sharp contrast, DADT singled out (1) a particular group of individuals, prohibiting only them from identifying according to their sexual orientation (2) in any manner whatsoever. In other words, the DADT policy, by affecting the ability of sexual minorities, and no others, to choose whether, how, and when to self-identify, unlike the dress regulation at issue in *Goldman*, was both targeted in purpose and all-encompassing in effect.

The Supreme Court in *Goldman* concluded that the military's interest in uniformity and discipline, as pursued through the dress regulation, outweighed the Jewish captain's rights of expression under the First Amendment. However, it is highly unlikely that the Court would have upheld the regulation if it had prohibited the plaintiff from expressing his Jewish identity in any way while on duty and, more crucially, in his civilian life. In addition, as law professors David Cole and William Eskridge note, the "dress regulation did not target religious minorities (though it was insensitive to their concerns), and it is unlikely that the Court would have upheld the ban if it selectively barred the wearing of yarmulkes."[9] But that is precisely what DADT did: it selectively prohibited sexual minorities, and no others, from expressing their sexual identity in any manner whatsoever. Further, it is unimaginable, as Wolff notes, that the Supreme Court would have upheld the dress regulation if it had compelled Goldman to pretend he was a Christian. But once again, that is precisely what DADT did: it forced sexual minorities to adopt the default identity of heterosexuality by prohibiting them to speak (or act) in any way that might suggest to others that they were lesbian, gay, or bisexual.[10]

Given all of this, it would have been reasonable to assume that courts would grapple, seriously and extensively, with the question of whether DADT passed constitutional muster under the First Amendment. Instead, the federal appellate courts (the issue never reached the Supreme Court) consistently gave the First Amendment challenges to DADT short shrift. Rather than focusing on the severe effects that the policy had on the ability of sexual minority service members to participate in public debates and in choosing whether, how, and when to self-identify, the courts contended that the policy was nothing more than a means for regulating same-sex sexual conduct. From the courts' perspective, the policy targeted same-sex sexual conduct rather than self-identifying gay speech.

The courts reasoned that the speech in question was relevant under the policy only to the extent it constituted evidence that the individuals who self-identified as lesbian, gay, or bisexual engaged in same-sex sexual conduct. Because the military was ostensibly concerned with conduct and not with speech as such, the courts concluded it was permissible under the First Amendment for officials to use the self-identificatory statements of gay, lesbian, and bisexual service members as the sole basis for dismissal from military service.[11]

It is truly remarkable that the courts, in assessing the constitutionality of DADT, blinded themselves to the ways in which self-identificatory statements by sexual minorities constituted protected speech under the First Amendment. For the courts, the speech in question was nothing more than evidence of conduct. But in actuality, as already noted, the regulated speech was crucially linked to the identity and status of being a sexual minority, as well as to the ability of lesbian, gay, and bisexual service members to participate in public discourses. As one dissenting judge succinctly put it, "DADT severely burdens speech. It unquestionably has the effect of chilling speech by homosexual service members—speech that is of tremendous importance to the individuals involved, speech that goes to their right to communicate the core of their emotions and identity to others."[12]

As explored in Chapter 3, courts in many of the gay civil servant cases from the 1970s, as well as in the Rhode Island prom case, understood the link between sexual minorities' coming out speech and their identity and status. Unlike the courts in the DADT cases, the earlier courts did not allow the government's constitutional authority to regulate same-sex sexual conduct, as it was generally understood before the Court struck down sodomy laws in *Lawrence v. Texas*, to blind them from the effects on expressive rights of policies aimed at keeping sexual minorities silent.

It is difficult to explain precisely why most judges who heard the DADT cases failed to perceive, much less grapple with, the policy's grave free speech implications. It is possible that courts were swayed by the traditional judicial deference to the military, as well as by the Supreme Court's failure to recognize the constitutional rights of LGBT people in *Bowers v. Hardwick*. But ultimately, there is no satisfying explanation for the federal courts' failure to engage seriously with the free speech challenges to DADT. After all, the Supreme Court had made it clear that members of the armed forces, despite the judicial deference owed to the military, retained constitutional rights after joining, including those protected by the First Amendment.[13] In addition, there were many ways in which the courts, had they been so inclined, could have distinguished the sodomy regulation at issue in *Bowers* from the speech restrictions at issue in the DADT cases.

Regardless of the precise causes, the failure of the DADT free speech litigation showed the limits of the protections afforded by the First Amendment to LGBT people. It was not until the Court overruled *Bowers* in *Lawrence*, that courts began to meaningfully question the constitutionality of DADT. And they did so primarily not on free speech grounds, but on those of substantive due process.[14] Shortly thereafter, Congress repealed the DADT statute.

Fortunately, despite the invidiousness of the DADT policy, it represented, by the time it was adopted, a largely anomalous effort to explicitly use state authority to prevent sexual minorities from speaking, associating, mobilizing, and organizing. But even after efforts by state actors to silence sexual minorities by interfering with their rights to free speech and association largely came to an end outside of the military context, there remained in place a myriad of government policies that sought to keep LGBT people in the closet. Those laws included sodomy statutes that rendered all sexually active lesbians, gay men, and bisexuals criminals, and marriage bans that denied LGBT individuals the hundreds of rights and benefits that the state allocates through the institution of marriage. The fact that these laws generally did not entail direct government efforts to silence LGBT people meant that they were not easily amenable to free speech challenges.[15]

However, the general inapplicability of the First Amendment to many of the antigay laws that remained on the books did not mean that considerations of free speech—in particular, the *exercise* of free speech rights through speaking, associating, mobilizing, and organizing—ceased to be important for the LGBT movement. In the remainder of the chapter, I explore some representative examples of sodomy, AIDS, and marriage equality activism to illustrate the ways in which the waning of pro-LGBT rights First Amendment litigation did not reflect a diminishment in the importance of free speech rights for the LGBT movement.

Sodomy Repeal Activism

In analyzing the impact of social movements, the sociologist Mary Bernstein distinguishes between their political, mobilization, and cultural effects. Political impact can be measured by changes in laws and policies. In contrast, mobilization outcomes relate to organizational successes that permit social movements to continue to engage in collective action into the future. For their part, cultural outcomes "are changes in social norms and behaviors, which alter public understandings of an issue and create a collective consciousness among activists."[16]

As Bernstein points out, the three categories of movement outcomes do not always align with each other. It is possible, for example, for a social movement to gain political successes without enjoying mobilization benefits or promoting cultural changes. It is also possible for a movement to make organizational and cultural changes without gaining positive policy outcomes, at least in the short term.

Bernstein uses the example of advocacy aimed at repealing sodomy laws to illustrate the different types of social movement outcomes and how they do not always correspond with each other. In doing so, Bernstein focuses on two different periods: between 1961 and 1977, during which seventeen state legislatures repealed their sodomy laws; and between 1986 and 1991, during which no legislature did so. LGBT activists, in the first period, did not generally engage the state on questions of sodomy regulation. One explanation for this lack of advocacy was a practical one: the LGBT movement during this era lacked the resources to push for reforms at the national or state level. Instead, the movement was able to effect political change only at the local level, which explains why its first legislative successes came in the form of local ordinances prohibiting discrimination on the basis of sexual orientation and why much of the early political activism focused on stopping harassment and entrapment by local police departments.

The lack of antisodomy advocacy during the first period also had an ideological explanation: many LGBT activists at the time were gay liberationists or lesbian feminists who opposed engaging the state through the seeking of gradual political reforms; instead, many of the early advocates wanted wholesale (that is, more radical) changes to how society dealt with sexuality and gender hierarchies that went far beyond the repeal of sodomy laws.[17]

As Bernstein points out, the fact that seventeen legislatures repealed their sodomy statutes between 1961 and 1977 was not the result of LGBT movement activism; instead, it was the result of what she calls elite engagement on the sodomy issue, that is, the way in which academics and lawyers, most prominently those involved in the drafting of the Model Penal Code, criticized the criminalization of consensual sexual conduct on privacy grounds.[18] Although many state legislatures embraced the Model Penal Code, often through its in toto incorporation into their respective criminal laws, and in the process repealed sodomy proscriptions, those political successes did not translate into mobilization gains because they did not promote or strengthen the ability of the movement to engage in ongoing activism. The legislative repeals also did not lead to positive cultural outcomes for the movement. As Bernstein explains, "even where the sodomy laws were removed, the cultural consensus that condemned homosexuality had to shift to solidify change. Because repeal rested on notions of victimless crimes and a right to privacy, which were not incompatible with views of homosexuality as immoral, decriminalization alone did not halt repressive police practices. Repeal of the sodomy laws removed one key state justification for permitting discrimination and harassment of lesbians and gay men, but a shift in cultural understanding was still needed to make the repeal meaningful."[19]

In order to understand the role that the exercise of free speech rights has played in creating the necessary conditions for making principles of equality applicable in the context of sexual orientation, it is important to pay particular attention to the ways in which that exercise has worked to change social and moral understandings of the lives and relationships of sexual minorities. Two questions in particular are relevant in this regard: First, did the exercise of First Amendment rights succeed in reducing the stigma associated with being a sexual minority? Second, did the exercise effectively respond to the contention that same-sex sexual relationships and conduct were immoral? If the answer to one or both of those questions in any particular LGBT advocacy context was yes, then it is likely that the exercise of First Amendment rights meaningfully promoted gay equality in political and legal spheres by helping to persuade decision-makers and the broader public that how society treated and regulated sexual minorities was constrained by equality principles.

Before proceeding, it is necessary to pause for a moment to note that I am here using the phrase "exercise of First Amendment rights" as a catchall phrase for particular acts, such as speaking, associating, mobilizing, and organizing. It is in part because I recognize that the phrase "exercise of First Amendment rights" is somewhat ambiguous that I try in the remainder of this chapter to provide specific examples of how LGBT rights supporters engaged in that exercise on particular issues.

Although there was not much speaking, associating, mobilizing, or organizing by LGBT activists around the issue of sodomy in the 1970s and into the 1980s, that changed in 1986, almost overnight, following the Supreme Court's ruling in *Bowers v. Hardwick* that the Constitution did not protect the ability of lesbians, gay men, and bisexuals to engage in consensual sexual intimacy in private. Importantly, the exercise of free speech rights on sodomy issues that took place after *Bowers* did not focus exclusively on relatively abstract considerations relating to privacy rights and the lack of harm associated with victimless crimes, which were the main arguments supporting the Model Penal Code's call for eliminating consensual sodomy laws. Instead, the LGBT rights activism on sodomy regulations following *Bowers* also aimed to address the moral objections to same-sex sexuality and conduct and to *replace* those objections with a different moral understanding that emphasized the full humanity of LGBT people.

Sixteen days after the Court decided *Bowers*, LGBT rights activists met in New York City to start planning a march on Washington, D.C. A few weeks later, march organizers mailed a call-to-action letter to LGBT organizations around the country containing the following theme: "For Love and For Life, We're not Going Back." The march, which took place the following year and brought more than two hundred thousand openly LGBT people and their heterosexual allies to the nation's capital, was organized around two main themes: to demand that the government respond to the AIDS crisis with the necessary resources and to protest against the Supreme Court's failure in *Bowers* to recognize the constitutional rights of gay people.[20] Movement leaders, by bringing together the biggest congregation of LGBT people in the country's history, showed the nation that large numbers of sexual minorities were willing to hit the streets and, in the process, identify themselves publicly in order to demand equal treatment.

Also after *Bowers*, the National Gay and Lesbian Task Force (NGTLF) made the strategic decision to emphasize matters related to gay sexuality, rather than hide behind abstract concepts such as "privacy" and "human rights," as part of its efforts to end sodomy laws. The NGTLF did this by, among other things, pointing out that those laws contributed to the spread of HIV because they deterred testing among gay men; distributing literature that rejected society's moral condemnation of same-sex sexual conduct and relationships (one flyer stated: "Anti-sodomy laws define love and sexual intimacy as criminal, unnatural, perverse, and repulsive. That's the real crime"); and distributing T-shirts at the 1987 march that read "So Do My Friends, So Do My Neighbors" to emphasize the hypocrisy of condemning lesbians, gay men, and bisexuals for engaging in sodomy despite the large number of heterosexual Americans who also engaged in oral and anal sex.[21] In addition, the NGLTF organized a series of annual rallies, lobbying days, and demonstrations throughout the country to bring public attention to the injustice that inhered in the criminalization of gay people's sexual conduct.

As Bernstein explains, "strategies varied according to locale, but in most places, post-*Bowers* sodomy law reform efforts showed a markedly more open approach to discussing and defending same-sex sexuality."[22] In addition, the activism around sodomy laws following *Bowers* led to the mobilization of lesbians and gay men in states and localities where there had been little political activism earlier.[23] That mobilization created organizational structures that soon began working on issues that went beyond sodomy, including AIDS and, a few years later, marriage rights.

Although the post-*Bowers* sodomy activism did not lead to widespread repeals of sodomy laws (only two states, Nevada and Rhode Island, did so between 1986 and 2000), it showed that LGBT people were willing and able to respond directly to the accusations leveled against them regarding the supposed immorality of their sexual conduct and relationships. The activism might not have created enough political pressure to lead to widespread sodomy law reforms. But the activism showed LGBT people defining themselves and their lives in their own terms by refusing to leave unanswered accusations of sexual depravity and immorality leveled against them. In that process, LGBT activists repeatedly emphasized a different moral understanding of sexual orientation, one that called on society both to tolerate sexual minorities and to disapprove of discrimination aimed at them.

Because government officials by this time were generally not seeking to limit the rights of LGBT people to speak, associate, and organize, and as a result, those First Amendment rights were no longer subject to political contestation and legal controversies, it is easy to miss their continued importance to the movement. That importance was linked to their very existence at a time when LGBT people, as sexual minorities, *had few other legally recognized rights*. The Supreme Court in *Bowers* had rejected out of

hand the idea that LGBT people were entitled to even the most basic constitutional privacy protections. Furthermore, at the time of *Bowers*, it was
legal in forty-nine states (the exception was Wisconsin) to discriminate
on the basis of sexual orientation.

In addition, courts were generally unwilling to recognize sexual
minorities as a protected class under the Equal Protection Clause, a desig-
nation that would have required heightened judicial scrutiny of laws that
classified individuals on the basis of sexual orientation. There were two
principal reasons for this refusal. First, courts reasoned that if the state
could criminalize the conduct (namely, sodomy) that ostensibly defined
the class, it would be incongruous to provide the class with heightened
protection under the Equal Protection Clause.[24] Second, courts generally
concluded that sexual orientation, unlike race and gender, was a mutable
trait that was under the control of individuals and, therefore, regulations
that classified on the basis of sexuality were not worthy of heightened
judicial scrutiny.[25]

Although LGBT people had few legally recognized rights to privacy or
equality, by the 1980s, they did have clearly established First Amendment
rights as a result of the judicial victories explored earlier in this book. The
post-*Bowers* antisodomy activism showed how the movement—through
rallies, demonstrations, canvassing, organizing, leafleting, and lobbying—
was able to exercise First Amendment rights in ways that were starting
to change how growing segments of society viewed their lives and relationships. It was that activism that eventually made it clear to increasing
numbers of policy-makers, judges, and citizens that protections afforded
by privacy and equality principles applied to LGBT people too.

After years of activism aimed at replacing the traditional and negative
social and moral understandings of LGBT people with new and positive
ones—activism involving not only ridding society of sodomy laws, but
also fighting against discrimination aimed at people with AIDS and pushing for equal marriage rights—the Supreme Court struck down sodomy
laws in *Lawrence v. Texas*.[26] The Court, clearly influenced by years of LGBT
activism inside and outside of the courts, recognized that sexual minorities, like heterosexuals, had dignity-based interests in exercising their
autonomy while choosing sexual partners that protected them from governmental coercion. The *Bowers* Court, reflecting widespread social and
moral understandings of gay people that viewed them as little more than
sexual deviants defined primarily by their physical urges, had rejected the

notion that gay people were similarly situated to heterosexuals in matters related to sexual intimacy. In contrast, the *Lawrence* Court recognized the full humanity of LGBT people, one that included the need for sexual and intimate relationships. These were precisely the types of arguments that many LGBT rights advocates had been making for years not only in seeking to repeal sodomy laws, but also in political activism engendered by the AIDS epidemic and, shortly thereafter, by marriage inequality.

AIDS Activism

By the time the Supreme Court ruled in *Bowers*, the AIDS epidemic was devastating LGBT communities throughout the country. In the years leading up to the AIDS crisis, it had been possible for some lesbians and gay men, in particular those living and working in predominantly LGBT neighborhoods in large cities, to lead relatively open lives without risking rampant discrimination. But AIDS laid bare the vulnerability to discrimination and stigmatization of even relatively privileged and well-to-do members of the LGBT community. The spread of HIV also brought out some of the worst prejudice in those who thought that individuals who engaged in same-sex sexual conduct were perverse and morally depraved. To make matters worse, the early years of the AIDS epidemic coincided with the modern emergence of the Christian evangelical political movement, whose leaders frequently claimed that HIV was God's punishment for those who engaged in immoral sexual conduct. As the Reverend Jerry Falwell, the head of the Moral Majority, starkly put it in 1983 when speaking about the AIDS epidemic, "when you violate moral, health, and hygiene laws, you reap the whirlwind. You cannot shake your fist in God's face and get away with it."[27] For his part, Senator Jesse Helms of North Carolina declared that "Americans who don't want to risk being killed by AIDS have a clear choice and a safe bet available: reject sodomy and practice morality."[28]

At the beginning of the AIDS crisis, there were almost no laws that protected LGBT people from discrimination. Although the federal Rehabilitation Act of 1973 prohibited disability discrimination by the federal government acting as an employer and by programs that received federal funds, it was not clear whether those protections—and those offered by state disability antidiscrimination laws—applied to a communicable disease such as AIDS.[29] Furthermore, the typical response by officials at all levels of government for many years after the appearance of HIV was one of general indifference at the devastation that the virus was wreaking in the lives of marginalized individuals—including gay men, intravenous drug users, and racial minorities—an indifference most prominently and harmfully manifested in an unwillingness to commit the necessary financial resources to study and treat the disease. The courts did not help matters by upholding the closing of gay establishments and allowing hospitals to fire gay health-care employees suspected of being HIV positive, rulings that institutionalized discrimination without advancing public health objectives.[30]

The one source of legal protection that early AIDS activists, the majority of whom were LGBT, enjoyed was the First Amendment and its guarantee of the rights to speak, mobilize, and organize on behalf of individuals living with AIDS. Although the AIDS epidemic had rendered sexual minorities, especially gay and bisexual men, even more vulnerable than they had been before to losing jobs, housing, and health insurance, they were nonetheless generally free to speak on issues of sex and sexuality, while advocating for greater governmental involvement in protecting the health and rights of people with HIV.

Given that many political and religious leaders placed much of the blame for the health crisis on the sexual activities of gay men, AIDS activists had no alternative but to respond by explaining and defending the nature of gay sexuality. It was not possible to advocate for the interests of people living with AIDS without having frank discussions about the sexual lives of gay men and about how best to reach and educate them regarding the need to take voluntary steps to prevent the transmission of the virus. Activists therefore agitated for the development and implementation of AIDS programs that explicitly accounted for the existence, and the unique needs of, the gay male population. For that reason, AIDS activists angrily denounced a successful effort by Senator Helms to attach an amendment to a 1988 appropriations bill prohibiting the Centers for Disease Control and Prevention from funding AIDS programs "that promote or encourage, directly, homosexual activities."[31] At the same time, AIDS activists worked to disabuse policy-makers and the general public of the view that AIDS was somehow a "gay disease" by repeatedly pointing out that it affected individuals regardless of sexual orientation or identity, a position supported by the fact that most people who eventually developed the disease around the world engaged in opposite-sex sexual conduct.

When government and private institutions failed to provide adequate care to people living with AIDS, the LGBT community rose to the occasion by creating and staffing social services organizations whose mission was to reduce, as much as possible, the suffering, isolation, and fear that came with the disease. The organizations, such as the Gay Men's Health Crisis (New York City), the Whitman-Walker Clinic (Washington, D.C.), AIDS Action Center (Boston), and the AIDS Project (Los Angeles), focused on providing medical, housing, and legal services to affected communities and on educating the public about the disease and its means of transmission.

However, it was clear from the early days of the epidemic that protecting and providing for people with AIDS was not something that the LGBT community could do on its own. It was therefore necessary to engage politically in order to get the attention of the broader society. At first, the AIDS activism was relatively muted. In 1983, for example, activists organized candlelight vigils in several cities, including New York, San Francisco, Houston, and Chicago. The participants in the New York march walked from Greenwich Village to the federal building in lower Manhattan with the objective of mourning the dead, raising public awareness, and demanding more federal funds for the medical treatment of people living with HIV.[32]

But the spread of the disease continued at a frightening pace. By the end of 1985, there had been more than twelve thousand AIDS-related deaths in the United States, and the disease had become the leading cause of death among twenty-five to forty-four year olds in the country. The following year, about the same number of people died of AIDS as had died in the previous five years combined, laying bare the exponential growth of the disease. As the devastating death toll continued to climb, there were increasing calls from growing segments of the AIDS and LGBT communities for the activism to move beyond vigils and become more confrontational.

The Supreme Court's decision in *Bowers* was a further impetus for action. The Court's dismissive rejection of the notion that gay people had a constitutional right to sexual privacy had a galvanizing effect on lesbian and gay communities. For many LGBT people, *Bowers* came both as a moral shock and a clarion call for action. As the sociologist Deborah Gould explains, "it was deeply shocking that the state would declare [that gay people lacked rights to sexual privacy] precisely when lesbians and gay communities were suffering such immense devastation and death and were desperately requesting state assistance that, it was assumed, would have been forthcoming for other citizen groups."[33]

Several hours after the Court issued its *Bowers* ruling, two thousand people participated in a demonstration in San Francisco in which speakers lashed out at the Court and at the government's inertia in confronting AIDS. The day after, in the largest gay rights demonstration in New York City since the early 1970s, several thousand lesbians and gay men marched in Greenwich Village, at one point sitting down on the street and bringing vehicular traffic to a halt. A few days later, on July 4th, about ten thousand lesbian and gay protestors, angrily chanting "Civil rights or Civil war!," marched in lower Manhattan near where government dignitaries, including President Ronald Reagan and several Supreme Court justices, had gathered to mark the one hundredth anniversary of the Statute of Liberty.[34]

In the months following *Bowers*, direct-action AIDS organizations sprang up across the country. A group of lesbians and gay men in San Francisco formed Citizens for Medical Justice, which staged a sit-in at the offices of Governor George Deukmejian to protest his veto of a bill that would have prohibited discrimination on the basis of HIV status and his failure to take action on several AIDS bills that would have helped people living with AIDS.[35] In early 1987, activists in New York formed ACT UP (the AIDS Coalition to Unleash Power); within a matter of weeks, several ACT UP chapters sprang up in cities across the country. The group's first demonstration, involving about six hundred protestors, was held on Wall Street to denounce the slow development of AIDS medications. The police arrested nineteen people after they laid down on the street blocking traffic.[36]

The 1987 gay rights march on Washington, which drew more than two hundred thousand participants, was led by people with AIDS, many of them in wheelchairs. That weekend, four thousand protestors participated in a civil-disobedience action in the plaza in front of the Supreme Court (where demonstrations, ironically enough, are not allowed).[37] The police arrested more than six hundred individuals, making it the largest civil disobedience action in the United States since the Vietnam War.[38] During the 1987 march, the AIDS Quilt, a massive quilt (by then already the size of two football fields) containing almost two thousand smaller quilts, each recognizing the life of a person who had died of the disease, was displayed for the first time.[39]

The following year, hundreds of loud and angry ACT UP demonstrators from across the country converged on the headquarters of the Food and Drug Administration (FDA) in suburban Washington demanding that the agency speed up its cumbersome process for approving AIDS medications. The protestors' banners and placards contained slogans such as "AIDS Doesn't Discriminate. The Government Does" and "The Government has Blood on its Hands. One AIDS Death Every Half an Hour." Some protestors laid down on the street and held cardboard tombstones accusing the FDA of responsibility for AIDS deaths. The ten-hour protest received nationwide media coverage and led to the arrest of 176 activists for loitering. Government officials had no choice but to pay attention to the large demonstration. Indeed, law professor Lewis Grossman has argued that the protest "sparked a profound transformation in the government's approach to regulating treatments for serious illnesses."[40]

It is important to keep in mind that at this time members of LGBT communities in general, and people living with HIV in particular, enjoyed almost no legal protections, whether constitutional or statutory, against discrimination. In addition, the Supreme Court had held that the constitutional right to privacy that applied to the marriages and relationships of heterosexuals was not relevant to those who engaged in "homosexual sodomy." The one weapon that ACT UP and other direct-action groups *did* have was to speak out and engage in demonstrations and protests with the objective of bringing attention to the AIDS crisis and the human devastation and invidious discrimination that it wrought. During the last years of the 1980s and the first few of the 1990s, AIDS activists, for example, chained themselves to drug company's trucks, demonstrated with cardboard tombstones in front of government buildings, draped Senator Helms's house with a gigantic condom, dressed in drag and lobbed flowers at New York City Cardinal John O'Connor (who opposed the distribution of condoms and other AIDS prevention measures), and held "political funerals" in which protestors marched on the streets of New York and San Francisco while holding up canisters that contained the ashes of their loved ones who had died of AIDS. These were admittedly confrontational forms of protest, never before seen in LGBT political activism, with the possible exception of the zaps organized by gay liberation groups in the early 1970s. But desperate times called for robust forms of protests and demonstrations. Although not all of the activism was shielded by the

First Amendment, much of it was, thus providing a significant source of legal protection for activists to express their anger and frustration. It was also generally understood that when AIDS demonstrators engaged in illegal forms of protests (for example, by trespassing or blocking traffic), they were engaging in the type of civil-disobedience actions that had a long and distinguished pedigree in the American free speech tradition. As a result, authorities quickly released the majority of AIDS activists whom they arrested and later dropped many of the criminal charges filed against them.

The AIDS epidemic awakened LGBT people politically. Gay people were literally fighting for their lives, and early on in the epidemic, the only viable and effective way of doing so was by criticizing, cajoling, and embarrassing government officials and corporate leaders who were in a position to help. Indeed, ACT UP's slogan of "SILENCE = DEATH" brilliantly captured the stakes for LGBT people of remaining quiet in the face of the epidemic. The disease, and the responses of either raging homophobia or benign neglect that it engendered among many Americans, encouraged tens of thousands of lesbians, gay men, and bisexuals to work collectively by organizing, mobilizing, and protesting in order to fight for their lives and those of their friends. As John-Manuel Andriote puts it, "AIDS brought the gay community *as* a community out of the closet."[41]

One of the ironies of the AIDS epidemic is that its devastating impact on LGBT people and communities eventually contributed to the humanization, in the eyes of large segments of the American population, of sexual minorities. Although committed homophobes remained convinced that gay people had no one to blame but themselves for the disease, large numbers of Americans eventually came to sympathize with the human suffering caused by AIDS and to respect the efforts by sexual minorities to care for, and advocate on behalf of, their own. The epidemic also laid bare the dire consequences of the law's general unwillingness to protect LGBT people from discrimination and to recognize same-sex relationships and families.[42]

After several years of concerted activism by members of LGBT communities on behalf of people with AIDS, and after, unfortunately, the deaths of thousands of Americans from the disease, many of them under the age of forty, the activism led to crucial and much-needed changes in government policies. In 1990, Congress enacted the Americans with Disabilities Act, the most important federal civil rights statute since the

1960s. The Act prohibited employers, state and local governments, and places of public accommodation from discriminating against individuals with disabilities, including those who were HIV positive. AIDS organizations formed an important part of the broad coalition of civil rights and disability groups that pushed and lobbied for the new law. Several state and local governments around this time also adopted laws prohibiting discrimination against people with AIDS. In addition, in the early 1990s, especially after Bill Clinton became president, the federal government began investing significantly more funds in AIDS research and treatment. As the government started responding with greater urgency to the now decade-old health crisis, AIDS political activism lost some of its more confrontational characteristics. With government now serving more as an ally than an opponent, a growing number of AIDS advocates began working closely with officials and scientists in funding, organizing, and carrying out large and multifaceted drug studies in search for a cure. This work eventually led to the development of medical treatments that turned AIDS, for those who have access to the medications, from a deadly disease to a treatable, albeit chronic, illness.

As the legal protections for people with HIV were put in place at the federal, state, and local levels, and as the worst manifestations of irrational discrimination against people living with AIDS began to decrease, activists' exercise of First Amendment rights became less important in protecting the needs and interests of people with AIDS. But it was the activists' vigorous exercise of those rights that led the government to respond in ways that eventually made the need for protests, mobilization, and organizing less pressing. As has happened consistently throughout the history of the LGBT movement in the United States, the exercise of free speech came first and equality protections came second.

Marriage Activism

Before three same-sex couples in Hawai'i constitutionally challenged their state's same-sex marriage prohibition in the early 1990s, most Americans had never thought of, much less grappled with, the question of whether same-sex couples should be permitted to marry. No presidential candidate from the major political parties, for example, had ever broached the subject. Similarly, no state legislature had ever addressed the implications for lesbians and gay men of being denied marital rights. It was widely assumed that marriage was, by definition, a union of a man and a woman and any suggestion to the contrary was simply not part of mainstream political, policy, or legal debates.

All of that changed when the Hawai'i lawsuit, to everyone's surprise, led the state supreme court to issue a ruling questioning the constitutionality of denying same-sex couples the opportunity to marry.[43] Seemingly overnight, the question of whether same-sex couples should be permitted to marry became a topic of ongoing, and oftentimes heated, discussions around kitchen tables, on the floors of legislatures, on the Internet, and on the streets.[44]

It had been possible, before marriage equality became a topic of widespread debates and conversations, to promote important parts of the LGBT rights agenda without engaging in discussions about the nature of committed same-sex relationships. It had been possible, for example, to push for employment and housing discrimination protection without discussing, explaining, or elaborating on the intimate relationships of LGBT people.[45] But it was much more difficult to advocate for marriage equality, inside and outside of courtrooms, without bringing attention to the love and commitment that were part of many same-sex intimate relationships and of families headed by lesbians and gay men. In pursuing marriage equality, the LGBT movement for the first time placed the relationships and families of lesbians and gay men front and center and, by doing so, showed that there was much more to LGBT people than just an amalgamation of sexual acts and desires. Through the process of formally demanding admission into the institution of marriage, sexual minorities showed the American public that they were capable of entering and remaining in committed relationships—and for those who had them, of raising children—in ways that did not differ fundamentally from the experiences of heterosexuals.

In the years following the Hawai'i litigation, no advocacy effort on behalf of LGBT rights did more than marriage equality advocacy to challenge social and moral stereotypes of sexual minorities and to replace them with new and positive understandings. Much of that advocacy was centered on acknowledging and celebrating the full humanity of LGBT people, a humanity characterized in part by the need to love and be loved by another person. Marriage equality activists, in multiple, methodical, consistent, and persistent ways, made the point that the institution of marriage, at its core, was about neither gender nor sexual orientation as claimed by the traditional moral order; instead, the institution was primarily about providing structure and support for individuals in life-long relationships built around intimacy and love. In addition, advocates emphasized that same-sex couples were as capable of building and maintaining those relationships as opposite-sex couples, and that there was nothing morally problematic about same-sex intimate relationships. What was morally wrong and unjust was a marital exclusionary policy that assumed lesbians and gay men lacked the ability to enter and remain in the kind of committed and valuable relationships that society recognized as marital.

Although judicial challenges constituted the driving force behind the push for marriage equality—ending with the Supreme Court's 2015 ruling in *Obergefell v. Hodges* striking down as unconstitutional laws prohibiting same-sex couples from marrying—considerable marriage activism took place outside of the courts through the exercise of free speech rights. Some of that activism was addressed directly at legislatures. In early 2000, for example, a few weeks after the Vermont Supreme Court held that the state constitution required the state to provide same-sex couples with the same rights and benefits afforded to different-sex married couples,[46] dozens of lesbians and gay men from throughout the state testified before a joint committee of the Vermont legislature to explain to their elected representatives the discrimination they faced and the need for the law to protect their families. As one lesbian woman explained to the legislators, "I want my children to have the respect they deserve, to have parents that are married and can fully provide for them. . . . I urge you to support the right for same-sex couples to marry in order to ensure that my family is extended the same rights and privileges that opposite sex couples enjoy."[47] Over a two-day period, committee members heard from about a hundred speakers (each of whom spoke for about two minutes) who encouraged them to legally recognize same-sex relationships. (The committee also heard from about an equal number of opponents of such recognition.) As David Moats notes, the lesbians and gay men who spoke at those hearings "had answered the call to stand up at the State House, declaring who they were before the cold stares of those who would condemn them. . . . For some House members unsure of how to vote, fearful of the voters' wrath, unclear whether gay and lesbian Vermonters deserved the rights they were seeking, the moral force of the promarriage speakers at the two public hearings was persuasive."[48]

There were other ways in which marriage equality activists worked outside the courtrooms to achieve their objectives. As early as 1987, a Los Angeles–based LGBT group organized a rally called "The Wedding" during that year's gay rights march in Washington, D.C., under the slogan "Love Makes a Family, Nothing Else, Nothing Less." At that event, held symbolically in front of the IRS building, several hundred same-sex couples participated in a group wedding ceremony to protest the lack of legal rights for same-sex couples.[49] In 1998, two days before Valentine's Day, the Lambda Legal Defense and Education Fund sponsored a Freedom to Marry Day, encouraging supporters in about forty cities across the country to tie ribbons around trees, lampposts, and doors. As Lambda's executive director explained, "every person who 'Ties the Knot,' on February 12 will be starting conversations. When someone asks what the ribbon represents, each of us can explain: it represents support for the Freedom to Marry, equality for lesbians and gay men, and love."[50]

In San Francisco, activists helped mark Freedom to Marry Day by having same-sex couples go to city hall to request marriage licenses. For the next few years, the couples returned around Valentine's Day as a way of bringing attention to marriage inequality. In February 2004, San Francisco Mayor Gavin Newsom ordered city clerks to grant marriage licenses to the same-sex couples, a decision that led to the issuance of licenses to thousands of lesbians and gay men until the state supreme court, about a month later, ordered the city to cease doing so. In addition, for several years into the 2000s, demonstrations on Freedom to Marry Day in several cities included "groups of same-sex couples dressed in wedding gowns and tuxedos strolling down city streets. The Lambda Legal Defense and Education Fund even published a 'Strolling Wedding Party Guide' touting the efficacy of street theater for stimulating discussion of same-sex marriage."[51]

In Vermont in the early 2000s, the state's Freedom to Marry Task Force organized speakers' bureaus to place lesbians and gay men in front of social clubs, church groups, and other organizations in order "to put a human face on the issue of gay rights."[52] A few years later, marriage equality groups in Massachusetts defeated a push by conservative activists to have the state legislature vote in favor of amending the state constitution to prohibit same-sex marriages. The LGBT rights organizations did so by "using tactics that included door-to-door canvassing, electoral campaigning in support of pro-equality candidates, organizing constituent-legislator meetings, lobbying legislators, and rallying outside the State House."[53]

Although marriage equality activists succeeded in derailing efforts to amend the Massachusetts constitution, their opponents, during the first decade of the new century, succeeded in persuading voters in about half the states to adopt constitutional amendments banning same-sex marriages. Many of the states that adopted the amendments, like Alabama and Mississippi, were deeply conservative, and as a result, LGBT rights proponents had little chance of prevailing. But voters in considerably more liberal states, like Oregon and California, also approved the amendments. For the most part, leaders of the "vote no" campaigns made the strategic decision to frame the issue around abstract concepts such as equality and fairness rather than focus on the lives and relationships of gay people and the human impact of the proposed amendments on sexual minorities.[54]

For marriage equality proponents, the most distressing and worrisome of these ballot losses was California's in 2008. The voters' approval of Proposition 8—a constitutional amendment banning same-sex marriages—brought to an end the issuing of marriage licenses to same-sex couples in the nation's largest state that had begun several months earlier after the California Supreme Court struck down the statutory marriage ban because it violated the state constitution.[55] Unlike much of the campaign against Proposition 8 *before* the vote, the LGBT activism *after* its approval centered specifically on the lives and relationships of sexual minorities, and on how marriage inequality impacted them. Following the vote, LGBT activists organized daily demonstrations throughout California calling for equal marriage rights. On November 15, 2008, activists organized coordinated demonstrations in cities across the country, with thousands of participants hitting the streets to demand marital rights. In December, California activists organized a demonstration called "Day without Gay," in which "gay rights supporters stayed home from work, called in 'gay,' and spent their day volunteering for the movement. Determined to win back marriage equality in California, the young activists began canvassing the state door-to-door, telling residents the stories of gay people."[56]

In 2012, marriage equality advocates for the first time won several ballot campaigns. Maine citizens voted to enact a marriage equality statute; voters in Maryland and Washington defeated efforts to overturn legislative enactments of marriage equality; and in Minnesota, voters defeated a ballot initiative that would have amended the state constitution in order to ban same-sex marriages. The marriage equality campaigns in these four states differed from the earlier campaigns. For example, although earlier marriage campaigns in other states had focused on neutral themes of equality and the protection of civil rights for all citizens, Minnesotans United for all Families, the leading organization that worked to defeat the constitutional amendment in Minnesota, focused "the entire campaign— even the phone banks—on personal stories about how the amendment would hurt" LGBT people and their loved ones.[57] In the months leading up to the vote, the group sought to have its volunteers engage in one million conversations across the state to help residents understand the impact the amendment would have on the daily lives of sexual minorities.[58] The group also organized more than one thousand house parties and encouraged marriage equality supporters to have one-on-one conversations with those who planned to vote for the amendment.[59]

LGBT rights activists pursued a similar strategy in Maine. Door-to-door canvassing was an essential component of the campaign by Mainers United for Marriage. Between May 2011 and May 2012, the organization's representatives had more than 72,000 conversations with voters at their homes.[60] As occurred in the other states with marriage initiatives on the ballot in 2012, LGBT rights advocates in Maine "adopted a new approach to canvassing, one that attempted to persuade through open-ended conversations rather than merely identifying supporters and moving on."[61] In addition, Mainers United for Marriage sponsored a rally in Portland held several weeks before the election and attended by hundreds of supporters of the marriage equality law.[62] Whether in large rallies or in one-on-one conversations, advocates emphasized that the issue before voters was not just about equality and tangible benefits, but also about human relationships of commitment and love.

The society-wide debates on the intersection of marriage and equality impacted how legislatures and courts came to understand the institution of marriage in relation to sexual minorities. In striking down the Defense of Marriage Act in *United States v. Windsor*, the Supreme Court emphasized the role that changing social understandings of sexual minorities played in the adoption by states like New York of marriage equality laws: "After a statewide deliberative process that enabled its citizens to discuss and weigh arguments for and against same-sex marriage, New York acted to enlarge the definition of marriage to correct what its citizens and elected representatives perceived to be an injustice that they had not earlier known or understood."[63] The Court added:

> It seems fair to conclude that, until recent years, many citizens had not even considered the possibility that two persons of the same sex might aspire to occupy the same status and dignity as that of a man and woman in lawful marriage. . . . For others, however, came the beginnings of a new perspective, a new insight. Accordingly some States concluded that same-sex marriage ought to be given recognition and validity in the law for those same-sex couples who wish to define themselves by their commitment to each other. The limitation of lawful marriage to heterosexual couples, which for centuries had been deemed both necessary and fundamental, came to be seen in New York and certain other States as an unjust exclusion.[64]

Two years after *Windsor*, the Court in *Obergefell* also came to see the marriage bans as unjust exclusions. In doing so, the Court recognized, in the ruling's very first sentence, the role that identity and its expression plays in determining the scope of constitutionally protected liberty: "The Constitution promises liberty to all within its reach, a liberty that includes certain specific rights that allow persons, within a lawful realm, to define and express their identity."[65] The Court also emphasized how the state for most of the twentieth century condemned same-sex intimacy as immoral, and in the process denied gay people "dignity in their own distinct identity." Under those circumstances, "a truthful declaration by same-sex couples of what was in their hearts had to remain unspoken."[66] In these passages, the Court recognized the constitutional problems that inhered in laws aimed at silencing sexual minorities by forcing them to hide their identities.

Obergefell explicitly acknowledged the crucial role that the leading of open lives by sexual minorities, and the extensive debates over marriage equality, played in both changing social and moral understandings of sexual minorities and in framing the constitutional issues for the judiciary branch. As the Court explained, "in the late 20th century, following substantial cultural and political developments, same-sex couples began to lead more open and public lives and to establish families. This development was followed by a quite extensive discussion of the issue in both governmental and private sectors and by a shift in public attitudes toward greater tolerance. As a result, questions about the rights of gays and lesbians soon reached the courts, where the issue could be discussed in the formal discourse of the law."[67]

The Court's ruling in *Obergefell* recognized the full humanity of LGBT people as it relates to their intimate and committed relationships; as the Court explained, "there is dignity in the bond between two men or two women who seek to marry and in their autonomy to make such profound choices."[68] Several decades of marriage equality activism led the Court to recognize what had been clear to sexual minority communities for a long time: that the same-sex marriage bans demeaned and harmed LGBT people and their loved ones. This was a view that the Court was not in a position to understand, much less accept, in 1972 when it summarily upheld a lower court's rejection of the claim, raised by Michael McConnell and Jack Baker, that the prohibition on same-sex marriages was unconstitutional.[69] But it was a view that the Court embraced in 2015 after four decades of concerted activism on behalf of LGBT equality, much of which took place outside of the courts.

It was the exercise of free speech rights by LGBT rights advocates that, after decades of debates and discussions, led to fundamental changes in the ways in which large segments of society and many public officials and judges morally understood and valued same-sex relationships and families headed by LGBT individuals. These changes, in turn, revealed the extent to which the marriage bans impermissibly interfered with equality and liberty rights protected by the Constitution.

Although the campaign for marriage equality began in earnest in Hawai'i in the early 1990s with a lawsuit and ended, in 2015, with the Supreme Court's ruling in *Obergefell*, much of the activism took place outside of courtrooms as activists exercised their First Amendment rights in the pursuit of LGBT equality. In this sense, marriage equality activism followed in the footsteps of earlier efforts, including those aimed at repealing sodomy laws and at pushing the government and society to respond adequately to the AIDS epidemic, which used advocacy, association, agitation, and mobilization as means for the attainment of equality goals. All of these campaigns show how the exercise of First Amendment rights remained a crucial tool for LGBT activists long after free speech and association litigation became less prevalent, that is, after government officials generally ceased engaging in direct efforts to silence sexual minorities.

PART II

From LGBT Equality to the First Amendment

CHAPTER FIVE

The Race and Gender Precedents

THE FIRST PART of this book explored how the LGBT movement attained and exercised free speech rights in ways that helped persuade growing segments of society that sexual minorities were entitled to equal treatment under the law. The second part of the book focuses on how the adoption of LGBT equality measures has increasingly led opponents of LGBT rights to turn to the First Amendment, and its corresponding values and principles, to try to circumscribe the state's ability to promote LGBT equality.

The gains in legal rights for sexual minorities have not, of course, taken place overnight. It has been a gradual process characterized by slow and methodical change, starting, at its most embryonic stage, with the Supreme Court's refusal to uphold government censorship of gay publications in the late 1950s and early 1960s, and culminating with the Court's ruling in *Obergefell* v. *Hodges* in 2015 recognizing that LGBT people have a constitutional right to marry the individuals of their choice. During that span of more than fifty years, dozens of local governments and about twenty states adopted sexual orientation and gender identity antidiscrimination laws; some state legislatures repealed and several courts voided sodomy laws and marriage bans; several states and the federal government included sexual orientation and gender identity within the scope of hate-crimes laws; and the federal government prohibited its agencies and contractors from discriminating on the basis of sexual orientation and gender identity, while Congress repealed the military's discriminatory Don't Ask, Don't Tell policy.

As the breadth of LGBT equality measures expanded, social and religious conservatives began to sound the alarm about what that expansion meant for those who morally object to same-sex sexual conduct and relationships. In particular, critics argued that LGBT equality measures threatened the rights to speech, association, and the free exercise of religion of moral traditionalists. This meant that as the need for LGBT advocates to challenge government measures under the First Amendment decreased, their political opponents saw an increased need to challenge state action under that amendment, and its corresponding values and principles, with the objective of slowing down or carving out exceptions to laws and policies aimed at promoting the equality rights of sexual minorities. Interestingly, as we will explore in Chapters 6 and 7, the reliance by social and religious conservatives on the First Amendment has become as central to their pursuit of political and legal objectives as it was for the LGBT movement in earlier decades.

It is easy to overlook (or forget), as our society grapples with contemporary controversies pitting LGBT equality against the rights of speech, association, and the free exercise of religion of those who oppose that equality, that our nation through the decades has repeatedly dealt with difficult questions related to how best to balance the equality rights of some against the liberty interests of others. Indeed, the contemporary disputes over the proper scope of the state's authority to promote LGBT equality in the face of liberty-based objections are only the latest iterations of a continuing debate in American law and policy over the reach of antidiscrimination laws.

As we will explore in some detail in Chapter 7, LGBT rights opponents for some time now have been claiming that the expansion of LGBT equality, in particular marriage equality, must be accompanied by broad provisions exempting religious organizations, small businesses, and government employees from legal obligations arising from sexual orientation antidiscrimination laws. Behind this claim is the notion of "same-sex marriage exceptionalism," that is, the contention that the issue of marriage equality presents society with novel and unique questions regarding the intersection of antidiscrimination laws and religious freedom in ways that demand new forms of exemptions from those laws. It is therefore argued that exemptions, for example, should allow businesses owned by religious individuals to refuse to provide goods and services to celebrate same-sex marriages and permit religious government employees to refuse to issue licenses to same-sex couples.

It is true that the particulars of the contemporary debates over the intersection of LGBT equality and liberty claims are relatively new—the tension between equality and liberty in the context of LGBT rights could not arise before there were equality protections for sexual minorities in place. Sexual orientation antidiscrimination laws are of relatively recent vintage, and therefore the conflict between LGBT equality and religious freedom, for example, is also of relatively recent vintage.

But even if the particulars of the debates are relatively new, the broader question of how to enforce antidiscrimination laws while accommodating liberty-based interests, including those related to religious freedom, is an old and recurring one in American history. The purpose of this chapter is to explore some of the most important debates in American history pitting the government's interest in promoting equality through antidiscrimination laws against the liberty interests of those who dissent from that objective. The history shows that there is nothing particularly new or novel about contemporary LGBT disputes over the scope of the government's authority to promote equality in the face of liberty-based objections. Although the particulars of the debates may change, the fundamental, underlying normative questions of how to protect basic liberties while promoting equality have remained constant through the decades. As I will argue in Chapter 7, the current controversies over LGBT rights and religious freedom should be addressed without adding new and expansive accommodations that depart significantly from the ways in which our country has in the past accommodated liberty concerns while seeking to attain antidiscrimination objectives.

Given that our country has grappled with liberty-based limits, including First Amendment ones, to the application of antidiscrimination laws at many different times during our history, there is no need for same-sex marriage exceptionalism. Such weighing of equality versus liberty considerations took place during the adoption of the Civil Rights Act of 1875; during the enactment of the Civil Rights Act of 1964; during the controversy, in the early 1980s, that arose when the federal government denied tax benefits to Bob Jones University and other religious educational institutions because of their racial policies; during the 1980s and 1990s as courts grappled with the application of gender antidiscrimination laws to all-male organizations; and during the last fifty years as courts have developed and implemented the ministerial exception to antidiscrimination laws, which constitutionally protects the ability of religious organizations to choose their ministers free of the application of antidiscrimination regulations. This chapter canvasses these earlier controversies over the enactment and enforcement of race and gender antidiscrimination laws and policies with the purpose of gleaning insights and lessons that can help us better understand and assess similar contemporary disputes over the scope of the government's authority to promote LGBT equality.

This chapter, in showing that there is nothing particularly new or novel about contemporary LGBT disputes over the scope of the government's authority to promote equality in the face of liberty objectives, explores how First Amendment values and principles have limited the state's authority to attain equality objectives. At different points in our nation's history, legislatures and courts have limited the government's ability to attain equality goals in order to protect freedom of speech, association, or religious exercise.[1] These limitations illustrate the dual nature of the First Amendment's relationship to equality. On the one hand, as we saw throughout Part I, the amendment can be of great assistance to marginalized minorities in articulating and pursuing equality claims in ways that can be eventually recognized by legislatures and courts. On the other hand, as this chapter shows, legislatures and courts have sometimes limited the attainment of equality objectives in the name of First Amendment principles and values.

The Civil Rights Act of 1875

Of all the political, economic, social, and legal challenges confronting the nation in the aftermath of the Civil War, none was greater than that of how to fully incorporate former slaves into the American society. The first important legal steps in that process of incorporation were the adoption in 1865 of the Thirteenth Amendment, prohibiting slavery and indentured servitude, and the enactment of the Civil Rights Act of 1866, granting all persons born in the United States the same rights to contract, sue, and inherit, own, and lease property as, in the words of the statute, was "enjoyed by white citizens."

Although the adoption of the Thirteenth Amendment crucially codified slavery's abolishment into the Constitution, it was an insufficient step in two important ways. First, it did not explicitly address the status of former slaves under the law. Second, it did not, on its face, grant the federal government the constitutional authority to enact equality-promoting measures such as the Civil Rights Act of 1866. The Thirteenth Amendment's limitations led to the adoption of the Fourteenth Amendment, a measure that, among other things, made clear that all individuals born in the United States were citizens, prohibited states from denying "any person within [their] jurisdiction the equal protection of the laws," and authorized Congress to enact legislation enforcing its provisions. A few months after the Fourteenth Amendment was ratified in 1868, Congress proposed the Fifteenth Amendment that, when ratified by the states, prohibited the abridgment of the right to vote "on account of race, color, or previous condition of servitude."

The initial impact of these measures was significant, as former slaves were permitted, for the first time, to marry, enter into enforceable contracts, own property, and vote. (The right to vote was then limited to men, and the ability of married women, regardless of race, to enter into contracts and own property was significantly limited by law.) However, it was initially unclear to what extent the new measures addressed discrimination by private entities. In order to address this apparent limitation in the ability of federal law to promote racial equality, Charles Sumner, the former abolitionist and Republican senator from Massachusetts, introduced a bill in 1870 that would prohibit racial discrimination by certain entities, including railroads, inns, and theaters. Congress proceeded to debate different versions of Sumner's bill at different points during the following five years.[2] It finally adopted a public accommodation antidiscrimination law during the lame duck session of the 43rd Congress in 1875, following both Sumner's death and the landslide election victory the previous November by Democratic opponents of racial equality in the House of Representatives. Eight years later, the Supreme Court struck down the Civil Rights Act of 1875 as unconstitutional in the *Civil Rights Cases*.[3] By that time, the forces of racism and reaction were in firm political control of Southern states, successfully dismantling most of the racial equality gains achieved during the early Reconstruction period.

Three aspects of the debates over the Civil Rights Act of 1875 are reflected in contemporary disputes over the state's pursuit of LGBT equality and its impact on dissenters, showing the shared normative and policy themes, once we move beyond the particulars of the debates, between the nineteenth century disputes involving racial equality and contemporary disputes implicating LGBT rights. First, congressional opponents of the nineteenth-century public accommodation law claimed that it impermissibly and unconstitutionally sought to promote "social rights" rather than "civil rights" by interfering with the autonomy and freedom of citizens in their private lives. Although the terminology has changed—we no longer, for example, speak of "social rights" to describe private spheres of action that are (or should be) beyond the government's regulatory reach—the basic disagreement at the core of many contemporary LGBT rights disputes also revolve around the proper scope of governmental authority to promote equality rights and its ability to impose legal obligations on those who object to those rights.

Second, like many contemporary opponents of LGBT rights, congressional foes of the Civil Rights Act of 1875 relied on their religious faith to criticize expansive understandings of the government's authority to promote equality. Third, because Sumner's original bill sought to prohibit incorporated churches from discriminating on the basis of race among their members (a provision eliminated from the final bill approved by Congress), opponents claimed that the measure violated citizens' rights to religious liberty protected by the First Amendment. As we will explore in some detail in Chapter 7, many contemporary opponents of LGBT rights also claim that sexual orientation equality measures threaten the rights of dissenters to freely exercise their religion.

An Early Cry for Associational Freedom: The Civil Rights versus Social Rights Debate

Congressional opponents of the Civil Rights Act of 1875 raised two main, and related, arguments against the statute. The first was that the government's authority to promote equality only extended to requiring places of public accommodation to make their goods and services available to blacks, something that many of these businesses were already doing.[4] According to the bill's critics, as long as railroads, inns, and theaters, for example, offered blacks goods and services that were comparable to the ones they offered whites, there was no need or justification for government intervention.[5] From this perspective, Congress should reject the civil rights bill because it went beyond guaranteeing access to goods and services and instead demanded that blacks and whites *share* in the accommodations provided by private entities. This criticism, of course, reflected the kind of reasoning that would later support the "separate but equal" ideology that served as a normative foundation for Jim Crow segregation.

The notion that considerations of equality were met once business owners granted access regardless of race overlapped with a second main objection to the bill: that it sought to promote social rather than civil equality. Both supporters and opponents of the bill agreed that the federal government had the constitutional authority to protect civil rights but lacked the power to promote social ones.[6] The fundamental disagreement between the two sides was over the proper definition of each category of rights. For many of the bill's opponents, civil rights were limited to those protected by the Civil Rights Act of 1866, namely, rights to have the law enforce contractual obligations and protect property interests. From the opponents' perspective, Sumner's bill addressed issues not of civil rights but of social ones, granting black people the right to associate with white people who objected to such associations.[7] The public accommodation law was problematic, according to critics, because it intruded on matters of associational freedom.

It bears emphasizing that opposition to the Civil Rights Act of 1875 was an early manifestation of opposition to the expansion of equality on personal liberty grounds in general and associational freedom in particular. Although I have not found evidence that the bill's opponents, in raising the "social rights" critique, relied explicitly on the First Amendment, it is clear that their claims were grounded, in part, on the notion of associational freedom (in addition to other considerations such as property rights), which the Supreme Court eventually held is protected by the First Amendment.[8] Opponents of Sumner's bill claimed repeatedly that the government overreaches when it limits the ability of individuals to choose with whom to associate. Echoes of that nineteenth-century claim can be seen in twentieth-century disputes, including in the successful argument made by the Boy Scouts of America before the Supreme Court that the application of a sexual orientation antidiscrimination law to its exclusion of openly gay scoutmasters violated its rights of association.[9]

As for supporters of Sumner's bill, they rejected the idea that the Civil Rights Act of 1866 sufficiently accounted for the civil rights of black Americans or that the proposed statute promoted social equality.[10] For supporters, it was both necessary and appropriate for federal law to undo the vestiges of slavery and mitigate the many powerful manifestations of racism left in its wake by prohibiting places of public accommodation from segregating their customers on the basis of race. These were not issues of social rights, but of civil equality: The entrenched racial prejudice that was part and parcel of Southern society could not be addressed simply by granting black Americans the right to enforce contracts and own property. (It bears noting that while racism was by no means limited to the South, much of the debate over Sumner's bill involved how best to address the consequences of slavery in the South.) True civic equality was possible only if both state actors *and* private businesses were prohibited from making distinctions on the basis of race.[11]

This point was made by Senator Sumner himself when he argued on the senate floor that "equality is where all are alike. A substitute can never take the place of equality." Sumner added that "any rule excluding a man on account of his color is an indignity, an insult and a wrong."[12] In response, Senator Joshua Hill from Georgia complained that Sumner's "definition of rights differs materially from my own. What he terms a right might be the right of any man that pleases to come into my parlor and to be my guest. This is not the right of any colored man upon earth, nor of any white man, unless it is agreeable to me."[13]

Sumner retorted that questions of personal associations were distinct from those of equal rights; the former were matters of private taste, friendships, and social equality that were not the government's business, but the latter were a different matter altogether: "I cannot deny any human being, the humblest, any right of equality. He must be equal before the law or the promises of the Declaration of Independence are not yet fulfilled."[14] Congressman Henry Pratt of Iowa agreed, noting that "the negro does not seek nor does this bill give him any of your peculiar social rights and privileges. You may still select your own society and invite whom you will at your table. . . . [But] if you choose to sit down at a public table at a public inn open to all comers who behave themselves, you must be content to sit beside or opposite to somebody whose skin or language, manners or religion, may shock your sensibilities."[15]

However, opponents insisted that the bill promoted social equality at the price of personal autonomy and freedom by regulating matters that should be left to the preferences and choices of individuals. Representative Aylett Buckner of Missouri claimed that the bill called for such extensive "interference with the rights of private property and the rules and regulations of society that no free people would tolerate such mischievous intermeddling. No parallel or counterpart of such legislation can be found outside of the most despotic governments and of the most absolute tyranny."[16] For his part, Representative Milton Durham of Kentucky claimed that "we have no more right or power to say who shall enter a theater or a hotel and be accommodated therein than to say who shall enter a man's private house or enter into any social amusement to pass away an evening's hour. These are matters purely of local legislation or of private contract."[17]

It bears noting that Sumner's original bill prohibited racial discrimination not only by places of public accommodation like railroads and inns, but also by public schools. If that provision had made it into law (and survived constitutional scrutiny and political backlash), the forces of equality would have struck a blow against racial segregation in education almost a century before *Brown v. Board of Education*. Many senators and congressmen in the 1870s, however, believed that the issue of whether black children had the right to attend schools with white children was one of social rather than civil rights. From this perspective, the question of civil rights was limited to whether black children had the right to attend schools of equal quality as those serving white families. But the additional step of requiring the integration of schools, it was argued, was one of social equality because it involved forcing white children to associate and interact with black children over their parents' objections.[18] In the end, the civil rights bill that became law in 1875 was stripped of the language that would have rendered it applicable to schools.

Debates over the difference between civil rights and social rights also took place outside of Congress. During the Reconstruction era, several Southern courts upheld the validity of antimiscegenation laws when challenged under federal law, partly on the ground that the new federal constitutional amendments and statutes granted African Americans civil but not social rights. As the Georgia Supreme Court explained in rejecting a challenge to the state's prohibition on interracial marriages, "the most absolute and despotic governments do not attempt to regulate social status by fixed laws, or to enforce social equality among races or classes without their consent."[19]

Similarly, the U.S. Supreme Court, in striking down the Civil Rights Act of 1875 eight years after its enactment, explained that Congress lacked the constitutional authority to adopt legislation covering "the whole domain of rights appertaining to life, liberty, and property, defining them and providing for their vindication. That would be to establish a code of municipal law regulative of all private rights between man and man in society."[20] The Court in the *Civil Rights Cases* distinguished the statute before it from the Civil Rights Act of 1866, which had not sought "to adjust what may be called the social rights of men and races in the community; but only to declare and vindicate those fundamental rights which appertain to the essence of citizenship, and the enjoyment or deprivation of which constitutes the essential distinction between freedom and slavery."[21]

Justice John Marshall Harlan, the sole dissenter in the *Civil Rights Cases*, did not question the majority's distinction between the government's proper protection of civil rights and its improper codification of social rights. Instead, Harlan took issue with the Court's categorization of the Civil Rights Act of 1875 as one that promoted social rights: "No government ever has brought, or ever can bring, its people into social intercourse against their wishes. Whether one person will permit or maintain social relations with another is a matter with which government has no concern."[22] What the statute instead endeavored to accomplish, in Harlan's view, was to make sure that black people could access railroads and other businesses in the same way they were entitled, after the enactment of the Fourteenth Amendment, to access public institutions: without the fear of racial discrimination.

Several Southern states, prior to the *Civil Rights Cases*, had enacted laws granting businesses the freedom to choose whom they wanted to serve and how they did so. Congress's enactment of the Civil Rights Act of 1875 presumably rendered those laws invalid. But the Court's striking down of the federal statute emboldened Southern opponents of racial equality to flex their political muscles by enacting laws that *mandated*, rather than simply allowed, the separation of the races. In the early 1880s, Southern legislatures began adopting Jim Crow laws requiring many businesses to segregate their customers on the basis of race.[23]

When the constitutionality of those laws reached the Supreme Court in *Plessy v. Ferguson* in 1896, the justices continued to assess the ability of federal law to prescribe equality based on the distinction between civil and social rights. In upholding the constitutionality of a Louisiana law that criminalized the presence of black people in railroad cars designated as "Whites Only," the Court explained in *Plessy* that although the

Fourteenth Amendment was intended "to enforce the absolute equality of the two races before the law, . . . it could not have been intended to abolish distinctions based upon color, or to enforce social, as distinguished from political, equality, or a commingling of the two races upon terms unsatisfactory to either."[24] For his part, Justice Harlan, writing once again in solitary dissent, rejected the notion that his interpretation of the Fourteenth Amendment, which did not allow for laws that rendered blacks second-class citizens, promoted "social equality."[25] As Harlan explained, "the arbitrary separation of citizens, on the basis of race, while they are on a public highway, is a badge of servitude wholly inconsistent with the civil freedom and the equality before the law established by the constitution. It cannot be justified upon any legal grounds."[26]

After the turn of the twentieth century, the lexical and normative distinctions between civil and social rights lost political and legal resonance, yet there continued to be fierce political and legal disagreements over how to distinguish "public spheres," which were properly subject to government regulation, from "private spheres," which were beyond the government's regulatory reach. These disagreements were in stark view at the beginning of the century, when the Supreme Court began to routinely strike down progressive-era laws aimed at promoting public health and safety on the ground that they impermissibly interfered with the right of individuals to enter into contractual arrangements as they saw fit. The disagreements flared up again in the context of government promotion of racial equality in debates surrounding Congress's enactment of the Civil Rights Act of 1964 (as we will soon see). Similar disagreements over proper spheres of government regulation and corresponding limits on the state's authority to promote equality have been at the center of contemporary debates over how the government should accommodate the views of LGBT rights opponents while actively promoting equality for sexual minorities.

It is clear, in viewing the long arc of these recurring debates in the nation's history, that the ambit of what was deemed by many late-nineteenth-century Americans to constitute the sphere of "social rights" has gradually diminished. Almost no one today contends that the government improperly intrudes in private spheres when it demands that African-American children have the opportunity to attend public schools with white children and that places of public accommodation make goods and services available to everyone regardless of race. In contrast, the question of the state's authority to promote LGBT equality at the expense of the liberty interests—in particular, those associated with rights of speech, association, and religion—of social and religious conservatives is the subject of much ongoing controversy. Does the government go too far, for example, when it requires business owners who have religious objections to same-sex sexual relationships and conduct to hire LGBT individuals or to provide goods and services that facilitate marriages by same-sex couples? This is the contemporary version of the heated debates, framed around the distinction between civil and social rights, that took place almost 150 years ago regarding whether the federal government had the authority to prohibit racial discrimination by places of public accommodation.

The (Supposed) Word of God

The link between the two eras is evident in other ways, including the deployment of religious doctrine to oppose equality. Much of the opposition to the Civil Rights Act of 1875 was grounded in religious doctrine. Indeed, the statements by opponents were full of references to the supposed Word of God. For example, Senator Thomas Norwood of Georgia claimed that "I do not believe that there is a man here who does not feel the superiority of the white over the black race. While we accord to the latter political rights, . . . there is a distinction which has been marked by the Almighty Himself . . . between the two races. If you adopt this [bill], what distinction between them remains?"[27] Senator Francis Blair of Missouri reasoned similarly when he claimed that the proposed "legislation sought to reverse the decrees of the Almighty, to make white people out of black, to take away from people those instincts implanted by the Deity and intended to keep these races apart and prevent their amalgamation and degradation."[28]

Opponents of the civil rights bill frequently coupled references to God's will with the question of interracial marriage. Although the bill did not address the legal status of marriages that crossed racial lines or prohibit states from banning such marriages, its critics repeatedly raised the specter of interracial marriages to try to embarrass the bill's supporters. In doing so, opponents repeatedly claimed that God was on their side. For example, in addressing the question of interracial marriages while explaining his opposition to the civil rights bill, Senator Hill stated, "I am one of those who have believed that when it pleased the Creator of heaven and earth to make different races of men it was His purpose to keep them distinct and separate."[29] For his part, Representative John Atkins of Tennessee, in arguing that the states had the constitutional authority to keep the races apart and that there was nothing the federal government, consistently with the Constitution, could do about it, proclaimed that "God has stamped the fiat of his condemnation upon the issue of [interracial] marriages too unmistakably to be denied—the original progenitors of both races being superior every way to the mixed offspring."[30]

The religious views expressed on the floor of Congress by opponents of the federal civil rights bill were neither surprising nor unusual. After all, in earlier days, supporters of slavery had routinely invoked their understandings of Christian doctrine to justify that bastion of white supremacy. And several years later, Jim Crow supporters routinely relied on similar understandings of Christianity to defend the strict legal and social separation of the races. What is notable about the debate surrounding the Civil Rights Act of 1875 is that it constituted the first time, at least at the federal level, that opponents of an antidiscrimination law relied on their Christian beliefs to support narrow understandings of the government's authority to prohibit discrimination.

Much of the contemporary opposition to the expansion of LGBT equality in general, and marriage equality in particular, has also been grounded in conservative religious tenets that view same-sex relationships and sexual conduct as morally tainted and sinful. To provide just three of many examples of religious-based objections to LGBT rights positions, as Congress in 1996 debated the Defense of Marriage Act (DOMA) and the purported need to "defend" American marriages and families from LGBT people and their relationships, Senator Robert Byrd of West Virginia stood on the Senate floor and, after reading from the Bible, decried the notion that two individuals of the same gender could marry. The Bible made clear, Byrd claimed, that marriage could only be between a man and a woman, and "woe betide that society . . . that fails to honor that heritage and begins to blur that tradition which was laid down by the Creator in the beginning."[31] (It is worth noting that Senator Byrd also read from the Bible on the Senate floor in opposing the Civil Rights Act of 1964, contending that "God's statutes . . . recognize the natural separateness of things.")[32] And while speaking in support of DOMA, Congressman Steve Buyer of Indiana claimed that "we as legislators and leaders for the country are in the midst of a chaos, an attack upon God's principles. God laid down that one man and one woman is a legal union. That is marriage, known for thousands of years. That God-given principle is under attack. . . . There are those in our society that try to shift us away from a society based on religious principles to humanistic principles; that the human being can do whatever they want, as long as it feels good and does not hurt others."[33] For his part, Representative Tom Coburn added that "I come from a district in Oklahoma who [sic] has very profound beliefs that homosexuality is wrong. . . . They base that belief on what they believe God says about homosexuality. . . . [T]hey believe . . . that homosexuality is based on perversion, that it is based on lust."[34]

There are many other examples of the ways in which conservative political and religious leaders have relied on particular religious understandings to oppose the expansion of LGBT rights. In contemporary times in the context of LGBT rights, as in earlier times in the context of racial antidiscrimination laws, many on the right have marshaled out the purported Word of God to argue against government policies that seek to promote equality.[35] By pointing this out, my objective is not to argue that there is a moral equivalence between the religious-based racism of opponents of racial equality in the nineteenth century and more contemporary religious-based objections to LGBT equality. I am simply noting that, historically, in our debates over issues of discrimination and the scope of the government's authority to promote equality, it has been common for many conservatives to rely on their understanding of the Word of God to argue in the public square against the adoption of egalitarian policies. The tension between the pursuit by the government of equality for traditionally subordinated groups and the religious views of equality dissenters that the nation is experiencing in the context of LGBT rights raises issues that our nation has confronted before.

Covering Churches

Although it is now a largely forgotten historical footnote, the initial federal antidiscrimination bill introduced by Senator Sumner in 1870 prohibited incorporated churches from discriminating on the basis of race. Sumner believed that incorporated churches should not be allowed to exclude members on racial grounds for two main reasons. First, the racial discrimination carried out by many white churches was part of a broader system of white supremacy that viewed black people as inferior and that subjected them to deep injuries and stigmatization. As Sumner explained, in typically eloquent fashion, "it is the prejudice of color which pursues its victim in the long pilgrimage from the cradle to the grave, closing the school, barring the hotel, excluding from the public conveyance, insulting at the theater, shutting the gates of science, and playing its fantastic tricks even in the church where he kneels and the grave where his dust mingles with the surrounding dust."[36]

Second, Sumner believed that because the churches covered by his bill had requested and received incorporation privileges from the state, it was appropriate for the government, in return, to impose antidiscrimination obligations on them. As Sumner explained, "show me a legal institution, anything created or regulated by law, and I show you what must be opened to all without distinctions of color."[37] This did not mean, as the Massachusetts Republican made clear, that the government could either tell churches how to worship "or interfere with any religious observance," but it did mean that incorporated churches should not be allowed to exclude individuals on the basis of race.[38] As Sumner explained, "whenever a church organization seeks incorporation it must submit to the great political law of the land. Here is nothing of religion—it is the political law, the law of justice, the law of equal rights."[39] To allow incorporated churches to discriminate freely on the basis of race "because they are the homes of religion, of Christianity . . . [is] a vindication of caste, and caste in one of its most offensive forms."[40]

Not surprisingly, many of Sumner's colleagues, including several who otherwise supported the civil rights bill, objected to the inclusion of churches. That opposition was grounded largely in the notion that imposing nondiscrimination obligations on churches violated the First Amendment's Religion Clauses. For these legislators, the inclusion was inconsistent with antiestablishment principles because it made religious affairs the state's business. It also interfered with the liberty rights of Christians to worship as they pleased. It was the framers' intent, Senator Matthew Carpenter of Wisconsin explained, to "carefully . . . exclude the whole subject of religion from Federal control or interference."[41] Carpenter agreed with Sumner that a church that excluded members on the basis of race acted deplorably. But that was not the issue; instead, the question was "whether a church organized upon this exclusive creed can be overhauled by enactment of Congress, can be compelled to furnish its communion table to persons whom it believes not entitled to admittance thereto. . . . The precise question is whether the Senator [Sumner] and myself, being in Congress, have any constitutional power to enforce our theory upon those who may conscientiously differ with us."[42] For his part, Senator Frederick Frelinghuysen of New Jersey argued that "the two great doctrines of human progress and religious freedom should not be antagonized, and we should hesitate long before passing the first law affecting in any manner perfect freedom in the exercise of religion."[43] Senator Oliver Morton of Indiana added that because Americans had the constitutional right to "say how they will worship, what they will worship, and with whom they will worship," the provision in question was unconstitutional.[44]

In the end, opposition to the inclusion of churches in the bill proved too strong. After Senator Frelinghuysen proposed an amendment deleting churches from the bill, his proposal quickly gathered majority support.[45]

For our purposes, the debate over the inclusion of churches in the nineteenth-century civil rights law is important for two reasons. First, it constitutes yet another link with contemporary disputes involving the state's authority to promote LGBT equality. Admittedly, the particulars of the disputes have changed. Today it is clear, for example, that the government lacks the constitutional authority to force religious organizations to admit members whom they do not want to admit. It is also clear that the Religion Clauses prevent the state from interfering with the ability of religious organizations to choose their ministers.[46] Rather than debating whether the government, through the enforcement of antidiscrimination laws, can force religious organizations to accept ministers or members whom they do not want to accept, contemporary policy-makers and commentators are debating, for example, whether for-profit entities owned by religious owners should be exempted from antidiscrimination obligations. But the crucial underlying normative questions of how to accommodate religious liberty as the state promotes equal opportunity are essentially the same today as they were in 1875. Again, the type of tension between equality and liberty that we are seeing today in the context of LGBT rights issues is not particularly new or novel.

Second, the removal of churches from Sumner's bill constituted the *first time* in American history that arguments and claims based on First Amendment values and principles were used to successfully limit the scope of the government's authority to promote equality. Long before

LGBT rights activists began to routinely turn to the First Amendment to successfully agitate in favor of the adoption of LGBT equality measures, and more than a century before social and religious conservatives turned to the First Amendment to try to slow down or counteract the nation's growing embrace of LGBT equality, critics of broad antidiscrimination laws relied on the First Amendment to successfully limit the state's ability to promote racial equality.

The Civil Rights Act of 1964

After the Supreme Court struck down the Civil Rights Act of 1875 as unconstitutional, Congress did not enact another significant antidiscrimination law until almost a century later. It took the political and social agitation engendered by the civil rights movement, along with the growing concern of many Americans in the face of the repeated violence and harassment suffered by civil rights activists at the hands of Southern white segregationists, to finally persuade Congress in 1964 to enact a comprehensive civil rights law.[47] In many ways, the Civil Rights Act of 1964 constituted the fulfillment of some of the most important promises of racial equality that the country had made to black Americans after the Civil War but failed, for decades, to deliver.

The two most important provisions of the 1964 statute are Title II, which prohibits certain places of public accommodation, including hotels, restaurants, and theaters, from discriminating on the basis of race, color, national origin, or religion; and Title VII, which prohibits employers of more than fifteen employees from discriminating on the same bases and on that of sex.

Title II was controversial among some at the time of its enactment because it represented a renewed effort by the federal government to require large numbers of businesses to serve all customers regardless of race. (Although thirty-two states by 1964 had adopted laws prohibiting places of public accommodation from discriminating on the basis of race, none of them were Southern states.)[48] Some of the objections to the law were grounded in federalist concerns about the limits of congressional authority in matters that, critics argued, fell under the exclusive jurisdiction of state governments. But opponents also claimed, in ways that would presage contemporary debates over measures aimed at promoting sexual orientation equality, that Title II trampled on the liberty rights—in particular, rights to property and free association—of those who opposed racial equality. A review of those claims can help us better understand and assess the political, legal, and moral issues that are at stake in today's controversies involving the state's authority to force those who oppose LGBT equality on grounds of conscience to abide by antidiscrimination regulations.

Even though some critics of the 1964 statute also objected to the federal government's prohibition of employment discrimination because of its impact on the liberty rights of employers, those arguments were similar to the ones raised in the context of Title II. What is most pertinent about the history of Title VII's enactment to contemporary clashes over LGBT equality is the scope, and the reasons for the adoption, of what I will refer to here as the "Title VII compromise," one that permits religious organizations to hire only coreligionists for all of their employment positions, not just those directly linked to the pursuit of their spiritual missions.

Places of Public Accommodation (Again)

Although the lexical and normative distinctions between civil and social rights, which permeated the debates over the Civil Rights Act of 1875, were no longer part of public debates by the 1960s, the underlying normative disagreement regarding whether the federal government, in particular, could require individuals to engage in commercial transactions against their will framed much of the debate over Title II. Rather than speaking of the "social rights" of public accommodation owners and their white customers, opponents of the Civil Rights Act of 1964 emphasized the property and associational rights of business owners. As a conceptual matter, the twentieth-century objections were quite similar to their nineteenth-century counterparts: They were grounded in the contention that the federal government, in seeking to enforce the equality rights of some, was impermissibly trampling on the liberty interests of others.[49] Like critics had argued almost a century earlier in the context of the Civil Rights Act of 1875, Title II opponents claimed that Congress, by seeking to impose nondiscrimination mandates that interfered with the private choices of individuals, was attempting to improperly regulate private spheres of conduct.

Critics of Title II raised other objections, including ones based on federalism concerns and the need to limit the regulatory authority of the national government. Some opponents to Title II also raised an additional argument, one that, ironically enough, was based on the Thirteenth Amendment: to force businesspeople to serve customers against their will, it was argued, constituted a form of involuntary servitude.[50] Not surprisingly, the Supreme Court eventually rejected that particular claim without any trouble.[51] But most conservative critics of Title II more generally argued that it threatened the liberty rights of individuals.

The future federal judge (and unsuccessful Supreme Court nominee) Robert Bork, in a 1963 article published in the *New Republic*, articulated some of the objections, grounded in associational freedoms, to Title II. Bork complained that proponents of civil rights laws ignored their negative impact on "a vital area of personal liberty" by forcing some "to deal with and serve persons with whom they do not wish to associate."[52] For Bork, the issue was "not whether racial prejudice or preference is a good thing but whether individual men ought to be free to deal and associate with whom they please for whatever reasons appeal to them."[53] The problem with promoting the public good by protecting individuals from the harms caused by discrimination was that there was no logical limiting principle; this understanding of the public good, Bork claimed, would sacrifice liberty in the name of fighting prejudice every time.

The bill's congressional opponents were similarly troubled by its impact on associational freedoms. For example, conservative members of the House Judiciary Committee argued that the bill promoted the freedom of some by impermissibly limiting the freedom of others and that it gave the federal government "the power to completely dominate the lives" of millions of Americans.[54] For his part, in objecting to the bill's scope, Senator Strom Thurmond of South Carolina quoted from a recent concurring opinion by the second Justice Harlan arguing that "freedom of the individual to choose his associates or his neighbors, to use and dispose of his property as he sees fit, to be irrational, arbitrary, capricious, even unjust in his personal relations are things all entitled to a large measure of protection from governmental interference."[55] For Thurmond, the civil rights bill violated the rights of individual liberty and property as protected by the Fifth Amendment. According to the senator, it would eliminate "freedom of individual choice" and replace it with "federal compulsion."[56]

As law professor Christopher Schmidt explains, conservative critics of the civil rights bill, in effect, defended a right to discriminate on

constitutional and philosophical grounds rooted in liberty considerations.[57] According to these critics, business owners had associational
and property-based rights that allowed them to choose their employees
and customers free of government interference. Although courts had no
difficulty in rejecting the notion of "a right to discriminate," arguments
on behalf of that right nonetheless framed much of the opposition to
the Civil Rights Act of 1964.[58] As an Alabama Supreme Court justice contended at the time, "in a free society, great care should be taken to secure
the individual's freedom. The owner of a neighborhood drug store, or
dress shop, or soda fountain . . . has the right to choose his customers as
he sees fit. Call this a property right, or a right of privacy, or a right of free
association. It too is a civil right."[59]

It bears noting that some of the objections to Title II were also based
on assertions of religious doctrine and values. Although by 1964 few
members of Congress were willing to articulate their opposition to civil
rights laws on the basis of Christian values, as countless federal and state
legislators had done during the Reconstruction and Jim Crow eras, some
business owners objected to Title II's mandates on religious grounds.
One of the most prominent of these dissenters was Maurice Bessinger,
the owner of four barbecue restaurants in South Carolina, who claimed
that the mixing of the races in public places was inconsistent with Christian teachings. After a group of African-American plaintiffs sued Bessinger under Title II for prohibiting them from entering his restaurants,
he argued in court that the statute was unconstitutional, in part because
it violated his right to the free exercise of religion. A federal district court
rejected that claim, explaining that while Bessinger had "a constitutional
right to espouse the religious beliefs of his own choosing," he could not
exercise those rights in ways that violated the rights of others.[60] The
Supreme Court agreed with that conclusion, deeming Bessinger's religious freedom claim to be "patently frivolous."[61]

Congressional supporters of Title II, in responding to the contention
that it violated business owners' rights to association, pointed out that
those rights, once owners made their goods and services available to the
general public, did not limit the power of the government to prohibit discrimination. The bill's proponents were confident that courts would find
that the right to be free from racial discrimination outweighed the rights
of association of those who "have knowingly and for profit opened their
doors to the public."[62]

In emphasizing the harms inflicted by racial discrimination, Title II supporters pointed not only to economic injuries, but also to dignitary harms caused by discrimination. As one group of congressmen put it, "on moral grounds, and from the standpoint of upholding human dignity, the U.S. Congress cannot tolerate" racially discriminatory practices engaged in by restaurants, hotels, and similar establishments.[63] The Senate report accompanying the bill reasoned similarly when it explained that "the primary purpose of [the bill] is to solve . . . the deprivation of personal dignity that surely accompanies denials of equal access to public establishments. Discrimination is not simply dollars and cents, hamburgers and movies; it is the humiliation, frustration, and embarrassment that a person must surely feel when he is told that he is unacceptable as a member of the public because of his race or color."[64]

It is worth keeping three aspects of the debates over Title II of the Civil Rights Act of 1964 in mind when assessing recent disputes over the government's authority to promote LGBT equality in the face of objections grounded in First Amendment values and principles. First, as with the debates over the Civil Rights Act of 1875, and as with contemporary disputes over LGBT rights, the debates over Title II laid bare disagreements about the extent to which associational and religious freedom rights should limit the scope of the government's authority to promote equality for traditionally marginalized groups.

Second, with the passage of time, the question of whether the government can appropriately prohibit places of public accommodation from discriminating on the basis of race, despite the prohibition's impact on the liberty interests of business owners, has been entirely settled. Indeed, in 2004, when the House of Representatives issued a proclamation honoring the fortieth anniversary of the Civil Rights Act, only one member, the libertarian Congressman Ron Paul of Texas, voted against it.[65] And six years later, commentators across the political spectrum criticized his son and future senator from Kentucky Rand Paul for claiming that Title II impermissibly trampled on the liberty rights of business owners.[66] Although the fact that there now exists a broad consensus that Title II constitutes an entirely legitimate and proper exercise of governmental authority does not, by itself, prove that the liberty-based objections to it were meritless, it does show that what may seem to one generation like deeply divisive clashes between the need to promote equality on the one hand and to protect liberty on the other hand may seem, to another generation, like a nonissue.

Third, although the right of association and other related liberties played a prominent role in the policy and legislative debates leading to the enactment of the Civil Rights Act of 1964, they did not gain much traction in the judicial arena. Indeed, when the Supreme Court considered the constitutionality of Title II, it quickly rejected objections based on rights to liberty and property and focused instead on the question, which the Court answered affirmatively, of whether Congress could enact Title II under its authority to regulate interstate commerce.[67]

In contrast, as we will explore in Chapter 6, in later cases involving government efforts to promote LGBT equality, the Supreme Court grappled extensively with claims that the First Amendment shielded certain organizations from laws aimed at promoting sexual orientation equality. One of the reasons that may explain this difference is that the cases from the 1960s challenging Title II were brought by commercial enterprises. In contrast, the parties that later raised First Amendment objections to the enforcement of LGBT equality measures were noncommercial associations, such as the organizers of Boston's St. Patrick's Day Parade and the Boy Scouts. Although the Court has held that expressive associations, in some circumstances, have the right to exclude individuals who belong to classes protected by antidiscrimination laws, it has never ruled that for-profit enterprises have a constitutional right to discriminate. I return to this issue in Chapter 6.

The Title VII Compromise

The Civil Rights Act of 1964 grew out of a proposed bill that President John Kennedy had sent to Congress the previous summer. Kennedy's bill primarily addressed discrimination by places of public accommodation and did not include a provision prohibiting employment discrimination in the private sector. However, a majority of the members of a subcommittee of the House Judiciary Committee, the committee to which Kennedy's bill was referred, wanted the new civil rights law to address employment discrimination by private employers. As a result, the subcommittee adopted the language of an earlier bill prohibiting employment discrimination, which had stalled before the House Rules Committee. The earlier bill categorically exempted "religious corporations, associations, or societies" from employment antidiscrimination obligations without any further qualifications.[68] This is notable because the exemption, on its face, was not limited to the question of whether religious organizations could take religion into account in making employment decisions; instead, the exemption, if enacted into law, would have allowed religious entities to make distinctions not only on the basis of religion, but also on that of any other protected trait under the statute, including race.[69]

The categorical exemption for religious corporations, associations, and societies received little attention during deliberations of the bill in the House of Representatives. One of the few exceptions took place when Representative George Grant of Alabama, a bill opponent, asked during a Rules Committee hearing why the legislation did not apply to religious organizations: "If this [law] is so wonderful, why exempt anyone or any group? Why not let it apply to all?"[70] However, the Rules Committee did not propose any amendments to the bill, and the full House eventually approved the categorical religious exemption.

During the floor debate, Representative Graham Purcell of Texas, after noting that the exemption did not seem to apply to religious *educational* institutions because they might not be included within the meaning of religious "corporations, associations, or societies," offered an amendment to exempt such institutions from the obligation not to discriminate on the basis of religion in filling *all* of their employment positions. Purcell expressed concern that courts might interpret another of the bill's provisions, which allowed employers to take religion (as well as sex and national origin) into account when it "is a bona fide occupational qualification," to apply only when religious schools hired administrators or teachers but not other workers such as clerks and janitors. To require religious educational institutions to hire "an atheist or a member of a different faith" for any position, Purcell claimed, would violate the First Amendment's right to free religious exercise and its requirement of separation between church and state.[71]

Speaking in opposition to Purcell's amendment, Representative Emanuel Celler of New York, the chair of the Judiciary Committee, argued that it went too far because it allowed religious schools to discriminate in filling positions that had nothing to do with their religious missions. Celler complained that "if we adopt this amendment, we may well be building in the bill a legal discrimination which we have worked so long to eliminate."[72] However, a majority of the representatives who spoke on Purcell's amendment supported its passage by arguing that Title VII should allow religious schools to hire only coreligionists if they so chose. As Representative John Roush of Indiana explained, a religious "college should have the right to compel [all] the individuals it employs to adhere to its beliefs, for that college exists to propagate and to extend to the people with whom it has influence its convictions and beliefs. To force [it] to hire an 'outsider' would dilute if not destroy its effect and thus its very purpose for existence."[73] The House voted in favor of Purcell's amendment and, two days later, passed the entire bill by a 290 to 130 vote.

When the bill reached the Senate, supporters were committed to avoiding its Judiciary Committee, which was dominated by conservatives and was known as the "graveyard of civil rights legislation."[74] After overcoming a filibuster on the procedural question of whether to bypass the Judiciary Committee, the bill's supporters succeeded in sending it directly to the floor. Supporters then worked intensely behind the scenes to persuade prominent conservative senators from non-Southern states—prominent among them Senator Everett Dirksen, the Republican Minority Leader from Illinois—to support the legislation. Out of that process, a substitute bill emerged that, among other changes, narrowed Title VII's categorical exemption for religious corporations, associations, and societies in two important ways. First, the bill allowed such entities to hire coreligionists only, but did not permit them to make employment decisions on the basis of protected traits other than religion, such as race and sex. Second, the bill limited the exemption to the organization's "religious activities,"[75] making it applicable only to instances in which religious organizations filled positions directly related to the pursuit of their religious missions. The amendment, in other words, aimed to apply to religious organizations when they hired ministers, for example, but not when they hired clerks and other employees not directly involved in religious activities. (The substitute bill left in place Purcell's amendment exempting religious educational institutions in their hiring for all positions.)

The question of religious exemptions received almost no attention during the Senate floor debates. After supporters overcame yet another filibuster—the longest in the history of the Senate, lasting 534 hours, 1 minute, and 51 seconds—the bill passed by a vote of 73 to 27.[76] The Senate bill was then introduced in the House, which quickly approved it.

Congress returned to the question of religious exemptions in 1972 when it considered and approved several changes to Title VII, including covering public employers, reducing the minimum number of employees necessary to trigger coverage of an employer from 25 to 15, and authorizing the Equal Employment Opportunity Committee (EEOC) to sue employers in federal court.[77] Supporters of broader religious exemptions than those contained in the original statute saw Congress's reconsideration of Title VII as an opportunity to advance their views. Senators James Allen of Alabama and Samuel Ervin of North Carolina introduced an amendment that, like the House's original 1964 bill, would have categorically exempted all religious organizations from any antidiscrimination obligations under Title VII, including those that pertained to race and sex. In defending the proposed amendment, Senator Ervin reiterated the position taken by opponents of the federal antidiscrimination law in 1964, namely, that it promoted the interests of some individuals at the expense of the freedom of others.[78] Referring specifically to small business owners, Ervin argued that individuals of a particular race or national origin do not do "anything evil or . . . iniquitous" when they only hire employees of their own race or national origin. The same was true, Ervin claimed, when business owners of a particular religion only hire employees of their own religion.[79]

Ervin added that the EEOC should not have the power "to compel a Christian denomination to employ a Mohammedan [Muslim] secretary or to employ an atheist as a secretary or to employ an agnostic as a secretary."[80] The North Carolina senator claimed, repeatedly and emphatically, that to force religious organizations to hire employees, regardless of their job functions, against the organizations' will violated the separation of church and state.[81] He claimed that, in contrast, Senator Allen's and his proposal, by completely exempting religious organizations from Title VII's scope, would protect their religious exercise rights. It was crucial, Ervin explained, to take "the political hands of Caesar [off of] the things that belong to God."[82] Senator Allen also argued that imposing nondiscrimination obligations on religious entities violated the separation between church and state while impermissibly trampling on religious freedom.[83]

Senator Harrison Williams of New Jersey took the lead in opposing the Allen/Ervin amendment. Williams argued that the government did not compromise the "religious integrity" of religious organizations when it required them to offer equal employment opportunities to everyone while filling positions unrelated to their religious activities.[84] The senator noted that some religious organizations ran hospitals and provided other "purely secular services to the general public without regard to religious affiliations, and that most of the many thousands of persons employed by these institutions perform totally secular functions."[85] There was no reason for a religiously affiliated hospital, for example, to use religious criteria to hire janitors. Williams added that "of all the institutions in this country [that] should be setting the example of equal employment opportunity, of equal opportunity for that matter in all aspects of life, it is America's religious institutions. I am confident that the Houses of God in this country do not shirk that responsibility nor should we."[86]

Whereas Ervin and Allen contended that requiring religious organizations to comply with antidiscrimination laws violated the Establishment Clause, Williams argued that it was the *granting* of broad exemptions from civil rights laws to such organizations that was inconsistent with the separation of church and state.[87] At the same time, Williams reasoned that the narrower exemption contained in the Civil Rights Act of 1964, limited to the organizations' religious activities, sufficiently protected their free exercise rights because it recognized their interests in determining, without governmental intervention, who engaged in religious activities on their behalf.[88]

In the end, the Senate voted against the Allen/Ervin amendment by a vote of 55 to 25.[89] Several weeks later, Senator Allen proposed a second, narrower amendment, one that would allow religious organizations to take religion (but not race, national origin, or sex) into account by hiring, if they so chose, only coreligionists for *all* employment positions. Although Senator Williams also opposed the new amendment on grounds that were similar to his objections to the broader exemption, he conceded that the measure had enough support—the Senate had approved a similar provision two years earlier by a vote of 43 to 28—to justify its passage without a roll call.[90] The House of Representatives eventually agreed to adopt the Senate's language on the religious exemption, and that provision remains the law today.

In sum, Congress grappled with three different possible exemptions under Title VII. The broadest measure, proposed in both 1964 and 1972 but not adopted into law, would have completely exempted religious organizations from any Title VII obligations, including the duty not to discriminate on the basis of race or sex. The narrowest, in place between 1964 and 1972, allowed religious organizations to hire coreligionists exclusively, but only for positions related to the groups' religious activities.[91] In both 1964 and 1972, Congress chose middle positions, not allowing religious organizations to take race or sex into account in making employment decisions while permitting them to hire coreligionists only. The middle position adopted by Congress in 1972 also did not limit the exemption to religious activities; instead, it allowed religious entities to take religion into account in making employment decisions without distinguishing among different categories of positions.

There are five aspects of the Title VII religious exemption compromise that are worth noting. First, as had happened with the Civil Rights Act of 1875, and as has happened more recently in the context of LGBT rights, the Title VII religious exemption debates involved the question of how to balance the government's promotion of equality against the liberty interests of those who opposed that equality. Second, exemption supporters relied heavily on First Amendment considerations (primarily related to the Free Exercise Clause, but also to the Establishment Clause) in seeking to limit the ability of the government to promote equality. Third, the legislative outcome was a *compromise*: although arguments were made for both broader and narrower exemptions, Congress ultimately chose a middle ground that balanced the need to promote rights to equality against the importance of protecting religious liberty.

Fourth, the compromise was centered on the religious nature of the exempted organizations. Although some conservative legislators, such as Senator Ervin, expressed the view that small business owners should be permitted to make employment decisions based on their religious views, Congress did not, in either 1964 or 1972, seriously consider expanding the exemption beyond traditional religious organizations in order to cover profit-making enterprises. As I will elaborate on in Chapter 7, this is a point worth remembering when assessing contemporary efforts to exempt religious owners of for-profit entities from sexual orientation antidiscrimination obligations: such exemptions go significantly beyond what Congress considered, much less enacted, in the context of Title VII.

Finally, and perhaps most important, the Title VII compromise has on the whole worked well. It has provided important protection, beyond what is constitutionally required, to religious entities by allowing them to make some employment decisions based on their religious views. (As discussed at the end of this chapter, the constitutionally mandated ministerial exception to antidiscrimination laws protects the ability of religious organizations to choose ministers free from government interference, but does not apply to other employment positions. The Title VII compromise goes beyond what is constitutionally required by allowing religious organizations to hire coreligionists exclusively in filling *all* of their employment positions without incurring antidiscrimination liability.) At the same time, the exemption has not significantly interfered with the ability of the statute to provide Americans with equal employment opportunities. This is largely because the exemption has two crucial limitations. First, it is limited to the ability of religious organizations to hire coreligionists and does not cover discrimination on the basis of other traits, such as race and sex, protected by the statute. Second, in benefitting only religious "corporations, associations, or societies" and not for-profit business entities, it applies to a relatively small number of employers.

The debates over federal civil rights laws from the 1870s to the 1970s illustrate the ways in which our nation has repeatedly struggled with the question of how to balance the equality rights of some against the liberty interests of others. The debates show that First Amendment values and principles have been important sources of limitations on the state's ability to promote equality for traditionally marginalized groups. At the same time, the history shows that the current controversies over the scope of LGBT equality measures raise legal and policy questions that our country has grappled with repeatedly in other antidiscrimination contexts. Our experiences as a nation with these issues make it unnecessary to reinvent the wheel, so to speak, in matters related to exemptions from the application of antidiscrimination laws. Instead, decision-makers and citizens should look to how our predecessors dealt with these questions to help find the appropriate balance between equality and liberty in the context of the state's promotion and protection of LGBT rights. I will return to this point in Chapter 7.

The Bob Jones University Controversy

The next big clash between government measures aimed at promoting equality and the asserted liberty interests of those who dissented from such measures arose in the context of tax exemptions. Federal law exempts nonprofit institutions from taxation, a benefit that not only allows them to avoid paying federal taxes, but also permits donors to deduct their contributions to those institutions from their federal income taxes.

The racial desegregation of public schools in the South during the 1960s led to the creation of so-called white-flight private schools, some of which operated under the auspices of Christian denominations, that catered to white parents who did not want their children attending schools with black children.[92] In 1969, a group of black parents in Mississippi whose children attended public schools sued the Treasury Department, challenging the Internal Revenue Service's grant of tax exemptions to private schools that discriminated on the basis of race. After a federal court issued an injunction prohibiting the IRS from awarding tax-exempt status to private schools in Mississippi unless they made it clear they did not discriminate on the basis of race, the agency announced that it would withhold tax exempt status from private schools across the country that lacked racial nondiscrimination policies.[93] The IRS took the position that educational institutions that discriminated on the basis of race were in violation of clearly declared federal policy, and as a result, they should not be deemed "charitable" within the meaning of the tax code and its regulations.

One of the institutions affected by the IRS's new policy was Bob Jones University (BJU), a Christian fundamentalist school of about five thousand students located in Greenville, South Carolina.[94] The university's educational mission was grounded in a literal interpretation of the Bible that aimed to "combat all atheistic, agnostic, pagan and so-called scientific adulterations of the Gospel [while] unqualifiedly affirming and teaching the inspiration of the Bible."[95] The university required its teachers to be "born again" Christians; screened student applicants based on their religious beliefs; and did not permit students to dance, play cards, smoke cigarettes, watch movies, listen to rock or jazz music, or walk with a student of the opposite sex "on campus unless both of them have a legitimate reason for going in the same direction."[96] From its founding in the 1920s until 1971, the university also did not admit black students, believing that racial integration was inconsistent with biblical commands. In 1971, BJU modified its policy by admitting married black students (as long as they were married to other African Americans), but left in place its exclusionary policy regarding single black students.

After the IRS rescinded BJU's tax exempt status, the university sued contending that the agency did not have the statutory authority to deny the exemption on racial discrimination grounds and that even if the tax code authorized the denial of the exemption, such authority violated the Free Exercise Clause. As the lawsuit made its way through the federal courts, the Supreme Court held in a different case that the Civil Rights

Act of 1866 prohibited private secular schools from discriminating on the basis of race.[97] Although the Court in that case explicitly refused to decide whether the civil rights statute could constitutionally be applied to religious schools that discriminated on the basis of race, BJU had by then announced that it would accept applications from black students regardless of their marital status.[98] But as the university lifted its ban on black students, it simultaneously instituted a policy that called for the expulsion of students who married or dated across racial lines, as well as students who promoted or encouraged other students to do so.[99] According to the government, the school's new policy against interracial marriage and dating justified the continued denial of the tax exemption. (The Supreme Court eventually consolidated the BJU case with that of a religious freedom challenge to the IRS policy brought by the Goldsboro Christian School, a K–12 school in North Carolina. That institution did not admit racial minorities as students on the ground that "cultural or biological mixing of the races is . . . a violation of God's command.")[100]

The IRS under President Jimmy Carter demanded that private schools prove that they were complying with federal antidiscrimination policies— by reporting how many black students attended the schools in relation to the black population in their regions—in order to be eligible for the tax exemption.[101] But after Ronald Reagan became president, the IRS changed course, announcing it would now grant exemptions to the roughly one hundred private schools that the agency had previously determined were discriminating on the basis of race.[102] While the Republican administration's change in policy pleased its Christian fundamentalist supporters, its decision to grant the exemptions created a political firestorm as liberals and civil rights advocates accused the federal government of subsidizing racism.[103]

Meanwhile, the administration asked the Supreme Court to dismiss the BJU lawsuit, contending that the case was now moot. The Court, however, refused to do so in apparent recognition that the tax code might authorize the IRS to deny the exemption despite the administration's belief to the contrary. The justices asked William Coleman, the chairman of the NAACP Legal Defense Fund, to make the legal case on behalf of the constitutionality of denying the tax exemption to religious schools that discriminated on the basis of race.

After hearing from all sides, the Court held that the tax code permitted the denial of the tax exemption to racially discriminatory schools and that the denial was constitutional. The Court pointed out that all three branches of the federal government had made it eminently clear that racial discrimination was inconsistent with national public policy. The Court also concluded that the government's interest in discouraging racial discrimination was compelling and that it outweighed whatever burden the denial of the tax benefit imposed on the ability of university members to exercise their religion.[104] In doing so, the Court noted that while the denial imposed a financial cost on schools that discriminated, it did not prevent them "from observing their religious tenets."[105]

Although the BJU case has now receded into history, it constituted one of the most disputed civil rights controversies of its time. By the early 1980s, few individuals were willing to publicly defend BJU's racist views. But for many, there was an important principle at stake: the need to protect religious institutions from state-mandated equality.[106] At the same time, most civil rights supporters argued that it was unacceptable, given the nation's history of racism and discrimination, for the government to subsidize institutions, even religious ones, that insisted on retaining racially discriminatory policies.

It is clear, then, that the *Bob Jones University* case represents yet another instance in American history in which the government's promotion of equality came to be in tension with First Amendment values and principles. Although the Court ultimately held that the amendment did not render unconstitutional the IRS's equality-promoting policy, the more expansive understanding of the amendment's protections of religious liberty urged by BJU's supporters, if it had been accepted by the justices, would have made it impermissible for the government to promote equality by denying tax benefits to religious organizations that implemented racially discriminatory policies.

There are at least two ways of understanding the impact of *Bob Jones University* on contemporary debates over LGBT equality and the First Amendment. The first, and narrow, way is to view the case as standing for the proposition that race is special, that is, that racial discrimination represents a uniquely socially corrosive and immoral practice that has made it impossible for the nation, until relatively recently, to live up to its ideals of equal citizenship. From this perspective, the government has the constitutional authority to institute expansive measures to discourage private parties from engaging in racial discrimination. At the same time, it is argued, the government does not have a similar broad constitutional authority to prohibit sexual orientation discrimination, especially when it interferes with the rights of conscience of those who oppose the equal treatment of sexual minorities.

A second, and broader, understanding of *Bob Jones University* views it as prioritizing the government's interest in eradicating invidious discrimination, in particular the types of discrimination that have been deeply rooted in the nation's history, social norms, and laws, and about which there is a clear (or at least emerging) consensus regarding their moral wrongness. From this perspective, the reasoning of *Bob Jones University*, if not its holding, supports the notion that the government has expansive constitutional authority to prohibit discrimination on the basis of sexual orientation even in instances when it might limit the ability of dissenters to engage in conduct that results in the differential treatment of individuals based on their sexual orientation.

Although the applicability of *Bob Jones University* to questions associated with LGBT equality remains disputed, the Supreme Court's ruling in that case helped to forge a national consensus about the social and moral unacceptability of racial discrimination by private parties and the corresponding appropriateness of state action to discourage it. Indeed, when George W. Bush gave a speech at BJU as a way of seeking the support of fundamentalist Christians during the presidential campaign of 2000, he was heavily criticized for doing so after the media revealed that the university retained its policies prohibiting interracial marriages and dating. (Bush later apologized for the appearance, and the university shortly thereafter rescinded its interracial policies and apologized for its past racially discriminatory views and actions.)[107] Two years later, Senator Trent Lott of Mississippi resigned from his position as Senate Minority Leader following the media's revelation, after Lott had made controversial statements in support of the segregationist Senator Strom Thurmond, that he had filed an amicus brief with the Supreme Court fifteen years earlier in support of BJU's lawsuit against the government.[108] Shortly after the Court's ruling, Lott had insisted that the case was not about racial discrimination, but about religious freedom.[109]

As had occurred with the dissipation of controversy after the passage of Title II of the Civil Rights Act of 1964, the relatively quick emergence of a broad consensus on the question of tax exemptions for racially discriminatory schools does not, by itself, mean that the Court got it right in *Bob Jones University*. But that consensus shows the extent to which some of the most highly disputed conflicts pitting the promotion of equality against the protection of liberty frequently lose their intensity with the passage of time. Although it is true that those who prioritized antidiscrimination values prevailed both in the case of Title II and in that of BJU, a similar broad consensus emerged after Congress's adoption of the Title VII compromise, one that did not prioritize antidiscrimination values to the maximum extent possible, but instead exempted religious organizations from the obligation to refrain from discriminating on the basis of religion as applied to *all* of their employment positions. What all three instances do have in common is that the country generally made its peace with the decisions of either Congress or the Court and then moved on to other matters. This historical pattern suggests that the nation might reach a similar degree of consensus once legislatures and courts make defensible decisions on how to best balance LGBT equality against the liberty-based rights and interests of those who oppose that equality.

The Case of Gender Discrimination

During the oral arguments in *Bob Jones University*, Justice Lewis Powell expressed interest in finding a "limiting principle" that would cabin the ability of the government to withhold tax exemptions from institutions that had policies with which it disagreed. In doing so, he asked William Coleman whether the government could deny a tax exemption to an organization because it discriminated on the basis of gender. Coleman, whose immediate objective was to defend the government's decision to deny a tax exemption to BJU, responded by claiming that racial discrimination presented special and unique circumstances justifying more assertive government policies aimed at prohibiting such discrimination. As he put it to the justices that day, "we didn't fight a civil war over sex discrimination."[110]

Shortly after its ruling in *Bob Jones University*, the Court was presented with two cases raising the question of how far the government could go in promoting gender equality in the face of First Amendment objections. In the first case, *Hishon v. King & Spalding*, a female attorney sued her former law firm under Title VII, contending that it had refused to promote her to partner because she was a woman. In defending themselves from the discrimination claim, the firm's all-male partners argued that they had a constitutionally protected right of association that allowed them to choose new partners without interference from civil rights laws. The

Court unanimously rejected that argument by explaining, in effect, that there is no constitutional right to discriminate.[111]

Although the Court in the second case, *Roberts v. United States Jaycees*, also sided with government efforts to promote gender equality through the application of antidiscrimination laws in the face of First Amendment objections, it did so after engaging in a more detailed analysis of the constitutional issues at stake. *Roberts* was a more difficult case than *Hishon* because whereas the latter involved a for-profit law firm, the former implicated the admissions policies of a nonprofit organization created to promote the interests of young men.[112]

In 1974, the St. Paul and Minneapolis chapters of the Jaycees (also known as the Junior Chamber of Commerce) began to admit women as members in violation of the national organization's bylaws. The Jaycees "considered itself to be a young men's leadership training organization, serving the goals of individual development, community development, and development of management ability."[113] The organization, which limited membership to men between the ages of 18 and 35, placed great emphasis in the recruitment of members and had almost 300,000 members nationwide.[114]

After the two Minnesota chapters started admitting women, the national group began taking steps to revoke their charters. The chapters then filed an action before the Minnesota Human Rights Department, claiming that the national organization's gender policy violated a state statute prohibiting places of public accommodation from discriminating on the basis of sex. The Jaycees responded by suing state officials in federal court, claiming that its First Amendment rights to free expression and association precluded the application of the state civil rights law to it.

Roberts is a crucial case because, in confronting the question of how the First Amendment limits the application of an antidiscrimination law, the Court made clear that the government must satisfy a high burden when it seeks to apply such a law in ways that require expressive associations—that is, associations that pursue "a wide variety of political, social, economic, educational, religious, and cultural ends"—to admit members whom they do not want to admit.[115] In doing so, the Court pointed to *NAACP v. Alabama* (the 1950s case in which state officials had tried to force the NAACP's Alabama chapter to reveal its membership list), among other cases, to support the proposition that expressive associations have considerable discretion in setting membership admission criteria.[116]

In writing for the Court, Justice William Brennan in *Roberts* explained that the First Amendment rights to speak, worship, and petition would not have much meaning if individuals did not enjoy the "correlative freedom" to engage in those activities with others in pursuit of common objectives. As a result, the Minnesota antidiscrimination statute "plainly implicated" the rights of organizations like the Jaycees to be protected from governmental regulation of their internal affairs. As Brennan explained, "there can be no clearer example of an intrusion into the internal structure or affairs of an association than a regulation that forces the group to accept members it does not desire. Such a regulation may impair the ability of the original members to express only those views that brought them together. Freedom of association therefore plainly presupposes a freedom not to associate."[117]

Roberts represents yet another example of how government efforts to promote equality through antidiscrimination regulations came to be in tension with First Amendment values and principles. The reasoning of *Roberts* leaves little doubt that the First Amendment limits the ability of the state to promote equality in ways that interfere with the ability of associations to express themselves. Indeed, the Court placed a heavy burden on the government in these types of cases, requiring it to show the existence of "compelling state interests, unrelated to the suppression of ideas, that cannot be achieved through means significantly less restrictive of associational freedoms."[118]

However, the *Roberts* Court ultimately upheld the application of the antidiscrimination law against the First Amendment challenge for three reasons. First, the state had a compelling interest in eradicating discrimination against its female citizens. In making clear that the government has a compelling interest in eradicating gender discrimination, the Court concluded, in effect, that racial discrimination is not unique for these purposes and that eradicating other forms of discrimination can constitute such an interest.

Second, the goal of the civil rights law was to protect citizens from the economic, social, and dignitary harms caused by discrimination, not to suppress speech or limit the expression of particular viewpoints. Third, the state's pursuit of its compelling interest had a limited impact on the associational freedoms of the Jaycees's male members.

In making this last point, the Court emphasized that admitting women would not impair the Jaycees's ability to pursue its objective of promoting the leadership skills and community interests of young men, to continue to take public positions on diverse political and social issues that did not implicate questions of gender, and to exclude individuals (both men and women) whose viewpoints differed from those of the organization. The Court added that the Jaycees's contention that the presence of women in the organization as members would alter the group's message was based "on unsupported generalizations about the relative interests and perspectives of men and women."[119]

Roberts made clear that the First Amendment limits the ability of the state to pursue equality objectives: it grants those who associate for expressive purposes the right to exclude classes of individuals protected by antidiscrimination laws when inclusion would affect the messages they choose to convey. Importantly, this limitation on state authority imposed by the First Amendment applies *even if the government's equality objective constitutes a compelling state interest.* The Court's analysis made clear that if it had concluded that the forced admission of women as members impacted the Jaycees's ability to express its views, it would have sided with the organization even though it had already held that the eradication of gender inequality was a compelling state interest.

Although the Court in *Roberts* determined that the ability of the Jaycees to express its views was not affected by the forced admission of women as members, the Court in subsequent cases ruled that sexual orientation antidiscrimination laws could not be used to require the organizers of St. Patrick's Day parades to allow gay organizations to march under their own banners or to force the Boy Scouts of America to permit openly gay men to serve as scoutmasters.[120] In both instances, the Court determined that the organizations' First Amendment rights trumped the government's equality objectives as pursued through the application of sexual orientation antidiscrimination laws. I explore both of these cases in Chapter 6.

Roberts, then, reflects the dual character of the First Amendment's relationship to equality. On the one hand, the Court's reasoning makes it possible, in some circumstances, to deploy the First Amendment as a shield against the application of antidiscrimination laws. On the other hand, the case makes clear that the eradication of discrimination against traditionally marginalized groups in contexts other than race can constitute a compelling state interest that, in some circumstances, can trump speech and associational claims. For reasons explored later in this book, both of these considerations have become highly relevant to contemporary LGBT rights disputes.

The Ministerial Exception

The First Amendment limits the government's authority to attain equality objectives not only through the protection of the right of association, but also through its requirement that there be a "ministerial exception" to antidiscrimination laws. Although the Title VII compromise protects the ability of religious organizations to hire only coreligionists if they so wish, it does not immunize them from liability if they make employment distinctions on the basis of race, sex, or national origin. As a result, religious organizations such as the Catholic Church and the Southern Baptists, for example, could be liable under the statute's wording for refusing to hire women as priests or ministers. Starting in 1972, however, federal appellate courts began to rule consistently that the Free Exercise Clause or the Establishment Clause, or a combination of the two, prevented the government from interfering with the ability of religious organizations to choose their ministers. Although the courts' precise reasoning has varied, this constitutional limitation on the state's authority to eradicate discrimination has generally been grounded in the need to protect the autonomy interests of religious organizations by giving them unfettered discretion to choose employees who are involved in advancing their religious missions free from governmental interference.

As the case law in this area developed, lower federal courts applied the ministerial exception in ways that protected not only organizations that ran houses of worship, such as churches, synagogues, and mosques, but also religiously affiliated groups that operated other institutions, such as schools. In addition, it quickly became clear that the protection was not limited to ordained religious leaders, but also affected other employees whose job responsibilities included the carrying out of the institutions' religious missions. Courts therefore relied on the ministerial exception to dismiss discrimination lawsuits brought by, for example, the communications manager for the Catholic Archdiocese of Chicago, the principal of a Catholic school, and the choir director of a Methodist church.[121]

Every federal circuit court that considered the issue embraced the ministerial exception. The Supreme Court, faced with lower court unanimity, did not weigh in on the matter until a federal court of appeals in

2010 held that the exception did not prevent a fourth-grade teacher at a Lutheran school from suing her employer under the Americans with Disabilities Act because she was not a "minister" within the meaning of the exception.[122] The teacher in *Hosanna-Tabor Evangelical Lutheran Church and School v. EEOC* had taken a leave of absence from the school where she worked after she developed narcolepsy. A disagreement eventually arose between school administrators and the teacher regarding whether she was physically able to return to work. The school ended up dismissing the teacher after she told the principal that she had consulted a lawyer and would pursue her legal rights. According to the school, she had "violated the Synod's belief that Christians should resolve their disputes internally."[123]

The Supreme Court in *Hosanna-Tabor* unanimously held that the ministerial exception barred the teacher's antidiscrimination claim. The Court pointed to several of its earlier rulings that had rejected government interference with the ability of churches to select their leaders.[124] Although those cases did not involve the application of antidiscrimination laws, they illustrated the constitutional limits of the state's authority to regulate churches in ways that impacted their freedom to choose ministers. Those precedents, when combined with the historical background and the purposes of the Religion Clauses, led the Court to conclude that the government is constitutionally barred from enforcing antidiscrimination laws against religious organizations in their choice of ministers. As the Court explained, "by imposing an unwanted minister, the state infringes the Free Exercise Clause, which protects a religious group's right to shape its own faith and mission through its appointments. According the state the power to determine which individuals will minister to the faithful also violates the Establishment Clause, which prohibits government involvement in such ecclesiastical decisions."[125] The Court also concluded that the teacher in *Hosanna-Tabor* was a minister within the meaning of the exception because the religious school had held her out as a minister and because her duties included conveying the church's religious message and carrying out its spiritual mission.

It is important to note that the application of the ministerial exception to religious organizations under the Religion Clauses serves a similar function as does the application of the right of association to expressive associations under the Free Speech Clause. In both instances, the First Amendment acts as a shield that, in certain circumstances, protects the ability of organizations to exclude individuals whose presence is inconsistent with their religious or secular missions. In both instances, the government's interest in promoting equality gives way to considerations of religious or associational freedom.[126]

As explored in Chapter 6, the application of the doctrine of associational freedom in the context of LGBT equality has been controversial, especially after the Supreme Court held it was unconstitutional to apply a sexual orientation antidiscrimination law to the Boy Scouts.[127] In contrast, the fact that the ministerial exception limits the reach of sexual orientation antidiscrimination laws has not been the subject of much controversy. This is because the exception is consistent with the view, shared by almost everyone in the debates involving the intersection of LGBT equality and rights to religious liberty, that the government should not interfere with the ability of religious institutions to choose their ministers or to decide how to practice their religion. This means that the government lacks the constitutional authority, for example, to require conservative religious institutions to hire LGBT individuals to serve in ministerial capacities. It also means that the government cannot force ministers representing religious institutions and organizations that oppose marriages by same-sex couples to solemnize those marriages.

It is not possible to fully understand the nature and implications of recent controversies about the scope of the state's authority to promote LGBT equality over the objection of dissenters without understanding how legislators and courts have dealt with similar clashes between equality and liberty going back to the post–Civil War period. Three overarching points emerge from the history explored in this chapter. First, that the clash between equality and liberty is a recurring issue in the history of American antidiscrimination law, rendering the ongoing debates over LGBT equality neither exceptional nor surprising. Second, that First Amendment values and principles place limits on the ability of the state to pursue equality objectives. Third, that it has been possible in the past to reach workable compromises between the pursuit of equality for marginalized groups and the protection of important liberty interests enjoyed by opponents of that equality.

Any such compromise, whether legislatively crafted (as in the Title VII compromise) or judicially mandated (as in the ministerial exception), can be criticized for being too narrow or too broad. Nonetheless, the generally reasonable compromises that legislatures and courts have implemented in this area have had two distinct benefits. First, they have helped to calm the waters, so to speak, by reducing the social and political conflict that accompanies the initial, and seemingly inevitable, clash between equality and liberty in the application of American antidiscrimination law. Second, most of the compromises have provided important protections to religious organizations and expressive associations without significantly interfering with the government's efforts to eradicate racial and gender discrimination. This historical record provides grounds for optimism that the nation will be able to reach reasonable and workable compromises on how best to balance equality and liberty in the context of LGBT rights that, although not satisfying the concerns of advocates on all sides, end up being generally accepted as fair and appropriate.

CHAPTER SIX

LGBT Equality and the Right to Exclude

I N 1978, two lesbian, gay, and bisexual student organizations at Georgetown sought official recognition from the university. After school officials turned down the recognition requests, the student groups sued. Unlike in the gay student group cases explored in Chapter 2, all of which involved public universities, the First Amendment was of no use to the LGBT Georgetown students because it does not apply to private entities. As a result, the students based their suit on a sexual orientation antidiscrimination law enacted in 1977 by the Council of the District of Columbia, the first state-level measure of its kind in the country. That law prohibited certain places of public accommodation, including educational institutions, from discriminating on the basis of sexual orientation.

Georgetown has been a Catholic institution since its founding in 1789 (the same year the Constitution was ratified). Although being Catholic has never been a requirement to work or study at the university, at the time of the lawsuit, all of its presidents had been Catholic, several had been Bishops, and since 1825, all had been Jesuits. The university viewed itself as "fulfilling a secular educational role without abandoning its religious heritage."[1] Part of that heritage entailed moral disapproval of same-sex relationships and conduct.

Although the gay students could not turn to the First Amendment for help, the same was not true of the Catholic university, which insisted from the start of the litigation that the application of the antidiscrimination law to its policies violated its rights under the amendment. Georgetown argued that to recognize the gay student groups meant to approve their messages and objectives. As a result, the university claimed that if the government required it to recognize the gay groups, the mandate would violate both its right not to be compelled to speak under the Free Speech Clause and its right to operate according to its religious principles under the Free Exercise Clause. Georgetown's claims meant that the lawsuit filed by its LGBT student groups became the first legal controversy in American history raising the question of whether the enforcement of a sexual orientation antidiscrimination law violated a defendant's First Amendment rights to free speech and religion.

The case, which included a trial and two rulings by the District of Columbia Court of Appeals, took many years to litigate and received widespread public attention.[2] The second, and final, appellate court ruling in *Gay Rights Coalition of Georgetown University Law Center v. Georgetown University* led each of the court's seven judges to write a separate opinion. The controlling opinion, penned by Judge Julia Cooper Mack, has been described as "Solomonic."[3] On the one hand, Judge Mack concluded that the District of Columbia law required the university to provide the gay student groups all of the rights and benefits that it afforded to other student organizations; anything less would violate the law's equality mandate. On the other hand, Judge Mack reasoned, the application of the civil rights law would be unconstitutional if it required not just the equal distribution of rights and benefits, but also official recognition. On that point, Judge Mack agreed with Georgetown that the antidiscrimination law could not, consistently with the Constitution, require the university to recognize organizations that it believed had values and objectives that were inconsistent with its own.

The *Georgetown* case, as law professor Nan Hunter puts it, was "a proverbial canary in a coal mine" because it was the first lawsuit to raise an issue that has been the subject of much dispute and controversy in the decades that followed: whether the government goes too far in promoting LGBT equality when it imposes antidiscrimination obligations on entities whose leaders and members have moral or religious objections to same-sex relationships and conduct.[4] At first, cases like *Georgetown* were relatively unusual, largely because in the 1980s, and into the 1990s, there were few state-level laws that prohibited sexual orientation discrimination. A First Amendment defense can only arise in this context, after all, if there are laws on the books aimed at promoting LGBT equality. As the number of antidiscrimination measures increased, and then later as the number of states allowing same-sex couples to marry grew, there was a corresponding increase in both the frequency and intensity with which those with conscience-based objections to same-sex relationships and conduct turned to First Amendment values and principles to claim that they were entitled to constitutional or statutory exemptions from LGBT equality measures.

Earlier in this book, we explored the extensive and multifaceted campaigns by government agencies and officials during the middle part of the twentieth century to persecute, intimidate, and silence lesbians, gay men, and bisexuals. In the 1950s and 1960s, the state accomplished its antigay objectives through several means, including bar raids, arrests, and general police intimidation, aimed at impeding the ability of sexual minorities to associate with each other and to organize into groups in order to advance their causes. While such overt and outrageous forms of government coercion became less frequent in the 1970s, there were other ways in which state actors tried to harass and silence LGBT people, including by refusing to recognize their organizations and by dismissing gay employees who publicly acknowledged their sexual orientation. As we saw in Chapters 1 through 3, LGBT activists ended up challenging many of these government efforts under the First Amendment, mostly successfully.

Starting in the 1980s and 1990s, when dissenters from LGBT equality began seeking constitutional protection from state action they also turned to the First Amendment. That they did so is not particularly surprising. By that time, the LGBT movement, through speaking, associating, mobilizing, and organizing, was starting to persuade growing segments of society that sexual minorities were entitled to equal treatment. Changing social and moral understandings of sexual orientation led to the enactment of a growing number of state and local laws prohibiting discrimination on the basis of sexual orientation. In response, opponents of LGBT equality began arguing with some frequency that the government's sexual orientation equality mandates were requiring entities and individuals, in violation of the First Amendment, to send messages of tolerance toward or approval of sexual minorities that were inconsistent with their moral, religious, or political beliefs.

By the 1990s, almost no groups (other than fringe ones like the Ku Klux Klan) had policies explicitly excluding individuals on the basis of race and few on that of sex. But there were still mainstream organizations that remained extremely wary of sexual minorities. Some of those organizations used the First Amendment as a shield against the enforcement of LGBT equality measures. This chapter explores the three legal controversies regarding the application of sexual orientation antidiscrimination laws and policies to dissenters from LGBT equality that reached the Supreme Court between 1995 and 2010. The dissenters in the three cases were, respectively, the organizers of the Boston St. Patrick's Day Parade, the national leaders of the Boy Scouts, and a religious student group at a California public law school.

Although there were important differences among the cases, they all raised the fundamental question of whether the First Amendment granted the entities in question the right to exclude sexual minorities in ways that trumped the application of antidiscrimination laws and policies. I argue that the Supreme Court was correct in concluding that the organizers of the St. Patrick's Day Parade had a First Amendment right to exclude gay organizations from the march and that the religious law student group did not have a constitutional right to school-provided subsidies if they excluded LGBT students. (At the same time, I explain why the law school should have granted an exemption to the religious student group, even if it was not constitutionally required to do so.) I also contend that the Supreme Court improperly granted the Boy Scouts a constitutional right to discriminate against gay men. But I also explain how the LGBT movement, in the long run, ended up gaining more than losing as a result of the litigation defeat in the Boy Scouts case.

It is true, of course, that reasonable people often disagree on whether the Supreme Court decides any particular legal dispute correctly. Indeed, there are deep disagreements running through the extensive law review literature on the three Supreme Court cases explored in this chapter. But regardless of what constitutes the appropriate outcome in any particular case, it is important to recognize, as a foundational matter, that the First Amendment's mandate requiring state neutrality in response to private expression on matters related to sexuality, which proved so helpful to the early LGBT movement's ability to start gaining equality protections for sexual minorities, also limits the government's authority to promote that equality when doing so affects the ability of equality opponents to express their views. The question, therefore, is not *whether* the First Amendment limits the scope of the government's authority to promote LGBT (and other forms of) equality; instead, the question is *how* it should do so.

Although it is both proper and necessary for the state to promote equality for traditionally subordinated groups, that promotion cannot come at the expense of the ability of equality opponents to express their views. Admittedly, as this chapter (and the next) shows, it can sometimes be difficult to determine the appropriate limits of state authority in this area and where the line should be drawn between, for example, constitutionally protected expression and unprotected discriminatory conduct. But the challenges that sometimes accompany the drawing of these lines should not occlude the basic point that LGBT rights opponents in the twenty-first century are entitled to the same type of state neutrality in matters of private expression on matters of sexuality that the LGBT movement demanded in the twentieth century. In the end, the First Amendment's relationship to equality is a dual one: it both helps to create the conditions for greater equality and places limits on the ability of the state to promote equality.

The Saint Patrick's Day Parade

In 1990, New York City's chapter of the Ancient Order of the Hibernians (AOH), the group that organized the city's St. Patrick's Day Parade, turned down a request by an Irish gay organization to participate in the following year's parade. After city officials asked AOH to reconsider, it allowed the gay group to march, not as an independent unit, but as the guest of another organization. The 1991 parade was marred by recurring verbal altercations between some members of the gay group and some hostile audience members who watched the parade as it progressed along the city's streets.[5]

After AOH the following year again refused to allow the gay group to march as an independent unit under its own banner, the New York City Commission on Human Rights began an investigation that culminated with a finding that the parade organizers were in violation of the city ordinance prohibiting discrimination on the basis of sexual orientation by places of public accommodation. This finding led city officials to grant the parade permit to another organization, one that seemed inclined to allow the gay group to march. In response, AOH filed a federal lawsuit claiming that the city's actions violated its First Amendment rights to free expression and association. The federal district court agreed, issuing an injunction ordering city officials to grant AOH the marching permit and prohibiting them from requiring that organization to include a group in the parade that it had not approved.[6]

Meanwhile, a group of Irish LGBT individuals in Boston formed an organization in 1992 called the Irish-American Gay, Lesbian, and Bisexual Group of Boston (GLIB). The group's main purposes were gaining entry into the city's St. Patrick's Day Parade, showing that some Bostonians were proud of both their Irish and gay identities, and expressing solidarity with the New York City gay Irish group. In 1992, the organization that planned the Boston parade, the South Boston Allied War Veterans Council, refused to allow GLIB to march. Its reasons for doing so would change with time. The council first claimed that including the gay group raised safety concerns due to possible physical and verbal altercations with members of the public, only to later argue that groups "with sexual themes" were inconsistent with the parade's religious and social values.[7] (Similarly, the AOH gave shifting explanations for not allowing the gay group to march in New York: first because there was a waiting list, then because of safety concerns, and finally because the gay group's message was inconsistent with "the parade sponsor's [message] and the Catholic faith.")[8]

After the council rejected GLIB's application to march, the gay group sued in state court, claiming the decision violated the Massachusetts statute prohibiting public accommodations from discriminating on the basis of sexual orientation. During the 1970s and 1980s, several states, including Massachusetts, expanded their public accommodation laws to increase both the types of activities covered and the classes of individuals protected. By the time of GLIB's lawsuit, the Massachusetts statute covered not only traditional places of public accommodation, such as inns and theaters, but also "a boardwalk or other public highway" as well as "a place of public amusement, recreation or entertainment."[9] (The state courts later concluded that this language made the St. Patrick's Day Parade a place of public accommodation within the meaning of the state law.) The statute also provided protection from discrimination not only on the basis of race, but also, unlike Title II of the Civil Rights Act of 1964, on that of sex and sexual orientation.

In response to the lawsuit, the council argued that the First Amendment barred the statute's application to its decision to deny GLIB the opportunity to participate in the parade because the admission of the gay group would alter the parade's message. The council claimed that the Constitution protected its right to determine the parade's message without government interference. The presence of GLIB in the march, argued the council, sent the message that it approved or endorsed the gay organization's views, a message that the council did not want to convey.

The state courts concluded that the council did not have a constitutional right to exclude the gay organization in contravention of the state antidiscrimination law because the council had never bothered to adopt admissions criteria and, as a result, had failed to be selective in choosing which groups could participate.[10] Recent St. Patrick's Day parades in Boston had included a wide spectrum of participants and sponsors, including businesses, veterans groups, athletic associations, unions, churches, bars, and a right-to-life group. The council had allowed some organizations to march after they made financial contributions without filling out applications, and permitted other groups, like the Boston Bruins hockey team, to march after simply showing up at the parade. Since 1947, when the council took over the responsibility of organizing the event from the city, it had rejected the applications of only two groups: the Ku Klux Klan and an organization opposed to busing children as a way of racially integrating public schools. For the state courts, the organizers' lack of selectivity and the corresponding absence of a discernible message behind the parade, other than perhaps a general pride in being Irish, meant that GLIB's presence in the parade could not be inconsistent with the parade's message. To the state courts, the council denied GLIB's application, not because of the gay organization's views, but because its members were lesbian, gay, and bisexual, a form of exclusion that was explicitly prohibited by Massachusetts law.

The U.S. Supreme Court, however, unanimously reversed in *Hurley v. GLIB*. The Court reasoned that parades are intrinsically expressive events, negating the need for organizers to convey a specific or coherent message to be eligible for First Amendment protection. The council had the constitutional right to determine which organizations participated in the parade because the presence of particular groups affected the message conveyed by the parade as a whole. The council had not waived this constitutional right by being admittedly lax in exercising its right to exclude organizations with particular messages. It was for the council to determine the parade's message, and it was therefore up to it to decide whether to include a group whose clear message was to promote equality and tolerance for sexual minorities.[11]

The Court also noted that the council did not exclude individuals on the basis of sexual orientation, which was the harm that the statute was meant to address.[12] The council allowed lesbians, gay men, and bisexuals to march with nongay organizations. The council's objection was limited to allowing an LGBT group to march under its own banner because of the message conveyed by such participation. As the Supreme Court saw it, the way in which the state courts had applied the antidiscrimination law turned the council's speech itself into a place of public accommodation subject to regulation, a result prohibited by the First Amendment. That amendment blocked the state's effort, in effect, to append another group's message onto the council's message.

The Court made two other important points in supporting its holding. First, it determined that it was reasonable to believe that members of the public would perceive GLIB's participation in the parade as resulting from the council's support for, or approval of, the gay group's message.[13] Second, it concluded that although the government was entitled to ban discriminatory conduct, its aim could not be to create a society free of discriminatory views. As the Court explained, "the very idea that a . . . speech restriction be used to produce thoughts and statements acceptable to some groups or, indeed, all people, grates on the First Amendment, for it amounts to nothing less than a proposal to limit speech in the service of orthodox expression. The Speech Clause has no more certain antithesis."[14]

The controversy in *Hurley* initially arose because of the broad reach of the state's public accommodation law as interpreted by the state courts. It can be argued that private parades should not be included within the scope of civil rights statutes. At the same time, it was in many ways to be expected that, as the country grew more diverse, and as demands for equal treatment went beyond issues of racial discrimination to cover gender and sexuality discrimination, the sites of conflict over the limits of the government's authority to promote equality expanded to include new venues and organizations. Indeed, it is not particularly surprising that the sites of conflict over public accommodations shifted from sites traditionally covered by equal treatment obligations (either under the common law or early statutes), such as inns and theaters, to large organizations (like the Junior Chamber of Commerce and the Boy Scouts) and events (like the St. Patrick's Day Parade) that make available economic, social, or cultural benefits to members and participants.[15]

The controversies over the St. Patrick's Day parades in New York and Boston illustrate how, by the 1990s, the LGBT movement in growing parts of the country (particularly in many urban areas) had succeeded in persuading state actors to take their side on questions of discrimination. Government agencies and elected officials in most large American cities were now largely in favor of gay equality. In a growing number of states and municipalities, the government was increasingly taking sides with the LGBT community not just through the enactment and enforcement of antidiscrimination laws, but also by helping to increase public pressure on organizations that insisted in retaining exclusionary policies. In 1991, for example, when the organizers of the New York St. Patrick's Day Parade allowed the gay Irish group to march as the guest of another organization, Mayor David Dinkins chose to walk with the gay group rather than at the head of the parade, where mayors had traditionally marched.[16] And when parade organizers the following spring refused to allow the gay group to march at all, many New York elected officials showed their support for LGBT equality by attending a gay rights demonstration held immediately prior to the parade.[17] Also in 1992, many of those officials started a tradition (replicated by many of their counterparts in Boston), which remained firmly in place for decades, of skipping the St. Patrick's Day Parade altogether to communicate disapproval of discrimination against sexual minorities. It was in confronting this challenging, if not hostile, political environment that the organizers of the New York and Boston parades turned to the First Amendment for protection.

The Court was correct in both describing parades as intrinsically expressive events and in not demanding that parade organizers have a clear and cohesive message before recognizing their right to exclude viewpoints with which they disagreed. For purposes of putting together a private parade, it should be enough for organizers to believe that the message conveyed by the excluded group is inconsistent with the message that the organizers want to send. (It bears noting that the intrinsically expressive nature of parades is one of several important distinctions between *Hurley* and the Boy Scouts case that followed in its wake, to be discussed next.) Courts are not well equipped to assess the cohesiveness or effectiveness of many forms of speech that are intrinsically expressive, including not only parades, but also art and literature. As the Court in *Hurley* put it, an articulable message cannot be a precondition of free speech protection because, if so, it "would never reach the unquestionably shielded painting of Jackson Pollock, music of Arnold Schöenberg, or Jabberwocky verse of Lewis Carroll."[18]

The Court also appropriately emphasized that the council, although prohibiting gay organizations from parading under their own banners, did not exclude gay people as a whole from marching. The distinction between excluding organizations because of their professed views and excluding individuals because of their status is a generally valid one. For example, it is not clear that organizers of a parade discriminate on the basis of race or ethnicity if they prohibit racial equality groups from marching but permit African Americans, Latinos, and Asians to do so as individual members of "approved" organizations. Indeed, to attempt to apply a civil rights statute in such a situation seems, as the Court reasoned in *Hurley*, to turn the organizers' message of exclusion into the "place of public accommodation" subject to government regulation, an effort that cannot survive scrutiny under the First Amendment.

It is true that sexual orientation complicates the distinction between an exclusionary policy that is grounded in the excluded group's message and one based on the status of the excluded individuals. This is because sexual minorities often have to identify themselves in some way in order to make their presence known. It can be argued, therefore, that there is little difference, from an equality perspective, between completely excluding lesbians, gay men, and bisexuals from certain venues and allowing them to participate as long as they do not identify themselves as sexual minorities. This suggests that there may be something particularly invidious about a policy, like the council's exclusion of gay groups, that discourages individuals from conveying their sexual identity at a place of public accommodation.

However, the First Amendment difficulty arises because *the process through which LGBT individuals identify themselves is almost always an expressive one*. This is one of the lessons learned from the cases (such as the gay college student group lawsuits, some of the public employee cases, and the high school prom litigation) discussed in Part I in which courts concluded that the public self-identification of gay people in certain contexts contained sufficient expressive purpose and meaning so as to become eligible for protection under the First Amendment. If those cases were correctly decided, as almost everyone now agrees they were, that suggests that the outcome in *Hurley* was also the correct one. It is frequently the case that when LGBT people publicly identify themselves as such—as GLIB members clearly intended to do if they had been allowed to march in the St. Patrick Day's Parade under the organization's banner—they send a message in favor of inclusion of, and tolerance for, sexual minorities that may contradict the message of those who believe that such inclusion and tolerance is misguided or inappropriate. Although the government cannot constitutionally seek to silence the self-identification, it also cannot constitutionally seek to displace or limit speech that is in contradistinction to it.

Indeed, when *Hurley* is placed alongside the judicial rulings explored in Part I rejecting government efforts to silence the voices and expression of sexual minorities, it becomes clear that the Free Speech Clause demands government neutrality in regulating private expression as it relates to sexuality. As we saw in Part I, early LGBT equality proponents benefited immensely from the courts' general unwillingness to allow government actors to promote their understanding of sexual morality in ways that limited the ability of sexual minorities to speak, agitate, and associate. *Hurley* illustrates how constitutionally required governmental neutrality, in response to private expression in matters of sexuality, can help not only proponents of LGBT equality, but opponents as well. As the Court explained in *Hurley*, it is one thing for the government to demand that certain private entities not discriminate on the basis of sexual orientation (and other protected traits). It is another matter altogether for the government, in seeking to attain equality objectives, to attempt to alter the sexuality-related messages that those private entities wish to convey. In many ways, cases like *Hurley* are the (relatively limited) price that the LGBT movement has had to pay in order to enjoy the many (more) positive legal and political outcomes that have resulted from the type of government neutrality in these matters required by the First Amendment.

At first blush, *Hurley* seemed like a defeat for the LGBT movement because the Court interpreted the First Amendment in a way that allowed parade organizers to exclude gay organizations without incurring antidiscrimination liability. But the principle behind the ruling—that the First Amendment protects the right of private speakers to express their views on sexuality issues without governmental interference—is unassailable. It is that principle, as we saw in Part I, which permitted the early LGBT rights movement to successfully begin agitating for LGBT equality. Indeed, it is that principle that made possible the enactment of laws like the Massachusetts public accommodation antidiscrimination law at issue in *Hurley*. It is both appropriate and necessary, therefore, to keep the principle in mind when considering how the government's authority to promote equality should be limited.

This is not to suggest that the application of the principle in *Hurley* was straightforward. That application was complicated by the need to ascertain the impact of the forced inclusion of an LGBT rights group in a parade whose organizers had not before the lawsuit taken a clear position on questions of sexuality and LGBT equality. Indeed, a crucial part of the legal analysis required an exploration of the following question: Is it reasonable to believe that when an organization recognizes or admits LGBT groups or individuals, it sends a message of endorsement or support of pro-LGBT rights views? It is impossible to answer that question in the abstract because the ultimate conclusion depends on many different factors, including the organization's size, purposes, and selectivity, as well as, interestingly enough, how socially controversial the open presence of sexual minorities is at any given place and time.

As a general matter, the bigger the organization, the broader its purposes and objectives, and the less selective it is, the less reasonable it is to conclude that members of the public will believe that the presence of LGBT groups or individuals constitutes a form of endorsement or support by the organization. For example, the fact that the council welcomed the participation or sponsorship of dozens of groups that represented wide cross-sections of society, with different messages, priorities, and values, cut against the view that members of the public would have reasonably understood GLIB's participation in the parade as a manifestation of the council's endorsement or approval of pro-LGBT rights positions. At the same time, the growing success of the LGBT movement in increasing the visibility of sexual minorities throughout society at the time of *Hurley*, and the accompanying controversies engendered by that growing visibility, made it difficult for socially visible and important organizations to welcome LGBT people without being perceived as purposefully supporting greater toleration of sexual minorities.[19]

The passage of time can also be relevant in analyzing the social meaning of inclusion in two potentially countervailing ways. First, to the extent that the passage of time allows for social norms to become more tolerant of sexual minorities, then inclusion at a later time will be less likely to contain an implicit message of endorsement or support for pro-gay rights positions than an earlier inclusion. Second, it can be argued that if the inclusion is *legally mandated*, especially after a high-profile lawsuit, it is less reasonable to believe that the public will equate inclusion of members of a particular class with endorsement of the view that the class in question is entitled to certain rights and protections. But the passage of time may help to counteract this conclusion: the fact that the inclusion was legally required at an earlier point may, with the passage of time, become less culturally, socially, and politically salient, making it, in turn, more likely that the inclusion will later be interpreted as a form of approval or support, especially if the presence remains controversial. The complicated and shifting cultural, social, and political meanings associated with the presence of openly gay people in particular settings suggest that law professors Andrew Koppelman and Tobias Barrington Wolff may be correct when they argue that the question of whether the presence of openly gay people in certain settings conveys particular messages is one that sounds more in cultural anthropology than in law.[20]

In any event, it is clear that the courts, in applying the type of multifactor test called for by cases that pit constitutional rights to free speech and association against the state's interest in protecting the equality rights of its citizens, must be willing, in appropriate circumstances, to refuse to equate legally mandated inclusion of sexual minorities with the affected organizations' endorsement of pro-LGBT messages. For example, it was one thing to conclude, as the Court did in *Hurley*, that the general public in the 1990s could reasonably believe, after observing a gay organization march in a St. Patrick's Day parade under its own banner, that the parade's organizers favored tolerance toward sexual minorities. It would have been much more questionable for the Court to have concluded that reasonable observers would have deemed *the mere presence of a few openly gay individuals*, among the thousands of parade participants, as signaling the organizers' support for greater tolerance in matters of same-sex sexuality. And yet, that is precisely the type of odd reasoning that the Court embraced five years after *Hurley* in the Boy Scouts case.

The Boy Scouts

By the time the Supreme Court in 2000 addressed the question of whether a state civil rights law could be used to prohibit the Boy Scouts of America (BSA) from excluding gay scoutmasters, that organization had been involved in years of controversy and litigation regarding not only issues of sexual orientation, but also whether it could use gender and atheism as reasons for denying access to its leadership positions.[21] If the Boy Scouts had been a small sectarian organization, its exclusionary policies would have received much less public attention. But because the Boy Scouts was the country's largest youth organization, and because it had historically been associated with values, such as hard-work, courage, and determination, that were embraced by large and diverse segments of the American society, the controversies that surrounded its membership policies were the focus of much political, legal, and media attention.

James Dale joined the organization in 1978 at the age of eight as a Cub Scout in Monmouth County, New Jersey; he became a Boy Scout at the age of eleven; and when he turned eighteen, the BSA approved his application to be an assistant scoutmaster. At around this time, Dale left home to attend Rutgers University. While in college, Dale acknowledged to himself and others that he was gay. He eventually became copresident of the university's gay student group. In 1990, he attended a seminar on the health and psychological needs of LGBT teenagers. A reporter for the *Star-Ledger*, New Jersey's largest newspaper, was also present at the seminar. She wrote a story about the meeting that quoted Dale, included his picture, and identified him as copresident of the Rutgers gay student organization.[22]

Although the story did not mention either the Boy Scouts or Dale's participation in that organization, a few weeks later his local Boy Scouts Council sent him a letter stating that he would no longer be permitted to serve as an assistant scoutmaster. While the letter did not explain the reason for the council's decision, Dale later learned that it was because the newspaper story had identified him as a gay man.

The following year, New Jersey enacted a sexual orientation antidiscrimination law that, among other mandates, prohibited places of public accommodation from making distinctions on the basis of sexual orientation. Dale sued the BSA under the statute, seeking reinstatement. In defending itself, the BSA contended that it was not a place of public accommodation within the meaning of the New Jersey law and that, even if it was, it had a First Amendment right to exclude an "avowed homosexual and gay rights activist" such as Dale from the organization.[23]

The litigation lasted eight years and included a trial and three appeals, culminating with the U.S. Supreme Court's ruling in *Boy Scouts of America v. Dale*. During all that time, there was much disagreement between the two sides on the crucial, threshold question of whether the BSA had an official policy that deemed being gay to be inconsistent with the group's values and objectives. As already noted, the First Amendment does not allow the state to promote its equality objectives in ways that impair the ability of organizations and individuals to express their moral, religious, or political beliefs in matters related to sexuality. If the BSA's values and beliefs called for the condemnation of same-sex relationships and conduct, that strengthened its First Amendment defense to the antidiscrimination claim because it would bolster its argument that the forced admission of Dale would undermine its ability to determine and express its values without government interference.

In contrast, if condemnation of same-sex relationships and conduct were not connected to BSA's values and beliefs, then the First Amendment did not provide it with a safe harbor to discriminate. After all, the mere fact that an organization excludes individuals on the basis of sexual orientation (or race or gender) cannot be enough to afford it complete First Amendment immunity from antidiscrimination laws; otherwise, any entity that discriminates on any basis would be able to claim that the Constitution protects it from the reach of civil rights statutes.

The New Jersey Supreme Court ruled in Dale's favor. After concluding that the BSA was a place of public accommodation under New Jersey's expansive definition of that term, which covered entities that invite the public at large to join and that engage in advertising and public promotion, the state's high court proceeded to reject BSA's First Amendment defense.[24] But less than a year later, five members of the U.S. Supreme Court accepted the BSA's constitutional claim and overturned the state court's decision.

As a result of cases such as *Roberts v. United States Jaycees* (explored in Chapter 5), it was clear, by the time of *Dale*, that the freedom of association under the First Amendment protected the ability of expressive associations with antiegalitarian values to exclude entire classes of individuals. The organization usually used to illustrate this point is the Ku Klux Klan: the government cannot force the KKK to admit African Americans, Jews, and Catholics because that organization is constructed around an ideology of white and Protestant supremacy.

But the Supreme Court had also made clear that the Constitution does not protect the right of most organizations to discriminate in ways that interfered with the government's ability to promote meaningful racial equality. It was one thing for the KKK to have a constitutional right to discriminate on the basis of race because *its very purpose* was to promote the notion of white supremacy. But it was quite another thing to grant a constitutional right to discriminate to organizations, such as most unions, political parties, and private schools, whose purposes and objectives were not centered on the need to promote discriminatory values and beliefs. In cases involving all three of these types of organizations, the Court had either rejected or ignored the constitutional claim that the groups enjoyed First Amendment rights to discriminate on the basis of race.[25] Indeed, it would have been unfathomable for the Supreme Court in 2000 to have held that civil rights laws could not have been constitutionally applied to the Boy Scouts had that organization excluded scoutmasters on the basis of race.[26] As a result, the fact that the Court granted the Boy Scouts constitutional immunity to discriminate on the basis of sexual orientation raised the following perplexing question: Why would the First Amendment protect one viewpoint (that gay people, in the words of the Boy Scouts, were not "morally straight") from the application of civil rights laws while not protecting another viewpoint (that white people were superior to black people)?

During the course of the litigation, BSA contended that being gay was inconsistent with the provision in its Scout Oath that urged members to be "morally straight" and in its Scout Law that required them to be "clean." The difficulty for the BSA was that the *Boy Scouts Handbook* defined both terms *without mentioning sexuality*. According to the handbook, "morally straight" related to "honesty, purity, and justice" and showing respect for others, and "clean" referred to physical cleanliness and avoiding "foul language and harmful thoughts."[27] Nonetheless, a majority of Supreme Court justices concluded that it was for the BSA to determine whether being an "avowed homosexual" (as the Court put it) was inconsistent with being "morally straight" and "clean." The fact that BSA claimed during the litigation that there was such an inconsistency was enough for the Court to hold that the antidiscrimination law could not constitutionally be applied to it.

Similarly, the Court refused to question BSA's contention that the presence of a gay scoutmaster—who had never spoken about issues related to sexuality in general or about his sexual orientation in particular while engaged in Boy Scouts activities—affected the ability of an organization with close to five million members and hundreds of thousands of participating adults to express its values and views. For the Court, the fact that the Boy Scouts wanted to exclude gay men and that Dale was an "avowed homosexual" was enough to constitutionally protect the BSA's decision to terminate his relationship with the organization.[28] What the Court either ignored or missed was that its highly deferential posture toward an entity charged with illegal discrimination regarding the impact of the application of an antidiscrimination law on its ability to express itself made it possible, in theory, for any expressive association (commercial or noncommercial, large or small) to claim that being forced by the government to include a member of a class when the entity had (secular, ideological, moral, or religious) objections to the inclusion violated its First Amendment rights. The Court, in effect, held that if an expressive association claims, during the course of discrimination litigation, that the application of the antidiscrimination law in question is inconsistent with its values, that by itself constitutes a valid basis for a First Amendment right not to have to obey that law.

In assessing the soundness of the Court's holding, it is worth emphasizing that it likely would not have allowed a large organization such as the Boy Scouts, if it had wanted to exclude members on the basis of race, to use the exclusion itself as the basis for constitutional immunity from antidiscrimination laws. The Court's reasoning in *Dale* might be explained, therefore, by the fact that perhaps the majority viewed the elimination of sexual orientation discrimination as constituting an insufficiently important governmental interest, in contrast to the elimination of race discrimination, to justify requiring expressive associations to provide equal opportunities to sexual minorities against their will. But if that is what a majority of the justices believed, their ruling lacked the courage of their convictions because the opinion left the question of the importance of the government interest in eradicating sexual orientation discrimination completely unaddressed.

Although critics of *Roberts* have contended that the Court was too quick to conclude that the forced inclusion of women into the Junior Chamber of Commerce did not significantly affect the organization's ability to decide which messages to convey and which priorities to pursue, the *Roberts* Court at least dedicated several pages of its ruling to balancing the state's interest in combating gender discrimination against the impact of the enforcement of the civil rights law on the Jacyees's ability to express its views and attain its objectives.[29] In sharp contrast, the Court in *Dale* did not even acknowledge the existence of a state interest, compelling or otherwise, in addressing sexual orientation discrimination, much less engage in the type of balancing that its own precedent in *Roberts* required.

It is fortunate that, as a practical matter, *Dale* has had a limited impact. As Koppelman and Wolff have shown, lower courts in subsequent years limited its precedential value either by distinguishing the facts in *Dale* from those of the disputes before them or by being "unwilling to follow th[e] opinion's logic to its conclusions."[30] Furthermore, the Court in its unanimous 2006 ruling in *Rumsfeld v. FAIR* seemed determined to limit the scope of *Dale*. *Rumsfeld* involved a First Amendment challenge brought by law school administrators and faculty to the Solomon Amendment, a law that denied federal funds to educational institutions that barred the military from any of their campus' units. The challengers claimed that the Solomon Amendment impermissibly burdened their rights of free speech and association because it required them to facilitate military recruitment despite their support for LGBT equality and their objections to the military's Don't Ask, Don't Tell policy.[31] The Court disagreed, noting that the enforcement of the statute did not affect the challengers' ability to express their views on matters related to LGBT equality and military policy. In rejecting the challengers' claim, the Court in *Rumsfeld* walked itself back from the precipice created by its reasoning in *Dale* that a principled objection to the application of a law is a valid basis for a First Amendment right not to have to obey that law.

Even if improperly applied by the Court in *Dale*, it is important to keep in mind that the freedom of association has a proper role to play in limiting the authority of the state to promote equality: The government should not force expressive associations that hold clear antigay views to accept LGBT individuals as members. In such situations, the government would be requiring the organizations in question to send a message of tolerance in matters related to sexual orientation that they do not wish to send. The First Amendment, in our contemporary era of growing LGBT equality, requires the government to allow antigay expression by private organizations and individuals in the same way that it required the government, in earlier times of LGBT inequality, to allow progay expression by private parties.

Dale proved to be an exceedingly controversial case, as reflected not only in the justices' fractured 5 to 4 vote, but also in the extensive legal commentary that followed the case, some of which vigorously defended the Court's ruling and some of which forcefully criticized it.[32] Despite the disagreements about the appropriateness of the outcome in the case, there are two overarching principles that emanate from it. First, that organizations express themselves through their membership rules and rolls, and as a result, expressive associations with antigay views are constitutionally entitled to exclude LGBT people. The majority and the dissent did not disagree on this point; their disagreement instead centered on whether BSA had sufficiently articulated an antigay message so that it was entitled to First Amendment immunity from the application of sexual orientation antidiscrimination laws. Second, the Supreme Court, in recognizing the BSA's First Amendment rights, implicitly acknowledged what lower courts in earlier cases (involving gay college students, gay public employees, and the high school prom explored in Part I) had recognized: that the act of coming out by an LGBT person can be intrinsically expressive and imbued with political and social meaning.[33] Although the first principle clearly limits the ability of the state to promote LGBT equality, the second principle promotes that equality because it constitutionally protects the ability of LGBT people to express and assert their identities from governmental efforts to suppress them. *Dale*, then, encapsulates the ways in which the First Amendment both promotes and limits LGBT equality. The case, in other words, reflects the First Amendment's dual relationship with that equality.

Although many equality advocates were disappointed with the outcome in *Dale*, that outcome, in hindsight, seems to be an example of what law professor Douglas NeJaime has categorized, in assessing the impact of some litigation defeats on social movements, as "winning through losing."[34] It seems clear that, in the long run, the LGBT movement gained more than it lost as a result of its defeat in *Dale*. Although the BSA prevailed in its constitutional claim, it came at a steep price: the legal victory required the organization, for the first time in its history, to take explicit public positions in favor of excluding gay men. Prior to it being sued by Dale and other gay plaintiffs, BSA had what can be described fairly as an ambiguous policy with regards to the sexual orientation of its scoutmasters. That ambiguity had served the organization well as it tried to maintain the support of, and participation by, countless sponsors and families throughout the country, many of whom supported LGBT equality and many of whom did not. The organization's legal victory in *Dale* came at the price of losing its ability to remain purposefully ambiguous on controversial social issues associated with sexual orientation in order not to alienate either side in the gay culture wars. But following its victory before the Supreme Court, the BSA became a poster child for discrimination:

its by then clearly articulated exclusionary policy subjected it to severe criticism not only by LGBT activists, but also by elected officials, private charitable organizations, corporate funders, newspaper editorialists and columnists, parents of children in the Boy Scouts, and by many of its own members who disapproved of its discriminatory policy.[35]

If the BSA had lost in *Dale*, it would have been able to paint itself as the "victim" of coercive government efforts to promote equality at the expense of associational freedom. Instead, the BSA won its constitutional claim, but largely lost in the court of public opinion. Under mounting public pressure, the organization in 2013 considered lifting its categorical exclusion of gay men and youth by allowing local councils to decide whether to accept gays as leaders and scouts. The news that the organization was rethinking its categorical exclusionary policy led to a firestorm of opposition from many social and religious conservatives. As a result, the BSA decided instead to lift only the ban on membership by gay youth across the country.[36] But once the organization recognized that it was possible to be gay and a boy scout, and that therefore being gay was, in fact, not inconsistent with the group's understanding of what it means to be "morally straight" and "clean," it once again became vulnerable to antidiscrimination lawsuits by openly gay men who were denied the opportunity to serve as scoutmasters. As pressure continued to mount on the Boy Scouts, it decided in 2015 to no longer categorically prohibit gay men from serving as scoutmasters and instead to allow local councils to set their own policy on the issue.[37]

The events surrounding the Boy Scouts' exclusionary policy following *Dale* shows how the granting of antidiscrimination exemptions, at least in the case of highly visible organizations, allows, and perhaps even encourages, continued public scrutiny of discriminatory policies. In a society that is quickly moving toward greater acceptance of sexual minorities, that continued public attention usually works in favor of the LGBT rights movement. Indeed, after more than two decades of controversy and criticism, the organizers of the St. Patrick's Day parades in Boston and New York allowed LGBT groups to march in 2015 for the first time.[38] The changes in policies by the parade organizers and the Boy Scouts shows that the granting of exemptions to highly visible organizations does not necessarily prevent the attainment of equality objectives over the long run.[39]

Although the LGBT movement, in the case of the Boy Scouts, "won through losing," it is important not to minimize or ignore the harm that resulted from the Supreme Court's use of the First Amendment in *Dale* to limit the ability of the government to promote equality. As a result of that ruling, hundreds of highly qualified and capable gay men like James Dale were denied the opportunity to contribute their energy and talents to an organization aimed at improving and enriching the lives of millions of American boys. The denial, in turn, resulted in depriving countless numbers of those boys the benefits of learning from individuals whose ability to serve as leaders and role models, despite the BSA's vague suggestions to the contrary, was not affected by their sexual orientation. In addition, the Court's holding left in place an exclusionary policy that contributed to the stigmatization and sense of inferiority of the gay and bisexual boys in the organization. That policy communicated to those boys, loudly and unambiguously, that their sexual orientation rendered them less worthy and capable than their heterosexual peers. The fact that the Boy Scouts, many years after Dale filed his lawsuit, chose to allow local councils to decide whether gay men should be welcomed into the organization as leaders did not mitigate the harm that its categorical exclusionary policy inflicted on gay and bisexual youth for decades.

The Christian Legal Society

In 2004, a handful of students at the Hastings School of Law, a public law school within the University of California system, formed a local chapter of the Christian Legal Society, a national organization of Christian lawyers and law students. The national group required members of its chapters to sign a Statement of Faith and to abide by certain principles, including the belief that sexual conduct should only take place within marriage by a man and a woman. As such, the national organization required its chapters to exclude those who engaged in what it called "unrepentant homosexual conduct," as well as those whose religious views were inconsistent with its Statement of Faith.[40]

Shortly after the Hastings law students formed the Christian Legal Society chapter (CLS), they asked the school to recognize their group as a "registered student organization" (RSO). The law school provided RSOs with certain benefits, including financial assistance, the use of school channels of communication (such as newsletters and participation in a student fair used by student groups to recruit new members), and the use of the school's name and logo. In return for these benefits, Hastings required that RSOs be noncommercial, be composed only of students, and not discriminate on the basis of "race, color, religion, national origin, ancestry, disability, age, sex or sexual orientation." Although the law school did not provide the already-mentioned benefits to non-RSO student organizations, it did allow them to use its facilities for meetings, as well as its chalkboards and generally available bulletin boards to announce their events.

Hastings denied RSO status to CLS because the group barred students on the basis of sexual orientation and religion in violation of the school's nondiscrimination policy. The student group then formally asked the school to exempt it from that policy. In doing so, CLS became the first student group to ask for a waiver of the nondiscrimination policy since the school adopted it in 1990. Hastings denied the exemption request, leading CLS to file a federal lawsuit contending that the denial violated its rights to free speech, expressive association, and the free exercise of religion under the First Amendment. During the course of the litigation, the parties stipulated that Hastings interpreted its nondiscrimination policy to require all RSOs to accept all students who were interested in joining (the all-comers policy).[41] Although CLS was unwilling to change its admission criteria in order to gain RSO status, the group continued to operate in the absence of school recognition by, for example, holding meetings on campus, sponsoring a lecture on Christian values, and organizing social events.[42]

After losing in the lower federal courts, CLS persuaded the Supreme Court to hear its case. More than a decade earlier, the Court had considered an appeal involving a First Amendment challenge brought by a Christian student group at the University of Virginia following the school's decision to deny it funds, collected from student fees, to help defray costs associated with printing and distributing the group's magazine. Although the university made funds available to other student organizations for a wide range of purposes, it did not grant the requested benefit to the Christian group on the ground that doing so would impermissibly fund religious activities in violation of the Establishment Clause. The Court, in *Rosenberger v. University of Virginia*, concluded that the university, by agreeing to fund the activities of many student groups, had created a "limited public forum."[43]

As explained in Chapter 2, the modifier "limited" is used to distinguish traditional public forums, such as streets and parks, from other government-created forums in which it encourages or allows the expression of views. The Court applies strict scrutiny to regulations that limit access to traditional public forums (unless the regulations are neutral on their face).[44] In contrast, the Court upholds access restrictions that apply to limited public forums as long as they are reasonable and viewpoint neutral. In *Rosenberger*, the Court held that the exclusion of the Christian student group from the limited public forum was not viewpoint neutral because it was grounded in the fact that the organization's message was a religious one. The Court also held that the university's disbursement of funds to help pay for the publication of the religious group's magazine did not violate the Establishment Clause.

A majority of the Court in *Christian Legal Society v. Martinez* thought it appropriate to apply the *Rosenberger* analysis to Hastings's RSO scheme, which everyone involved in the litigation agreed constituted a limited public forum.[45] The Court concluded that the all-comers policy was reasonable because (1) it ensured that the educational, social, and leadership opportunities offered by the law school were available to all students and (2) encouraged tolerance and cooperation among students. The policy also permitted the school to implement its nondiscrimination requirement in ways that avoided the administratively cumbersome process of trying to determine the reasons (for example, whether because of status or because of belief) why particular organizations might exclude particular students. In addition, the Court concluded that the all-comers policy, because it applied to all the organizations and protected all students, was by definition viewpoint neutral. All student groups, regardless of their ideologies and objectives, had to abide by the policy.

The Court also noted that unlike the public accommodation law at issue in *Dale*, the policy challenged by CLS did not require the organization to admit members it did not want to admit. Instead, the policy implicated the question of how a public entity allocates subsidies. In deciding how to distribute subsidies, the school could constitutionally condition the funds on student groups agreeing not to turn away students who were interested in joining. As the Court explained, it was constitutionally relevant that "Hastings, through its RSO program, is dangling the carrot of subsidy, not wielding the stick of prohibition."[46]

There are some clear parallels between the CLS lawsuit and the gay student group cases from the 1970s discussed in Chapter 2. Like CLS, the gay student groups sued under the First Amendment after some public universities refused to recognize them. In addition, CLS had views on questions of sexual morality that departed significantly from prevailing majoritarian views in some areas around the country (including in San Francisco, where Hastings is located). Similarly, the gay student organizations in the years following Stonewall advocated views on sexuality that departed significantly from the views of the majority in society.

However, there is a crucial difference between the CLS case and the prior gay student group disputes: the earlier cases arose because the universities in question targeted the gay groups for differential treatment based on their beliefs. The school administrators in those cases made clear that they disagreed with, and disapproved of, the gay groups' views, and worried that recognition of the groups amounted to university support or endorsement of those views. In contrast, Hastings did not adopt its nondiscrimination policy in order to target or silence its conservative Christian students. Indeed, the fact that the policy prohibited discrimination on the basis of religion shows that the school aimed, in part, to *protect* religious students. The law school denied CLS the benefits of RSO status not because of its members' views, but because of its decision to engage in exclusionary conduct. As the Court noted in *Hurley*, antidiscrimination regulations "do not, as a general matter, violate the First or Fourteenth Amendments [because they do] not, on [their] face, target speech or discriminate on the basis of its content, the focal point of [their] prohibition being rather on the act of discriminating against individuals . . . on the proscribed grounds."[47]

The crucial difference in the government's objective in *Christian Legal Society* and its aim in the earlier cases involving gay student groups can be further elucidated through the following hypothetical: Suppose the gay student groups in the 1970s had decided to exclude heterosexual students from their organizations and that some public universities had denied them recognition solely on that basis. It seems clear that school administrators would have been on much firmer constitutional ground if they had refused to recognize gay student groups because of their exclusion of heterosexual students (to say nothing of African-American or Catholic students) rather than, as actually happened, because of their progay messages.

The difference between targeting viewpoints or beliefs and targeting conduct is crucial in assessing the constitutionality of regulations under the First Amendment. Indeed, it is worth noting that the Solomon Amendment, the statute at issue in *Rumsfeld v. FAIR* that denied federal funding to educational institutions that did not permit the military to recruit students on their campuses, was an equal access law comparable to antidiscrimination regulations in that it aimed to deter exclusionary conduct. The Solomon Amendment, like Hastings's nondiscrimination policy, required recipients of government subsidies to abstain from excluding certain individuals. The government's objective was similar in both cases: to deter the exclusion of military recruiters (in *Rumsfeld*) and law students (in *Christian Legal Society*). Equal access laws aimed at exclusionary conduct rather than at viewpoints or beliefs do not violate the First Amendment. As Chief Justice John Roberts explained in *Rumsfeld*, "the Solomon Amendment regulates conduct, not speech. It affects what law schools must do—afford equal access to military recruiters—not what they may or may not say." Roberts added that the law "neither limits what law schools may say nor requires them to say anything."[48] Similarly, Hastings's all-comers policy was aimed at discouraging discriminatory conduct rather than targeting the ability of student organizations to express their views.

Law professors Erwin Chemerinsky and Catherine Fisk correctly note that "antidiscrimination laws are motivated by and targeted toward ending harmful conduct, not toward silencing the view that discrimination is desirable." Although it is the case that prohibiting discrimination has an impact on discriminatory conduct engaged in for expressive purposes (conduct aimed, in part, at expressing racial or gender superiority, for example), the effect is an incidental one "just as laws that prohibit nudity or peyote use have the incidental effect of prohibiting nudity and peyote use where they are expressive. . . . If discrimination is inherently expressive such that antidiscrimination laws are necessarily targeted toward silencing that expression, then all antidiscrimination laws are constitutionally suspect."[49] Law professor Robert Post makes a similar point when he notes that, under the First Amendment, "requiring that bakers or landlords not discriminate against patrons is paradigmatically categorized as a simple regulation of conduct. It does not matter whether the owner of an inn regards leasing rooms as expressive; First Amendment coverage is not triggered by the application of a general rule requiring landlords to lease rooms without discrimination. First Amendment doctrine does not conceive these kinds of conduct regulations as preventing or inhibiting expression, political or otherwise."[50]

Rumsfeld and *Christian Legal Society*, then, stand for an important limitation in First Amendment restrictions on the state's authority to promote equality: When the government seeks to promote equality through the allocation of subsidies, the First Amendment allows it to take into account discriminatory conduct on the part of potential recipients.[51] At the same time, the First Amendment prohibits the government from interfering with the ability of associations to express their views. It therefore mattered that CLS members were free to believe whatever they wanted about the intersection of Christian doctrine and sexuality. It was also crucial that the organization and its members were free to express those beliefs in a myriad of ways, both inside and outside the law school, including by trying to persuade their fellow students through discussions and debates, inviting guest speakers, distributing publications, and posting their views on the Internet. The one thing they could not do, and still be eligible for law school subsidies, was to exclude other students from the organization.

The CLS argued throughout the litigation that the application of the school's policy constituted viewpoint discrimination, in violation of the First Amendment, because the policy had a disparate impact on conservative religious groups, a claim that the dissenting justices agreed with.[52] To put it simply, CLS contended that the effect of the law school's policy aimed at guaranteeing inclusion for all was to place greater burdens on organizations with views that departed from the mainstream. The position taken by CLS was consistent with that taken by those who claim that LGBT equality measures, in effect, discriminate against entities and individuals that abide by traditional religious values. As one supporter of this view argues, "gay-rights laws (in marriage or other contexts) may be facially neutral and generally applicable, but like other generally applicable laws their effects fall disproportionately on those religious individuals and groups—in this case, religious traditionalists—whose practices conflict with them."[53]

It is correct, as a factual and logical matter, that laws which prohibit discrimination place greater burdens on those who would like to exclude individuals belonging to groups protected by those laws. That is the way antidiscrimination laws work: they require those who want to exclude to modify their conduct by admitting rather than excluding, while they leave undisturbed the conduct of those who do not wish to exclude. If courts were to accept the proposition that the "disparate impact" arising from the application of antidiscrimination laws on those who dissent from their mandates constitutes grounds, under the First Amendment, for constitutionally exempting the dissenters from their scope, it would bring the application of antidiscrimination law, as we know it, to a grinding halt. This is because antidiscrimination laws, by definition, have a greater impact on those who engage in the proscribed differential treatment than on those who do not.

Hastings's nondiscrimination policy was not intended to penalize groups like CLS for their views. This lack of intent matters both legally and morally. It matters legally because, under the Supreme Court's interpretation of the First Amendment, the purposeful targeting of speakers due to the content of their speech almost never survives constitutional scrutiny, whereas facially neutral regulations that are not intended to squelch particular viewpoints almost always survive that scrutiny, even when the regulations have a greater impact on some speakers than on others.[54] It matters morally because the government acts unjustly when it targets speakers because it disapproves of their views and beliefs. In contrast, the government does not act unjustly when, in attempting to ensure equal treatment for traditionally subordinated groups, it adopts nondiscrimination regulations that have a greater impact on some than on others.

The first, and most important, difference between the CLS case and the earlier gay student group disputes, then, is that university administrators in the earlier cases targeted the gay groups because of their beliefs. A second difference is that the gay student groups in the earlier cases demanded equal treatment from their universities—that is, they did not ask for an exemption from a generally applicable rule; instead, they argued that the First Amendment required the university to apply the same recognition criteria that it applied to other student organizations. In contrast, CLS's claim was based on the assertion that the law school had a constitutional obligation to exempt it from the nondiscrimination requirement that applied to all other student groups. Whereas the gay groups in the earlier cases demanded equal treatment, CLS requested a special exemption.

The fact that CLS demanded an exemption also has legal and moral implications. As a legal matter, the Court has made clear (as we will explore in Chapter 7) that the Free Exercise Clause does not require the government to exempt religious believers from generally applicable and neutral laws.[55] Antidiscrimination laws fall under this category because they are broadly applicable and do not target religious exercise.

As a moral matter, a claim (such as the one made by the gay student groups in the earlier cases) that says "treat me like everyone else" has greater normative force than one that says, in effect, "you can apply this regulation to everyone else, but not to me." Exemptions, by their very nature, relieve their beneficiaries from obligations that everyone else must comply with and, as a result, they entail a claim to preferential treatment. This does not mean that religious exemptions are always problematic and should never be granted; but it does mean that courts and legislatures should grant them carefully and sparingly, especially in the context of antidiscrimination laws.

The next chapter addresses in much more detail questions related to religious exemptions from LGBT equality measures. I want to end this chapter by making the point that although I believe the Supreme Court was correct in concluding that CLS was not *constitutionally entitled* to an exemption from the law school's antidiscrimination policy, the question of whether school administrators, in their discretion, should have granted the exemption is a different one. I believe the law school should have granted the exemption for three reasons. First, as a practical matter, it was unlikely that openly gay, lesbian, or bisexual students would have been interested in joining an organization that morally condemned same-sex relationships. As a result, it was unlikely that the granting of the exemption would have led to actual discrimination against LGBT students.

Second, in the unlikely event that CLS would have had the opportunity to turn away LGBT students who expressed interest in joining the organization, the injury experienced by those students would have been different in kind and in degree from the harm suffered by sexual minorities when employers deny them jobs or when places of public accommodation refuse to provide services to them because of their sexual orientation. Membership in a student organization enjoyed while attending an educational institution does not carry with it the same economic, social, and dignitary importance as finding employment or being served by places of public accommodation without fear of discrimination.

Finally, although it may be reasonable for government officials to be concerned that granting religious exemptions from antidiscrimination policies to one organization may lead other groups to request exemptions, thus threatening the objectives of those policies, that concern did not seem particularly pressing in the CLS case. This is because it was unlikely that many other law student organizations at Hastings would have been interested in excluding sexual minorities on religious grounds. Indeed, as already noted, no student group other than CLS had ever requested an exemption from the school's nondiscrimination policy on any grounds. All of this makes it likely that administrators could have granted CLS an exemption from the nondiscrimination policy without exposing gay, lesbian, and bisexual students to a meaningful risk of harmful discrimination.

This chapter has explored some of the ways in which the First Amendment can limit the ability of the government to promote LGBT equality. We have seen that the First Amendment's demand that the state remain neutral vis-à-vis private expression on matters of sexuality, a neutrality that was extremely helpful to the early LGBT rights movement, prohibits the state from promoting equality by requiring expressive associations to admit LGBT individuals when doing so conveys a message that is inconsistent with the associations' values and beliefs. We have also seen that the balancing of free speech/association and equality considerations in this area sometimes requires the making of difficult assessments regarding the impact of forced inclusion of sexual minorities on the ability of organizations to express themselves as they wish on issues related to sexuality. Finally, we have explored how the First Amendment distinguishes, in the context of government subsidies, between unprotected discriminatory conduct and protected expression that seeks to defend the differential treatment of sexual minorities.

CHAPTER SEVEN

Marriage Equality and Religious Liberty

I N 2006, Misti Collinsworth and Vanessa Willock, a lesbian couple living in New Mexico, began planning a commitment ceremony. In doing so, they went online and found a photography business in Albuquerque called Elane Photography. The website contained sample wedding photographs taken by Elaine Huguenin, who had opened the business with her husband six months earlier, as well as information about her experience with and approach to photography.

Having liked what she saw on the website, Willock wrote an email: "We are researching potential photographers for our commitment ceremony on September 27, 2007, in Taos, New Mexico. This is a same-gender ceremony. If you are open to helping us celebrate our day we'd like to receive pricing information. Thanks." Unbeknown to Willock and Collinsworth, the Huguenins had religious objections to marriages by same-sex couples and had agreed between themselves not to photograph events that were inconsistent with their religious views. A few hours after receiving Willock's email, Elaine Huguenin wrote back: "Hello Vanessa. As a company, we photograph traditional weddings, engagements, seniors, and several other things such as political photographs and singer's portfolios. Elaine."[1]

Willock was unsure whether Huguenin's message meant that Elane Photography did not provide its services to same-sex couples. Two months later, she wrote again: "Hi Elaine. Thanks for your response below of September 21, 2006. I'm a bit confused, however, by the wording of your response. Are you saying that your company does not offer photography services to same-sex couples? Thanks. Vanessa." That same day, Huguenin replied with a clarifying message: "Hello Vanessa. Sorry if our last response was a confusing one. Yes, you are correct in saying we do not photograph same-sex weddings, but again, thanks for checking out our site! Have a great day. Elaine."[2]

In an effort to determine whether Huguenin would respond differently to a potential customer who did not reveal her sexual orientation, Collinsworth the next day emailed Huguenin to inquire whether she would photograph her upcoming wedding, without mentioning the sex of her partner. Huguenin wrote back stating that she would be happy to provide her services. The message also included pricing information and an offer to meet to discuss the matter further.

A few weeks later, Willock filed a charge against Elane Photography with the New Mexico Human Rights Division, arguing that the company had violated the state law prohibiting places of public accommodation from discriminating on the basis of sexual orientation. Her complaint asked that the division order the business to cease discriminating and require it to reimburse her for attorney fees and costs. After the state agency ruled in Willock's favor, Elane Photography appealed to a trial court, an intermediary appellate court, and then to the state supreme court, arguing at each stage that application of the antidiscrimination law violated its constitutional rights to free speech and the free exercise of religion because the Huguenins opposed same-sex marriages on religious grounds.

The speech claim was based on the assertion that the First Amendment protects intrinsically expressive activity like photography and that by forcing the business to take photographs at a same-sex commitment ceremony, the state was compelling it to speak in ways it did not want to speak. The religious claim was based on the proposition that religious freedom protections required the state to exempt the Huguenins's business from the application of the civil rights law because the couple had religious-based reasons for withholding their services to same-sex couples.

All nine judges who heard the case, at both the trial and appellate levels, rejected Elane Photography's speech and religious freedom arguments. In doing so, they explained that the government did not require the Huguenins to speak against their will; instead, the government required them, once they chose to make their photography services available to the general public, not to make distinctions based on the customers' race, sex, sexual orientation, and other protected traits. As the state supreme court explained, "if Elane Photography took photographs on its own time and sold them at a gallery, or if it was hired by certain clients but did not offer its services to the general public, the law would not apply to [its] choice of whom to photograph or not."[3] In addition, the New Mexico courts pointed out that the government is not constitutionally required to provide exemptions to laws, such as antidiscrimination statutes, that are generally applicable and do not target religious beliefs.[4]

For many conservatives, *Elane Photography* crystallized their worst fears about the application of sexual orientation antidiscrimination laws at a time of increasing acceptance of marriage equality. Critics claimed that to force individuals who believe, on religious grounds, that same-sex marriages are morally wrong to participate in the celebration of such marriages is to require them to be complicit in the committing of a moral wrong. From this perspective, when the state mandates that business owners who have religious objections to same-sex marriages provide goods and services in ways that assist in the celebration of those unions, it violates their rights to religious liberty.

Social and religious conservatives in the last years of marriage inequality in the United States engaged in a concerted, two-prong campaign: first, they continued arguing, as they had for decades, that the state should only allow opposite-sex couples to marry; and second, they repeatedly claimed that marriage equality threatened the religious liberty rights of those who believe that same-sex marriages are morally wrong. Although the first part of the campaign aimed to prevent the government from granting same-sex couples the opportunity to marry altogether, the second part sought to limit the impact and effect of such recognition.[5] As the number of states that allowed same-sex couples to marry increased, social and religious conservatives became more vehement about the need to enact broad exemptions from sexual orientation antidiscrimination obligations for individuals and entities that oppose same-sex marriage on religious grounds.

Supporters of religious exemptions argue that to force business owners to provide goods and services in ways that violate their religious beliefs is to discriminate against those of religious faith. After all, the same-sex couple in *Elane Photography* was free to choose another provider of photography services for their commitment ceremony, as they in fact did. From the perspective of exemption supporters, the government presented the Huguenins with a Hobson's choice: they either had to provide the photography services to the lesbian couple in contravention of their deeply held religious beliefs or they had to close their business. As a result, the argument goes, the real victims of discrimination in these cases are business owners of religious faith, not LGBT people.

The country's increased willingness to embrace liberal norms in matters of sexuality—including not only those related to same-sex relationships and conduct, but also those affecting heterosexuals (such as the engaging in sex outside of marriage and the use of contraceptives)—has led many conservative religious Americans to feel besieged and vulnerable. Religious conservatives have come to see many of the government's social policies that depart from traditional understandings of sexual morality as threats to their religious freedom. As a declaration signed by more than 150 interdenominational leaders of Christian Orthodox, Catholic, and Evangelical churches and organization puts it, "it is ironic that those who today assert a right to kill the unborn, aged and disabled and also a right to engage in immoral sexual practices, and even a right to have relationships integrated around these practices be recognized and blessed by law—such persons claiming these 'rights' are very often in the vanguard of those who would trample upon the freedom of others to express their religious and moral commitments to the sanctity of life and to the dignity of marriage as the conjugal union of husband and wife."[6] The United States Conference of Catholic Bishops made a similar point when it stated, in a Supreme Court amicus brief filed in *Obergefell v. Hodges*, that while a ruling striking down same-sex marriage "might enhance the equal treatment of gays and lesbians, [it would do so] by subtracting from the First Amendment liberties of religious institutions and believers."[7]

Elane Photography was only one of several contentious disputes pitting LGBT equality against religious liberty that arose as the nation began embracing full legal equality for sexual minorities. Not all of the clashes between the promotion of LGBT equality and claims to religious liberty revolved around the recognition and celebration of same-sex relationships. In Massachusetts, for example, Catholic Charities in 2006 stopped providing adoption services rather than comply with a state law prohibiting adoption agencies from discriminating on the basis of sexual orientation in adoption placements.[8] Five years later, the Illinois Catholic Charities stopped taking state money to provide adoption and foster care services rather than assist lesbians and gay men with becoming parents. In explaining the organization's decision, the bishop of Springfield, Illinois, complained that "in the name of tolerance, we are not being tolerated."[9]

But most of the LGBT rights controversies raising questions of religious freedom have arisen in the context of the recognition or celebration of same-sex unions. In 2007, for example, a dispute arose in New Jersey when an association affiliated with the Methodist Church, which rented out its beachfront boardwalk pavilion to members of the public for many different kinds of events and celebrations including marriages, refused to permit a same-sex couple to celebrate their civil union at its facility.[10] In addition, like the Huguenins, several religious owners of wedding-related businesses (such as florists and bakers), objecting to marriages by same-sex couples on religious grounds, have refused to provide their services to lesbian and gay couples.[11] Furthermore, some government employees with similar religious views have argued that they should be exempt from having to issue marriage licenses to same-sex couples.

Questions related to religious exemptions have lately received an immense amount of attention from elected officials, conservative and liberal activists, and the media. The topic has also been the subject of several books and dozens of scholarly articles. I cannot in one chapter address all of the legal, political, and moral complexities raised by religious exemptions. As a result, this chapter has two modest objectives: First, to explain, as a descriptive matter, when, how, and why issues of religious freedom became part of marriage equality debates in the United States. As a legal matter, for reasons explained in the first part of the chapter, the question of whether those who object to marriages by same-sex couples on religious grounds are entitled to exemptions from antidiscrimination obligations is largely one of legislative discretion rather than constitutional obligation. In matters related to LGBT equality, as the middle part of the chapter explains, exemption supporters have attempted to gain accommodations through two types of statutes in particular: laws recognizing the right of same-sex couples to marry and so-called religious liberty statutes. This part of the chapter also includes a discussion of the implications for questions related to religious exemptions from LGBT equality of *Obergefell v. Hodges* and *Burwell v. Hobby Lobby*. In the first case, the Supreme Court held that same-sex couples have a constitutional right to marry; in the second, it ruled that privately held, for-profit corporations have religious exercise rights under the federal Religious Freedom Restoration Act.

The chapter's second objective is to defend the proposition that, in accommodating religious dissenters from legal obligations arising from marriage equality, it is neither necessary nor appropriate to depart significantly from the traditional ways in which American antidiscrimination law has for decades accommodated the views of those who dissent from the attainment of equality objectives on religious grounds.[12] In defending this proposition, the last part of the chapter details five important characteristics of the ways in which American antidiscrimination law, before the advent of same-sex marriage, sought to accommodate religious dissent while pursuing equality objectives. In my view, those principles should guide the determination of how the law should accommodate religious dissent in the context of LGBT equality.

The last part of the chapter also critiques two arguments raised frequently by supporters of expansive religious exemptions in the context of LGBT rights: first, that it is frequently possible to exempt religious actors from sexual orientation antidiscrimination obligations without harming sexual minorities; and second, that religious exemptions in the context of sexual orientation merit more serious consideration than in that of race because most religious actors who believe, on conscience grounds, that it is proper to make distinctions on the basis of sexual orientation act in good faith (that is, they are not homophobic), while those who believe it is proper to make racial distinctions always act in bad faith (that is, they are racists).

As explained in Chapter 5, there is nothing new or distinct about the clash between equality goals and liberty norms that our nation is currently working through in the context of LGBT rights. Indeed, the country, since the Civil War, has repeatedly struggled with how to balance the pursuit of antidiscrimination objectives and the protection of liberty interests, including those related to religious freedom. Although it is certainly possible to criticize particular policy outcomes arising from that balancing, the basic approach of American antidiscrimination law to questions of religious exemptions is reasonable, has worked well, and is time tested. There is no need to develop new exemption regimes for implementing LGBT antidiscrimination measures that depart from the framework that is already in place for racial and gender discrimination. In other words, there is no need for LGBT rights exceptionalism in matters related to religious exemptions.

Religious Exemptions and the Free Exercise Clause

As interpreted by the Supreme Court, the Constitution does not require the government to accommodate religious actors when implementing neutral and generally applicable laws. The Court made this clear in a 1990 case called *Employment Division v. Smith*.[13] That lawsuit raised the question of whether the Free Exercise Clause entitled individuals who ingested peyote for sacramental purposes as part of religious ceremonies at their Native American church to an exemption from the application of a state law that criminalized the drug's use. In writing for the Court, Justice Antonin Scalia rejected the notion that "religious motivation" for engaging in conduct immunizes that conduct from the application of an otherwise valid law. Scalia reasoned that "the government's ability to enforce generally applicable prohibitions of socially harmful conduct, like its ability to carry out other aspects of public policy, cannot depend on measuring the effects of a governmental action on a religious objector's spiritual development."[14]

Part of the Court's concern in *Smith* was that there seemed to be no limits to the types of neutral and generally applicable laws that might incidentally burden the ability of individuals to live according to their religious principles, including tax laws, health and safety regulations, social welfare legislation, environmental regulations, and "laws providing for equality of opportunity for the races." To argue that all those laws were presumptively invalid when they conflicted with the religious views of some individuals, Scalia reasoned, was a recipe for "courting anarchy," especially in a society, such as the American one, with a rich multiplicity of religious beliefs.[15]

For the *Smith* Court, the question of whether to exempt religious objectors from neutral and generally applicable laws was an issue of legislative policy rather than constitutional mandate. The Court acknowledged that its holding left religious believers who have conscience-based objections to certain laws at the mercy of majoritarian will, an outcome that might particularly disadvantage small religious communities that lack political clout. But, Scalia noted, "that unavoidable consequence of democratic government must be preferred to a system in which each conscience is a law unto itself or in which judges weigh the social importance of all laws against the centrality of all religious beliefs."[16]

The *Smith* case serves as a crucial backdrop to the question of religious exemptions from LGBT equality laws. Those laws are neutral and generally applicable. Neither sexual orientation antidiscrimination laws nor marriage equality ones target religious beliefs or conduct. Both sets of laws also generally impose legal obligations on wide sectors of society. It is true, of course, that some individuals believe that complying with LGBT antidiscrimination laws, especially in the context of marriage equality, is inconsistent with their religious values. But the existence of such "incidental" effects (a term relied on by the Court in its First Amendment cases to describe the effects of otherwise valid laws that are not intended to target expression or belief) is not enough to render unconstitutional the application of antidiscrimination laws to individuals who object to them on conscience grounds.[17]

The bottom line is this: the federal Constitution does not generally require that either legislatures or courts grant exemptions to those who object to LGBT equality laws on religious grounds. The exceptions to this general principle are relatively narrow and straightforward. One such exception is reflected in the "ministerial exception," which deprives the government of the authority to prohibit religious organizations to discriminate in their choice of ministers. As a result of that exception, the government cannot require, for example, a religious organization that believes same-sex relationships are sinful to hire a minister who is in such a relationship. In addition, although the case has never arisen, it seems clear that the government cannot constitutionally require houses of worship and ministers to solemnize marriages that are inconsistent with their religious views. Outside of the relatively narrow contexts of how religious organizations hire ministers and which relationships they choose to solemnize and sanctify, the Free Exercise Clause, after *Smith*, does not require the government to exempt those who object to same-sex relationships or conduct on religious grounds from LGBT equality laws.

To the extent, then, that the law should provide religious exemptions to religious dissenters from LGBT equality, it must do so as a result of legislative choice rather than constitutional mandate. This is one of the reasons, as we will see later in the chapter, why many of the controversies over religious exemptions to LGBT equality measures have arisen in the context of laws that seek to "restore" religious freedom following *Smith*. Given the importance of these measures in recent LGBT rights debates, it is helpful to explore briefly Congress's enactment in 1993 of the first such law.

The Religious Freedom Restoration Act

The Court's ruling in *Smith* was met with strong criticism from many religious leaders, legal academics, and elected officials across the political spectrum. Those who prioritized religious liberty claimed that the Court was insufficiently cognizant of the ways in which generally applicable laws (from health regulations to zoning laws) could interfere with the ability of individuals of faith to exercise their religion. And those who prioritized equality and nondiscrimination protections for people of all faiths criticized the Court for leaving religious minorities, who generally lack the political power to gain statutory exemptions, at the mercy of legislatures. The widespread dissatisfaction with *Smith* led Congress to enact the Religious Freedom Restoration Act of 1993 (RFRA), a bill that received overwhelming congressional support (only three senators voted against the measure, while the House passed it on a voice vote) and was supported by President Bill Clinton, who enthusiastically signed it into law. The new federal statute prohibited the government from enforcing a generally applicable rule that substantially burdened a person's exercise of religion unless it could show that the regulation advanced a compelling state interest and constituted the least restrictive means of attaining that interest, that is, that it restricted religious exercise as little as possible.[18]

Although Congress intended for RFRA to apply to all levels of government, the Supreme Court held in *City of Boerne v. Flores* that Congress lacked the constitutional authority, under the Fourteenth Amendment, to make the statute applicable to state and local governments.[19] As a result, RFRA only restricts the actions of the federal government.

In order to address this gap in the law, nineteen states during the 1990s enacted their own versions of RFRA. No state legislature passed such a bill again until Arizona and Mississippi did so in 2014, and Arkansas and Indiana in 2015. By that time, as explored later in this chapter, religious freedom statutes had become inextricably and controversially linked to the question of LGBT rights and marriage equality. This was because those who supported religious exemptions came to see religious freedom laws as crucial sources of protection for small business owners (such as the photographer in *Elane Photography v. Willock*) and other individuals who had religious-based objections to facilitating same-sex marriages. In contrast, opponents of such exemptions came to see the religious freedom laws as threats to the hard-earned equality gains of sexual minorities.

Given that the expansion of marriage equality across the country led to heated controversies in many states over whether it was appropriate to use religious freedom laws to carve out exemptions from the application of LGBT equality measures, it is helpful to explore whether the members of Congress who voted for RFRA intended for that statute to limit the scope of antidiscrimination laws. The provision's language would seem to make it applicable to all rules of "general applicability" because it does not contain an exception for antidiscrimination laws (or any other generally applicable laws). There are several reasons to believe, however, that Congress did not intend RFRA to limit the scope of antidiscrimination laws. First, the only reference to antidiscrimination laws in RFRA's Senate and House committee reports made clear that it was *not* the committees' intent for the statute to apply to the Civil Rights Act of 1964.[20] Second, the subject of antidiscrimination laws and their impact on religious observants did not arise during the bill's lengthy floor debates. Although those discussions referred to several different types of laws and regulations that would be subject to RFRA, no legislator suggested that the measure applied to antidiscrimination laws. Instead, bill supporters focused on the burdens imposed on religious believers by other types of regulations, including zoning laws that excluded places of worship from residential neighborhoods, regulations requiring autopsies over the religious objections of survivors, road safety regulations that required the Amish to affix lights and bright warning signs on their buggies in violation of their religious principles, and food preparation regulations that impacted some religious groups like Orthodox Jews.[21]

Finally, it seems highly unlikely that congressional liberals (such as Senator Ted Kennedy of Massachusetts, one of the bill's cosponsors and strongest proponents) would have supported legislation intended to limit the scope of civil rights laws. Indeed, the bill attracted the support of liberals precisely because they viewed it as a measure aimed primarily at *preventing* discrimination—especially against small religious denominations that, although lacking much political power on their own, reflected America's rich religious diversity—rather than allowing it. In short, there is no legislative history suggesting that Congress intended RFRA to apply to civil rights laws.[22]

Although there is no evidence that Congress believed RFRA would limit the scope of antidiscrimination laws, the same cannot be said about its consideration in 1999 of the Religious Liberty Protection Act (RLPA). That bill sought to provide protection for religious exercise in the application of state and local laws. (Bill supporters hoped to work around the Court's ruling in *City of Flores v. Boerne* by relying on Congress's authority to legislate under the Commerce and Spending Clauses rather than the Fourteenth Amendment.) But the broad consensus that led to the easy passage of RFRA six years earlier had evaporated by the time Congress considered RLPA. The biggest source of contention was the new bill's implications for issues of civil rights in general and LGBT equality in particular.

Much happened in the area of LGBT rights between Congress's enactment of RFRA in 1993 and its consideration of RLPA in 1999. First, the Hawai'i Supreme Court issued a ruling questioning the constitutionality of same-sex marriage bans, leading to a powerful conservative backlash as reflected, most prominently, in the passage of the Defense of Marriage Act of 1996.[23] (We will return to these developments in the next section.) Second, the Supreme Court struck down a Colorado constitutional amendment that would have deprived lesbians, gay men, and bisexuals, but no others, of the protections afforded by antidiscrimination regulations.[24] Third, several states and many municipalities enacted laws prohibiting discrimination on the basis of sexual orientation. Finally, a federal appellate court held that the Free Exercise Clause protected religious landlords who objected to cohabitation outside of marriage from laws that prohibited housing discrimination on the basis of marital status.[25] This ruling was of great concern to civil rights proponents because it suggested that the Constitution granted religious individuals a right to discriminate.

In short, what had been possible in 1993—to debate a law aimed at protecting rights to religious liberty without considering its impact on the enforcement of antidiscrimination laws in general and LGBT equality measures in particular—had become impossible by 1999. Liberal organizations like the ACLU, which had enthusiastically supported RFRA six years earlier, withheld their support from RLPA unless legislators amended the bill to limit its possible impact on the enforcement of civil rights laws.[26] Representative Jerrold Nadler of New York proposed such an amendment, but the House approved the bill without it. In the absence of support from the civil rights community, the bill stalled after it reached the Senate.[27]

The type of conflict that arose from the intersection of religious liberty and LGBT equality in the context of RLPA would only become more frequent and intense as a growing majority of Americans, after the turn of the century, embraced full equality rights for sexual minorities. The issue that, by far, did the most in engendering concerns for religious liberty on the right and hopes for LGBT equality on the left was that of same-sex marriage.

Same-Sex Marriage: Litigation, Statutes, and Religious Exemptions

Although some members of the LGBT community pushed for marital rights in the years following the Stonewall riots, marriage equality was not a priority for most LGBT organizations and activists prior to the 1990s.[28] The LGBT movement during the 1970s focused on issues such as the enactment of local laws prohibiting discrimination on the basis of sexual orientation and ending police harassment of LGBT people. In the 1980s, the movement also pushed for discrimination protection for people living with AIDS and for the enactment of domestic partnership laws. In many ways, the question of marriage was thrust upon the LGBT movement after three same-sex couples in Hawai'i in 1990, working with local activists, showed up at the marriage bureau in Honolulu requesting marriage licenses.

After officials denied the applications, the couples approached legal rights organizations, including the ACLU and the Lambda Legal Defense & Education Fund, seeking legal representation in order to constitutionally challenge the denials. The organizations, believing that a lawsuit would be futile, refused to represent them. The couples then turned to a local civil liberties attorney, who agreed to file a lawsuit on their behalf despite his lack of experience litigating LGBT rights cases.[29] To everyone's surprise, the Hawai'i Supreme Court in 1993 issued a ruling questioning the constitutionality of denying same-sex couples the opportunity to marry.[30]

The difficulty that the Hawai'i couples had in gaining legal representation illustrated the reluctance that many LGBT rights organizations had in embracing the issue of marriage equality—into the 1990s, the issue seemed to have greater resonance among many members of the LGBT community than among movement leaders. Some of the leaders worried that neither the country nor the courts were ready to consider the possibility of marriage for same-sex couples. Other activists, in particular lesbian feminists, had ideological objections to prioritizing the institution of marriage and, in the process, further stigmatizing those who chose to order their personal and familial lives outside of marriage. By the middle of the 1990s, however, a growing number of LGBT rights organizations, facing both the surprising prospect of marriage equality in Hawai'i and a growing conservative backlash against marital rights for same-sex couples, quickly turned the pursuit of marriage equality into their most important objective.

The movement's prioritization of marriage was initially followed by many more defeats than victories. In Hawai'i, the progress in the courts was stymied by a constitutional amendment authorizing the legislature to define marriage as the union of a man and a woman. In addition, Congress in 1996, after conducting a vitriolic debate in which conservative legislators repeatedly claimed there was a pressing need "to defend" marriages and families from LGBT people and their relationships, enacted the Defense of Marriage Act (DOMA). That law prohibited the federal government from recognizing the state-sanctioned marriages of same-sex couples (at a time when there were no such marriages), while seeking to exempt states from any obligation to recognize the validity of marriage licenses issued to same-sex couples by other jurisdictions. Between 1997 and 2000, fourteen states (including liberal ones such as California, Minnesota, and Washington) enacted laws prohibiting the recognition of marriages by same-sex couples.

While the marriage equality movement was experiencing a series of crushing political and legislative defeats, some of the nation's state supreme courts began accepting its constitutional claims. In 1999, the Vermont Supreme Court held that denying same-sex couples the rights and benefits that accompany marriage violated the state constitution.[31] The Vermont legislature responded the following year by enacting the nation's first civil union law, offering same-sex couples the same rights and benefits available to heterosexual married couples under state and local laws.

During the first decade of the new century, the question of whether same-sex couples should be permitted to marry became one of the most hotly contested political, social, and legal issues across the country. The

Massachusetts Supreme Court in 2003 became the first state supreme court to hold that the government was required by a state constitution to offer same-sex couples the opportunity to marry.[32] Although the supreme courts of California, Connecticut, and Iowa soon followed with similar rulings,[33] the highest courts of Maryland, New York, and Washington upheld the constitutionality of their states' same-sex marriage bans.[34] At around this time, voters in more than half the states approved constitutional amendments prohibiting the recognition of marriages by same-sex couples. One of those amendments, known as Proposition 8, received the support of a majority of California voters in 2008, bringing to an end the issuance of marriage licenses to same-sex couples that had followed the state supreme court's ruling of a few months earlier striking down the statutory marriage ban.

Not all the progress enjoyed by the marriage equality movement was the result of judicial victories. In 2007, the New Hampshire legislature, acting on its own rather than pursuant to a court ruling, followed neighboring Vermont's lead by adopting a civil union law. Emboldened by that victory, LGBT activists two years later pushed the New Hampshire legislature to enact a law allowing same-sex couples to marry.

The initial New Hampshire marriage bill made clear that religious clergy who opposed marriages by same-sex couples would not be required to solemnize such marriages. But some legislators complained that the bill's religious exemption was too narrow, and Governor John Lynch threatened to veto the bill unless it was broadened.[35] As a result, the bill's religious exemption was expanded to allow religious organizations, associations, and societies, as well as nonprofit institutions associated with religious organizations, to refuse "to provide services, accommodations, advantages, facilities, goods, or privileges" related to the solemnization of marriages that were inconsistent with the entities' religious views. The exemption also applied to the provision by religious entities of "counseling, programs, courses, retreats, or housing designated for married individuals."[36]

Most marriage equality activists in New Hampshire supported the broadening of the religious exemption, believing it necessary to get the law enacted. For some moderate opponents of same-sex marriage (such as Governor Lynch, who had earlier supported civil unions but not marriage for same-sex couples), the broadening of the exemption led them to support the marriage equality bill. But many conservative legislators and activists remained opposed to the bill, with some arguing that the exemption was not broad enough because it did not include small business owners, such as photographers and bakers, who did not want to provide their goods and services for use in the celebration of same-sex unions.[37] Nonetheless, the legislature approved the law in 2009, making New Hampshire the first state to enact a marriage equality law without being required to do so by court order.

Connecticut, Vermont, and the District of Columbia also enacted marriage equality laws in 2009 that contained similar exemptions for religious organizations.[38] In 2011, New York followed suit and became, by far, the biggest state in the country to enact a marriage equality law. As in New Hampshire, many LGBT rights supporters in New York, including Governor Andrew Cuomo, came to the conclusion that the legislature would not enact a marriage equality law without significant exemptions for religious organizations. (In 2009, a marriage equality bill that only contained an exemption for clergy failed to pass the New York legislature.)[39] After language was added to the New York marriage equality bill, similar to that contained in the New Hampshire law, exempting religious organizations from having to provide goods, services, and accommodations for the solemnization or celebration of marriages that were inconsistent with their religious views, a handful of undecided Republican state senators announced their support for the bill, leading to its passage.[40]

It bears noting that the religious exemptions included in marriage equality laws by the New Hampshire, New York, and other state legislatures do not distinguish between different "types" of marriages, that is, they do not treat marriages by same-sex couples differently from other marriages. Under the statutes, a religious organization that owns a meeting hall, for example, is as free to refuse to rent its facility for the celebration of marriages that run across racial lines as it is free to deny the use of its property for the celebration of marriages by same-sex couples (as long as the marriages in question are inconsistent with the organization's religious beliefs).

For many supporters of religious exemptions, the accommodations of religious dissenters enacted alongside the marriage equality laws in states like New Hampshire and New York were insufficient. A group of prominent religious liberty law scholars, for example, wrote letters to officials in states that were considering marriage equality laws urging them to include two additional forms of religious accommodations.[41] First, the scholars proposed that the exemptions cover businesses whose owners objected to marriages on religious grounds. Specifically, the scholars argued that the businesses should be exempted from providing goods and services related to the solemnization and celebration of those marriages; counseling or other services that "directly facilitate the perpetuation of" those marriages; benefits to the spouses of employees in such marriages; and finally, housing to couples in such marriages. Second, the scholars proposed that government employees—the concern here was primarily about justices of the peace and clerks in government marriage offices— who object to marriages on religious grounds be exempted from the obligation to solemnize those marriages. As one of the scholars explained, "it is abundantly clear that existing religious liberty protections do not go far enough to protect individuals outside religious organizations. Legislators have largely ignored the plight of judges, government employees, and those in the wedding industry who cannot assist with a same-sex marriage because of a 'relationship with Jesus Christ'—or for any other sincerely held religious reason."[42]

The scholars made two clarifying points about their proposals. First, the exemptions would only apply if there were other business owners or government officials in the area who were willing and able to provide the goods and services in question. Second, although the proposed exemptions, like the exemptions enacted as part of the marriage equality laws in states like New Hampshire and New York, would be triggered by religious objections to *any* marriage, the scholars made clear that their main concern was the impact of same-sex marriages in particular on religious liberty rights. As the scholars explained, "the conflicts between same-sex marriage and religious conscience will be both certain and considerable if adequate protections are not provided. Without adequate safeguards, many religious individuals will be forced to engage in conduct that violates their deepest religious beliefs, and religious organizations will be constrained in crucial aspects of their religious exercise."[43]

In the two years following the enactment of New York's marriage equality statute, eight additional states adopted laws allowing same-sex couples to marry. All eight states included religious exemptions in their new laws, although none of them covered businesses or government clerks. Five of the states (Hawai'i, Maryland, Minnesota, Rhode Island, and Washington) adopted language similar to that contained in the New Hampshire and New York statutes by generally exempting religious organizations from having to provide goods, services, and facilities for the celebration of marriages;[44] two states (Illinois and Maine) adopted somewhat narrower exemptions;[45] and the last state (Delaware) only exempted clergy and judges from solemnizing marriages that violated their religious principles.[46]

Most LGBT rights supporters opposed religious exemptions that would allow businesses and government employees to make distinctions on whom they served on the basis of sexual orientation. From their perspective, exempting for-profit businesses from antidiscrimination obligations threatened to undermine the ability of civil rights laws to achieve their objectives. Similarly, LGBT rights proponents argued that government employees have an obligation to serve the entire public and that it would set a dangerous precedent to allow them to pick and choose whom they serve.

The states that enacted marriage equality statutes between 2009 and 2013 were relatively liberal ones. Although it was not clear at the time whether the LGBT movement would be able to achieve similar legislative victories in more conservative states, several political and judicial victories seemed to quickly change the dynamics of the nationwide debates over marriage rights for same-sex couples, with proponents of marriage equality for the first time starting to clearly gain the upper hand.

The Tide Turns: Marriage Equality Expansion and Religious Freedom Laws

One of the first important events contributing to the change in the dynamics of the same-sex marriage debates—with opponents of those marriages, to put it simply, being forced to shift from playing offense to playing defense—took place in 2012 when President Barack Obama became the first sitting president to embrace equal marriage rights for same-sex couples. At around that time, polls showed that for the first time a majority of Americans supported granting same-sex couples the right to marry. And marriage equality supporters, who had won *only one of more than thirty* ballot-box measures in the previous decade, prevailed in all four such measures—in Maine, Maryland, Minnesota, and Washington State—placed before voters in 2012.

These political milestones were followed by two judicial victories before the Supreme Court in 2013. In the first case, the Court held that supporters of California's Proposition 8 did not have legal standing to defend its constitutionality, a ruling that left in place the district court's finding that the measure violated the federal constitution.[47] In the second case, the Court struck down the DOMA provision prohibiting the federal government from recognizing state-sanctioned marriages by same-sex couples on the ground that it violated the Equal Protection Clause.[48] Between that ruling and the end of 2014, more than twenty federal courts, both at the trial and appellate levels, struck down same-sex marriage bans. As a result, the number of states allowing same-sex couples to marry more than doubled in 2014, increasing from sixteen to thirty-five.

As marriage bans fell in state after state as a result of judicial invalidation, conservative opponents of LGBT rights were deprived of the opportunity to seek religious exemptions from LGBT equality obligations through the enactment of marriage equality laws. This led conservatives to turn their attention to the types of religious liberty statutes enacted in the 1990s following the Supreme Court's ruling in *Employment Division v. Smith.*

The first battle over the enactment of a religious liberty statute in the era of same-sex marriage took place in Arizona in 2014. Raising concerns about the impact of same-sex marriages on the rights of those who objected to them on religious grounds, conservative legislators in Arizona proposed amendments to the state's religious liberty law with the objective of preventing discrimination suits brought against religious business owners for refusing to serve same-sex couples. The original Arizona religious liberty statute enacted in 1999, like the federal RFRA, required the government to show the existence of a compelling state interest when it enforced a rule of general applicability in ways that substantially burdened a person's exercise of religion. The original provision defined "person" to include "a religious assembly or institution," but did not mention for-profit enterprises.[49] The 2014 bill proposed to expand the definition of "person" significantly by including partnerships, corporations, and "any other legal entity" within its scope.[50] In addition, because the original statute could be interpreted to protect religious believers from state actors and not to create exemptions from antidiscrimination laws, which are generally enforced through *private* litigation, the 2014 bill, in the name of religious liberty, limited the ability of plaintiffs to pursue private lawsuits, presumably including ones based on discrimination claims.

The proposed amendments to Arizona's religious freedom statute, introduced during the highly polarized political environment created by the increasingly successful push for marriage equality nationwide, met fierce resistance. Opponents of the measure expressed grave concerns that the new law would allow discrimination not only against LGBT people, but against other groups as well. Opponents included both civil rights organizations and also some prominent Republicans (including former presidential candidates John McCain and Mitt Romney), almost all Democrats, many Arizona and national businesses (as well as the Arizona Chamber of Commerce), and many newspaper boards around the country. In addition, the National Football League, which was planning to hold the Super Bowl in Arizona in 2015, announced that it would reconsider its decision if the bill became law.

Despite the loud and widespread opposition to the bill, the Republican-controlled state legislature, under intense pressure from religious conservatives, approved the measure. In the end, however, Republican governor Jan Brewer, concerned about the national criticism of the state engendered by the religious liberty bill and its possible negative economic consequences for Arizona, vetoed the measure.[51]

Conservative activists, growing increasingly concerned about the number of states required by federal courts to allow same-sex couples to marry, and seemingly undaunted by their defeat in Arizona, continued to push for laws in other states that would exempt religious dissenters from having to abide by LGBT equality measures. In response, conservative legislators introduced more than twenty such bills across the country. One of those bills, which essentially tracked the federal RFRA, was enacted by the Mississippi legislature in 2014.[52] But in 2015, the Arkansas and Indiana legislatures adopted broader religious freedom laws.[53] Not coincidentally, federal courts in both states had recently ruled that same-sex marriage bans were unconstitutional.[54]

The actions by the Arkansas and Indiana legislatures engendered the same type of uproar that followed the passage of the similar Arizona bill. In Indiana, many prominent figures, including business leaders, university presidents, and heads of sports organizations, spoke out forcefully against the measure after Governor Mike Pence signed it into law. The NCAA, which has its headquarters in Indianapolis and was about to hold its men's basketball Final Four tournament there, expressed displeasure with the law, as did the chief executives of large companies, including Apple, Nike, and PayPal.[55] As the pressure mounted, Governor Pence and Republican legislative leaders scrambled to address the political firestorm.

Several days later, the legislature enacted an amendment to the law, signed by the governor, explicitly stating that the religious liberty statute did not authorize businesses to deny services, goods, employment, and housing on the basis of several traits, including race, sex, religion, disability, sexual orientation, and gender identity.[56]

The Arkansas religious liberty bill met with a similar fate. Governor Asa Hutchinson, after initially expressing support for the law, backtracked following loud opposition led by important businesses (including most prominently Wal-Mart, the state's largest corporation) and civil rights organizations.[57] Governor Hutchinson asked the legislature to make changes to the bill, which it did by adopting a version that, in tracking the language of the federal RFRA, contained two crucial modifications: first, it did not expressly allow for the religious freedom law to be used as a defense in private litigation; and second, it did not include corporations within the meaning of "a person" protected by the statute.[58]

Whereas the controversies in Arkansas and Indiana centered on the question of whether business owners should be permitted to deny goods and services to same-sex couples, Republican legislators in North Carolina and South Carolina introduced bills that would allow government employees—such as judges, magistrates, and county clerks—who opposed same-sex marriages on religious grounds to refuse to solemnize those marriages.[59] Meanwhile, some elected officials went so far as to question whether state employees had to comply with federal court rulings ordering that same-sex couples be permitted to marry. In 2015, Republican legislators in Oklahoma, South Carolina, and Texas introduced legislation prohibiting state and local government employees from issuing marriage licenses to same-sex couples despite the federal courts' rulings, applicable to those states, striking down the marriage bans.[60] Although the proposals did not become law, they called to mind the kind of willful resistance by Southern officials to federal integration mandates during the civil rights era.

The question of whether state officials had to follow orders issued by federal courts in same-sex marriage cases was the subject of much attention and dispute in Alabama. After a federal judge in early 2015 struck down that state's same-sex marriage ban, the chief justice of the Alabama Supreme Court issued a letter calling on the state's probate judges to ignore the federal ruling by refusing to issue licenses to same-sex couples.[61] Some probate judges, faced with conflicting legal guidance, decided to follow the federal court's ruling while others refused to do so. This confusing state of affairs meant that whether Alabama same-sex couples could marry depended on their county of residence.[62] A few weeks later, the Alabama Supreme Court issued an order prohibiting probate judges from granting marriage licenses to same-sex couples, putting a halt to the issuance of such licenses across the state.[63] In the meantime, LGBT rights groups petitioned the federal courts to require state officials to comply with federal constitutional law.[64] The state/federal impasse remained in place right up to the Supreme Court's ruling in *Obergefell v. Hodges* striking down same-sex marriage bans as unconstitutional. And even after *Obergefell*, several probate judges in Alabama continued to refuse to issue any marriage licenses on the ground that the Court's ruling was inconsistent with their religious views.[65]

There was also activity at the federal level. Ten days before the Court issued its ruling in *Obergefell*, congressional conservatives introduced a bill called the First Amendment Defense Act (FADA). The bill quickly garnered cosponsorship support from more than 130 representatives and 35 senators. The measure aims to prohibit the federal government from taking any "discriminatory action" against a person "who believes or acts in accordance with a religious belief or moral conviction that marriage is or should be recognized as the union of one man and one woman, or that sexual relations are properly reserved to such a marriage."[66] The proposed bill is both narrower and broader than the religious freedom restoration statutes. It is narrower because it protects only *some* religious views: those grounded in the notion that male/female marriage is the only form of acceptable marriage. But the bill is also broader than the freedom restoration statutes because the latter, assuming they apply to the enforcement of antidiscrimination laws, at least require religious persons to prove that the application of the law under challenge substantially burdens their freedom of religion while allowing the government to show that it has a compelling state interest in discouraging discrimination. In contrast, FADA would categorically preclude the federal government from denying a job, grant, contract, or benefit to persons who treat sexual minorities (and heterosexuals who have sex outside of marriage) differently as long as the reasons for doing so are grounded in religious or moral views regarding the inappropriateness of same-sex marriages and of having sex outside of male/female marriages.[67] If enacted, the legislation would, for example, prevent the federal government from enforcing equal treatment regulations against employers that refuse to provide health benefits to their employees' same-sex spouses and from denying subsidies to health clinics that refuse to provide contraceptives to unmarried women.[68]

Also shortly before *Obergefell*, the North Carolina legislature enacted a law, over the veto of the Republican governor, allowing magistrates and registers of deeds to recuse themselves from performing marriages "based upon any sincerely held religious objection."[69] At around the same time, Utah also adopted a law that allows county clerks to refuse to issue marriage licenses.[70] Both statutes require officials to make sure that someone is available to issue legally valid marriage licenses.

A few weeks after *Obergefell*, an Apostolic Christian county clerk in Kentucky drew national headlines following her announcement that her office would stop issuing marriage licenses because she opposed same-sex marriages on religious grounds.[71] A federal judge, responding to a lawsuit filed by same-sex couples living in the county, ordered the clerk to issue licenses to all eligible couples, rejecting her arguments that she had a right under the Constitution and the state Religious Freedom Restoration Act to refuse to issue the licenses. When the county clerk continued to refuse to issue licenses, the judge ordered her jailed for contempt.[72] The judge released her five days later after she allowed her assistants to issue licenses to same-sex couples.[73] In 2016, the Kentucky legislature, prompted by a newly elected Republican governor, enacted a statute that removed the names of county clerks from the marriage licenses issued by their offices.[74]

Also in 2016, the Republican governor of Georgia vetoed a religious freedom restoration law.[75] But a few days later, Mississippi enacted a law called the Protecting Freedom of Conscience from Government Discrimination Act. Unlike the religious freedom restoration statutes already discussed, which seek to protect the exercise of religion regardless of the religious beliefs motivating the exercise, the Mississippi statute, if deemed constitutional by the courts, would protect only three particular "religious beliefs or moral convictions," namely, that "(a) Marriage is or should be recognized as the union of one man and one woman; (b) Sexual relations are properly reserved to such a marriage; and (c) Male (man) or female (woman) refer to an individual's immutable biological sex as objectively determined by anatomy and genetics at time of birth."[76] The law would provide, by far, the broadest religious exemptions in the context of marriage and discrimination ever adopted by an American jurisdiction. The statute would prohibit state and local officials from taking "any discriminatory action" against any religious organization for refusing to hire or terminate employees, sell or rent property, or provide adoption or foster care services on the basis of the protected religious views.[77] The statute would also allow providers to refuse to make services related to gender transition, psychological counseling, or infertility that are inconsistent with the religious views protected by the statute. In addition, the measure would prohibit the government from "discriminating" against businesses that refuse to provide their services and goods for the celebration of marriages that are inconsistent with the protected religious views. Finally, among other provisions, the statute would allow clerks, judges, and justices of the peace to refuse to issue marriage licenses when that refusal is grounded in the religious views protected by the statute. Unlike the North Carolina and Utah laws, which allow designated officials to choose to cease issuing marriage licenses *altogether*, the Mississippi statute would permit individual government officials to choose whom to serve by marrying all couples that come before them *except for* same-sex ones.[78]

The Employment Non-Discrimination Act

In 1975, Representative Bella Abzug of New York introduced the first bill in Congress prohibiting employment discrimination on the basis of sexual orientation. Abzug's bill would have simply amended Title VII to include sexual orientation as a protected trait. In 1994, congressional supporters of LGBT rights proposed a stand-alone law, the Employment Non-Discrimination Act (ENDA), that would have prohibited employment discrimination on the basis of sexual orientation. (Later versions of the bill would have also prohibited discrimination on the basis of gender identity.) The 1994 ENDA bill, like similar ones introduced in subsequent years, completely exempted religious organizations from its scope.[79]

The ENDA bill was first introduced in a markedly different LGBT rights environment from that which existed a couple of decades later. In 1994, the push for marriage equality was at its early stages, with few people, on either side of the debate, believing that same-sex couples would soon gain the right to marry. At the same time, questions related to religious exemptions from the few LGBT equality measures then on the books received little attention. All of that changed as the number of states that allowed same-sex couples to marry grew, first relatively slowly, and then, after the Supreme Court's 2013 ruling in *United States v. Windsor* (striking DOMA down), breathtakingly quickly. Around that time, supporters of religious exemptions embraced ENDA's broad carve out for religious organizations. For example, when President Obama was considering issuing an executive order prohibiting federal contractors from discriminating on the basis of sexual orientation and gender identity, religious exemption supporters urged him to adopt ENDA's expansive exemption for religious organizations.[80]

In contrast, as the question of religious exemptions continued to arise in political and legal debates over LGBT equality, gay rights supporters began expressing concerns that ENDA's religious exemption was significantly broader than that contained in Title VII. As we saw in Chapter 5, the latter limited the antidiscrimination carve out to cases involving *religious* discrimination, while leaving unaffected proscriptions against race and sex discrimination. In contrast, ENDA's religious exemption would have allowed religious organizations to discriminate on the basis of *sexual orientation*. I return to this distinction later in the chapter.

In the summer of 2014, several leading LGBT rights organizations, a few weeks after the Supreme Court's ruling in *Burwell v. Hobby Lobby* raised the prospect, as discussed in the following section, that courts in future cases might conclude that even for-profit entities were entitled to religious exemptions from LGBT equality measures, withdrew their support for ENDA because of its religious exemption. A year later, many LGBT rights activists rallied around a new bill introduced in Congress called the Equality Act.[81] That bill would amend the Civil Rights Act of 1964, among other federal antidiscrimination statutes, by adding sexual orientation and gender identity as protected categories without changing existing religious exemptions included in federal antidiscrimination laws. Unlike ENDA, the Equality Act's scope is not limited to employment discrimination; it also applies, for example, to discrimination by landlords and by places of public accommodation. Most commentators agreed that the liberal Equality Act, like the conservative First Amendment Defense Act, was unlikely to become law in the near future.

Meanwhile, Back at the Supreme Court

The dispute in *Hobby Lobby* arose over a regulation, issued under the Patient Protection and Affordable Care Act of 2010 (known as Obamacare), requiring most employers of more than fifty employees to provide their workers with health insurance coverage that includes free access to

FDA-approved contraceptives. The owners of the Hobby Lobby Corporation, a privately held company that operates 500 arts-and-crafts stores in
thirty-nine states, has a workforce of 13,000 employees, and estimated
annual revenues of $2 billion, objected to the use of some of the contra-
ceptives on religious grounds because they believed them to induce abor-
tions. The corporation argued that the regulation requiring it to help its
employees gain access to the contraceptives forced it to facilitate abor-
tions in violation of its religious liberty rights under RFRA.

The legal challenge to the contraceptive regulation brought by Hobby
Lobby and a handful of other for-profit corporations created a perfect
storm in American political and legal circles by bringing together three
contested areas of government policy. First, it involved a regulation
implementing Obamacare, the most controversial social welfare legislation adopted by Congress since it instituted Medicaid and Medicare in
the 1960s. As had happened fifty years earlier, Republican critics assailed
federal involvement in the provision of health care, calling it a threat
both to individual liberty and state's rights. Second, the case involved the
question of women's access to contraceptives. Although the vast majority of American women of procreative age use contraceptives and polls
consistently show overwhelming support for their use, some social and
religious conservative activists and elected officials object to government
efforts to make access to contraceptives easier and cheaper. Finally, *Hobby
Lobby* raised a question that had become central to the debate over the
intersection of LGBT equality and religious liberty: whether legislatures
should grant religious owners of for-profit enterprises exemptions from
LGBT equality measures.

The Religious Freedom Restoration Act makes its protections available to "a person" without defining the meaning of that term. The Court
in *Hobby Lobby* determined that closely held for-profit corporations can
exercise rights to religious liberty and that Congress intended to include
them within the meaning of "person."[82] It is possible that *Hobby Lobby*
represents a new judicial willingness to exempt for-profit corporations
from obligations arising from neutral and generally applicable laws in the
name of religious liberty. It will be interesting to see how that question
plays out, especially given the apparent tension between the reasoning
in *Hobby Lobby* and the Court's statement, in an earlier case, that "when
followers of a particular sect enter into commercial activity as a matter of choice, the limits they accept on their own conduct as a matter of

conscience and faith are not to be superimposed on the statutory schemes [that] are binding on others in that activity."[83] But be that is it may, there are reasons to believe that the Court is not favorably disposed to reading religious liberty statutes so broadly that they grant exemptions from antidiscrimination obligations to for-profit entities.

The Court in *Hobby Lobby* took the trouble of distinguishing between the contraceptive regulation before it and laws prohibiting racial discrimination. In responding to Justice Ruth Bader Ginsburg's concern, expressed in dissent, about the impact of the Court's ruling on many laws of general applicability, including antidiscrimination statutes, the Court stated that the government's interest in guaranteeing equal opportunity in the workplace on the basis of race was compelling and would not be affected by its holding.[84] This suggests that a majority of the justices may not be so quick to conclude that for-profit entities enjoy religious-based rights to discriminate against groups protected by antidiscrimination laws.

The *Hobby Lobby* Court limited its dictum to racial discrimination, even though Justice Ginsburg expressed concern about the impact of the majority's ruling on antidiscrimination laws more broadly, including protections against gender and sexual orientation discrimination.[85] The Court has not had the opportunity to weigh the state's interest in eradicating sexual orientation discrimination against the religious liberty rights of for-profit actors in the commercial marketplace.[86] However, when one looks at the cumulative holdings and reasoning of the Court's LGBT rights cases over the last twenty years, it clearly believes that the differential treatment of individuals on the basis of sexual orientation is highly problematic. In *Romer v. Evans* (1996), the Court struck down a state constitutional amendment that would have denied antidiscrimination protection to sexual minorities.[87] In doing so, the Court was troubled by the effort to target lesbians, gay men, and bisexuals for a form of differential treatment that denied them, but no others, the opportunity to seek the equal protection of the laws. In striking down sodomy statutes in *Lawrence v. Texas* (2003), the Court noted the ways in which those criminal laws had been used to justify discrimination against an entire class of individuals whose consensual sexual intimacy rendered them criminals before the law.[88] Ten years later, the Court in *United States v. Windsor* (2013) decried the ways in which the Defense of Marriage Act demeaned and stigmatized the committed relationships of same-sex couples.[89] And finally, the Court in *Obergefell v. Hodges* (2015) held that same-sex couples did not differ from opposite-sex ones in their constitutionally protected interests in having the state recognize their relationships as marital and, in the process, provide those relationships with the support, stability, and protection that accompanies the legal status of marriage.[90] (The next section discusses *Obergefell* in greater detail.) Although it was possible to argue that the state did not have a compelling interest in addressing sexual orientation discrimination a few decades ago, that position is increasingly untenable given that the Court has made clear, in different ways, that sexual orientation does not impact either the capabilities or dignitary interests of human beings. The conclusion that the state has a compelling interest in eradicating sexual orientation discrimination would make it significantly less likely that the Court will conclude that for-profit entities enjoy religious-based rights to discriminate against sexual minorities.

The Supreme Court Strikes Down Same-Sex Marriage Bans

Several months after its ruling in *Hobby Lobby*, the Court agreed to consider the constitutionality of state laws banning the recognition of same-sex marriages. The issue in *Obergefell v. Hodges* was whether those bans violated equality and liberty protections afforded by the federal Constitution. The Court had last grappled with the constitutionality of marriage bans that impacted minority groups in 1967 when it struck down interracial marriage laws in *Loving v. Virginia*. At the time, no one argued that individuals who objected to interracial marriages on religious grounds should be exempted from having to treat interracial couples equally, even though much of the opposition to such marriages was based on the notion that God purportedly intended for the races to remain apart.[91] In contrast, the question of religious exemptions from sexual orientation antidiscrimination laws, although not directly at issue in *Obergefell*, served as an important backdrop to the case.

A group of prominent religious liberty scholars filed an amicus brief in *Obergefell* urging the Court to strike down the marriage bans, while also "tak[ing] responsibility for the resulting issues of religious liberty."[92] During oral arguments, Justice Scalia repeatedly pressed Mary Bonauto, the lawyer representing the same-sex couples, on whether a victory for her clients would mean that states could require ministers to solemnize same-sex marriages. Although no jurisdiction in the nation's history has ever imposed a requirement that ministers marry all eligible couples who come before them (and therefore the issue has never been litigated), the answer to Scalia's question is obvious: The First Amendment's Religion Clauses prevent the government from forcing ministers to participate in marriages that are contrary to their religious beliefs, a right not affected by the fundamental right to marry.

An example illustrates why this is so clear: No one disputes that two individuals of different religious faiths have a constitutional right to marry. As a result, the government does not have the constitutional authority to prohibit interreligious marriages. But that lack of constitutional authority does not mean that interreligious couples, or the state acting on their behalf, can force ministers who oppose interreligious marriages to officiate their marriage ceremonies.

The Court in *Obergefell* held that the fundamental right to marry protects the ability of lesbians, gay men, and bisexuals to marry the individuals of their choice. The Court also held that to exclude same-sex couples from the institution of marriage violated equal protection principles. In doing so, the Court acknowledged that "many who deem same-sex marriage to be wrong reach that conclusion based on decent and honorable religious or philosophical premises," and made clear that it did not intend to disparage "neither they nor their beliefs."[93] The majority in *Obergefell* also spoke directly to religious opponents of same-sex marriage to assure them that their rights to believe, advocate, and teach were in no way impaired by the ruling. As the majority explained, "those who adhere to religious doctrines, may continue to advocate with utmost, sincere conviction that, by divine precepts, same-sex marriage should not be condoned. The First Amendment ensures that religious organizations and persons are given proper protection as they seek to teach the principles that are so fulfilling and so central to their lives and faiths, and to their own deep aspirations to continue the family structure they have long revered."[94]

However, these assurances were not enough for the dissenting justices. Justice Clarence Thomas charged that "the majority's decision threatens the religious liberty our Nation has long sought to protect."[95] For his part, Chief Justice John Roberts claimed that the ruling "creates serious questions about religious liberty" and found it "ominous[]" that the majority, although acknowledging that dissenters from same-sex marriages on religious grounds had the right to advocate and teach their views, did not refer to their right to *exercise* religion.[96] Roberts added that "hard questions arise when people of faith exercise religion in ways that may be seen to conflict with the new right to same-sex marriage—when, for example, a religious college provides married student housing only to opposite-sex married couples, or a religious adoption agency declines to place children with same-sex married couples."[97]

Although Roberts was correct that the intersection of religious freedom and LGBT equality can raise difficult legal and policy questions, the history explored in Chapter 5 shows that they are neither novel nor intractable. We have, as a nation, repeatedly faced the question of how to attain equality objectives while respecting the basic liberty rights of dissenters, including those associated with religious freedom. That this tension between equality and liberty has arisen with some frequency is not surprising in a nation whose norms, including, perhaps most prominently, its constitutional norms, value both equality and liberty. It makes sense, in addressing contemporary controversies over the state's authority to promote LGBT equality, to look to how American antidiscrimination law has traditionally sought to balance equality and liberty concerns.

History as a Guide on Religious Exemptions from Antidiscrimination Laws

Our country, since the Civil War, has repeatedly struggled with how to balance the pursuit of antidiscrimination objectives and the protection of liberty interests, including those related to religious freedom. Although particular policy outcomes arising from that balancing can always be criticized, the basic approach of American antidiscrimination law to questions of religious exemptions is reasonable, has worked well, and is time tested. Legislatures and courts have deliberated over and revisited these issues through the decades and have, on the whole, reached reasonable and workable solutions that have allowed for the attainment, in the context of race and gender, of important equality objectives while respecting important liberty interests of equality dissenters. It is therefore appropriate to look to how the law has accommodated religious dissent in the context of race and gender equality for guidance in determining how the law should accommodate religious dissent in the context of LGBT equality. My focus here is on prudential or discretionary exemptions rather than on constitutionally required accommodations. For the reasons already noted, constitutional mandates play a relatively minor direct role in setting the scope of religious exemptions from antidiscrimination laws. It is still the case, however, that discussions of discretionary exemptions are properly informed by First Amendment values and principles.

There are five important characteristics to the ways in which American antidiscrimination law has sought to accommodate religious dissent while pursuing equality objectives, characteristics that were firmly in place by the time marriage equality began to spread across the country. First, the exemptions have granted religious organizations some accommodations from antidiscrimination obligations that go beyond what is constitutionally required. Second, the exemptions have generally distinguished between the discretion of religious organizations to make distinctions on the basis of religion and their ability to take other protected traits, such as race and gender, into account. Third, the exemptions have applied to a broad category of religious organizations, not just to houses of worship. Fourth, the exemptions have been limited to nonprofit religious organizations. Finally, the exemptions have not allowed government officials to decide which members of the public to serve based on the officials' religious views.

After discussing each of these traditional characteristics of religious exemptions that have been part of American antidiscrimination law for decades, the chapter ends by making two other points: first, that in assessing the need to grant exemptions from antidiscrimination laws to religious dissenters from LGBT equality, it is essential to keep in mind the harm to sexual minorities that may be caused by the granting of those exemptions; and second, that it is problematic, as exemptions supporters sometimes do, to try to distinguish religious-based justifications for the differential treatment of individuals according to their race and religious-based justifications for differential treatment according to their sexual orientation.

1. Accommodations beyond Those That Are Constitutionally Required. As explored in Chapters 5 and 6, the First Amendment provides important protections for equality dissenters. The right of association, which the Court has derived from the Free Speech Clause, protects expressive associations, including religious organizations, from being forced by the government to admit members whose presence interferes with their ability to express their views, values, and beliefs. In addition, the government, under the ministerial exception to antidiscrimination laws mandated by the Religion Clauses, lacks the authority to interfere with the ability of religious organizations to choose their ministers. Furthermore, although the case has never arisen, it is clear that the government cannot constitutionally require houses of worship and ministers to solemnize marriages that are inconsistent with their religious views.

Moving beyond constitutional requirements, there are many precedents in the racial and gender contexts for granting so-called prudential or discretionary exemptions to religious dissenters from antidiscrimination obligations. The Title VII coreligionist exemption, given that it applies to *all* of a religious organization's employees and not just to those involved in religious activities, is an example of such a discretionary exemption.[98] Similarly, many state employment antidiscrimination laws, and some state housing and public accommodations antidiscrimination laws, also provide exemptions that go beyond what is constitutionally required by allowing, for example, religious organizations to hire only those of the same faith for any position or to provide housing or services to only those of a certain religion.[99]

To argue that there should be no (or almost no) accommodation of religious actors beyond what is constitutionally mandated is inconsistent with the traditional ways in which American antidiscrimination law, for decades, has accommodated the views of those who dissent from the attainment of equality objectives on religious grounds. Given that the nation's laws have traditionally provided some discretionary exemptions to religious actors from antidiscrimination obligations, the Constitution in this area should serve as a floor and not a ceiling. In the same way that there is no obvious reason why sexual orientation discrimination issues require the adoption of new and expansive religious exemptions, there is no obvious reason why those same issues should lead to cutting back on the types of discretionary exemptions that American antidiscrimination law has traditionally afforded religious actors.

2. Distinctions Based on Religion as Opposed to on Other Protected Traits. American antidiscrimination law has generally recognized that religious organizations should be permitted to make distinctions, especially in the context of employment, that favor coreligionists. For example, the religious exemption contained in Title VII, the most important employment antidiscrimination law in the nation's history, allows religious organizations to hire only coreligionists if they so wish. At the same time, however, Title VII does not permit religious organizations to make distinctions on the basis of other protected traits.[100] Many state antidiscrimination statutes, in particular those that regulate employment, also allow religious organizations to prefer coreligionists but do not permit them to take other protected traits into account.[101] Similarly, when President George W. Bush in 2002 issued an executive order exempting religious organizations that contract with the federal government from a preexisting obligation, dating back to a 1965 executive order, not to engage in employment discrimination, he limited the exemption to the ability of such organizations to employ "individuals of a particular religion," leaving unaffected the obligation not to discriminate on the basis of other grounds, including race and sex.[102]

The proper application of coreligionist exemptions allows, for example, religious community centers and schools to exclusively hire individuals of their respective faiths without violating the law, but does not permit them to make distinctions on the basis of race or gender even if such discrimination is justified on religious grounds. (Antidiscrimination prohibitions, however, are limited by the constitutionally required ministerial exception, which grants religious organizations unfettered discretion to choose their ministers.) If coreligionist exemptions were to be interpreted in ways that allow covered entities to discriminate on the basis of race or gender, it would in effect swallow the antidiscrimination mandate, granting religious organizations complete dispensation from all antidiscrimination obligations.[103]

If religious exemptions from sexual orientation equality mandates are permitted to track the exemptions that have traditionally been part of American antidiscrimination laws, those exemptions would allow religious organizations to make employment decisions on the basis of religious faith as long as the decisions are not based on the sexual orientation of current or prospective employees. Under this approach, for example, it would be permissible for a Catholic school to refuse to hire individuals who engage in sex outside of marriage in contravention of Catholic religious doctrine. Such a policy is gender and sexual orientation neutral. As the Colorado Court of Appeals notes, "opposition to premarital romantic and sexual relationships, unlike opposition to same-sex marriage, is not tantamount to discrimination on the basis of sexual orientation."[104]

But under the approach called for by coreligionist exemptions, a Catholic school would not be allowed to fire employees because they entered into same-sex marriages; the government would be able to prohibit that type of discriminatory policy because it turns on the employees' sexual orientation.[105] In the same way that Title VII prohibits religious organizations from setting employment policies based on race or sex, sexual orientation antidiscrimination statutes should prohibit religious organizations from making employment decisions based on the sexuality of employees and job applicants. (The one important caveat, once again, is that antidiscrimination laws, under the ministerial exception, cannot be applied to ministers. If the employee in question is a minister within the meaning of that exception, religious organizations are constitutionally entitled to make hiring, firing, and promotion decisions on any ground, including sexual orientation.)

The same result is required if a religious organization refuses to pay for the health insurance benefits of its employees' same-sex spouses. As long as the organization is willing to pay for the health benefits of its employees' opposite-sex spouses, the law should deem its refusal to do the same in the case of same-sex relationships to constitute impermissible discrimination. This is because the distinction, once again, turns on the sexual orientation of the employees in question.

Note that the relevant distinction in these cases is not between conduct and belief. That is, under coreligionist exemptions contained in statutes such as Title VII, a religious organization is allowed to make distinctions based on an employee's conduct when that conduct is inconsistent with the organizations' religious beliefs *as long as it does not differentiate on the basis of race or gender.* For example, a religious organization can refuse to renew the contract of an employee who divorces and remarries if it considers such conduct to be sinful. What the organization cannot do is refuse to renew the contract of (nonministerial) female employees who remarry, but not male ones. This would be true even if the religious organization believed it is sinful for women to remarry, but not men.[106]

A Title VII case involving a claim of sex discrimination brought by a female teacher whose contract was not renewed by a Catholic school because she received in vitro fertilization treatment illustrates the distinction between the employment policies of religious organizations that are properly exempt under coreligionist exemption provisions and those that are not. Even if a Catholic school can make distinctions among employees on the basis of whether they have been involved in reproductive treatments that the Catholic Church believes are sinful (such as in vitro fertilization), the school may not apply its policy in ways that make distinctions on the basis of sex. As a result, the court permitted the female teacher to try to persuade a jury, which she ultimately did, that the Catholic school violated Title VII because it would not have refused to renew the contract of a male teacher who had been involved in his wife's in vitro fertilization treatment.[107]

I recognize that threads exist in the Title VII case law that might, at first glance, be understood to call for more expansive forms of religious accommodations than what I am describing here. For example, the U.S. Court of Appeals for the Third Circuit has concluded that, under Title VII, a religious organization can lawfully fire or refuse to hire individuals who have "publicly engaged in conduct regarded by [the organization] as inconsistent with its religious principles."[108] The court in that case held that the refusal by a Catholic school to renew the contract of a teacher of Protestant faith because she had remarried in contravention of Catholic doctrine did not violate Title VII. However, it bears noting that there was no evidence presented in the case showing that the school applied its "no remarriage rule" *in ways that took employees' gender into account.* That is, the school did not have a remarriage policy for women and another for men. It seems unlikely that the court would have been willing to apply Title VII's coreligionist exemption if the school allowed men but not women to remarry, even if such a gender-based distinction was mandated by the organization's religious principles.[109]

Sexual orientation, as a protected trait, should be treated in the same way that Title VII (and many state antidiscrimination statutes) regulates distinctions on the basis of race and sex: Religious organizations should be allowed to take religious doctrine into account in making employment decisions except when doing so leads to differential treatment on the basis of the employees' sexuality. In the same way that Title VII does not allow religious organizations to have one set of employment criteria for employees who are white or male and another set for those who are African American or female, religious exemptions from sexual orientation antidiscrimination laws should not permit religious organizations to implement one set of employment criteria for heterosexuals and another set for LGBT people.

3. Application to Broad Categories of Religious Organizations. There is a long tradition in the United States of religious organizations of all kinds pursuing their spiritual missions outside of houses of worship. To give just one example, the nation has a rich tradition of religious denominations, including Catholics, Lutherans, and Quakers, operating schools through which they seek to instill religious and moral values on children. As a result, Title VII broadly exempts religious corporations, associations, educational institutions, and societies. Based on the same reasoning, state law exemptions from employment antidiscrimination laws also generally apply to many different types of religious organizations that go beyond houses of worship.[110]

In determining whether any given organization qualifies for an exemption under Title VII, the courts ask whether the group's "purpose and character are primarily religious."[111] In answering that question, courts look to several factors (not all of which have to be present), including whether the organization is a nonprofit; if it has an explicitly religious purpose; if it is owned by or affiliated with a church or other house of worship; if it holds itself out as secular or sectarian; if its activities include prayer or other forms of worship; and if it is an educational institution, it includes religious instruction as part of the curriculum.[112] The same factors should be used to determine which organizations are eligible for exemptions from LGBT equality measures.

It is worth noting that the religious exemptions included in most of the marriage equality statutes adopted by state legislatures between 2009 and 2013 generally apply the Title VII model. Although those statutes are concerned with the provision of goods, services, and facilities, rather than with issues of employment, they are similar to Title VII in that they apply not just to churches and other houses of worship but also, in the words of the New York marriage equality statute, to "any religious or denominational institution or organization, or any organization operated for charitable or educational purposes, which is operated, supervised or controlled by or in connection with a religious organization."[113] Although in some close cases it may be difficult to determine whether an organization is sufficiently religious to be eligible for exemptions from the application of antidiscrimination laws, courts on the whole have been able to make these types of assessments without engendering much controversy or opposition. There is no reason to believe that they will be unable to do so in the context of LGBT rights issues.

4. Exemptions Limited to Nonprofit Entities. In 1972, when Congress was considering making changes to Title VII, Senator Sam Ervin of North Carolina argued that small business owners should be entitled to make employment decisions based on their religious views. Ervin claimed that when religious business owners only hire individuals of their own faith, they do not discriminate but instead simply conduct their businesses according to their religious beliefs. As Ervin put it, "I ... happen to believe that a person of a particular religion ought to have—and that he will have, in a free society—the right to employ a person whose religious beliefs are similar to his."[114]

Despite his views on the issue, Ervin did not propose an amendment that would have exempted businesses owned by religious individuals from Title VII, perhaps because he knew that most of his colleagues would not vote to approve it. (It probably did not help that Ervin also suggested that small business owners should be permitted to hire only those of their own race.)[115] This meant that Congress did not consider exempting for-profit enterprises from the scope of the statute.[116]

As we saw in Chapter 5, the Title VII compromise adopted by Congress allowed religious organizations to prefer coreligionists in making all employment decisions. The statute, however, limits that special dispensation to *nonprofit* religious entities; as already noted, courts look to whether an entity is a nonprofit, among other criteria, to determine whether it qualifies as a religious organization eligible to benefit from the religious exemption to Title VII. No court has held that a for-profit corporation is entitled to a religious exemption under Title VII. Indeed, as one commentator notes, there is "only one published case where a for-profit corporation [has] even sought the exemption."[117]

The same is true of religious exemptions under the federal Fair Housing Act, enacted in 1968. That statute allows religious organizations to sell or rent noncommercial properties to individuals of the same religion, but does not extend the exemption to for-profit enterprises.[118] Similarly, when Congress, more than twenty years later, enacted Title I of the Americans with Disabilities Act, which prohibits employment discrimination on the basis of disability, it limited the religious exemption to the same types of religious organizations exempted under Title VII.[119]

Many state antidiscrimination laws also exempt nonprofit religious organizations from their scope in some circumstances, but none exempt for-profit enterprises.[120] The same is true of religious exemptions contained in the marriage equality statutes enacted by about a dozen state legislatures between 2009 and 2013. Although most of those statutes exempt religious organizations from having to provide goods and services for the solemnization or celebration of marriages that are inconsistent with their religious views, they do not explicitly extend the exemptions to cover for-profit businesses, nor have courts interpreted the provisions in that way.

The same distinction between nonprofit religious organizations and for-profit entities is reflected in the constitutionally mandated ministerial exception. That exception, as explored in Chapter 5, allows a religious entity to choose employees involved in pursuing the organization's religious mission free of constraints imposed by antidiscrimination laws. Although courts have for decades immunized religious organizations from antidiscrimination liability under the ministerial exception, no court has ever extended the constitutional doctrine to for-profit entities.

The exclusion of for-profit entities from the scope of religious exemptions in matters related to the application of antidiscrimination laws is also consistent with the Supreme Court's multiple rulings on the lack of a constitutional right enjoyed by for-profit actors to discriminate. In the specific context of religious freedom, the Court has summarily dismissed the idea that the Free Exercise Clause protects business owners from the obligation not to discriminate under Title II of the Civil Rights Act of 1964.[121] And the Court has repeatedly reached the same conclusion when assessing other constitutional claims that would exempt for-profit entities from the application of antidiscrimination laws. As early as 1904, the Court upheld a California law prohibiting places of public amusement or entertainment from denying admission to paying members of the public (unless they were intoxicated or engaged in "boisterous conduct") from a constitutional challenge brought by a corporation that operated a race track. In doing so, the Court rejected the claim that the for-profit entity had either a liberty- or property-based right to exclude certain members of the public.[122] The justices reached the same conclusion more than sixty years later when assessing the constitutionality of Title II. A for-profit entity, the Court concluded, "has no 'right' to select its guests as it sees fit, free from governmental regulation."[123] In the years that followed, the Court rejected the notion that "commercially operated" schools had a First Amendment right, grounded in the freedom of association, to maintain racially exclusionary policies or that applying Title VII to the operation of a law firm by requiring it to provide equal opportunities to women violated the male law partners' rights of expression and association.[124] As Justice Sandra Day O'Connor has explained, "the Constitution does not guarantee a right to choose employees, customers, suppliers, or those with whom one engages in simple commercial transactions, without restraint from the State. [For example], a shopkeeper has no constitutional right to deal only with persons of one sex."[125]

Under both federal and state constitutional and statutory law, therefore, religious exemptions from antidiscrimination obligations have been limited to nonprofit religious organizations to the exclusion of for-profit entities. American antidiscrimination law, in carving out exemptions for religious dissenters, has repeatedly made distinctions between nonprofit religious organizations and for-profit entities. There is no apparent reason to treat issues related to discrimination on the basis of sexual orientation (or gender identity) any differently.

I want to make it clear that my claim is limited to the granting of discretionary religious exemptions *from antidiscrimination obligations* to for-profit entities. My argument is not that for-profit entities should be ineligible to receive First Amendment protections, such as that recognized by the Supreme Court in the controversial case of *Citizens United v. Federal Elections Commission*, involving the constitutionality of election finance laws that limit the use of general corporate treasury funds for electioneering expenditures.[126] The extent to which for-profit corporations should enjoy First Amendment protections goes beyond the scope of this book. In addition, I am not arguing that for-profit corporations should never be granted religious exemptions in *any* context; whether they should also goes beyond the scope of this book.[127] Instead, my claim is limited to the relatively narrow contention that the granting of religious exemptions from antidiscrimination obligations to for-profit entities is unprecedented in American history. There is no obvious reason why religious exemptions in the context of sexual orientation antidiscrimination laws in particular should depart from that tradition.

It is undoubtedly the case that those who support exempting for-profit entities from sexual orientation antidiscrimination obligations have been emboldened by the Court's ruling in *Hobby Lobby*. However, there are two aspects to *Hobby Lobby*'s reasoning that will likely limit its impact on the question of whether legislatures and courts should grant for-profit entities religious exemptions from antidiscrimination obligations. First, as already noted, the Court distinguished antidiscrimination laws—at least those involving race—from the contraceptive mandate at issue in the case. This suggests that the Court may not be so quick to conclude that for-profit entities enjoy (either constitutional or statutory) religious freedom rights to discriminate against groups protected by anti-discrimination laws.

Second, the Court's reasoning was based on the conclusion—perhaps the word "assumption" would be more accurate—that the granting of the exemption to closely held, for-profit entities would not harm third parties. Justice Samuel Alito, in writing for the majority, claimed that the impact on female employees of the granting of a religious exemption to their corporate employers "would be precisely zero."[128] For his part, Justice Anthony Kennedy, who provided the crucial fifth vote in *Hobby Lobby*, explained in his concurrence that religious liberty should not be promoted through exemptions in ways that "unduly restrict other persons, such as employees, in protecting their own interests."[129] Because Kennedy agreed that the Religious Freedom Restoration Act required the exemption, he also seemed to assume that the accommodation would not negatively impact the ability of the government to promote the interests of women in having free access to contraceptives.

As critics have pointed out, the Court was incorrect to surmise that the exemption did not harm third parties: In the months following the Court's ruling, many women who worked for exempted for-profit corporations, as well as their employees' female dependents, were harmed because they were unable to gain free access to contraceptives as the government worked to put in place an alternative mechanism for their provision.[130] It seems likely that courts, going forward, will not be so quick to assume that the granting of religious exemptions from antidiscrimination obligations to for-profit entities will not harm traditionally marginalized minorities, such as LGBT people. I return to the intersection of discrimination, exemptions, and harms below.

5. No Antidiscrimination Exemptions for Government Employees. Like proposed laws that would exempt for-profit entities from antidiscrimination obligations based on the owners' religious views, exemptions granting government employees the authority to refuse to serve *particular members of the public* based on the employees' religious views, in ways that allow them to escape the obligations of antidiscrimination obligations, are unprecedented in American history. Prior to the legal recognition of marriages by same-sex couples, no state had ever enacted a law allowing government officials to rely on their religious beliefs to refuse to serve groups protected by antidiscrimination laws.

It is true that Title VII, which applies not only to the private-sector but also to the public one, requires that employers accommodate religious employees unless doing so would constitute an undue hardship.[131] However, courts in interpreting Title VII's protections against religious discrimination have been generally skeptical of the notion that the statute requires the government to permit public servants to pick and choose whom to serve based on their religious views.[132] This skepticism seems particularly apt when the reason given by the government employee is linked to how particular members of the public self-identify.[133]

It is quite telling that, prior to the advent of same-sex marriage, there were no serious proposals to exempt government officials from antidiscrimination obligations in ways that would allow them to rely on their religious beliefs to decide which members of the public to serve. The absence of historical precedents is hardly surprising. Indeed, it is hard to imagine that any reasonable person would take seriously, for example, an exemption claim made by a Christian government employee who refuses, for religious reasons, to serve self-identified Jewish or Muslim members of the public because they engage in certain conduct. The same should hold true when assessing an exemption claim made by a religious government employee who refuses to serve members of the public who wish to marry someone of the same gender.

Sexual minorities, like all individuals, have rights under the federal Constitution, as well as all state constitutions, to equal treatment by the government. If the government as a whole cannot constitutionally deny benefits or services to LGBT people, it is unclear why the government should permit some of its representatives to refuse to serve them. For government officials to refuse to provide particular classes of individuals with services they are legally entitled to receive based on the officials' personal views, including those grounded in religious doctrine, constitutes a paradigmatic denial of the equal protection of the laws.[134]

Government employees, when exercising their official capacities, represent and speak for the state. On the question of marriage, the state is constitutionally required to treat same-sex couples on an equal footing with different-sex couples. To grant government employees the right to decide whom to serve based on sexual orientation is to permit the government to discriminate on that basis. For that reason, provisions such as the one enacted by Mississippi in 2016, which allows religious government officials to solemnize all marriages except those of same-sex couples, violate the Equal Protection Clause.[135]

Interestingly, even the legal claims raised by the Kentucky county clerk who garnered national attention in 2015 after her office stopped issuing marriage licenses implicitly recognized that government officials should not be permitted to pick and choose whom to serve based on the officials' religious views. Although the county clerk's religious objections were limited to same-sex marriages, she requested that she be accommodated by being allowed to stop issuing marriage licenses altogether. It is likely that the clerk and her lawyers asked for an accommodation that was much broader than that called for by her religious views (the clerk did not have religious objections to marrying different-sex couples) because they understood that a narrower exemption (one limited to same-sex couples) would be discriminatory and impermissible under *Obergefell*. Even the Kentucky county clerk and her lawyers seemed to understand that to grant her the accommodation that was actually tailored to her religious views would have placed the government in the constitutionally untenable position of discriminating on the basis of sexual orientation in the issuing of marriage licenses.[136]

It is true that provisions, such as those enacted by North Carolina and Utah, that allow the relevant government officials to decide not to issue *any* marriage licenses, when their reasons for doing so are religious in nature, do not permit government employees to pick and choose whom to marry. Nonetheless, *the context* in which these laws have been enacted is troubling. Although the North Carolina and Utah provisions are facially neutral (that is, the scope of the exemptions are not textually linked to the gender of the prospective spouses, as is the case with the Mississippi law), there is no doubt that the two state legislatures enacted the exemptions in order to allow government officials who object to same-sex marriages *in particular* to cease issuing marriage licenses. Even if the North Carolina and Utah provisions do not allow government officials to serve different-sex couples while turning away same-sex ones, the *purpose* of the statutes was to grant officials the discretion to decide whether they want to serve same-sex couples.

The accommodation of civil servants who object to same-sex marriages on religious grounds in ways that allow them to refuse to serve sexual minorities can reasonably lead LGBT people to question whether they are equal citizens entitled to equal treatment or whether theirs is a second-class citizenship. The demands for exemptions for government workers in matters related to same-sex marriages, after all, are not being made in a context in which the government has, until now, been impeccably neutral in how it views and treats sexual minorities. Instead, the government, at different levels and in different ways, has until recently enacted, implemented, and defended a series of laws and regulations (sodomy laws, policies that excluded LGBT people from civil service rolls, and same-sex marriage bans, to name just a few) intended to subordinate, silence, and humiliate sexual minorities who dared to be open about their sexual orientation. Viewed in that historical context, the refusal by some government officials to treat same-sex couples on an equal basis carries similar symbolic meanings and practical effects as would refusals to serve racial or religious minorities.[137]

It is also true that the North Carolina and Utah statutes require officials to make sure that someone is available to issue legally valid marriage licenses. But the availability of alternative officials does not make the exemptions any less troubling. Suppose, for example, that a government official has a religious objection to providing Christians or Muslims (or African Americans or Asians or Latinos) with public benefits they are otherwise entitled to receive. The fact that there are other officials in the same government office who are willing to assist all members of the public does not render a religious civil servant's refusal to serve particular classes of individuals who are otherwise legally entitled to the benefits in question any less problematic.

As with the question of religious exemptions benefitting for-profit entities, my argument here is a relatively narrow one. I am not contending that religious public employees should never be accommodated in ways that affect how they carry out their official duties.[138] Instead, my point is a more circumscribed one: we do not in this country have a tradition of enacting religious exemptions with the purpose of allowing civil servants to decide whether *to serve classes of individuals* who are otherwise both entitled to the service in question and protected by antidiscrimination laws. .

I have argued here that policy-makers and citizens, in assessing contemporary controversies over the state's authority to promote LGBT equality, should look to how American antidiscrimination law has traditionally sought to balance equality and liberty concerns. It is true, of course, that the mere fact that American antidiscrimination law has traditionally granted religious accommodations that go beyond what is constitutionally required; distinguished between the ability to hire coreligionists and the discretion to take other protected traits into account; allowed a broad category of religious organizations to benefit from exemptions and not just houses of worship; limited the beneficiaries of those accommodations to nonprofit organizations; and refused to exempt religious government employees from antidiscrimination obligations does not conclusively establish, as a normative matter, that the same should apply to religious exemptions from antidiscrimination laws in all circumstances, including those involving sexual minorities. But these time-tested characteristics of exemptions from antidiscrimination obligations create a strong presumption that they should be followed in determining the scope of exemptions in matters related to LGBT rights.

This means that if a proponent of LGBT equality contends that religious exemptions from sexual orientation antidiscrimination laws should be *narrower* than the exemptions that legislatures have granted religious dissenters in the past in matters related to race and gender—for example, by not extending exemptions beyond those that are constitutionally required or by limiting the beneficiaries of those exemptions to houses of worship, to the exclusion of other types of religious organizations—the proponent should have the burden of showing why LGBT equality should be treated differently from other forms of equality.[139]

Similarly, if an opponent of LGBT equality contends that religious exemptions from sexual orientation antidiscrimination laws should be *broader* than the exemptions that legislatures have granted religious dissenters in the past in matters related to race and gender—for example, by making religious exemptions available to for-profit entities or to government employees—the burden should be on the opponent to show why LGBT equality should be treated differently from other forms of equality. As law professor Alan Brownstein aptly puts it, "the contention that religious objectors to same-sex marriage must receive special accommodations beyond those that would be provided to others in comparable circumstances raises questions about preferentialism and equity that need to be addressed and resolved."[140] In short, if there is going to be LGBT rights exceptionalism when it comes to the scope of religious exemptions from antidiscrimination laws, the burden should be on proponents of that exceptionalism to establish why it is required.

Although I believe that applying the five principles that underlie the ways in which American antidiscrimination law, before the advent of same-sex marriage, sought to accommodate religious dissent while pursuing equality objectives, should guide the determination of how the law should accommodate religious dissent in the context of LGBT equality, I recognize that such an application will not, by itself, resolve all of the contemporary disputes in this area. For example, there is the question of whether religious organizations that provide goods, services, and facilities used to celebrate weddings should be allowed to make distinctions on whom to serve based on their religious beliefs. As noted earlier, about a dozen states enacted such exemptions as part of their adoption of marriage equality statutes between 2009 and 2013.

On the one hand, it could be argued that exemptions for religious organizations that provide goods, services, and facilities used to celebrate weddings are consistent with the limited scope of religious exemptions traditionally afforded by American antidiscrimination law. In particular, they benefit only nonprofit organizations of a religious nature and thus do not apply to the vast majority of photographers, bakers, and other *for-profit* wedding vendors. The exemptions also only apply to the actual solemnization or celebration of marriages, as opposed to the provision of goods, services, and facilities during the much longer *life of the marriage*.[141] On the other hand, it can be argued that the exemptions are inconsistent with the traditional way in which American antidiscrimination law has dealt with these issues because most public accommodation laws in the United States, including Title II of the Civil Rights Act of 1964, do not contain *any* exemptions for religious actors.[142]

Although exemptions for religious organizations that make wedding-related goods, services, and facilities available to the general public present a close case, it seems to me they are permissible under the traditional principles that undergird American antidiscrimination law's accommodation of religious actors for two main reasons. First, although most public accommodation antidiscrimination statutes do not allow for any religious exemptions, some do.[143] This makes exemptions for religious organizations that provide wedding-related goods, services, and facilities less of a historical outlier than, for example, exempting for-profit entities from antidiscrimination obligations. Second, the exemptions in question are limited to goods, services, and facilities associated with the solemnization or celebration of marriages, making them generally analogous to the constitutional protection that applies to the officiating of marriages. If the nation's tradition is not to force religious organizations to solemnize marriages that are inconsistent with their religious beliefs, then it seems acceptable for a legislature to go a little further by allowing the same organizations to decline to provide goods, services, and facilities to be used for the solemnization or celebration of marriages when doing so violates their religious beliefs.[144]

Although some progressive critics have argued that legislatures have been too accommodating of religious actors in some contexts (including through the exemptions contained in several marriage equality statutes),[145] it has been much more common for supporters of religious exemptions to criticize the insufficiency of existing exemptions. In fact, in my estimation, it has been supporters of religious exemptions who have sought, with much greater frequency and vehemence than opponents, to depart from the traditional ways in which American antidiscrimination law before the advent of same-sex marriage sought to accommodate religious dissent while pursuing equality objectives. For this reason, I end the chapter by critiquing two arguments raised frequently by supporters of expansive religious exemptions: first, that it is usually possible to exempt religious actors from sexual orientation antidiscrimination obligations without harming sexual minorities; and second, that religious exemptions in the context of sexual orientation merit more serious consideration than in that of race because most religious actors who believe, on conscience grounds, that it is proper to make distinctions on the basis of sexual orientation, in particular when it comes to marriage, act in good faith (that is, they are not homophobic), whereas those who believe it is proper to make racial distinctions always act in bad faith (that is, they are racists).

Discrimination and Its Harms

In assessing the merits of proposals calling for more expansive religious exemptions in matters related to LGBT equality than have been adopted in the past in the context of race and gender discrimination, it is important to keep in mind that religious exemptions from generally applicable laws are particularly problematic when granting them undermines the attainment of the state's interests behind those laws. The principal objective of antidiscrimination laws is to avoid the types of economic, social, and dignitary harms that discrimination imposes on its victims.[146] The denial of jobs, benefits, and services to members of certain classes of individuals has been one of the paradigmatic ways in which our society, unfortunately, has promoted racial, gender, and sexual orientation hierarchies and subordination. That turning away leaves members of traditionally stigmatized groups experiencing economic harms, social stigma, and the indignities associated with being considered second-class citizens.

Those who support granting exemptions benefiting religious actors in commercial contexts, such as the owner of the photography business in the *Elane Photography* case with which this chapter began, frequently contend that the exemptions would not usually harm LGBT people because they can find other providers willing to serve them. Exemption supporters claim that in these cases, the refusal to serve causes nothing more than, in the words of a leading religious liberty scholar, a "mere inconvenience."[147] Or as another academic supporter of religious exemptions from LGBT antidiscrimination measures puts it, "in most cases, the offended [same-sex] couple can go to the next entry in the phone book or the Google result" to find another merchant who is willing and able to provide the services or goods in question.[148]

It is important to note how anomalous it is to determine the appropriate outcome of a discrimination claim based on the availability of nondiscriminating actors in the same marketplace. Indeed, it is worth remembering that, even before the enactment of the Civil Rights Act of 1964, there were some areas of the South, in particular sections of large cities like Atlanta and Memphis, in which significant numbers of merchants, including white ones, were willing and able to serve black customers. But no one argued then that the availability of those alternative providers somehow lessened the harms, especially those related to dignity and the imposition of social stigma, associated with the original refusal of service.

In addition, merchants in the United States today generally serve black customers on equal terms with their white customers. An African American who is today refused service by a place of public accommodation, therefore, will in many instances be able to find alternative providers. Yet no one argues that fact justifies exempting religious owners of public accommodations from having to abide by racial antidiscrimination laws. In contrast, support for religious exemptions from LGBT equality measures is frequently premised on the notion of the "lone-wolf discriminator," that is, on the idea that because most business owners do not have religious objections to serving LGBT people, it is appropriate to exempt the few owners for whom such service is inconsistent with their religious values.[149]

The notion of the "lone-wolf discriminator" depends on rather speculative assertions grounded in the assumption that when religious business owners refuse to provide goods and services to LGBT people, the latter will usually be able to find alternative providers without difficulty. Whether those assertions are correct will likely vary by region depending on different factors, including prevailing social mores regarding sexual orientation, the applicability and enforcement of antidiscrimination laws, and even the extent to which there are legislatively mandated religious exemptions that apply to for-profit entities. It is not unreasonable to believe that the very existence of legislative carve outs from antidiscrimination obligations will encourage additional business owners to seek their protections. The availability of religious exemptions for providers of wedding goods and services will leave sexual minorities living in some areas of the country at the mercy of unpredictable marketplaces and vulnerable to the denial of those services and goods.

Supporters of religious exemptions from LGBT equality measures also minimize or ignore the dignitary harms associated with the initial refusal.[150] The crucial point is that the existence of alternative providers does not mitigate the dignitary harms associated with the original denial of the services or goods in question. As Chai Feldblum explains, "if I am denied a job, an apartment, a room at a hotel, a table at a restaurant, or a procedure by a doctor because I am a lesbian, that is a deep, intense, and tangible hurt. That hurt is not alleviated because I might be able to go down the street and get those [services] from someone else. The assault to my dignity and my sense of safety in the world occurs when the initial denial happens. That assault is not mitigated by the fact that others might not treat me in the same way."[151]

In distinguishing between permissible differentiation and wrongful discrimination, the theorist Deborah Hellman asks whether the distinctions in question demean others. According to Hellman, whether differential treatment demeans those affected depends on social contexts and meanings. As she explains, "whether the characteristic one uses to classify has the potential to demean is determined largely by how that characteristic has been used to separate people in the past and the relative social status of the group defined by the characteristic today."[152] That is why, for example, to ask racial minorities to sit at the back of the bus constitutes wrongful discrimination but asking teenagers to do the same does not.

Religious objections to same-sex relationships have traditionally been linked to understandings of sexual minorities that view them as sinners and as individuals who are morally compromised and tainted by their intimate relationships and sexual conduct. This is why, as law professors Douglas NeJaime and Reva Siegel note, when a person of faith refuses to serve LGBT individuals on moral grounds, those individuals "will immediately comprehend the social meaning that refusal expresses."[153] Such social meaning is driven by status-based judgments, that is, judgments grounded in the perceived moral unworthiness of sexual minorities as a class based on who and how they love. It is not surprising, therefore, that many LGBT people find service refusals by business owners to be demeaning and stigmatizing.[154] And when the law refuses to address the harms to dignity and self-worth that inevitably accompany the refusals, it engenders inferiority, vulnerability, and second-class citizenship in sexual minorities.

To claim that the harm suffered by sexual minorities when business owners, who make their goods and services available to the general public, refuse to serve them on religious grounds amounts to nothing more than a "mere inconvenience" (as long as there are other willing providers in the area) is to ignore the insight of those who enacted the Civil Rights Act of 1964 "that the primary purpose of [that law was] to solve . . . the deprivation of personal dignity that surely accompanies denials of equal access to public establishments."[155] As Congress recognized more than fifty years ago, to deny goods and services to members of the public because of who they are causes "humiliation, frustration, and embarrassment."[156] The Supreme Court has similarly recognized that discrimination by places of public accommodation "deprives persons of their individual dignity and denies society the benefits of wide participation in political, economic, and cultural life."[157]

Finally, it bears noting that when the Supreme Court, prior to *Employment Division v. Smith*, called for constitutionally-mandated religious exemptions from generally applicable laws, it did so only when the accommodations did not impose significant harms on third parties.[158] In addition, as already noted, the Supreme Court's ruling in *Hobby Lobby* was premised on the view that exempting closely held corporations owned by religious individuals from the obligation to provide female employees with free access to contraceptives did not harm the employees because the government had alternative ways of guaranteeing the access. It is not possible for the government to protect LGBT people from the harms associated with sexual orientation and gender identity discrimination other than by prohibiting that discrimination.

Those who support broad religious exemptions from LGBT equality obligations argue that the government must respect not only religious beliefs, but also religious conduct, including conduct in the commercial sphere. Some have analogized between the importance of religious identity and sexual orientation identity. In the same way that sexuality and intimate relationships help to define individuals while serving as sources of human dignity and autonomy, the argument goes, religion for many individuals helps to determine their identity and gives them a sense of dignity and purpose.[159] Furthermore, in both instances, the importance of the identity is not limited to matters of beliefs, but is instead intrinsically connected to conduct, specifically how individuals interact with others. It is then argued that, in the same way that the state does not sufficiently respect sexual minority identities when it tolerates their status but burdens their conduct, the government fails to acknowledge the importance of religion in the lives of individuals when it respects freedom of religious belief but prohibits conduct based on that belief. As one religious liberty scholar puts it, the religious believer, like the LGBT person, "has an interest in acting in accordance with her identity and deepest commitments."[160]

It is possible to concede, for purposes of argument, the validity of the identity analogy between sexual orientation and religion, and similarly concede that identity entails more than the holding of certain beliefs and views. But neither of those points justifies granting more expansive religious exemptions in the context of LGBT equality than those granted by legislatures and courts in the past in the context of race and gender discrimination. Engaging in same-sex sexual relationships or entering in a same-sex marriage does not harm third parties. The same cannot be said for denying goods and services to same-sex couples, to say nothing of firing employees because of their sexual orientation or because they have married someone of the same sex. In short, claims in favor of broad religious exemptions from LGBT equality measures, which go beyond the scope of traditional religious exemptions in American antidiscrimination law, have insufficiently accounted for the harms that those exemptions impose on third parties.

Distinguishing Race Discrimination and Questions of (Good) Faith

I am arguing here that accommodations of religious believers from LGBT equality mandates should generally track the types of accommodations traditionally granted to those who dissent, on religious grounds, from racial and gender equality. A critic may claim that there is a crucial difference between religious dissent from marriage equality and religious dissent from racial equality in particular: whereas racists, including religious ones, always act in bad faith, many individuals who object to serving same-sex couples on religious grounds act in good faith. As law professor Douglas Laycock puts it, "sometimes . . . refusals of service [to LGBT people] may be an act of bigotry or social protest, but very often, the claim to feel moral responsibility, or even fear of divine punishment, will be in complete good faith."[161] For his part, law professor Thomas Berg argues that those who, in earlier times, dissented on religious grounds "from basic racial equality showed an intransigence that bespoke a permanent dismissal of African-Americans as full humans." In contrast, religious dissenters from marriage equality act in good faith because "there is a serious debate about the relationship of sexuality and procreation to marriage, and about the relevance of the centuries of tradition—of accumulated social knowledge—which the world's great religions embody and which almost uniformly has treated marriage as a relationship between a man and a woman."[162] Similarly, law professor Robin Fretwell Wilson claims that "while the parallels between racial discrimination and discrimination on the basis of sexual orientation should not be dismissed, it is not clear that the two are equivalent in this context. The religious and moral convictions that motivate objectors to facilitate same-sex marriage simply cannot be marshaled to justify racial discrimination."[163]

In short, the claim is that arguments for racial inequality are (now) so beyond the pale that even religious-based claims of racial superiority reflect raw prejudice rather than good faith adherence to religious values.[164] In contrast, exemption proponents contend, reasonable people can (still) disagree about the appropriateness of maintaining marriage as a heterosexual institution. As a result, many of those who object to providing same-sex couples with goods and services for the celebration of their marriages do so in good faith and without prejudice.

The effort to distinguish religious-based objections to LGBT equality from religious-based objections to racial equality—in order to justify broader exemptions in the sexuality context—fails from the beginning because it is grounded in the notion that some religious views are more reasonable than others. Even if exemption proponents are correct in their assessment that the views of religious objectors to racial equality are unreasonable and bigoted while the views of many religious objectors to marriage equality are not, it is extremely problematic to set policies, including religious exemptions from generally applicable laws, on ostensible distinctions between reasonable and unreasonable religious views.

Indeed, it is difficult for outsiders to determine the degree of good faith with which individuals assert religious claims. Such a determination usually requires intrusive inquiries into the nature of and justifications for religious values, inquiries made even more problematic by the fact that religious beliefs are by their nature grounded in considerations of faith rather than in those of reason. As a result, courts are appropriately hesitant to scrutinize either the sincerity of religious litigants or the reasonableness of their views.[165]

It is hard to know with any certainty whether the line between bigotry and good faith on the question of religious objections to marriage equality is as clearly demarcated as exemption proponents claim. Assessments regarding the reasonableness of religious views (by which I mean whether religious views are, in effect, beyond the pale) are inevitably affected by the passage of time and changing social norms. Our assessments of what constitutes "beyond the pale" arguments change as more information becomes available, new ways of thinking are proposed, and new equality claims are made. In other words, our assessments of the line between bigoted and good faith opposition to equality measures change as society changes. Although exemption proponents seem confident in their view that the religious claims of many who oppose marriage equality, unlike individuals who opposed racial equality on religious grounds in earlier times, are not beyond the pale and that many religious opponents of same-sex marriage act in good faith, history's judgment may very well be different. In fact, it seems that growing segments of our society already view morals-based justifications for the differential treatment of LGBT people, even when religiously grounded, with the same kind of skepticism that they view morals-based beliefs about racial differences.

I have argued in this chapter that activists and commentators who contend that LGBT equality gains call for broader religious exemptions than those granted in the past in the context of racial and gender equality should have the burden to explain why that is the case. Efforts to do so based on the good faith of those who object to the application of LGBT equality mandates on religious grounds are insufficient.

At the end of the day, proponents of broad religious exemptions in the context of LGBT issues have failed to offer persuasive reasons for departing in significant ways from how antidiscrimination law has in the past accommodated religious dissenters in the context of race and gender. Well-established exemptions, such as the ministerial and Title VII exemptions, have provided important protections to religious organizations by allowing them to pursue their spiritual missions without having to abide by antidiscrimination obligations applicable to other entities. At the same time, the well-established religious exemptions have not interfered, to any significant degree, with the ability of antidiscrimination laws to achieve their objectives. The ways in which our country through the decades has balanced the pursuit of equality for marginalized groups against the liberty interests, including those associated with religious freedom, of equality opponents constitute time-tested, reasonable, and workable compromises that decision-makers and citizens should use as guides in addressing contemporary disputes arising from the tension between the attainment of LGBT equality and the protection of religious freedom. There is no need for LGBT rights exceptionalism when determining how religious liberty considerations should limit the scope and application of antidiscrimination laws.

Conclusion

THIS BOOK has explored the relationship between the exercise of First Amendment rights and the attainment of LGBT equality objectives. Long before the law recognized that LGBT people had rights to equality, courts started protecting the ability of sexual minorities to express themselves and to associate with each other. The courts' early recognition of the First Amendment rights of sexual minorities proved crucial in allowing LGBT activists to begin articulating claims to equal treatment and, eventually, to start persuading growing segments of the population that LGBT people were entitled to full legal equality.

Several decades later, the LGBT movement has attained remarkable achievements, including marriage equality for same-sex couples, the elimination of de jure sexual orientation discrimination, and the enactment by almost half the states of sexual orientation antidiscrimination laws. These achievements would have been impossible had it not been for the large shifts in the social and moral understandings of LGBT people and their sexuality—shifts that came about largely as the result of the exercise of First Amendment rights. It has been the speaking, associating, mobilizing, and organizing by increasingly vocal and outspoken members of LGBT communities, and their allies, that have persuaded large segments of the American public that sexual orientation does not affect the capabilities or moral worth of individuals, that same-sex relationships and intimacy are not morally problematic, and that discrimination on the basis of sexual orientation is morally wrong.

The fact that the First Amendment protects the rights of sexual minorities to speak and associate is by now well established and noncontroversial. But as Part I explored, that was not the case in the early decades of the LGBT movement. Early activists had to continuously assert and defend the rights of LGBT people to express themselves and to associate with each other. Starting in the late 1950s, courts began to provide, at first gradually and later more frequently, important protections to sexual minorities in the areas of free speech and association.

Several factors accounted for these early judicial victories by LGBT activists. First, by the time gay rights activism began, courts were growing increasingly skeptical of the government's contention that the promotion of public morality through obscenity law justified the suppression of same-sex political and erotic materials. Although courts did not question the moral condemnation of same-sex sexual conduct and relationships, they did begin to rule that the government could not rely on that condemnation to limit the ability of sexual minorities to express themselves and to associate with each other.

Second, early gay activists were able to build on the First Amendment protections that the Supreme Court had granted to civil rights activists. By the early 1960s, the Court was repeatedly voiding, on First Amendment grounds, efforts by Southern officials to restrict the ability of civil rights activists to agitate in favor of racial equality. Gay activists were able to use those legal precedents to gain protections for the small number of sexual minorities who were starting to challenge the ways in which society understood and regulated LGBT people.

Third, as the number of lesbians, gay men, and bisexuals who came out of the closet began increasing significantly in the 1970s, government officials, often acting in their capacity as employers or university administrators, moved to penalize them for their openness. This led LGBT employees and students, for example, to turn to the First Amendment by asserting that it protected their ability to self-identify and associate. The courts' record of protecting LGBT individuals in these contexts was a generally good one, with sufficient judicial victories along the way to place important restrictions on the ability of government officials to try to keep lesbian, gay, and bisexual people isolated and in the closet.

By the 1980s, it became relatively rare, outside of the military context, for government actors to attempt to directly interfere with the ability of sexual minorities to express themselves or to associate with each other. But the fact that it was clear by then that the First Amendment afforded protections to LGBT people did not minimize the practical importance of those protections for the movement. Indeed, LGBT activists repeatedly exercised those rights—through speaking, associating, mobilizing, and organizing—in order to bring attention to, and gain reforms in, several areas of law and policy, including sodomy regulations, AIDS funding and services, and marriage inequality.

The connection between LGBT equality objectives and free speech principles has been linked in crucial ways to shifting moral values. The moral understandings of LGBT people, their relationships, and their intimate conduct that prevailed for most of the twentieth century served as significant impediments to the early LGBT movement's ability to articulate, and to make progress on, equality claims. It was the exercise of First Amendment rights by early LGBT organizations and activists that allowed the movement, first, to express the moral need for equal treatment, and second, to begin to attain specific reforms that turned that moral vision into practice. Before sexual minorities could enjoy rights to equality, they first had to gain rights to speak, agitate, and associate. It was only after those First Amendment rights were firmly in place that the LGBT movement was in a position to start asserting and winning equality claims.

The ongoing and repeated exercise by sexual minorities of their First Amendment rights contributed in crucial ways to changing social and moral understandings of LGBT people, their sexual conduct, and their relationships. To put it simply, those understandings shifted, initially, from deep disapproval to tolerance and, later, to a growing acceptance of the equal moral worth of LGBT people and their relationships. With those changes came ever-increasing legal reforms, ones that generally eliminated the legally mandated differential treatment of sexual minorities and, in some jurisdictions, codified into law prohibitions against discrimination on the basis of sexual orientation and gender identity.

Of course, not everyone embraced these changes in the law. As in previous periods in American history, the expansion of equality rights for some led others to complain that such an expansion threatened their liberty rights. Opponents of LGBT equality measures have consistently relied on First Amendment values and principles to try to limit the scope of the government's authority to promote LGBT equality.

That authority, it has been argued, is circumscribed in crucial ways by the rights of LGBT equality opponents to speak, associate, and exercise their religion.

The First Amendment played a similar role in the early days of the LGBT movement as it has played more recently in the context of opposition to LGBT equality measures. In both instances, groups and individuals holding minority views on matters of sexuality relied on the amendment's values and principles to advance their normative and political positions. The First Amendment, among other things, serves to protect the rights of expression, association, and religious exercise of those whose views and priorities depart from majoritarian values. It stands to reason, therefore, that in earlier decades, it was LGBT activists who turned to the First Amendment to try to change a society that was deeply critical and fearful of same-sex relationships and conduct. As the American society became more tolerant of sexual minorities, and as that tolerance began to be reflected in laws and policies, it was dissenters from increasingly prevailing majoritarian views on the importance of LGBT equality who looked to First Amendment values and principles as means for advancing their beliefs and promoting their objectives.

This use of the First Amendment by both proponents and opponents of LGBT rights shows the duality of the amendment's relationship to sexuality equality. On the one hand, the amendment, by demanding that the state remain neutral in response to private expression on matters of sexuality, contributed in significant ways to the ability of the early LGBT movement to agitate in favor of equality for sexual minorities. On the other hand, that same neutrality requirement has made it possible for equality opponents, in some contexts, to limit the ability of the government to promote equality.

The history of the pursuit of LGBT rights in this country shows that not only do First Amendment values and principles promote the attainment of equality objectives, but they also can place limits on their scope. The right of association, which derives from the Free Speech Clause, allows expressive associations to exclude individuals whose presence limits or affects their ability to communicate political, social, or religious messages. And the Religion Clauses recognize the rights of religious organizations to choose the ministers who carry out their spiritual missions free from antidiscrimination obligations. Going beyond constitutional mandates, civil rights laws, especially in the employment context, frequently exempt religious organizations from some antidiscrimination obligations based on religious liberty considerations.

Although it may initially seem paradoxical that the First Amendment both makes equality possible and limits its scope, that apparent contradiction is one that, on reflection, makes sense. For historically stigmatized minorities, the freedom to agitate against discriminatory government laws and policies constitutes a crucial initial step in the process of challenging their subordination. As with racial minorities and women, the marginalization of LGBT people was historically predicated on successful efforts to silence them, including by making sure they were unable to advocate for their interests, articulate viable claims to equal treatment, or organize and mobilize in favor of legal and policy reforms. Under these circumstances, meaningful equality could not be obtained in the absence of recognized rights of free speech and association.

At the same time, the pursuit of equality at all costs can bring with it problematic outcomes, including the trampling on the legitimate liberty interests of those who dissent from that pursuit. In the end, under our constitutional structure, rights to free expression, association, and the free exercise of religion, on the one hand, and those to equality, on the other hand, are not absolute. Instead, legislatures, courts, and voters must make difficult decisions on how best to balance the promotion of equality against rights of expression, association, and religious freedom. Our country has grappled with these issues in the context of race and gender in earlier decades, is currently grappling with them in the context of sexual orientation, and will undoubtedly face them in new contexts in the future. Although these conflicts can be difficult and divisive, they are the price that our nation pays for valuing both equality and liberty.

There are some who have argued, in contradistinction to our nation's practices, that either liberty or equality should be *the* normative polestar in settling issues of discrimination. Some strict libertarians have contended that equality-based considerations should never (or almost never) trump the freedom of private individuals to contract and associate with whomever they wish. In contrast, some strict egalitarians have contended that the state should never (or almost never) tolerate discrimination of any kind against traditionally marginalized groups. The problem with these views is that it is impossible, at the end of the day, to enforce equality principles to the maximum extent possible without interfering in significant and problematic ways with liberty considerations. And the opposite is just as true: to enforce liberty to the maximum extent possible comes at the price of an unacceptable loss of equality.

We are fortunate that our tradition as a nation has been to grapple with difficult and socially contested questions associated with the proper scope of antidiscrimination protections by rejecting a strict and monolithic adherence to either liberty or equality considerations. Instead, our antidiscrimination tradition has been to balance equality concerns against liberty considerations. This tradition is reflected in both constitutional doctrine and statutory frameworks. Examples of the former include the right of expressive associations, in at least some circumstances, to choose their members free from governmental interference and the categorical right of religious organizations to choose their ministers free from antidiscrimination obligations. Examples of the latter include the many antidiscrimination statutes that contain religious exemptions that go beyond what is constitutionally mandated. As I argued in Chapter 7, policy-makers and citizens should look to the reasonable, workable, and time-tested ways in which American antidiscrimination law has grappled with the tension between equality and liberty for guidance in how to solve contemporary LGBT rights disputes that implicate the speech, association, and religious exercise rights of those who dissent from LGBT equality.

There are three final points worth emphasizing about the relationship between the First Amendment and LGBT equality explored in this book. First, it is essential that LGBT rights advocates continue to agitate vigorously for robust legal protections against discrimination. It is morally unacceptable that LGBT people who are today denied jobs, housing, or goods and services because of their sexual orientation or gender identity are not explicitly protected against discrimination by either federal law or by the laws of most states. At the same time, it is important for LGBT rights advocates to acknowledge that shifting social and moral views on matters of sexuality and gender identity have turned conservative positions on these issues, in some areas of the country and in some contexts, into distinctly minority views. Those who advocate in favor of rights for sexual and gender-identity minorities need to remember that not too long ago, it was LGBT equality positions that were the social and moral outliers. Now that the tables are turning, it is important that equality be defended and pursued in ways that do not trample on the rights of

expression and conscience of dissenters. The LGBT movement, in continuing to seek equality objectives through state action, should strive to
show respect for the rights of dissenters in ways that earlier opponents
of LGBT rights, in seeking antiequality objectives through state action,
never did. The First Amendment requires nothing less.

There are some LGBT rights proponents who seem to oppose *all*
exemptions benefiting opponents of LGBT equality. Indeed, some critics,
concerned with the efforts to limit LGBT equality and women's reproductive rights on religious liberty grounds, have called for a reconsideration
of the very idea that government should provide any accommodations to
religious observants.[1]

Such responses by some LGBT rights supporters are in many ways
understandable given that many committed opponents to LGBT equality
seem to be clutching onto religious liberty claims in a final, and seemingly
desperate, effort to try to preclude full legal equality for sexual minorities.
However, one of the purposes of this book has been to place contemporary
disputes over the scope of the state's authority to promote LGBT equality
in a broad, historical perspective. It seems to me that the history explored
in Part I should encourage progressives to approach the question of accommodations for those who dissent from LGBT equality on conscience
grounds in careful and open-minded ways. After all, not too long ago, it
was sexual minorities who were in great need of the protections afforded by
First Amendment values and principles in a society that was deeply skeptical and critical of the morality of LGBT people, their relationships, and
their forms of intimacy. The exercise by sexual minorities of their rights
to speech and association contributed in crucial ways to gradual changes
in that morality through the decades, changes generally characterized by a
moving away from disapproval and toward greater acceptance of same-sex
sexualities. These changes, in turn, led to significant equality gains.

Those gains would not have been possible had social and moral understandings of sexuality not shifted in fundamental ways toward the view
that sexual orientation is a benign trait and that sexual orientation discrimination is morally wrong. It is now those who dissent from this changing moral environment who are increasingly relying on First Amendment
values and principles to attain their legal and political objectives. It is
problematic to be unequivocally for protections grounded in those values and principles when they help the social movements we support, but
to be uniformly skeptical of them when they hinder those movements'

objectives, however laudable and worthy. In considering requests for exemptions from sexual orientation antidiscrimination mandates, it is necessary to keep in mind that majoritarian social and moral norms, as LGBT people know too well, can sometimes insufficiently account for the voices and interests of dissenters.

Second, the fact that both sides turned to the First Amendment for protection does not mean that dissenters from LGBT equality today are in a similar legal and moral position as were LGBT people in earlier decades. Some supporters of religious exemptions from LGBT equality measures have sought to draw parallels between the oppression faced by sexual minorities in earlier eras and the oppression that marriage equality purportedly imposes on religious conservatives in the absence of broad exemptions. As two prominent religious liberty scholars put it, without those exemptions, the result will be that "same-sex couples [will] oppress religious dissenters in the same way that those dissenters, when they had the power to do so, oppressed same-sex couples."[2]

It is important to question these types of rather simplistic analogies by distinguishing between the two very different types of government policies that have been at issue in LGBT rights controversies implicating First Amendment values and principles. The government campaigns to silence sexual minorities in earlier decades were part of concerted efforts to deprive LGBT individuals of their most basic constitutional and human rights in order to harass and intimidate them while making sure they stayed deep in the closet. There is no constitutional or moral equivalence between the government's coercive repression of LGBT individuals in the past and contemporary government efforts to recognize the rights to full citizenships of sexual minorities.

It is true, of course, that those efforts have caused distress among many social and religious conservatives who disagree with them, especially when the law calls on equality dissenters to abide by sexual orientation and gender identity nondiscrimination principles. Nonetheless, there are crucial differences in the nature and objectives of the state action in the two eras. The efforts to silence sexual minorities in earlier decades were part of broader government campaigns to silence, harass, and intimidate those who dared to be open about their emotional and sexual attraction to others of the same sex—campaigns that included not only efforts to squelch expression and punish association, but also to target LGBT people (in particular gay men and transgender women) for criminal prosecution and to expel sexual minorities from government jobs. The government's policies in the earlier period specifically targeted, subordinated, and silenced sexual minorities, doing so at a time when heterosexual privilege, despite its devastating effects on the lives of sexual and gender-identity minorities, was entirely taken for granted and was assumed to be the only acceptable moral position on these issues.

In stark contrast, the policies that many LGBT rights opponents today deem to be threats to their rights of conscience are the result of state efforts to guarantee basic equality for a traditionally subordinated minority. The objective today is to adopt laws and policies that address some of the most harmful structural and institutional manifestations of anti-LGBT bias, regulations that, by their very nature, are in tension with the views of those who oppose full equality for sexual minorities, but are not intended to target, subordinate, or silence social and religious conservatives.

It is important to keep in mind the differences related to the nature and objectives of the state action in the two eras when assessing the merits of the frequently raised claim by those on the right that LGBT equality measures "discriminate" against social and religious conservatives. In the same way that there was no constitutional or moral equivalence between the legal regime that created and protected racial segregation and white privilege from the legal regime that sought to dismantle it, there is no equivalence between laws and policies aimed to subordinate and silence sexual minorities and those aimed at guaranteeing them full citizenship rights.

It is true that in some parts of the country, and among certain segments of the population, anti-LGBT rights views are increasingly viewed with a great deal of skepticism and even opprobrium. But that does not mean that the enforcement of LGBT equality laws in those political and social environments "discriminate" against religious conservatives. The defense of the differential treatment of people on the basis of race in the United States also eventually came to be generally stigmatized and viewed by many with a great deal of opprobrium. As society becomes more inclusive, some defenses of inequality understandably come to be viewed with greater suspicion. That process is part and parcel of fulfilling the promise of equality to all Americans.

Finally, when we step back and look at the recurring and multifaceted intersections of First Amendment values and principles with LGBT equality objectives through the decades, it is clear that the amendment's protections have contributed to LGBT equality to a significantly greater extent than they have hindered its attainment. Although a narrow focus on contemporary LGBT rights disputes that also implicate the rights of social and religious conservatives may make it seem as if the First Amendment is more of a hindrance than a contributor to LGBT equality, the historically based perspectives provided in this book reveal that the amendment's protections contributed in crucial ways to the initiation and expansion of LGBT equality in the United States. It is only because the First Amendment, as an initial matter, made meaningful LGBT equality possible that it more recently has played a role in limiting, to some extent, the ability of the state to further promote that equality. The bottom line is this: without the First Amendment, LGBT equality as we know and experience it in the United States today would not exist.

NOTES

ACKNOWLEDGMENTS

INDEX

Notes

Introduction

1. Although this book focuses primarily on issues of sexual orientation, some of its content is relevant to questions of gender identity as well. As a general matter, therefore, I use broader and more inclusive terms (e.g., "LGBT movement" and "LGBT rights") rather than narrower and less inclusive ones (e.g., "gay movement" or "gay rights").

2. Other legal scholars have noted the importance of the First Amendment in the history and progress of the LGBT movement. See William N. Eskridge Jr., *Gaylaw: Challenging the Apartheid of the Closet* (Cambridge, MA: Harvard University Press, 1999), Ch. 3; Nan D. Hunter, "Identity, Speech, and Equality," 79 *Virginia Law Review* 1695 (1993). See also Dale Carpenter, "Expressive Association and Anti-Discrimination Law after *Dale*: A Tripartite Approach," 85 *Minnesota Law Review* 1515, 1528–1533 (2001).

3. As I explain in Chapter 7, the Free Exercise Clause plays a limited role in circumscribing the ability of the state to enforce antidiscrimination laws. For that reason, most of the ongoing disputes regarding religious exemptions from LGBT equality measures involve questions of legislative discretion rather than constitutional mandates. Although the First Amendment is not usually directly implicated in these disputes, its values and principles help to frame the legal and policy debates over the extent to which legislatures should exempt those who object to same-sex marriages on religious grounds from sexual orientation antidiscrimination laws.

4. One, Inc. v. Olesen, 355 U.S. 371 (1958); Manual Enterprises, Inc. v. Day, 370 U.S. 478 (1962).

5. Although this book generally focuses on the LGBT rights movement and not on other equality movements, the second section of Chapter 2 explains the role that the First Amendment played in helping the civil rights movement attain some of its objectives during the 1950s and 1960s.

6. Bowers v. Hardwick, 478 U.S. 186 (1986).

7. Hurley v. Irish-American Gay, Lesbian, and Bisexual Group of Boston, 515 U.S. 557 (1995); Boy Scouts of America v. Dale, 530 U.S. 640 (2000); Christian Legal Society v. Martinez, 561 U.S. 661 (2010).

Chapter 1: Moral Displacement and Obscenity Law

1. The first edition of *ONE* appeared six years after a Los Angeles woman, whose pseudonym was Lisa Ben (an anagram for "lesbian"), self-published nine issues of a publication, more of a newsletter than a magazine, called *Vice Versa*. On Ben and her publication of *Vice Versa*, see Rodger Streitmatter, *Unspeakable: The Rise of the Gay and Lesbian Press in America* (Boston: Faber & Faber, 1995), 1–16.

2. For a discussion of the background, scope, and impact of the federal obscenity statute, originally known as the Comstock Act, see Donna Dennis, *Licentious Gotham: Erotic Publishing and Its Prosecution in Nineteenth-Century New York* (Cambridge, MA: Harvard University Press, 2009), Ch. 7.

3. One, Inc. v. Olesen, 241 F.2d 772 (9th Cir. 1957).

4. One, Inc. v. Olesen, 355 U.S. 371 (1958); Manual Enterprises, Inc. v. Day, 370 U.S. 478 (1962).

5. See Christopher Wolfe, "Public Morality and the Modern Supreme Court," 45 *American Journal of Jurisprudence* 65 (2000). See also Patrick Devlin, *The Enforcement of Morals* (New York: Oxford University Press, 1965); H. L. A. Hart, *Law, Liberty, and Morality* (Stanford, CA: Stanford University Press, 1963).

6. For a comprehensive study of the lives of lesbians and gay men during World War II, see Allan Bérubé, *Coming out Under Fire: The History of Gay Men and Women in World War Two* (New York: Free Press, 1990).

7. Alfred C. Kinsey, Wardell B. Pomeroy, Clyde E. Martin, and Paul H. Gebhard, *Sexual Behavior in the Human Female* (Philadelphia: W. B. Saunders, 1953); Alfred C. Kinsey, Wardell B. Pomeroy, and Clyde E. Martin, *Sexual Behavior in the Human Male* (Philadelphia: W. B. Saunders, 1948).

8. For a comprehensive study of the federal government's effort to identify, harass, and dismiss lesbian and gay employees during the 1950s, see David K. Johnson, *The Lavender Scare: The Cold War Prosecution of Gays and Lesbians in the Federal Government* (Chicago: University of Chicago Press, 2004).

9. Subcommittee on Investigations of the Senate Committee on Expenditures in the Executive Department, "Interim Report: Employment of Homosexuals and Other Sex Perverts in Government" (1950).

10. Executive Order 10450 (1952).

11. John D'Emilio, *Sexual Politics, Sexual Communities: The Making of a Homosexual Minority in the United States, 1940–1970* (Chicago: University of Chicago Press, 1983), 44.

12. Ibid., 49–50. For explorations of the sex-crime panic that swept through the United States in the late 1940s and early 1950s, see Genny Beemyn, *A Queer Capital: A History of Gay Life in Washington, D.C.* (New York: Routledge, 2015), 130–132; George Chauncey, "The Postwar Sex Crime Panic," in *True Stories from the American Past*, William Graebner, ed. (New York: McGraw-Hill, 1993), 160.

13. On the founding of *ONE*, see Craig M. Loftin, *Masked Voices: Gay Men and Lesbians in Cold War America* (Albany: State University of New York Press, 2012), 20–21; C. Todd White, *Pre-Gay L.A.: A Social History of the Movement for Homosexual Rights* (Urbana: University of Illinois Press, 2009), 28–40.

14. White, *Pre-Gay L.A.*, 42–43. The articles are set forth in their entirety in Articles of Incorporation, ONE, Incorporated, filed with the California Secretary of State, February 7, 1953, available at http://www.tangentgroup.org/history/ONE%20Inc/ONEIncarticles.html.

15. Dale Jennings, "To Be Accused Is to Be Guilty," *ONE*, January, 1953, 13.

16. See, e.g., George Henry Mortenson, "To Be Accused Is to Be Guilty," *ONE*, May, 1953, 12–13; Lyn Pedersen, "Miami Hurricane," *ONE*, November, 1954, 4–8; "Miami Junks the Constitution," *ONE*, January, 1954, 16–21.

17. On the early efforts to distribute *ONE*, see Loftin, *Masked Voices*, 45–50.

18. For a large sample of readers' letters to *ONE*, see Craig M. Loftin, *Letters to ONE: Gay and Lesbian Voices from the 1950s and 1960s* (Albany: State University of New York Press, 2012).

19. For a detailed account of the FBI's investigation of *ONE* and its editors in 1953, see Douglas M. Charles, "From Subversion to Obscenity: The FBI's Investigations of the Early Homophile Movement in the United States, 1953–1958," 19 *Journal of the History of Sexuality* 262 (2010). The FBI renewed its interest in *ONE* several years later after it published an essay suggesting there were gay men working for the agency. The agency also investigated, and kept track of, the Mattachine Society and the Daughters of Bilitis. For internal documents relating to these investigations, see https://vault.fbi.gov/mattachine-society.

20. E. B. Saunders, "Marriage License or Just License?," *ONE*, August, 1953, 10–12.

21. Cover Statement, *ONE*, October, 1953.

22. "Law of Mailable Material," *ONE*, October, 1954, 5.

23. Ibid., 6.

24. It has been suggested that the Post Office renewed its investigation of *ONE* as a result of a letter written by Senator Alexander Wiley (R-WI) to the U.S. Postmaster complaining that the magazine should not be distributed via the mails because it "was devoted to the advancement of sexual perversion." Charles, "From Subversion to Obscenity," 276. Wiley also claimed that the gay magazine's "'lewd' and 'obscene' contents were inconsistent with

President Eisenhower's anti-homosexual internal security program." William N. Eskridge Jr., "Privacy Jurisprudence and the Apartheid of the Closet, 1946–1961," 24 *Florida State University Law Review* 703, 759–760 (1997).

25. Jane Dahr, "Sappho Remembered," *ONE*, October, 1954, 12. The short story is reproduced in its entirety in Albert B. Gerber, *Sex, Pornography, and Justice* (New York: Stuart, 1965), 136–139.

26. Brother Grundy, "Lord Samuel and Lord Montagu," *ONE*, October, 1954, 18. The poem is reproduced in its entirety in Gerber, *Sex, Pornography, and Justice*, 140–141.

27. Joyce Murdoch and Deb Price, *Courting Justice: Gay Men and Lesbians v. the Supreme Court* (New York: Basic Books, 2001), 31.

28. One, Inc. v. Olesen, 241 F.2d 772, 775–778 (9th Cir. 1957).

29. Editorial, *ONE*, February, 1957, 4.

30. For an exploration of the emergence of a physique culture in magazines and photographs in the late nineteenth century and its expansion into the twentieth century, see Thomas Waugh, *Hard to Imagine: Gay Male Eroticism in Photography and Film from Their Beginnings to Stonewall* (New York: Columbia University Press, 1996), 176–191.

31. David K. Johnson, "Physique Pioneers: The Politics of 1960s Gay Consumer Culture," 43 *Journal of Social History* 867, 871 (2010).

32. Ibid., 871. For an exploration of the development of gay physique magazines, see F. Valentine Hooven III, *Beefcake: The Muscle Magazines of America 1950–1970* (Los Angeles: Taschen, 1995).

33. James Lardner, "A Pornographer's Rise," *Washington Post*, January 12, 1978, A1, A24; Rodger Streitmatter and John C. Watson, "Herman Lynn Womack: Pornographer as First Amendment Pioneer," 28 *Journalism History* 56, 57 (2002).

34. The government, in its legal brief, provided detailed descriptions of the photographs in Womack's magazines. Brief for the Respondent, 5–7. A handful of the photographs at issue in *Manual Enterprises* are reproduced in Gerber, *Sex, Pornography, and Justice*, 164–167.

35. United States v. Womack, 211 F. Supp. 578, 580 (D.C. 1962).

36. Streitmatter and Watson, *Herman Lynn Womack*, 59. Although Womack's conviction was upheld on appeal, see Womack v. United States, 294 F.2d 204 (D.C. Ct. App. 1961), he persuaded the trial judge that he had mental problems, which allowed him to serve his sentence in a hospital rather than in a prison. Womack was released from the hospital after eighteen months. Lardner, *A Pornographer's Rise*, 24.

37. Johnson, *Physique Pioneers*, 876.

38. Ibid.

39. Transcript of Record, Manual Enterprises, Inc. v. Day, 370 U.S. 478 (1962), 35.

40. The District Court's ruling was not published. The appellate court's decision

is Manual Enterprises, Inc., v. Day, 289 F.2d 455 (D.C. Cir. 1961).

41. Roth v. United States, 354 U.S. 476 (1957); Kingsley International Pictures v. Regents of the University of the State of New York, 360 U.S. 684 (1959).

42. Commonwealth v. Sharpless, 2 Serg. & Rawle 91, 102 (Pa. 1815).

43. John Cleland, *Memoirs of a Woman of Pleasure* (1748).

44. Commonwealth v. Holmes, 17 Mass. 336 (1821).

45. Regina v. Hicklin, 3 Q.B. 360, 371 (1868).

46. Ibid., 372.

47. United States v. Bennett, 24 F. Cas. 1093 (Circ. Ct. S.D.N.Y. 1879). For other examples of American courts adopting the *Hicklin* test, see United States v. Clarke, 38 F. 732, 733–734 (E.D. Mo. 1889); People v. Muller, 96 N.Y. 408, 411 (1884). See also Knowles v. United States, 170 F. 409, 411–412 (8th Cir. 1909). For a detailed analysis of *Hicklin* and its influence on American courts, see Stephen Gillers, "A Tendency to Deprave and Corrupt: The Transformation of American Obscenity Law from *Hicklin* to *Ulysses II*," 85 *Washington University Law Review* 215 (2007).

48. Rosen v. United States, 161 U.S. 29 (1896).

49. Radclyffe Hall, *The Well of Loneliness* (New York: Blue Ribbon Books, 1928); People v. Friede, 133 Misc. 611 (N.Y. Magis. Ct. 1929).

50. For a discussion of the effort to censor *The Well of Loneliness* in both England and the United States, see Kim Emery, "Well Meaning: Pragmatism, Lesbianism, and the U.S. Obscenity Trial," in *Palatable Poison: Critical Perspectives on The Well of Loneliness*, Laura Doan and Jay Prosser, eds. (New York: Columbia University Press, 2001), 355–371; Nancy J. Knauer, "Homosexuality as Contagion: From *The Well of Loneliness* to the Boy Scouts," 29 *Hofstra Law Review* 401, 441–450 (2000).

51. *Friede*, 133 Misc. at 613.

52. Ibid., 614.

53. Laurence Tribe seems to have been one of the first commentators to use the phrase "thematic obscenity." Laurence Tribe, *American Constitutional Law* (Mineola, NY: Foundation Press, 1978), 665–666. The New York Court of Appeals embraced the notion of thematic obscenity in *People v. Wendling*, 180 N.E. 169 (N.Y. 1932).

54. *Friede*, 133 Misc. at 613.

55. "'Well of Loneliness' Cleared in Court Here," *New York Times*, April 20, 1929, 20; D'Emilio, *Sexual Politics*, 19.

56. Robin Bernstein, *Staging Lesbian and Gay New York*, in *The Cambridge Companion to the Literature of New York*, Cyrus R. K. Patell and Bryan Waterman, eds. (New York: Cambridge University Press, 2010), 202, 203.

57. For an extensive exploration of *The Captive* and the government's efforts to close down its performance on Broadway, see Kaeir Curtin, *"We Can Always Call Them Bulgarians": The Emergence of Lesbians and Gay Men on the American Stage* (Boston: Allyson Books, 1987), 43–64, 91–102.

58. Liveright v. Waldorf Theaters Corp., 221 N.Y.S. 194, 196 (App. Div. 1927).

59. United States v. Kennerly, 209 F. 119, 120 (S.D.N.Y. 1913).

60. United States v. Dennett, 39 F.2d 564 (2d Cir. 1930).

61. United States v. One Book Entitled *Ulysses* by James Joyce, 72 F.2d 705, 706–707 (2d Cir. 1934). For a detailed account of the campaign to prevent the sale of *Ulysses* in the United States, see Kevin Birmingham, *The Most Dangerous Book: The Battle for James Joyce's* Ulysses (New York: Penguin Press, 2014).

62. *One Book Entitled* Ulysses, 72 F.2d at 708.

63. United States v. Levine, 83 F.2d 156, 158 (2d Cir. 1936).

64. See, e.g., Brief for Morris L. Ernst as Amicus Curiae, Roth v. United States, 354 U.S. 476 (1957), 42. See also Commonwealth v. Gordon, 66 Pa. D & C. 101, 156 (1948) (holding that an obscenity statute could constitutionally be applied "only where there is a reasonable and demonstrable cause to believe that a crime or misdemeanor has been committed . . . as the perceptible result of the publication and distribution of the writing in question.").

65. United States v. Roth, 237 F.2d 796, 799 (2d Cir. 1956).

66. Ibid., 805. See also Commonwealth v. Gordon, 66 Pa. D and C. 101, 156 (1948).

67. After deciding three obscenity cases at the end of the nineteenth century, see Dunlop v. United States, 165 U.S. 486 (1897); Swearingen v. United States, 161 U.S. 446 (1896); and Rosen v. United States, 161 U.S. 29 (1896), the Supreme Court barely paid attention to the issue in the decades that followed. The Court returned to questions related to obscenity in 1948 with two rulings. In the first, it struck down on vagueness grounds a New York statute that deemed publications to be obscene if they consisted principally of "deeds of bloodshed, lust, or crime." Winters v. New York, 333 U.S. 507, 508 (1948). But the Court, in the second ruling, by an evenly divided vote and without issuing an opinion, affirmed an obscenity conviction under another New York statute based on the publication of a collection of interrelated short stories written by Edmund Wilson, a highly regarded literary critic, containing graphic sexual descriptions. Edmund Wilson, *Memoirs of Hecate County* (New York: Doubleday, 1946); Doubleday & Co. v. New York, 335 U.S. 848 (1948).

68. Brief for the United States, Roth v. United States, 354 U.S. 476 (1957), 8.

69. Brief for Petitioner, Roth v. United States, 354 U.S. 476 (1957), 8.

70. Roth v. United States, 354 U.S. 476, 484 (1957).

71. Ibid., 488.

72. On the *Howl* obscenity trial, see Ronald K. L. Collins and David M. Skover, *Mania: The Story of the Outraged & Outrageous Lives that Launched a Cultural Revolution* (Oak Park, IL: Top Five Books, 2013).

73. People v. Ferlinghetti (Mun. Court, S.F., Cal., Oct. 3, 1957), available at http://mason.gmu.edu/~kthomps4/363-s02/horn-howl.htm.

74. Butler v. Michigan, 352 U.S. 380 (1957).

75. *Kingsley*, 360 U.S. 684.
76. Kingsley International Pictures v. Regents of the Univ. of the State of New York, 151 N.E.2d 197, 201 (N.Y. 1959).
77. *Kingsley*, 360 U.S. at 689.
78. William B. Lockhart and Robert C. McClure, "Censorship of Obscenity: The Developing Constitutional Standard," 45 *Minnesota Law Review* 5, 100 (1960).
79. Although the Court in 1973 broadened the definition of obscenity by holding that the government did not have to prove that the materials in question were *"utterly* without redeeming social value," it did so without explicitly contending that the state had the authority to promote public morality. Miller v. California, 413 U.S. 15, 24 (1973) (emphasis added). And when the Court, also in 1973, held that the government could regulate the showing of obscene films in movie theaters, it sent mixed signals on the sufficiency of public morality as a justification for obscenity regulations. On the one hand, the Court emphasized the government's interest in prohibiting the commercial exploitation of materials that have "a tendency to injure the community as a whole . . . or to jeopardize [the ability] to maintain a decent society." In particular, the Court reasoned that the widely prevailing assumption that a "complete education" requires the reading of certain books comes with the "corollary assumption that commerce in obscene [materials] ha[s] a tendency to exert a corrupting and debasing impact leading to antisocial behavior." On the other hand, the Court described the government's authority to make these judgments as "a morally neutral" one. The Court also elaborated on morally neutral interests behind obscenity regulations, including "the interest of the public in the quality of life and the total community environment, the tone of commerce in the great city centers, and, possibly, the public safety itself." Paris Adult Theater v. Slaton, 413 U.S. 49, 58, 63 (1973).
80. One, Inc. v. Olesen, 355 U.S. 371 (1958).
81. One commentator, in writing about *Der Kreis*, notes that "no other magazine in the paranoid forties and fifties offered the same blend of ideas, art, and politics—and skin." Waugh, *Hard to Imagine*, 405. For an in-depth study of *Der Kreis*, which was published under different names between 1932 and 1967, see Hubert Kennedy, *The Ideal Gay Man: The Story of* Der Kreis (New York: Haworth Press, 2000).
82. *Roth*, 354 U.S. at 487.
83. Lockhart and McClure, *Censorship of Obscenity*, 113.
84. Manual Enterprises, Inc. v. Day, 370 U.S. 478, 482 (1962) (plurality opinion).
85. Ibid., 487.
86. Ibid., 490.
87. Ibid., 489–490 (emphasis added).
88. Ibid., 487, 482 (emphases added).
89. It is also worth noting that not all of the Supreme Court's obscenity decisions from this era sided with the publishers of gay materials. For example,

one of the doctrinal issues that arose in *Manual Enterprises* before the case reached the Supreme Court was whether the government had to show that the materials in question appealed to the prurient interests of the average members of the community as opposed to the publications' targeted audience. See Carlos A. Ball, "Obscenity, Morality, and the First Amendment: The First LGBT Rights Cases before the Supreme Court," 28 *Columbia Journal of Gender and Law* 229, 284–286 (2015). This was an important question in gay obscenity cases because although presumably gay men generally found gay erotic materials to be sexually stimulating, the same might not be true of the "average members" of the community. The Court in *Manual Enterprises* did not address the issue. However, several years later, the Court, in a case involving fifty pulp paperbacks, some of which were aimed at lesbian and gay readers and others at readers interested in sadomasochism, concluded that when materials were aimed at "a clearly defined deviant sexual group, rather than the public at large, the prurient-appeal requirement of the *Roth* test is satisfied if the dominant theme of the material taken as a whole appeals to the prurient interest in sex of the members of that group." Mishkin v. New York, 383 U.S. 502, 508 (1966). The fact that the Court in *Mishkin* (writing through Justice Brennan), in effect, described LGBT people as a "deviant sexual group" is further evidence that the free speech victories in cases like *One* and *Manual Enterprises* were not the result of the justices' embrace of more tolerant understandings of LGBT people.

90. In 1963, for example, the U.S. Court of Appeals for the Seventh Circuit upheld two convictions for conspiring to use the mails to distribute pictures of naked men. United States v. Zuideveld, 316 F.2d 873 (7th Cir. 1963). See also People v. G.I. Distributors, Inc., 228 N.E.2d 787 (N.Y. 1967). In addition, federal prosecutors in Minneapolis brought obscenity charges against two men for using the mails to distribute the first physique magazines that included photos of full frontal male nudity. After a bench trial, however, the judge found the defendants not guilty. Like Justice Harlan in *Manual Enterprises*, the judge agreed with the government that the magazines were aimed at a "deviant group." But that was not enough to render the publications obscene. As the judge explained, "the rights of minorities expressed individually in sexual groups or otherwise must be respected. With increasing research and study, we will in the future come to a better understanding of ourselves, sexual deviants, and others." Johnson, *Physique Pioneers*, 881. A few years later, the U.S. Court of Appeals for the Eighth Circuit reversed another obscenity conviction of the same two defendants. Spinar v. United States, 440 F.2d 1241 (8th Cir. 1971).

91. William Eskridge notes that the Court, in expanding the definition of proscribable obscenity in the early 1970s, upheld state obscenity prosecutions of materials that included gay erotica, among other types. See William N. Eskridge Jr., *Gaylaw: Challenging the Apartheid of the Closet* (Cambridge, MA:

Harvard University Press, 1999), 119, citing California v. Miller, 413 U.S. 15 (1973); Paris Adult Theater v. Slaton, 413 U.S. 49 (1973); and Kaplan v. California, 413 U.S. 155 (1973). Eskridge notes that "although [these cases] enabled southern jurisdictions [in particular] to go after homoerotica, [they] probably had little overall influence on its actual availability. By 1976 national mail-order homoerotic films and magazines were well-established." Eskridge, *Gaylaw*, 120. Eskridge also makes the important point that the Court's imposition during the 1960s of procedural requirements (for example, by prohibiting the seizure of allegedly obscene materials in the absence of a judicial hearing), made it more difficult for prosecutors to win obscenity cases. Eskridge, *Gaylaw*, 118.

92. John D'Emilio points to the growth in lesbian pulp fiction as an example of the explosion of published materials with lesbian and gay themes that took place during the 1960s. See D'Emilio, *Sexual Politics*, 135–136. On gay, lesbian, and transgender pulp fiction generally, see Susan Stryker, *Queer Pulp: Perverted Passions from the Golden Age of the Paperback* (San Francisco: Chronicle Books, 2001).

93. "The Homosexual in America," *Time*, January 21, 1966, 41.

94. Robert C. Doty, "Growth of Overt Homosexuality in City Provokes Wide Concern," *New York Times*, December 17, 1963, 1, 33.

95. Streitmatter, *Unspeakable*, 18.

96. D'Emilio, *Sexual Politics*, 114.

97. Johnson, *Physique Pioneers*, 870.

98. Jackie Hatton, "The Pornography Empire of H. Lynn Womack: Gay Political Discourse and Popular Culture 1955–1970," 7 *Thresholds: Viewing Culture* 8, 16 (1993).

99. Streitmatter and Watson, *Herman Lynn Womack*, 63.

100. Ibid. Another publication that combined political coverage, social activism, and homoerotic images was the *Los Angeles Advocate*, which later, as the *Advocate*, became a highly popular gay and lesbian magazine with a national audience. On the early days of the *Advocate*, see Streitmatter, *Unspeakable*, 87–88. Clark Polak, the publisher of *Drum*, closed down his magazine in 1969 after he was convicted of violating the state obscenity statute for publishing pictures of naked men. "Although *Drum* ran into legal trouble when it printed frontal male nudity, [other gay magazines such as] *Vector* and the *Advocate* got away with such nudity." Eskridge, *Gaylaw*, 118.

101. Johnson, *Physique Pioneers*, 883.

102. Eskridge, *Gaylaw*, 117.

103. D'Emilio, *Sexual Politics*, 5.

104. Brief of Petitioner, Bowers v. Hardwick, 478 U.S. 186 (1986), 20, 27, 36.

105. Bowers v. Hardwick, 478 U.S. 186, 190, 192, 194 (1986).

106. Ibid., 196.

107. Ibid. (Burger, C. J., concurring).

108. Lawrence v. Texas, 539 U.S. 558, 571 (2003).

109. Romer v. Texas, 517 U.S. 620, 632 (1996).

110. United States v. Windsor, 133 S. Ct. 2675, 2693 (2013). On the relationship between *Romer* and *Windsor* as it relates to the constitutional insufficiency of moral disapproval as a justification for the differential treatment of lesbians and gay men, see Linda C. McClain, "From *Romer v. Evans* to *United States v. Windsor*: Law as a Vehicle for Moral Disapproval in Amendment 2 and the Defense of Marriage Act," 20 *Duke Journal of Gender Law & Policy* 351 (2013).

111. *Windsor*, 133 S. Ct. at 2693 (quoting H.R. REP. NO. 104–664, at 12–13, 16 [1996]).

112. Ibid.

113. 44 Liquormart, Inc. v. Rhode Island, 517 U.S. 484, 512 (1996).

114. Roe v. Wade, 410 U.S. 113 (1973); Griswold v. Connecticut, 381 U.S. 479 (1965).

115. *Windsor*, 133 S. Ct. at 2692; *Lawrence*, 539 U.S. at 567.

Chapter 2: Coming Together and Free Expression

1. William Eskridge has also written about the important role that the right of association played in the lives of LGBT people leading up to Stonewall. See William N. Eskridge Jr., *Gaylaw: Challenging the Apartheid of the Closet* (Cambridge, MA: Harvard University Press, 1999), 112–116. For his part, Dale Carpenter has noted that the "development of gay political power . . . has depended in the first instance on the liberty of gays to organize in groups free of state regulation impinging on their internal affairs, including the content of their message and the composition of their membership." Dale Carpenter, "Expressive Association and Anti-Discrimination Law after *Dale*: A Tripartite Approach," 85 *Minnesota Law Review* 1515, 1527 (2001).

2. On the history and enforcement of the Sedition Act of 1798, see John C. Miller, *Crisis in Freedom: The Alien and Sedition Acts* (Boston: Little Brown, 1951); James Morton Smith, *Freedom's Fetters: The Alien and Sedition Laws and American Civil Liberties* (Ithaca, NY: Cornell University Press, 1956); Geoffrey R. Stone, *Perilous Times: Free Speech in Wartime* (New York: W. W. Horton, 2004), Ch. 1.

3. On the history and enforcement of the Espionage Act of 1917 and the Sedition Act of 1918, see Stone, *Perilous Times*, Ch. 3.

4. Schenck v. United States, 249 U.S. 47 (1919); Debs v. United States, 249 U.S. 211 (1919); Abrams v. United States, 250 U.S. 616 (1919). At around this time, the Court upheld the application of state criminal laws aimed at discouraging left-wing political activism in Gitlow v. New York, 268 U.S. 652 (1925), and Whitney v. California, 274 U.S. 357 (1927). Holmes and Brandeis took issue with the Court's reasoning in *Abrams*, *Gitlow*, and *Whitney*.

5. Brandenburg v. Ohio, 395 U.S. 444 (1969).

6. 80 U.S.C. §844 (1954).

7. Dennis v. United States, 341 U.S. 494 (1951). See also American Communications Association v. Douds, 339 U.S. 382 (1950). It was not until 1957 that the Court began expressing some skepticism of the government's anti-communist witch-hunts. See Yates v. United States, 354 U.S. 298, 318–320 (1957).

8. Michal R. Belknap, *Cold War Political Justice: The Smith Act, the Communist Party, and American Civil Liberties* (Westport, CT: Greenwood Press, 1977).

9. David Caute, *The Great Fear: The Anti-Communist Purge under Truman and Eisenhower* (New York: Simon & Schuster, 1978).

10. On the post–World War II persecution by the federal government of its gay and lesbian employees, see Genny Beemyn, *A Queer Capital: A History of Gay Life in Washington, D.C.* (New York: Routledge, 2015), Ch. 4; David K. Johnson, *The Lavender Scare: The Cold War Prosecution of Gays and Lesbians in the Federal Government* (Chicago: University of Chicago Press, 2004). See also Stacy Braukman, *Communists and Perverts under the Palms: The Johns Committee in Florida, 1956–1965* (Gainesville: University Press of Florida, 2012).

11. NAACP v. Alabama, 357 U.S. 449, 460–461 (1958). See also Bates v. Little Rock, 361 U.S. 516 (1960).

12. NAACP v. Button, 371 U.S. 415 (1963).

13. Shelton v. Tucker, 364 U.S. 479 (1960). For a detailed analysis of the NAACP cases implicating the First Amendment, see Harry Kalven Jr., *The Negro and the First Amendment* (Chicago: University of Chicago Press, 1965).

14. Michael J. Klarman, *From Jim Crow to Civil Rights: The Supreme Court and the Struggle for Racial Equality* (New York: Oxford University Press, 2004), 383.

15. Samuel Walker, *In Defense of American Liberties: A History of the* ACLU (New York: Oxford University Press, 1990), 241. It should be noted that the Court, before *NAACP v. Alabama*, had recognized and enforced the right of peaceful assembly made explicit in the First Amendment. See, e.g., De Jonge v. Oregon, 299 U.S. 353 (1937); Herndon v. Lowry, 301 U.S. 242 (1937). But the right of association recognized in *NAACP* went beyond the context of peaceful assemblies.

16. New York Times v. Sullivan, 376 U.S. 254, 270 (1964).

17. Harry Kalven Jr., "The *New York Times* Case: A Note on 'The Central Meaning of the First Amendment,'" 1964 *Supreme Court Law Review* 191, 208.

18. Edwards v. South Carolina, 372 U.S. 229 (1963).

19. Cox v. Louisiana, 379 U.S. 536 (1965).

20. See, e.g., Communist Party of the United States v. Subversive Activities Control Board, 367 U.S. 1 (1961) (rejecting a First Amendment challenge brought by the Communist Party against a federal statute requiring "subversive" organizations to register with the government and to reveal the names of their members). See also Scales v. United States, 367 U.S. 203 (1961); Barenblatt v. United States, 360 U.S. 109 (1959). It was not until

1967 that the Court recognized that communists were also protected by the freedom of association. See United States v. Robel, 389 U.S. 258 (1967).

21. William N. Eskridge Jr., "Law and the Construction of the Closet: American Regulation of Same-Sex Intimacy, 1880–1946," 82 *Iowa Law Review* 1007, 1020 (1997).

22. Ibid., 1021–1022.

23. Havelock Ellis, *Studies in the Psychology of the Sexes: Sexual Inversion* (Philadelphia: F. A. Davis, 3rd ed., 1915), 350, excerpted in Jonathan Ned Katz, *Gay American History: Lesbians and Gay Men in the U.S.A.* (New York: Meridien, 1992), 52.

24. Eskridge, *Law and the Construction of the Closet*, 1032.

25. See Gary L. Atkins, *Gay Seattle: Stories of Exile and Belonging* (Seattle: University of Washington Press, 2003), Ch. 3; Brett Beemyn, *A Queer Capital*, Ch. 3; *George Chauncey, Gay New York: Gender, Urban Culture, and the Making of the Gay Male World, 1890–1940* (New York: Basic Books, 1993); St. Sukie de la Croix, *Chicago Whispers: A History of LGBT Chicago before Stonewall* (Madison: University of Wisconsin Press, 2012), Chs. 12–14; Lillian Faderman and Stuart Timmons, *Gay L.A.: A History of Sexual Outlaws, Power Politics, and Lipstick Lesbians* (New York: Basic Books, 2006), Ch. 3; Elizabeth Lopovsky Kennedy and Madeline D. Davis, *Boots of Leather, Slippers of Gold: A History of a Lesbian Community* (New York: Routledge, 1993); Marc Stein, *City of Sisterly & Brotherly Loves: Lesbian and Gay Philadelphia, 1945–1972* (Chicago: University of Chicago Press, 2000), Ch. 2.

26. The Society for Human Rights, founded by Henry Gerber, likely never had more than ten members. On Gerber and his organization, see St. Sukie de la Croix, *Chicago Whispers*, Ch. 8; Jim Kepner and Stephen O. Murray, "Henry Gerber (1895–1972): Grandfather of the American Gay Movement," in *Before Stonewall: Activists for Gay and Lesbian Rights in Historical Context*, Vern L. Bullough, ed. (New York: Harrington Park Press, 2002), 24–34.

27. For a discussion of these laws, see Eskridge, *Law and the Construction of the Closet*, 1084–1086.

28. Chauncey, *Gay New York*, 340.

29. Nan Alamilla Boyd, *Wide-Open Town: A History of Queer San Francisco to 1965* (Berkeley: University of California Press, 2003), 116.

30. Allan Bérubé, "The History of Gay Bathhouses," 44 *Journal of Homosexuality* 33, 43 (2003). As Bérubé explains, this targeted enforcement effort in San Francisco proved futile as gay men soon found other establishments in different parts of the city in which to congregate.

31. St. Sukie de la Croix, *Chicago Whispers*, 166–167.

32. John D'Emilio, *Sexual Politics, Sexual Communities: The Making of a Homosexual Minority in the United States, 1940–1970* (Chicago: University of Chicago Press, 1983), 50.

33. "Miami Junks the Constitution," *ONE*, January, 1954, 21.

34. Lyn Pedersen, "Miami Hurricane," *ONE*, November, 1954, 4, 8.

35. Dal McIntire, "Tangents," *ONE*, December, 1955, 10.
36. Dal McIntire, "Tangents," *ONE*, October-November, 1956, 18, 19.
37. Sultan Turkish Bath v. Board of Police Commissioners, 169 Cal. App. 2d 188, 197 (Ct. App. 1959).
38. Dal McIntire, "Tangents," *ONE*, April, 1959, 17.
39. Boyd, *Wide-Open Town*, 121.
40. Stoumen v. Reilly, 222 P.2d 678, 682 (Ca. Ct. App. 1950) (quoting ruling by the Superior Court).
41. Stoumen v. Reilly, 234 P.2d 969 (Ca. 1951).
42. Bowers v. Hardwick, 478 U.S. 186 (1986).
43. For an in-depth analysis of the conduct/status distinction, see Janet E. Halley, "Reasoning about Sodomy: Act and Identity in and after *Bowers v. Hardwick*," 79 *Virginia Law Review* 1721 (1993).
44. *Stoumen*, 234 P.2d at 971.
45. Kershaw v. Department of Alcoholic Beverage Control, 318 P.2d 494, 497 (Ca. Ct. App. 1957).
46. Boyd, *Wide-Open Town*, 123, 127–133.
47. California Business and Professions Code §24200(e) (1957).
48. Boyd, *Wide-Open Town*, 141
49. Lyn Pedersen, "Court Upholds Gay Bars," *ONE*, March, 1959, 6, 7.
50. Vallerga v. Department of Alcoholic Beverage Control, 347 P.2d 909 (Ca. 1959).
51. See, e.g., *Kershaw*, 318 P.2d 494; Nickola v. Munro, 328 P.2d 271 (Ca. Ct. App. 1958). For similar cases from other jurisdictions, see In re Freedman, 235 A.2d 624 (Pa. Super. Ct. 1967); Cesaroni v. Smith, 202 A.2d 292 (R.I. 1964). For an extended discussion of the gay bar cases from the 1940s through the 1960s, see Rhonda R. Rivera, "Our Straight-Laced Judges: The Legal Position of Homosexual Persons in the United States," 30 *Hastings Law Journal* 799, 913–924 (1979).
52. One Eleven Wines & Liquors, Inc. v. Division of Alcoholic Beverage Control, 235 A.2d 12, 15 (N.J. 1967). Also in 1967, the New York Court of Appeals held that the mere presence of gay men at a bar did not justify the revocation of the establishment's liquor license. Kerma Restaurant Corporation v. State Liquor Authority, 233 N.E.2d 833 (N.Y. 1967). In contrast, a Florida appellate court that same year refused to strike down an outrageous Miami ordinance that prohibited a liquor licensee from (1) employing a gay person; (2) serving alcohol to a gay person; or (3) allowing two or more gay people to congregate in its place of business. Inman v. City of Miami, 197 So.2d 50 (Fla. App. 1967). However, five years later, another court held that the ordinance was unconstitutional. Eskridge, *Gaylaw*, 112.
53. *One Eleven Wines & Liquors*, 235 A.2d at 18.
54. Robinson v. California, 370 U.S. 660 (1962).
55. Boyd, *Wide-Open Town*, 132–133.

56. Ibid., 223–224.

57. Christopher Lowen Agee, *The Streets of San Francisco: Policing and the Creation of a Cosmopolitan Liberal Politics, 1950–1972* (Chicago: University of Chicago Press, 2014), 278n79.

58. D'Emilio, *Sexual Politics*, 189.

59. Boyd, *Wide-Open Town*, 225.

60. Ibid., 226.

61. Daniel E. Slotnick, "Jose Sarria, Gay Advocate and Performer, Dies at 90," *New York Times*, August 23, 2013, B9.

62. Boyd, *Wide-Open Town*, 211.

63. Slotnick, *Jose Sarria*, B9.

64. Boyd, *Wide-Open Town*, 221–222.

65. John D'Emilio, "Gay Politics and Community in San Francisco Since World War II," in *Hidden From History: Reclaiming the Gay and Lesbian Past*, Martin Bauml Duberman, Martha Vicinus, and George Chauncey Jr., eds. (New York: New American Library, 1989), 456, 462.

66. Boyd, *Wide-Open Town*, 213–214.

67. The Black Cat closed after yet another police raid and liquor investigation. See Stoumen v. Munro, 219 Cal. App. 2d 302 (1963). Stoumen tried to keep the establishment going without serving alcohol, but he was unable to make enough money to keep it open.

68. Boyd, *Wide-Open* Town, 228 (quoting Bill Beardemphl, "S.I.R.'s Statement of Policy," *Vector*, December 1964, 1). On the founding and philosophy of *Vector*, see Rodger Streitmatter, *Unspeakable: The Rise of the Gay and Lesbian Press in America* (Boston: Faber & Faber, 1995), 64–65.

69. Boyd, *Wide-Open Town*, 213 (quoting Bill Beardemphl, "Editorial," *Vector*, February 1965, 6).

70. Ibid., 227.

71. D'Emilio, *Gay Politics and Community in San Francisco*, 464.

72. Ibid., 465.

73. Ibid., 466.

74. Tracy Baim, "Chicago's Community Saw its Largest Growth during the Post-Stonewall 1970s," in *Out and Proud in Chicago: An Overview of the City's Gay Community*, Tracy Baim, ed. (Chicago: Surrey Books, 2008), 87–89.

75. Faderman and Timmons, *Gay L.A.*, Ch. 6.

76. Kristin G. Esterberg, "Associations and Organizations," in *Encyclopedia of Lesbian Histories and Cultures*, Bonnie Zimmerman, ed. (New York: Routledge, 1999), 76–77. The Combahee River Collective was a black women's group that included many lesbians as members.

77. Police efforts to harass gay activists in the 1970s were not completely unheard of. For example, in the summer of 1974, as the Fort Worth/Dallas Gay Council was holding the first statewide gay conference in Texas, Fort Worth police officers collected the license plate numbers of the attendees' cars. James T. Sears, *Rebels, Rubyfruit, and Rhinestones: Queering*

Space in the Stonewall South (New Brunswick, NJ: Rutgers University Press, 2001), 174. The police turned that information over to the *Fort Worth Star-Telegram*, hoping the newspaper would print the names and addresses of the attendants, something the paper refused to do. The conference organizers eventually sued the city, alleging that officials had violated their First Amendment rights. See Cyr v. Walls, 439 F. Supp. 697 (N.D. Tex. 1977).

78. On the Gay Liberation Front, see, e.g., Terence Kissack, "Freaking Fag Revolutionaries: New York's Gay Liberation Front," 62 *Radical History Review* 104 (1995); Toby Marotta, *The Politics of Homosexuality* (Boston: Haughton Mifflin, 1981); Donn Teal, *The Gay Militants: How Gay Liberation Began in America* (New York: Stein and Day, 1971).

79. Sewell Chan, "Revisiting 1969 and the Start of Gay Liberation," City Room Blog, *New York Times*, June 8, 2009.

80. Gay Activists Alliance v. Lomenzo, 320 N.Y.S.2d 994, 996–997 (Sup. Ct. 1971).

81. Owles v. Lomenzo, 329 N.Y.S.2d 181 (App. Div. 1972). The appellate division's ruling was affirmed by the New York Court of Appeals. See Gay Activists Alliance v. Lomenzo, 293 N.E.2d 255 (N.Y. 1973).

82. For a discussion of the role of sodomy laws in noncriminal contexts, see Diana Hassel, "The Use of Criminal Sodomy Laws in Civil Litigation," 79 *Texas Law Review* 813 (2001); Christopher R. Leslie, "Creating Criminals: The Injuries Inflicted by 'Unenforced' Sodomy Laws," 35 *Harvard Civil Rights-Civil Liberties Law Review* 103 (2000).

83. National Gay Task Force v. Board of Education of Oklahoma City, 729 F.2d 1270, 1274 (10th Cir. 1984).

84. Gay Lesbian Bisexual Alliance v. Pryor, 110 F.3d 1543, 1545 (11th Cir. 1997).

85. In re Thom, 337 N.Y.S.2d 588, 589, 590 (App. Div. 1972).

86. Application of Thom, 301 N.E.2d 542 (N.Y. 1973).

87. Ibid., 543.

88. Grant v. Brown, 313 N.E.2d 847, 849 (Ohio 1974).

89. Ibid.

90. Rivera, *Our Straight-Laced Judges*, 911.

91. For these and other accounts of universities' expulsions and harassment of students suspected of being gay, see Patrick Dilley, "20th Century Postsecondary Practices and Policies to Control Gay Students," 25 *Review of Higher Education* 409 (2002).

92. Ibid., 419. For the role that psychiatrists played in the treatment of gay students and faculty at the University of Kansas around the middle of the century, see Beth Bailey, *Sex in the Heartland* (Cambridge, MA: Harvard University Press, 1999).

93. Gerard Koskovich, "Private Lives, Public Struggles," 21 *Stanford Magazine* 32, 37 (1993).

94. Justin David Suran, "Coming Out Against the War: Antimilitarism and the

Politicization of Homosexuality in the Era of Vietnam," 53 *American Quarterly* 452, 464 (2001).

95. For the links between the antiwar and gay liberation movements, see Suran, *Coming Out Against the War*.

96. For an account of the early days of the Cornell group, see Brett Beemyn, "The Silence is Broken: A History of the First Lesbian, Gay, and Bisexual Student Groups," 12 *Journal of the History of Sexuality* 205 (2003). For an account of the first twenty years of the Rutgers gay student group, see David Nichols and Morris J. Kafka-Hozschlag, "The Rutgers University Lesbian/Gay Alliance 1969–1989: The First Twenty Years," 51 *Journal of the Rutgers University Libraries* 55 (1989). For an account of early gay activism on the Stanford campus, see Koskovich, *Private Lives, Public Struggles*, 37–40.

97. The first lawsuit challenging a university's refusal to recognize a gay student group was filed against Sacramento State College. For a comprehensive account of the background and implications of that case, see David A. Reichard, "'We Can't Hide and They Are Wrong': The Society for Homosexual Freedom and the Struggle for Recognition at Sacramento State College, 1969–1971," 28 *Law and History Review* 629 (2010).

98. Healy v. James, 408 U.S. 169 (1972).

99. Gay Students Organization of the University of New Hampshire v. Bonner, 509 F.2d 652, 659–660 (1st Cir. 1974).

100. Ibid., 661.

101. Ibid., 657–658.

102. Ibid., 661.

103. Ibid., 660.

104. Ibid., 662n6.

105. University of New Hampshire v. April, 347 A.2d 446 (N.H. 1975).

106. Gay Alliance of Students v. Matthews, 544 F.2d 162, 164 (4th Cir. 1976).

107. Ibid., 166.

108. Gay Lib v. University of Missouri, 558 F.2d 848, 854 (8th Cir. 1977).

109. Ibid., 855, 856.

110. See Gay and Lesbian Students Association v. Gohn, 850 F.2d 361 (8th Cir. 1988); Gay Student Services v. Texas A & M University, 737 F.2d 1317 (5th Cir. 1984); Gay Activists Alliance v. Board of Regents of the University of Oklahoma, 638 P.2d 1116 (Ok. 1981); Student Coalition for Gay Rights v. Austin Peay State University, 477 F. Supp. 1267 (M.D. Tenn. 1979). In 1982, the Supreme Court of Florida used the First Amendment to strike down a statute that prohibited the use of public money to fund an institution of higher learning that recognized or assisted any student group "that recommends or advocates sexual relations between persons not married to each other." Department of Education v. Lewis, 416 So.2d 455 (Fla. 1982).

111. Dilley, *20th Century Postsecondary Practices*, 410.

112. Beemyn, *The Silence Is Broken*, 223.

113. Toward a Gayer Bicentennial Committee v. Rhode Island Bicentennia

Commission, 417 F. Supp. 632, 633 (D.R.I. 1976).

114. Ibid., 635.

115. Pleasant Grove City v. Summum, 555 U.S. 460 (2009).

116. Rosenberger v. Rector and Visitors of the University of Virginia, 515 U.S. 819 (1995).

117. *Toward a Gayer Bicentennial Committee*, 417 F. Supp. at 640–641.

118. Ibid., 642. After the state commission, following the initial ruling, once again refused to allow the gay umbrella group to have access to the Old State House, the court issued an injunction ordering that the site be made available to the gay group for ninety minutes during the 1976 gay pride weekend. Toward a Gayer Bicentennial Committee v. Rhode Island Bicentennial Foundation, 417 F. Supp. 642 (D.R.I. 1976).

119. Brown v. Louisiana, 383 U.S. 131, 142 (1966); Cox v. Louisiana, 379 U.S. 536 (1965); Edwards v. South Carolina, 372 U.S. 229 (1963).

120. Alaska Gay Coalition v. Sullivan, 578 P.2d 951, 955 (Alaska 1978).

121. Ibid., 960.

122. Nan Hunter has made the conceptually distinct point that virtually all equality cases, including LGBT ones, are grounded in expressive identity claims. Nan D. Hunter, "Expressive Identity: Recuperating Dissent for Equality," 35 *Harvard Civil Rights-Civil Liberties Law Review* 1 (2000). Whereas Hunter's contention is that LGBT equality cases have crucial expressive implications, my claim is that LGBT free speech cases have crucial equality implications.

123. *Robinson*, 370 U.S. 660.

124. Romer v. Evans, 517 U.S. 620, 632 (1996); Lawrence v. Texas, 539 U.S. 558, 571 (2003).

125. Aristotle, *Politics* (New York: Modern Library), 307.

126. Ronald D. Rotunda and John E. Nowak, *Treatise on Constitutional Law: Substance and Procedure*, vol. 3, (Minneapolis: Thompson Reuters, 1999), 219.

127. The search for truth, and the corresponding notion of the marketplace of ideas, was articulated as a free speech principle by Justice Oliver Wendell Holmes in his famous dissent in *Abrams v. United States*, 250 U.S. 616, 630 (1919).

128. See, e.g., Police Department of Chicago v. Mosley, 408 U.S. 92 (1972).

129. Peter Westen, "The Empty Idea of Equality," 95 *Harvard Law Review* 537, 543–547 (1982).

130. In making this point, my objective is not, as it appears to have been Professor Westen's, to push equality off of its normative perch. In other words, my objective is not to question the social, political, or moral importance of equality principles. Instead, my point is that equality's normative bite is dependent on other (nonegalitarian) values and judgments. This dependency makes it impossible for government decision-makers, when applying equality norms, to abide by the kind of strict neutrality demanded by the Free Speech Clause. I explore the implications for questions of judicial

review of what I call "equality's dependence" on nonegalitarian normative judgments in Carlos A. Ball, "Why Liberty Judicial Review Is as Legitimate as Equality Review: The Case of Gay Rights Jurisprudence," 14 *University of Pennsylvania Journal of Constitutional Law* 1 (2011).

Chapter 3: Coming Out and Free Expression

1. Harper & Row v. Nation Enterprises, 471 U.S. 539, 559 (1986).

2. Alexander Meiklejohn, *Free Speech and its Relationship to Self-Government* (New York: Harper & Brothers, 1948), 26.

3. Owen Fiss, *Liberalism Divided: Freedom of Speech and the Many Uses of State Power* (Boulder: West View Press, 1996); Cass Sunstein, *Democracy and the Problem of Free Speech* (New York: Free Press, 1993).

4. Cass Sunstein, "Free Speech Now," 59 *University of Chicago Law Review* 255, 306 (1992).

5. C. Edwin Baker, "Scope of the First Amendment Freedom of Speech," 25 *UCLA Law Review* 964, 966 (1978). Baker elaborated on the autonomy-based understanding of free speech protections in C. Edwin Baker, *Human Liberty and Freedom of Speech* (New York: Oxford University Press, 1989) and in C. Edwin Baker, "Autonomy and Free Speech," 27 *Constitutional Commentary* 251 (2011).

6. David A. J. Richards, "Free Speech and Obscenity Law: Toward a Moral Theory of the First Amendment," 123 *University of Pennsylvania Law Review* 45, 62 (1974). Richards elaborated on the autonomy model of free speech in later work. See David A. J. Richards, "A Theory of Free Speech," 34 *UCLA Law Review* 1837 (1987); David A. J. Richards, "Public and Private in the Discourse of the First Amendment," 12 *Cardozo Studies in Law and Literature* 61 (2000).

7. Nan D. Hunter, "Identity, Speech, and Equality," 79 *Virginia Law Review* 1695, 1718 (1993). In later work, Hunter explained that expressive identities, such as those associated with sexual orientation, constitute "a shared viewpoint, not a set of opinions or a viewpoint specific to any particular topic or issue, but 'view-point' in a more literal, basic sense: a shared point of view(ing), a shared position from which one's views emerge. . . . What distinguishes the viewpoint embedded in expressive identity is its inextricable linkage to the identity itself." Nan D. Hunter, "Expressive Identity: Recuperating Dissent for Equality," 35 *Harvard Civil Rights-Civil Liberties Law Review* 1, 6 (2000). For an early articulation of the claim that the First Amendment protects the self-identification of sexual minorities based on considerations of "personhood," see José Gómez, "The Public Expression of Lesbian/Gay Personhood as Protected Speech," 1 *Law and Inequality* 121 (1983). For the questioning of the notion that there is a unifying (or unified) meaning in self-identifying

speech by sexual minorities, see James P. Madigan, "Questioning the Coercive Effect of Self-Identifying Speech," 87 *Iowa Law Review* 75 (2001).

8. See West Virginia State Board of Education v. Barnette, 319 U.S. 624 (1943); Wooley v. Maynard, 430 U.S. 705 (1977). For a critical analysis of the military's Don't Ask, Don't Tell policy from the perspective of compelled speech given that it forced lesbian, gay, and bisexual service members, through silence, to affirm a heterosexual identity, see Tobias Barrington Wolff, "Compelled Affirmations, Free Speech, and the U.S. Military's Don't Ask, Don't Tell Policy," 63 *Brooklyn Law Review* 1141 (1997). The free speech implications of the DADT policy are explored in Chapter 4.

9. Tobias Barrington Wolff, "Political Accountability and Representation under Don't Ask, Don't Tell," 89 *Iowa Law Review* 1633, 1652 (2004). For his part, William Eskridge notes that self-identification by sexual minorities is "crucial for the formation of a lesbian and gay nomos, consisting of discernibly gay history, institutions, and mores, and is essential to gay political power as well." William N. Eskridge Jr., "A Jurisprudence of 'Coming Out': Religion, Homosexuality, and Collisions of Liberty and Equality in American Public Law," 106 *Yale Law Journal* 2411, 2443 (1997). See also Fadi Hanna, "Gay Self-Identification and the Right to Political Legibility," 2006 *Wisconsin Law Review* 75, 79. For the equal protection implications of silencing LGBT voices, see Janet E. Halley, "The Politics of the Closet: Towards Equal Protection for Gay, Lesbian, and Bisexual Identity," 36 *UCLA Law Review* 915 (1989); Kenji Yoshino, "Assimilationist Bias in Equal Protection: The Visibility Presumption and the Case of 'Don't Ask, Don't Tell,'" 108 *Yale Law Journal* 485 (1998).

10. See, e.g., Dew v. Halaby, 317 F.2d 582 (D.C. Cir. 1963); Taylor v. U.S. Civil Service Commission, 374 F.2d 466 (9th Cir. 1967); Vigil v. Post Office Department, 406 F.2d 921 (10th Cir. 1969).

11. Norton v. Macy, 417 F.2d 1161 (D.C. Cir. 1969).

12. See, e.g., Schlegel v. United States, 416 F.2d 1372 (Ct. Cl. 1969); Richardson v. Hampton, 345 F. Supp. 600 (D.D.C. 1972). A class action lawsuit brought by the Society for Individual Rights (an organization discussed in Chapter 2) led the Civil Service Commission to change its policy so that "immoral conduct" was no longer a sufficient basis to justify the dismissal of federal employees. See Rhonda R. Rivera, "Our Straight-Laced Judges: The Legal Position of Homosexual Persons in the United States," 30 *Hastings Law Journal* 799, 821–822 (1979). It bears noting that in 1969, the California Supreme Court required school districts in the state to produce some evidence that teachers who engaged in same-sex sexual conduct were unable to fulfill their job responsibilities before they were dismissed. See Morrison v. State Board of Education, 461 P.2d 375 (Ca. 1969). For the ways in which California courts inconsistently applied *Morrison* in the 1970s, see Rivera, "Our Straight-Laced Judges," 862–864.

13. For details about the Baker/McConnell relationship, their quest to marry,

and their political activism, see Ken Bronson, "A Quest for Full Equality" (2004), available at https://www.qlibrary.org/wordpress/wp-content/uploads/2014/04/QuestforFull_Equality.pdf; Michael Boucai, "Glorious Precedents: When Gay Marriage Was Radical," 27 *Yale Law Journal of Law and the Humanities* 1, 23–29 (2015).

14. Letter from Gerald R. Nelson, Clerk of District Court, Hennepin County, Minnesota, to Richard John Baker, May 22, 1970 (included in Appellants' Brief and Appendix, Baker v. Nelson, Minnesota Supreme Court, No. 40039 (1971), Appendix, 1).

15. McConnell v. Anderson, 451 F.2d 193, 193 (8th Cir. 1971).

16. McConnell v. Anderson, 316 F. Supp. 809, 811 (D. Minn. 1970).

17. Ibid.

18. *McConnell*, 451 F.2d at 195n7.

19. Ibid., 196.

20. Pickering v. Board of Education, 391 U.S. 563 (1968).

21. The Minnesota Supreme Court rejected McConnell's and Baker's contention that the state's unwillingness to permit them to marry violated the federal Constitution, see Baker v. Nelson, 191 N.W.2d 185 (Minn. 1971), a ruling that was summarily affirmed by the U.S. Supreme Court. See Baker v. Nelson, 409 U.S. 810 (1972). The couple also lost a federal court claim asking for increased veterans' benefits for Baker on the ground that McConnell was his dependent spouse. See McConnell v. Nooner, 547 F.2d 54 (8th Cir. 1976).

22. Robert A. Rhoads, *Freedom's Web: Student Activism in an Age of Cultural Diversity* (Baltimore: Johns Hopkins University Press, 1998), 159, 163.

23. Petition for a Writ of Certiorari, Acanfora v. Board of Education, U.S. Supreme Court, 73–1843 (1974), 4.

24. Acanfora v. Board of Education, 491 F.2d 498, 500 (4th Cir. 1974).

25. Ibid., 501.

26. "Homosexual Gains Authority to Teach," *New York Times*, September 24, 1972.

27. Acanfora v. Board of Education, 359 F. Supp. 843, 847 (D. Md. 1973).

28. Ibid., 856–857.

29. *Acanfora*, 491 F.2d at 500–501.

30. Singer v. U.S. Civil Service Commission, 530 F.2d 247, 249, 256 (9th Cir. 1976). The Supreme Court vacated the Court of Appeals' ruling after the federal Civil Service Commission adopted new guidelines stating explicitly that engaging in same-sex sexual conduct was not, by itself, a sufficient ground for dismissal.

31. *Singer*, 530 F.2d at 256. The court in *Singer* rejected both the plaintiff's due process and free speech claims.

32. Aumiller v. University of Delaware, 434 F. Supp. 1273, 1289 (D. Del. 1977).

33. Ibid., 1283.

34. Ibid., 1301, 1313.

35. William N. Eskridge Jr., "Challenging the Apartheid of the Closet: Establishing Conditions for Lesbian and Gay Intimacy, *Nomos*, and Citizenship, 1961–1981," 25 *Hofstra Law Review* 817, 905 (1997).

36. Van Ooteghem v. Gray, 628 F.2d 488, 492–493 (5th Cir. 1980). Although the Fifth Circuit, after the panel decision, agreed to hear the case en banc (that is, agreed that all of the circuit's judges should hear the case) and therefore vacated the panel's ruling, it eventually agreed with the panel that the defendant had violated the plaintiff's rights of free speech under the First Amendment. See Van Ooteghem v. Gray, 654 F.2d 304 (5th Cir. 1981) (en banc).

37. As I do here, Eskridge in *Gaylaw* notes the equality implications of the 1970s gay civil servant cases that explicitly raised First Amendment issues. William N. Eskridge Jr., *Gaylaw: Challenging the Apartheid of the Closet* (Cambridge, MA: Harvard University Press, 1999), 124. Eskridge, however, focuses only on the unsuccessful challenges in *McConnell and Acanfora*, and does not address successful challenges in cases such as *Aumiller* and *Van Ooteghem*.

38. Gay Law Students Association v. Pacific Telephone and Telegraph Co., 595 P.2d 592, 610 (Ca. 1979).

39. Rowland v. Mad River Local School District, 730 F.2d 444 (6th Cir. 1984).

40. Rowland v. Mad River School District, 470 U.S. 1009, 1012 (1985) (Brennan, J., dissenting from denial of certiorari). See also Weaver v. Nebo School District, 29 F. Supp.2d 1279, 1284 (D. Utah 1998) (concluding that school's mandate that lesbian teacher not speak about her sexual orientation violated the First Amendment because the topic was one of public concern).

41. Nan D. Hunter, "Expressive Identity: Recuperating Dissent for Equality," 35 *Harvard Civil Rights-Civil Liberties Law Review* 1, 6 (2000).

42. Dudley Clendinen and Adam Nagourney, *Out for Good: The Struggle to Build a Gay Rights Movement in America* (New York: Simon & Schuster, 1999), 304.

43. David Aretha, *No Compromise: The Story of Harvey Milk* (Greensboro, NC: Morgan Reynolds Publishing, 2010), 76 (quoting from *The Times of Harvey Milk* documentary directed by Rob Epstein (Black Sands Production, 1984)).

44. Clendinen and Nagourney, *Out for Good*, 378

45. California Voters Pamphlet, General Election, November 7, 1978, 29.

46. Hunter, *Identity, Speech, and Equality*, 1704.

47. Ibid., 1705.

48. National Gay Task Force v. Board of Education, 729 F.2d 1270 (10th Cir. 1984).

49. Fred Fejes, *Gay Rights and Moral Panic: The Origins of America's Debate on Homosexuality* (New York: Palgrave Macmillan, 2008), 184–185.

50. Clendinen and Nagourney, *Out for Good*, 386–388.

51. For a description of the Dade County gay rights campaign, which emphasized abstract principles of "human rights" and "civil liberties" without directly tackling homophobia and prejudice through grassroots organizing, see Barry Adam, *The Rise of a Gay and Lesbian Movement* (New York: Twayne

Publishers, 1995), 104; Fejes, *Gay Rights and Moral Panic*, 118–119, 138.

52. For an exploration of the gay rights battle in Eugene in 1978, see The Gay Rights Writer's [*sic*] Group, *It Could Happen to You . . . An Account of the Gay Civil Rights Campaign in Eugene, Oregon* (Boston: Allyson Publications, 1983).

53. For a discussion of the different political strategies pursued by activists who emphasized human rights/civil liberties and those who focused on addressing homophobia directly during the anti–Briggs Initiative campaign, see Fejes, *Gay Rights and Moral Panic*, 196–197; Amber Hollibaugh, "Sexuality and the State: The Defeat of the Briggs Initiative and Beyond," 9 *Socialist Review* 55 (1979); Michael Ward and Mark Freeman, "Defending Gay Rights: The Campaign against the Briggs Initiative in California," 13 *Radical America* 11 (1979).

54. Hollibaugh, *Sexuality and the State*, 61.

55. Ramy K. Khalil, "Harvey Milk and California Proposition 6: How the Gay Liberation Movement Won Two Early Victories (Masters Thesis, Western Washington University, 2012), 91.

56. Elaine Herscher, "Witch-Hunt: Everyone's A Suspect," *Mother Jones*, November 1978, 7; Khalil, *Harvey Milk and California Proposition 6*, 108–115; Sara R. Smith, "Organizing for Social Justice: Rank-and-File Teachers' Activism and Social Unionism in California, 1948–1978" (Ph.D. dissertation, University of California at Santa Cruz, 2014), 396–397; Ward and Freeman, *Defending Gay Rights*, 22–23.

57. Amber L. Hollibaugh, *My Dangerous Desires: A Queer Girl Dreaming Her Way Home* (Durham, NC: Duke University Press, 2000), 43.

58. Transcript of Harvey Milk speech, Gay Freedom Day Parade, June 25, 1978, in Randy Shilts, *The Mayor of Castro Street: The Life and Times of Harvey Milk* (New York: St. Martin, 1982), 366.

59. Khalil, *Harvey Milk and California Proposition 6*, 73.

60. Smith, *Organizing for Social Justice*, 411 (quoting Doyle McManus, "Healdsburg's 'Weirdest Event': Briggs Debates Gay Teacher," *Los Angeles Times*, October 26, 1978).

61. Karen M. Harbeck, *Gay and Lesbian Educators: Personal Freedoms, Public Constraints* (Malden, MA: Amethyst Press, 1997), 78 (quoting "Senator Briggs Attacks Gay Teacher," *Gaysweek*, October 9, 1978).

62. Smith, *Organizing for Social Justice*, 411 (quoting Penelope McMillan, "Briggs Points to Gay Teacher in North as Example," *Los Angeles Times*, September 29, 1978).

63. Ward and Freeman, *Defending Gay Rights*, 20. Following the initiative's defeat, Berner sued Briggs for defamation. The case was settled out of court in 1982. See Finding Aid to the Lawrence Berner v. John Briggs Collection, 1940–2004, James C. Hormel Gay and Lesbian Center, San Francisco Public Library, available at http://pdf.oac.cdlib.org/pdf/csf/hglc/bernerbriggs.pdf.

64. Ward and Freeman, *Defending Gay Rights*, 20.

65. Smith, *Organizing for Social Justice*, 422–435.
66. Jackie Blount, *Fit to Teach: Same-Sex Desire, Gender and School Work in the Twentieth Century* (Albany: State University of New York Press, 2005), 138.
67. Fejes, *Gay Rights and Moral Panic*, 197.
68. Fricke v. Lynch, 491 F. Supp. 381, 383 (D.R.I. 1980).
69. Ibid.
70. Aaron Fricke, "One Life, One Prom," in *The Christopher Street Reader*, Michael Denneny, Charles Ortleb, and Thomas Steele, eds. (New York: Putnam, 1983), 21.
71. *Fricke*, 491 F. Supp. at 384–385.
72. Ibid., 387.

Chapter 4: Activism in and out of the Courts

1. One policy area that has continued to see the affirmative use of the Free Speech Clause by LGBT rights supporters involves the application of dress regulations to transgender students in public schools. See, e.g., McMillen v. Itawamba County School District, 702 F. Supp.2d 699 (N.D. Miss. 2010); Doe v. Yunits, 2000 WL 33162199 (Mass. Sup. Ct.). For the argument that freedom of speech principles prevent the government from regulating gender nonconformity in general, see Jeffrey Kosbie, "(No) State Interests in Regulating Gender: How Suppression of Gender Nonconformity Violates Freedom of Speech," 19 *William & Mary Journal of Women and the Law* 187 (2013).
2. 10 U.S.C. § 654 (1993).
3. In 1992, the year before the implementation of DADT, the military discharged 730 individuals on the ground that they were lesbian, gay, or bisexual (accounting for .040 percent of individuals in the active forces). By 2001, the number of annual discharges increased to 1,227 (accounting for .089 percent of those in the active forces, more than double the rate from nine years earlier). David F. Burrelli and Jody Feder, "Homosexuals and the U.S. Military: Current Issues," Congressional Research Service, July 22, 2009, 9–10.
4. 10 U.S.C. § 654(b)(2) (1993).
5. Tobias Barrington Wolff, "Political Accountability and Representation under Don't Ask, Don't Tell," 89 *Iowa Law Review* 1633, 1649–1650 (2004).
6. National Gay Task Force v. Board of Education, 729 F.2d 1270 (10th Cir. 1984).
7. Wolff, *Political Accountability*, 1652–1688.
8. Goldman v. Weinberger, 475 U.S. 503 (1986). The legal challenge in *Goldman* was based on the Free Exercise Clause.
9. David Cole and William N. Eskridge, Jr., "From Hand-Holding to Sodomy: First Amendment Protection of Homosexual (Expressive) Conduct," 29

Harvard Civil Rights-Civil Liberties Law Review 319, 342 (1994).

10. Wolff, *Political Accountability*, 1187–1188.

11. See Holmes v. California National Guard, 124 F.3d 1126, 1136 (9th Cir. 1997); Richenberg v. Perry, 97 F.3d 256, 263 (8th Cir. 1996); Thomasson v. Perry, 80 F.3d 915, 931 (4th Cir. 1996) (en banc). Earlier courts reached similar conclusions in assessing free speech challenges to the categorical ban of lesbian, gay, and bisexual service members that preceded DADT. See, e.g., Pruitt v. Cheney, 963 F.2d 1160, 1163–1164 (9th Cir. 1992).

12. *Holmes*, 124 F.3d at 1137 (Reinhardt, J., dissenting).

13. See *Goldman*, 475 U.S. at 507; Brown v. Glines, 444 U.S. 348, 354 (1980).

14. See Witt v. Department of the Air Force, 527 F.3d 806 (9th Cir. 2008); Witt v. Department of the Air Force, 739 F. Supp.2d 1308 (W.D. Wash. 2010); Log Cabin Republicans v. United States, 716 F. Supp.2d 884 (C.D. Cal. 2010), vacated on other grounds by 658 F.3d 1162 (9th Cir. 2011). But see Cook v. Gates, 528 F.3d 42 (1st Cir. 2008) (rejecting post-*Lawrence* constitutional challenge to DADT).

15. For the argument that the First Amendment prohibited not only the enforcement of DADT, but of sodomy laws as well, see Cole and Eskridge, *From Hand-Holding to Sodomy*.

16. Mary Bernstein, "Nothing Ventured, Nothing Gained? Conceptualizing Social Movement 'Success' in the Lesbian and Gay Movement," 46 *Sociological Perspectives* 353, 357 (2003).

17. Ibid., 361.

18. The one exception was California, which repealed its sodomy law as a result of the political activism of the LGBT movement. Ibid.

19. Ibid., 363.

20. Amin Ghaziani, *The Dividends of Dissent: How Conflict and Culture Work in Lesbian and Gay Marches on Washington* (Chicago: University of Chicago Press, 2008), 90–95.

21. Bernstein, *Nothing Ventured*, 366–367.

22. Ibid., 367.

23. Ibid., 367–368.

24. See, e.g., High Tech Gays v. Defense Indus. Sec. Clearance Office, 895 F.2d 563, 571 (9th Cir. 1990); Woodward v. United States, 871 F.2d 1068, 1076 (Fed. Cir. 1989).

25. See, e.g., *High Tech Gays*, 895 F.2d at 573–574.

26. Lawrence v. Texas, 539 U.S. 558 (2003).

27. John-Manuel Andriote, *Victory Deferred: How AIDS Changed Gay Life in America* (Chicago: University of Chicago Press, 1999), 68.

28. Editorial, "Senator Helms and the Guilty Victims," *New York Times*, June 17, 1987, A30.

29. Arthur S. Leonard, "Employment Discrimination against People with AIDS," 10 *Dayton University Law Review* 681 (1985).

30. See, e.g., Leckelt v. Board of Commissioners of Hospital District 1, 909 F.2d

820 (5th Cir. 1990); City of New York v. New Saint Mark's Bath, 497 N.Y.S.2d 979 (Sup. Ct. 1986).

31. The Labor-Health and Human Services Appropriations Act for Fiscal Year 1988, Public Law 101-202, §514(a) (1988). In 1989, the Helms Amendment was replaced with an ostensibly neutral provision that prohibited the use of federal monies for AIDS materials "designed to promote or encourage, directly, . . . sexual activity, homosexual or heterosexual." Public Law 100-436 (1988). The Helms Amendment, and the provision that replaced it, may have been impervious to a free speech challenge given the government's considerable authority, under the First Amendment, to determine how to fund social service programs. See, e.g., Rust v. Sullivan, 500 U.S. 173 (1991). However, in 1992, a federal court struck down a regulation issued by the Centers for Disease Control and Prevention that prohibited the funding of "offensive" materials on, inter alia, the ground that it was unconstitutionally vague under the Due Process Clause. See Gay Men's Health Crisis v. Sullivan, 792 F. Supp. 278 (S.D.N.Y. 1992).

32. Susan Chambré, *Fighting for Our Lives: New York's AIDS Community and the Politics of Disease* (New Brunswick, NJ: Rutgers University Press, 2006), 118.

33. Deborah B. Gould, *Moving Politics: Emotion and ACT UP's Fight against AIDS* (Chicago: University of Chicago Press, 2009), 139. As the *Advocate* put it, because of *Bowers*, "gays and lesbians are legal ghosts, essentially in the same predicament that blacks and women were in the 19th century." Ghaziani, *The Dividends of Dissent*, 90 (quoting Mark Vandervelden, "Civil Disobedience," *Advocate*, September 29, 1987, 48).

34. Gould, *Moving Politics*, 123–125.

35. Ibid., 128.

36. Chambré, *Fighting for Our Lives*, 122.

37. Hodge v. Talkin, 799 F.3d 1145 (D.C. Cir. 2015).

38. Ghaziani, *The Dividends of Dissent*, 120.

39. On the AIDS activist who created the quilt, see Cleve Jones and Jeff Dawson, *Stitching a Revolution: The Making of an AIDS Activist* (San Francisco: Harper, 2000).

40. Lewis A. Grossman, "AIDS Activists, FDA Regulation, and the Amendment of America's Drug Constitution," 42 *American Journal of Law and Medicine* (forthcoming, 2016). As Grossman explains, before "the AIDS movement took to the streets," the FDA viewed its primary responsibility to be protecting the public from dangerous and harmful products. "By the time AIDS activism waned in the early 1990s," the FDA also saw its role as "promoting the expeditious release of potentially effective treatments, both to advance public health and to enhance customer choice."

41. Andriote, *Victory Deferred*, 2.

42. George Chauncey, *Why Marriage? The History Shaping Today's Debate over Gay Equality* (New York: Basic Books, 2004).

43. Baehr v. Lewin, 852 P.2d 44 (Ha. 1993).

44. Carlos A. Ball, *From the Closet to the Courtroom: Five LGBT Lawsuits that Have Changed Our Nation* (Boston: Beacon, 2010), Ch. 4.

45. The campaigns that led to the enactment of the first two state statutes prohibiting sexual orientation discrimination, in Wisconsin (1982) and Massachusetts (1989), focused on behind-the-scene lobbying of key legislators with little public engagement of sexual orientation issues. See Peter M. Cicchino et al., "Sex, Lies and Civil Rights: A Critical History of the Massachusetts Gay Civil Rights Bill," 26 *Harvard Civil Rights-Civil Liberties Law Review* 549 (1991); Andrea Rottmann, "Passing Gay Rights in Wisconsin, 1967–1983" (thesis, Free University of Berlin, 2010). For a study of the factors that contributed to the passage of local ordinances prohibiting sexual orientation discrimination, see Kenneth D. Wald, James W. Button, and Barbara A. Rienzo, "The Politics of Gay Rights in American Communities: Explaining Antidiscrimination Ordinances and Policies," 40 *American Journal of Political Science* 1152 (1996). See also Mary Bernstein, "Celebration and Suppression: The Strategic Uses of Identity by the Lesbian and Gay Movement," 103 *American Journal of Sociology* 531 (1997).

46. Baker v. State, 744 A.2d 864 (Vt. 1999).

47. David Moats, *Civil Wars: A Battle for Gay Marriage* (New York: Harcourt, 2004), 170–171.

48. Ibid., 179.

49. On the 1987 "Wedding Protest," see Ghaziani, *The Dividends of Dissent*, 120–121.

50. "Lambda Press Release, Lesbians, Gay Men & Allies to Mark First National Event by 'Tying the Knot,'" January 12, 1998, available at http://www.lambdalegal.org/news/ny_19980112_national-freedom-to-marry-day. See also Verta Taylor, Katrina Kimport, Nella Van Dyke, and Ellen Ann Anderson, "Mobilization through Marriage," in *The Marrying Kind? Debating Same-Sex Marriage within the Lesbian and Gay Movement*, Mary Bernstein and Verta Taylor, eds. (Minneapolis: University of Minnesota Press, 2013), 228.

51. Taylor et al., *Mobilization through Marriage*, 229.

52. Moats, *Civil Wars*, 178.

53. Jeffrey Kosbie, "Discursive Community and Marriage Mobilization in Massachusetts," in Taylor et al., *The Marrying Kind?*, 109.

54. For a detailed analysis of the strategic decisions made by those who led the political campaigns against constitutional amendments banning same-sex marriages prior to 2009, see Amy L. Stone, *Gay Rights at the Ballot Box* (Minneapolis: University of Minnesota Press, 2012), Ch. 5.

55. In re Marriage Cases, 183 P.3d 384 (Ca. 2008).

56. Michael J. Klarman, *From the Closet to the Altar: Courts, Backlash, and the Struggle for Same-Sex Marriage* (New York: Oxford University Press, 2014), 125.

57. Baird Hegelson, "Rural Vote Crucial in Battle on Marriage," *Minneapolis-St. Paul Star Tribune*, June 17, 2012.

58. Baird Hegelson, "Amendment Foes Turn Up the Volume," *Minneapolis-St.*

Paul Star Tribune, June 24, 2012.

59. Baird Hegelson, "For Top Foe, Marriage Right is for Freedom," *Minneapolis-St. Paul Star Tribune,* October 5, 2012.

60. Judy Harrison, "Same-Sex Marriage Supporters Kick Off Maine Campaign by Going Door to Door," *Bangor Daily News,* May 15, 2012.

61. David Cole, *Engines of Liberty: The Power of Citizen Activists to Make Constitutional Law* (New York: Basic Books, 2016), 65.

62. Susan M. Cover, "Hundreds Rally for Same-Sex Marriage in Portland," *Portland Press Herald,* September 10, 2012.

63. United States v. Windsor, 133 U.S. 2675, 2689 (2013).

64. Ibid.

65. Obergefell v. Hodges, 135 S. Ct. 2584, 2593 (2015).

66. Ibid., 2596

67. Ibid.

68. Ibid., 2599.

69. Baker v. Nelson, 409 U.S. 810 (1972). I discuss Michael McConnell's employment discrimination/free speech lawsuit against the University of Minnesota in Chapter 3.

Chapter 5: The Race and Gender Precedents

1. Although this chapter focuses on the actions of Congress and of the Supreme Court, state legislatures, state courts, and lower federal courts have also periodically looked to First Amendment values and principles to limit the government's ability to pursue equality objectives.

2. The language of Sumner's bill went through modifications, large and small, through the five years during which Congress considered it. For the initial version of the bill, see Congressional Globe, 41st Cong., 2d Sess. 3434 (1870) (statement of Sen. Charles Sumner). For the version introduced in 1871, see Congressional Globe, 42nd Cong., 2d Sess. 244 (1872). For detailed accounts of the bill, and its modifications through the years, see Alfred Avins, "The Civil Rights Act of 1875: Some Reflected Light on the Fourteenth Amendment and Public Accommodations," 66 *Columbia Law Review* 873 (1966); Aderson Bellegarde François, "The Brand of Inferiority: The Civil Rights Act of 1875, White Supremacy, and Affirmative Action," 57 *Howard Law Journal* 573 (2014); Michael W. McConnell, "Originalism and the Desegregation Decisions," 81 *Virginia Law Review* 947 (1995); James M. McPherson, "Abolitionists and the Civil Rights Act of 1875," 52 *Journal of American History* 493 (1965).

3. The Civil Rights Cases, 109 U.S. 3 (1883).

4. See, e.g., Congressional Globe, 42nd Cong., 2d Sess. 428 (1872) (statement of Representative Stowell) ("Is the colored man anywhere excluded from places of public amusement, or from stagecoaches, railroads, or steamboats? . . . So long as [these businesses] are open to them, and they are not absolutely

excluded, it cannot be said that they are abridged of any right or denied the equal protection of the laws").

5. See, e.g., Congressional Globe, 42nd Cong., 2d Sess. 242 (1872) (statement of Senator Hill) (if a railroad placed a black man "in a car that was designed for colored people, and the car was equal in comfort to a first class passenger-class, there was no injustice done to him").

6. For a discussion of the distinction in late-nineteenth-century political and legal debates between civil rights and social rights, see Jack M. Balkin, "*Plessy, Brown*, and *Grutter*: A Play in Three Acts," 26 *Cardozo Law Review* 1689, 1694–1696 (2005); Reva Siegel, "Why Equality Protection No Longer Protects: The Evolving Forms of Status-Enforcing State Action," 49 *Stanford Law Review* 1111, 1198–1127 (1997); Mark Tushnet, "The Politics of Equality in Constitutional Law: The Equal Protection Clause, Dr. Du Bois, and Charles Hamilton Houston," 74 *Journal of American History* 884, 885–890 (1987). A third category of rights, those of political participation, had been seemingly addressed by the Fifteenth Amendment.

7. See, e.g., Congressional Globe, 42nd Cong., 2d Sess. 3251 (1872) (statement of Senator Blair) ("After we have secured to the Negro by previous bills the right of suffrage and all the civil rights which belong to any man, it is now proposed to give them social rights, to impose upon the whites of the community the necessity of a close association in all matters with the negroes."). See also Congressional Record, 43rd Cong., 2d Sess. 411 (1874) (statement of Representative Blount) ("Whatever inequality of public accommodations there may be is simply the result of an indisposition to social intercourse").

8. NAACP v. Alabama, 357 U.S. 449 (1958).

9. Boy Scouts of America v. Dale, 530 U.S. 640 (2000). I explore the *Dale* case in Chapter 6.

10. See, e.g., Congressional Globe, 42nd Cong., 2d Sess. 382 (1872) (statement of Senator Sumner) (arguing that the bill did not pose a "question of society; no question of social life; no question of social equality, if anybody knows what this means. The object is simply Equality before the law, a term which explains itself").

11. The first state statute prohibiting discrimination by places of public accommodation was enacted by Massachusetts in 1865. See Massachusetts State Statute 277 (1865). Shortly thereafter, some of the congressionally imposed state governments in the South enacted statutes requiring access to some public accommodations regardless of race. Between 1868 and 1873, Arkansas, Florida, Georgia, Louisiana, Mississippi, South Carolina, Tennessee, and Texas enacted such statutes. See Barbara Young Welke, *Recasting American Liberty: Gender, Race, Law, and the Railroad Revolution, 1865–1920* (New York: Cambridge University Press, 2001), 337. The Tennessee statute, for example, prohibited railroads and other common carriers from discriminating on the basis of race, and the South Carolina provision prohibited any businesses that required government licenses from doing the same. See Joseph William

Singer, "No Right to Exclude: Public Accommodations and Private Property," 90 *Northwestern University Law Review* 1283, 1355–1356 (1996). For excerpts from some of these statutes, see Richard Bardolph, *The Civil Rights Record: Black Americans and the Law, 1849–1970* (New York: Crowell, 1970), 72–75.

12. Congressional Globe, 42nd Cong., 2d Sess. 242 (1872) (statement of Senator Sumner).

13. Congressional Globe, 42nd Cong., 2d Sess. 242 (1872) (statement of Senator Hill).

14. Congressional Globe, 42nd Cong., 2d Sess. 243 (1872) (statement of Senator Sumner).

15. Congressional Record, 43rd Cong., 2d Sess. 4082 (1874) (statement of Representative Pratt).

16. Congressional Record, 43rd Cong., 2d Sess. 428 (1874) (statement of Representative Buckner).

17. Congressional Record, 43rd Cong., 2d Sess. 405 (1874) (statement of Representative Durham).

18. For a discussion of how the perceived distinction between civil rights and social rights framed much of the congressional debate over the Civil Rights Act of 1875 as it impacted on the question of education in public schools, see McConnell, *Originalism and the Desegregation Decisions*, 1014–1023.

19. Scott v. Georgia, 39 Ga. 321 (1869). See also Green v. State, 58 Ala. 190 (1877) ("The amendments to the Constitution were evidently designed to secure to citizens, without distinction of race, rights of a civil or political kind only—not such as are merely social, much less those of a purely domestic nature"); State v. Hairston, 63 N.C. 451 (1869) ("neither the Civil Rights Bill, nor our State Constitution was intended to enforce social equality, but only civil and political rights").

20. *The Civil Rights Cases*, 109 U.S. at 13.

21. Ibid., 22. In the *Civil Rights Cases*, the Supreme Court struck down the 1875 public accommodations law after concluding that the Thirteenth Amendment did not grant Congress the constitutional authority to enact the statute because the denial of public accommodations on the basis of race was not an incident of slavery. The Court also held that the Fourteenth Amendment only restricted the actions of the state and therefore did not restrict the conduct of private parties.

22. Ibid., 59.

23. For a detailed analysis of public accommodations laws in the second half of the nineteenth century, see Singer, *No Right to Exclude*.

24. Plessy v. Ferguson, 163 U.S. 537, 544 (1896).

25. Ibid., 561.

26. Ibid., 562.

27. Congressional Globe, 42nd Cong., 2d Sess. 819 (1872) (statement of Senator Norwood).

28. Congressional Globe, 42nd Cong., 2d Sess. 3252 (1872) (statement of Senator Blair).

29. Congressional Globe, 42nd Cong., 2d Sess. 242 (1872) (statement of Senator Hill).

30. Congressional Record, 43rd Cong., 2d Sess. 453 (1874) (statement of Representative Atkins).

31. 142 Congressional Record S10110, 104th Cong., 2d Sess. (September 10, 1996) (statement of Senator Byrd). According to the House Committee on the Judiciary's report on the Defense of Marriage Act, the proposed law appropriately reflected Congress's "moral disapproval of homosexuality, and a moral conviction that heterosexuality better comports with traditional (especially Judeo–Christian) morality." Report 104-664, Defense of Marriage Act, Committee on the Judiciary, U.S. House of Representatives, July 9, 1996, 16.

32. 110 Congressional Record S13207, 88th Cong., 2d Sess. (1964) (statement of Senator Byrd).

33. 142 Congressional Record H7486, 104th Cong., 2d Sess. (July 12, 1996) (statement of Representative Buyer).

34. 142 Congressional Record H7444, 104th Cong., 2d Sess. (July 11, 1996) (statement of Representative Coburn).

35. For an extensive study of the theological parallels between religious racism and religious homophobia, as well as of the supposed biblical foundations and doctrinal theories advanced by Southern Protestant denominations to support racial segregation and antimiscegenation regulations, see William N. Eskridge Jr., "Noah's Curse: How Religion Often Conflates Status, Belief, and Conduct to Resist Antidiscrimination Norms," 45 *Georgia Law Review* 657 (2011).

36. Congressional Globe, 42nd Cong., 2d Sess. 384 (1872) (statement of Senator Sumner).

37. Congressional Globe, 42nd Cong., 2d Sess. 242 (1872) (statement of Senator Sumner). See also Congressional Globe, 42nd Cong., 2d Sess. 384 (1872) (statement of Senator Sumner) ("I feel bound to insist upon the same equality in other public institutions of learning and science, also in churches and in the last resting-places of the dead. So far as any of these are public in character and organized by law, they must follow the general requirement. How strange that any institution of learning or science, or any church or cemetery should set up a discrimination so utterly inconsistent with correct principle").

38. Congressional Globe, 42nd Cong., 2d Sess. 823 (1872) (statement of Senator Sumner).

39. Congressional Globe, 42nd Cong., 2d Sess. 823 (1872) (statement of Senator Sumner).

40. Congressional Globe, 42nd Cong., 2d Sess. 823 (1872) (statement of Senator Sumner). Sumner was not the only senator who spoke in favor of prohibiting

churches from excluding individuals on the basis of race. See, e.g., Congressional Globe, 42nd Cong., 2d Sess. 843 (1872) (statement of Senator Sherman) (arguing that incorporated churches should be treated like all other incorporated organizations and that "any church association that would exclude a man because of his color from worshipping God within its walls is a heathen church; it is not a Christian Church"). Senator Sherman eventually supported an amendment to remove churches from the measure out of fear that the broader bill might otherwise be defeated. See Congressional Globe, 42nd Congress, 2d Sess. 897 (1872).

41. Congressional Globe, 42nd Cong., 2d Sess. 826 (1872) (statement of Senator Carpenter).

42. Ibid.

43. Congressional Globe, 42nd Cong., 2d Sess. 848 (1872) (statement by Senator Frelinghuysen).

44. Congressional Globe, 42nd Cong., 2d Sess. 898 (1872) (statement by Senator Morton).

45. For the amendment, see Congressional Globe, 42nd Cong., 2d Sess. 896 (1872). For the vote, see Congressional Globe, 42nd Cong., 2d Sess. 899 (1872).

46. Hosanna-Tabor Evangelical Lutheran Church and School v. EEOC, 132 S. Ct. 694 (2012).

47. On the legal and political backgrounds leading up to the enactment of the civil rights law, see Rebecca E. Zietlow, "To Secure These Rights: Congress, Courts, and the Civil Rights Act of 1964," 57 *Rutgers Law Review* 945 (2005).

48. Robert R. Bebermeyer, "Public Accommodations and the Civil Rights Act of 1964," 19 *University of Miami Law Review* 456 (1965).

49. Samuel Bagenstos has noted the conceptual link between the "social rights" claims raised by the opponents of the Civil Rights Act of 1875 and the arguments made by the opponents to Title II of the Civil Rights Act of 1964. See Samuel R. Bagenstos, "The Unrelenting Libertarian Challenge to Public Accommodations Law," 66 *Stanford Law Review* 1205 (2014).

50. The Thirteenth Amendment objection to Title II was raised by some legislators, see, e.g., Civil Rights Act of 1964, S. Rep. 88-872, 88th Cong., 2d Sess. (1964), 52–53 (individual views of Senator Thurmond); judges, see Browning v. Slenderella Systems, 341 P.2d 859, 869 (Wash. 1959) (Mallery, J., dissenting); and commentators, see Alfred Avins, "Freedom of Choice in Personal Service Occupations: Thirteenth Amendment Limitations on Antidiscrimination Legislation," 49 *Cornell Law Quarterly* 228 (1964). For a historical account of these claims, see Linda C. McClain. "Involuntary Servitude, Public Accommodations Law, and the Legacy of *Heart of Atlanta Motel, Inc. v. United States*," 71 *Maryland Law Review* 83 (2011).

51. Heart of Atlanta Motel, Inc. v. United States, 379 U.S. 241 (1964).

52. Robert Bork, "Civil Rights—A Challenge," *New Republic*, August 31, 1963, 22.

53. Ibid., 24.

54. Civil Rights Act of 1964, Minority Report to the House Judiciary Committee Report, H.R. 88-914, 88th Congress, 1st Sess. (Nov. 20, 1963), 69.

55. Civil Rights Act of 1964, S. Rep. 88-872, 88th Cong., 2d Sess. (1964), 46 (individual views of Senator Thurmond) (quoting Peterson v. City of Greenville, 373 U.S. 244, 250 (1963) (Harlan, J., concurring)).

56. Civil Rights Act of 1964, S. Rep. 88-872, 88th Cong., 2d Sess. (1964), 65.

57. Christopher W. Schmidt, "Defending the Right to Discriminate: The Libertarian Challenge to the Civil Rights Movement," in *Signposts: New Directions in Southern Legal History*, Sally E. Hadden and Patricia Hagler Minter, eds. (Athens: University of Georgia Press, 2013), 417. For a detailed assessment of the role that liberty-based objections played in the arguments of those who opposed school integration in Atlanta in the 1950s and 1960s, see Kevin M. Kruse, "The Fight for 'Freedom of Association': Segregationist Rights and Resistance in Atlanta," in *Massive Resistance: Southern Opposition to the Second Reconstruction*, Clive Webb ed. (New York: Oxford University Press, 2005), 99. See also Richard Cortner, *Civil Rights and Public Accommodations: The* Heart of Atlanta Motel *and* McClung *Cases* (Lawrence: University Press of Kansas, 2001).

58. For judicial opinions rejecting liberty-based objections to legal requirements not to discriminate on the basis of race, see, e.g., *Heart of Atlanta Motel*, 379 U.S. 241; Wills v. Pickrick Restaurant, 231 F. Supp. 396 (N.D. Ga. 1964).

59. Schmidt, *Defending the Right to Discriminate*, 417 (quoting Robert T. Simpson, "The Public Accommodations Section of the Civil Rights Bill," 25 *Alabama Lawyer* (1964), 308).

60. Newman v. Piggie Park Enterprises, 256 F. Supp. 941, 945 (D.S.C. 1966).

61. Newman v. Piggie Park Enterprises, 390 U.S. 400, 402 n.5 (1968).

62. Civil Rights Act of 1964, House Judiciary Committee Report, H.R. 88-914, 88th Cong., 1st Sess. (Nov. 20, 1963), 9.

63. Civil Rights Act of 1964, H.R. Rep. 88-914, 88th Cong., 2d Sess. (1964), Pt. 2, 8 (individual statement of Rep. William M. McCulloch et al.).

64. Civil Rights Act of 1964, S. Rep. 88-872, 88th Cong., 2d Sess. (1964), 16.

65. Honoring 40th Anniversary of Passage of Civil Rights Act of 1964, 150 Congressional Record 13,661–13,662 (2004). For a discussion of the resolution and Ron Paul's libertarian objections to the Civil Rights Act of 1964, see McClain, *Involuntary Servitude*, 141–145.

66. Even some libertarian commentators objected to Rand Paul's criticism of Title II. See Bagenstos, *The Unrelenting Libertarian Challenge*, 1222–1225.

67. *Heart of Atlanta Motel*, 379 U.S. 241; Katzenbach v. McClung, 379 U.S. 294 (1964).

68. See Civil Rights Act of 1964, Committee on Education and Labor Report, H.R. No. 88-570, 88th Cong., 1st Sess. (July 22, 1963), 4.

69. Interestingly, the report adopted by the Committee on Education and Labor states that this exemption, despite containing no language to this effect, was "intended to be applied only insofar as such activities are of a religious

nature or are related to religious endeavors." Civil Rights Act of 1964, Committee on Education and Labor Report, H.R. No. 88-570, 88th Cong., 1st Sess., (July 22, 1963), 4.

70. Hearings before the House Committee on Rules on H.R. 7152, 88th Cong., Pt. II (1964), 536.

71. 110 Congressional Record 2585 (1964). The House later approved an amendment stating that it was not unlawful for an employer to refuse to hire or employ atheists. 110 Congressional Record 2607–2611 (1964). The Senate bill that eventually became law did not include the atheist provision.

72. 110 Congressional Record 2587 (1964).

73. Ibid.

74. Charles W. Whalen and Barbara Whalen, *The Longest Debate: A Legislative History of the 1964 Civil Rights Act* (Cabin Jon, MD: Seven Locks Press, 1985), 4.

75. 110 Congressional Record 11931 (1964). The Senate bill also extended the same exemption to religious "educational institutions with respect to employment of individuals to perform work connected with the educational activities of such institution." Such an extension was seemingly unnecessary because the bill also retained the broader Purcell amendment that allowed religious educational institutions "to hire and employ employees of a particular religion" regardless of whether those employees were involved in their educational activities. As a result, Congress eventually removed the former provision, leaving the Purcell amendment as the only religious exemption that applied to educational institutions. H.R. Rep. No. 92-238, (1971), 19; S. Rpt. No. 92-415, (1971), 11.

76. Whalen and Whalen, *The Longest Debate*, 200.

77. Equal Employment Opportunity Act of 1972, Pub. L. 92-261, §§ 1-3.

78. 118 Congressional Record 1975 (1972).

79. Ibid., 1976.

80. Ibid., 1982.

81. Ibid., 1977–1980.

82. Ibid., 948.

83. Ibid., 1994.

84. Ibid., 1991.

85. Ibid., 1991–1992.

86. Ibid., 1992.

87. Ibid., 1992, 4813.

88. Ibid., 1992.

89. Ibid., 1995.

90. Ibid., 4813. Fifteen years later, the Supreme Court upheld the constitutionality of the Title VII religious exemption under the Establishment Clause. See Corporation of the Presiding Bishop of the Church of Jesus Christ of Latter-Day Saints v. Amos, 483 U.S. 327 (1987).

91. As noted, the 1964 statute allowed religious educational institutions to take religion into account in all of their employment decisions, not just those

related to religious activities.

92. On the Southern private schools created in the wake of the push for the racial integration of public schools, see David Nevin and Robert E. Bills, *The Schools that Fear Built: Segregationist Academies in the South* (Washington, D.C.: Acropolis Books, 1976).

93. For rulings arising from lawsuits filed by black parents against the Department of the Treasury, see Green v. Connally, 330 F. Supp. 1150 (D.D.C. 1971); Green v. Kennedy, 309 F. Supp. 1127 (D.D.C. 1970). For the IRS rule, see IRS Revenue Ruling 71-147 (1971).

94. On the history and mission of Bob Jones University, see Mark Taylor Dalhouse, *An Island in the Lake of Fire: Bob Jones University, Fundamentalism, and the Separatist Movement* (Athens: University of Georgia Press, 1996).

95. Bob Jones University v. United States, 468 F. Supp. 890, 893 (D.S.C. 1978).

96. Ibid., 894.

97. Runyon v. McCrary, 427 U.S. 160 (1976).

98. Ibid., 167.

99. Bob Jones University v. United States, 461 U.S. 574, 580–581 (1983).

100. Ibid., 583n6.

101. Aaron Haberman, "Into the Wilderness: Ronald Reagan, Bob Jones University, and the Political Education of the Christian Right," 67 *Historian* 234, 239 (2005).

102. Stuart Taylor Jr., "The School Tax Exemption Stalemate," *New York Times*, February 7, 1982.

103. Haberman, *Into the Wilderness*, 243–244.

104. *Bob Jones*, 461 U.S. at 603–604.

105. Ibid., 604.

106. For an eloquent critique of the Court's ruling in *Bob Jones University*, see Robert M. Cover, "*Nomos* and Narrative," 97 *Harvard Law Review* 4 (1997).

107. The university's apology can be found at http://www.bju.edu/about/what-we-believe/race-statement.php.

108. The Bush and Lott incidents are discussed in Martha Minow, "Should Religious Groups be Exempt from Civil Rights Laws?," 48 *Boston College Law Review* 781 (2007).

109. Jane Dailey, *The Theology of Massive Resistance: Sex, Segregation and the Sacred after* Brown, in Webb, ed., *Massive Resistance*, 171 (citing Lott interview in *Southern Partisan* (Fall 1984), 47).

110. Linda Greenhouse, "Rights Official Defends Tax Break for Racially Biased Schools," *New York Times*, October 13, 1982.

111. Hishon v. King & Spalding, 467 U.S. 69 (1984).

112. Roberts v. United States Jaycees, 468 U.S. 609 (1984).

113. United States Jaycees v. McClure, 534 F. Supp. 766, 769 (D. Minn. 1982).

114. *Roberts*, 468 U.S. at 613.

115. Ibid., 622.

116. NAACP v. Alabama, 357 U.S. 449, 462 (1958).

117. *Roberts*, 468 U.S. at 623.

118. Ibid.

119. Ibid., 628. In the years following *Roberts*, the Supreme Court decided two other cases upholding laws prohibiting gender discrimination by places of public accommodation in the face of constitutional objections based on the freedom of association. See New York State Club Association v. City of New York, 487 U.S. 1 (1988); Board of Directors of Rotary International v. Rotary Club of Duarte, 481 U.S. 537 (1987).

120. Hurley v. Irish-American Gay, Lesbian, and Bisexual Group of Boston, 515 U.S. 557 (1995); *Dale*, 530 U.S. 640.

121. Alicea-Hernandez v. Catholic Bishop of Chicago, 320 F.3d 698 (7th Cir. 2003); Pardue v. City Center Consortium Schools, 875 A.2d 669 (D.C. Ct. App. 2005); Starkman v. Evans, 198 F.3d 173 (5th Cir. 1999).

122. EEOC v. Hosanna-Tabor Evangelical Lutheran Church and School, 597 F.3d 769 (6th Cir. 2010).

123. *Hosanna-Tabor*, 132 S. Ct. at 694.

124. See Watson v. Jones, 13 Wall. 679 (1872); Kedroff v. St. Nicholas Cathedral of Russian Orthodox Church of North America, 344 U.S. 94 (1952); Serbian Eastern Orthodox Diocese for United States and Canada v. Milivojevich, 426 U.S. 696 (1976).

125. *Hosanna-Tabor*, 132 S. Ct. at 706.

126. The Obama administration took the position during the *Hosanna-Tabor* litigation that religious organizations were not constitutionally entitled to special immunity from antidiscrimination laws. Instead, the federal government argued that religious groups, like all expressive associations, are allowed, under the freedom of association, to exclude individuals whose inclusion impairs their ability to express and promote their viewpoints. Brief for the Federal Respondent, Hosanna-Tabor Evangelical Lutheran Church and School v. EEOC, 132 S. Ct. 694 (2012), 31. The Court rejected the administration's position, deeming it "untenable" because it rendered the Religious Clauses irrelevant to the crucial question of whether religious entities can choose their own ministers free from governmental interference. *Hosanna-Tabor*, 132 S. Ct. at 706. For criticism of the ministerial exception, see, e.g., Caroline Mala Corbin, "Above the Law? The Constitutionality of the Ministerial Exemption from Antidiscrimination Law," 75 *Fordham Law Review* 1965 (2007); Jane Rutherford, "Equality as the Primary Constitutional Value: The Case for Applying Employment Discrimination Laws to Religion," 81 *Cornell Law Review* 1049 (1996).

127. *Dale*, 530 U.S. 640.

Chapter 6: LGBT Equality and the Right to Exclude

1. Gay Rights Coalition of Georgetown University Law Center v. Georgetown University, 536 A.2d 1, 8 (D.C. Ct. App. 1987).
2. For a detailed exploration of the Georgetown case's background, ruling, and aftermath see Walter J. Walsh, "The Fearful Symmetry of Gay Rights, Religious Freedom, and Racial Equality," 40 *Howard Law Journal* 513 (1997).
3. Nan D. Hunter, "Pluralism and Its Perils: Navigating the Tension between Gay Rights and Religious Expression," 15 *Georgetown Journal of Gender and the Law* 435, 435 (2014); William N. Eskridge Jr., "Noah's Curse: How Religion Often Conflates Status, Belief, and Conduct to Resist Antidiscrimination Norms," 45 *Georgia Law Review* 657, 719 (2011).
4. Hunter, *Pluralism and Its Perils*, 435.
5. New York County Board of Ancient Order of Hibernians v. Dinkins, 814 F. Supp. 358, 362 (S.D.N.Y. 1993).
6. Ibid., 370.
7. Irish-American Gay, Lesbian, and Bisexual Group of Boston v. Boston, Massachusetts Superior Court, No. 92-1518 (December 15, 1993), 2.
8. *Ancient Order of Hibernians*, 814 F. Supp. at 362.
9. Massachusetts General Laws, Chapter 272, §92A.
10. Irish-American Gay, Lesbian, and Bisexual Group of Boston v. Boston, 636 N.E.2d 1293 (Mass. 1994).
11. Hurley v. Irish-American Gay, Lesbian, and Bisexual Group of Boston, 515 U.S. 557 (1995).
12. Ibid., 572.
13. Ibid., 575.
14. Ibid., 579.
15. Nan Hunter has noted that *Hurley* and the Boy Scouts case that followed in its wake, unlike earlier public accommodation disputes involving race and gender, did not involve questions of access to either physical spaces or material benefits. Instead, the two LGBT rights cases raised issues of access to "cultural or discursive" spaces and "a claim to cultural citizenship." Nan D. Hunter, "Accommodating the Public Sphere: Beyond the Market Model," 85 *Minnesota Law Review* 1591, 1627 (2001).
16. *Ancient Order of Hibernians*, 814 F. Supp. at 362.
17. Ibid., 363.
18. *Hurley*, 515 U.S. at 569.
19. Andrew Koppelman and Tobias Barrington Wolff, *A Right to Discriminate? How the Case of* Boy Scouts of America v. James Dale *Warped the Law of Free Association* (New Haven: Yale University, 2009), Ch. 2. For the argument that "the mere presence of an unwanted member in an organization almost never necessarily means that the organization accepts what that member stands for," see Hans Allhoff, "Membership and Messages: The (Il)logic of Expressive Association Doctrine," 15 *University of Pennsylvania Journal of*

Constitutional Law 1455, 1458 (2013).

20. Koppelman and Wolff, *A Right to Discriminate?*, Ch. 2.

21. See, e.g., Schwenk v. Boy Scouts of America, 551 P.2d 465 (Or. 1976) (exclusion of women); Quinnipiac Council, Boy Scouts of America v. Commission on Human Rights and Opportunities, 528 A.2d 352 (Conn. 1987) (exclusion of women); Welsh v. Boy Scouts of America, 993 F.2d 1267 (7th Cir. 1993) (exclusion of atheists); Seaburn v. Coronado Area Council, Boy Scouts of America, 891 P.2d 385 (Ka. 1995) (exclusion of atheists); Curran v. Mount Diablo Council of the Boy Scouts of America, 952 P.2d 218 (Ca. 1998) (exclusion of gay men). The Boy Scouts prevailed in all of these cases, primarily on the ground that its program did not constitute a place of public accommodation under the applicable state statutes.

22. Kinga Borondi, "Seminar Addresses Needs of Homosexual Teens," *Star-Ledger* (Newark), July 8, 1990, §2, 11.

23. Brief for Petitioners, Boy Scouts of America v. Dale, 530 U.S. 640 (2000), 20.

24. Dale v. Boy Scouts of America, 734 A.2d 1196 (N.J. 1999). The New Jersey Supreme Court affirmed a decision by the state's Appellate Division. See Dale v. Boy Scouts of America, 706 A.2d 270 (N.J. App. Div. 1998).

25. See Smith v. Allwright, 321 U.S. 649 (1944) (Democratic Party of Texas); Railway Mail Association v. Corsi, 326 U.S. 88 (1945) (union); and Runyon v. McCrary, 427 U.S. 160 (1976) (private school).

26. See Erwin Chemerinsky and Catherine Fisk, "The Expressive Interest of Associations," 9 *William and Mary Bill of Rights Journal* 595, 616 (2001).

27. *Dale*, 734 A.2d at 1203.

28. Boy Scouts of America v. Dale, 530 U.S. 640, 655–656 (2000).

29. Roberts v. United States Jaycees, 468 U.S. 609, 625–628 (1984). For criticism of the *Roberts* ruling for being insufficiently cognizant of the Jaycees's expressive and associational interests, see John D. Inazu, *Liberty's Refuge, The Forgotten Freedom of Assembly* (New Haven, CT: Yale University Press, 2012), 132–141.

30. Koppelman and Wolff, *A Right to Discriminate?*, 49.

31. Rumsfeld v. Forum for Academic and Institutional Rights, Inc., 547 U.S. 47 (2006).

32. For commentary defending *Dale*, see, e.g., David Bernstein, "Antidiscrimination Laws and the First Amendment," 66 *Missouri Law Review* 83 (2001); Dale Carpenter, "Expressive Association and Anti-Discrimination Law after *Dale*: A Tripartite Approach," 85 *Minnesota Law Review* 1515, 1564 (2001); Michael Stokes Paulsen, "Scouts, Families, and Schools," 85 *Minnesota Law Review* 1917 (2001). For commentary critical of *Dale*, see, e.g., Chemerinsky and Fisk, *The Expressive Interest of Associations*; Hunter, *Accommodating the Public Sphere*.

33. Other commentators have recognized the way in which the Court, in effect, deemed Dale's self-identification as a gay man to express a distinct message with First Amendment implications. See Carpenter, *Expressive Association*

and Anti-Discrimination Law, 1551–1553; Nancy J. Knauer, "'Simply So Different': The Uniquely Expressive Character of the Openly Gay Individual After *Boy Scouts of America v. Dale*," 89 *Kentucky Law Journal* 997 (2001). For the argument that Dale's coming out, by itself, failed to send a coherent or understandable message, see James P. Madigan, "Questioning the Coercive Effect of Self-Identifying Speech," 87 *Iowa Law Review* 75 (2001). It should be noted that even if Dale's self-identification as a gay man was a form of expression imbued with political and social meaning beyond the mere revealing of a fact about his sexuality, that does not mean that the Court was correct in siding with the Boy Scouts. This is because, for the Boy Scouts to prevail, it was not enough for Dale's self-identification to have recognizable political and social meanings; it was also necessary for the general public to have believed that the BSA's *failure to expel him* after he self-identified constituted an endorsement of the messages conveyed by his presence.

34. Douglas J. NeJaime, "Winning through Losing," 96 *Iowa Law Review* 941 (2011). Although NeJaime focuses on early defeats by the LGBT movement in sodomy and marriage litigation, and does not explore the consequences of the movement's loss in *Dale*, the repercussions of the Boy Scouts case are consistent with his thesis that social movements, over the long run, sometimes gain both legally and politically from litigation losses.

35. For a detailed account of the criticism heaped on the BSA following its legal victory in *Dale*, as well as the efforts of public and private sponsors to withdraw their support of the organization because of its exclusionary policy, see Richard J. Ellis, *Judging the Boy Scouts of America: Gay Rights, Freedom of Association, and the* Dale *Case* (Lawrence: University Press of Kansas, 2014).

36. For an exploration of the events leading up to the BSA's shift in policy on gay youth, see Ellis, *Judging the Boy Scouts of America*.

37. Erik Eckholm, "Boy Scouts End Ban on Gay Leaders, over Protests by Mormon Church," *New York Times*, July 27, 2015.

38. Katharine Q. Seelye and Jess Bidgood, "Boston Celebrates End of Ban as Gays March in St. Patrick's Parade," *New York Times*, March 15, 2015; Marc Santora, "Gay Groups to March in [New York's] St. Patrick's Day Parade as a Ban Falls," *New York Times*, September 3, 2014.

39. It bears noting that the same dynamic does not necessarily apply in the case of smaller entities, including small businesses that provide photography services, flowers, and cakes used in the celebration of weddings. Although the refusal of such businesses to serve same-sex couples may receive considerable public attention (especially if the refusal leads to litigation), it is not clear that the public spotlight would remain on those small businesses if judges or other decision-makers grant their requests for exemptions from sexual orientation antidiscrimination laws. In Chapter 7, I address the issue of religious exemptions from antidiscrimination laws.

40. *Christian Legal Society v. Martinez*, 561 U.S. 661, 671 (2010).

41. The stipulation's impact on the case proved to be controversial once it reached the Supreme Court. The majority, pointing to the stipulation, limited its constitutional analysis to the all-comers policy, leading the dissent to complain vehemently that the Court should have determined whether the application of the policy that protected certain classes of individuals from discrimination, rather than the all-comers policy, violated the Constitution.

42. *Christian Legal Society*, 561 U.S. at 673.

43. Rosenberger v. Rector and Visitors of the University of Virginia, 515 U.S. 819 (1995).

44. Police Department of Chicago v. Mosley, 408 U.S. 92 (1972).

45. The Court chose not to apply the freedom of association doctrine arising from cases such as *Roberts* and *Dale* because it required the application of heightened judicial scrutiny, a standard of judicial review that was inconsistent with the more relaxed form of review called for by cases involving limited public forums. *Christian Legal Society*, 561 U.S. at 681. For the argument that *Christian Legal Society* was, at its core, about the right of association, see Ashutosh Bhagwat, "Associations and Forums: Situating *CLS v. Martinez*," 38 *Hastings Constitutional Law Quarterly* 543 (2011).

46. *Christian Legal Society*, 561 U.S. at 683.

47. *Hurley*, 515 U.S. at 572.

48. *Rumsfeld*, 547 U.S. at 60.

49. Chemerinsky and Fisk, *The Expressive Interest of Associations*, 614.

50. Robert Post, "RFRA and First Amendment Freedom of Expression," 125 *Yale Law Journal Forum* 387, 391 (2016).

51. This principle is also supported by cases that allow the government to limit how organizations use public money. In *Rust v. Sullivan*, 500 U.S. 173 (1991), for example, the Court held that the First Amendment did not render unconstitutional a regulation prohibiting private organizations from using government money for abortion-related counseling, referrals, and advocacy.

52. The dissenting opinion in *Christian Legal Society* was written by Justice Alito and was joined by Chief Justice Roberts, Justice Scalia, and Justice Thomas. It bears noting that in the years following *Christian Legal Society*, Idaho, Kansas, North Carolina, Ohio, and Virginia enacted laws prohibiting postsecondary educational institutions from denying benefits to religious student groups on the ground that those groups require members to adhere to or comply with particular religious views. See Idaho Senate Bill 1078 (2013); Kansas Senate Bill 175 (2016); North Carolina Senate Bill 719 (2014); Ohio Revised Code § 3345.023; Virginia Code §23-9.2:12.

53. Thomas C. Berg, "What Same-Sex Marriage and Religious-Liberty Claims Have in Common," 5 *Northwestern Journal of Law & Social Policy* 206, 225 (2010).

54. Ward v. Rock Against Racism, 491 U.S. 781, 791 (1989) ("A regulation that

serves purposes unrelated to the content of expression is deemed neutral, even if it has an incidental effect on some speakers or messages but not others.").

55. Employment Division v. Smith, 494 U.S. 872 (1990).

Chapter 7: Marriage Equality and Religious Liberty

1. Willock v. Elane Photography, LLC, New Mexico Human Rights Commission, No. 06-12-20-0685, April 9, 2008, 4–5.

2. Ibid., 5.

3. Elane Photography, LLC v. Willock, 309 P.3d 53, 66 (N.M. 2013). The court further explained that the fact that photography, like many services ranging from the provision of floral arrangements to legal representation, involve creativity and expression does not immunize a photography business from antidiscrimination obligations. In addition, the judges explained that members of the public are unlikely to view a photography business's provision of its services for a fee at a wedding as an endorsement of that wedding. As the state high court explained, "it is well known to the public that wedding photographers are hired by paying customers and that a photographer may not share the happy couple's views on issues ranging from the minor (the color scheme, the hors d'oeuvres) to the decidedly major (the religious service, the choice of bride or groom)." *Elane Photography*, 309 P.2d at 69–70. The New Mexico Court of Appeals had earlier rejected the photographer's arguments on similar grounds. See Elane Photography, LLC v. Willock, 284 P.3d 428 (N.M. Ct. App. 2012).

4. Elane Photography also raised a statutory claim under the New Mexico Religious Freedom Restoration Act. The New Mexico Supreme Court rejected the claim on the ground that the statute did not apply to a lawsuit between two private litigants. *Elane Photography*, 309 P.2d at 76. As explored later in this chapter, the impact of so-called religious liberty statutes on matters of LGBT equality has been the subject of much controversy.

5. For a comprehensive assessment of how conservative politicians and activists used the question of religious exemptions as part of a larger strategy to both block the spread of marriage equality and to limit its impact, see Douglas NeJaime and Reva B. Siegel, "Conscience Wars: Complicity-Based Conscience Claims in Religion and Politics," 124 *Yale Law Journal* 2516 (2015).

6. Manhattan Declaration, available at http://www.manhattandeclaration. org/#0.

7. Brief Amicus Curiae of United States Conference of Catholic Bishops in Support of Respondents and Supporting Affirmance, Obergefell v. Hodges, 135 S. Ct. 2584 (2015) (No. 14-556), 31.

8. For an exploration of the Catholic Charities controversy in Boston, see Martha Minow, "Should Religious Groups Be Exempt from Civil Rights Laws?,"

48 *Boston College Law Review* 781 (2007).

9. Laurie Goodstein, "Bishops Say Rules on Gay Parents Limit Freedom of Religion," *New York Times*, December 28, 2011.

10. Bernstein v. Ocean Grove Camp Meeting, New Jersey Division of Civil Rights Docket PN34XB-03008 (2012). For an exploration of the Ocean Grove case, see Ira C. Lupu and Robert W. Tuttle, "Same-Sex Family Equality and Religious Freedom," 5 *Northwestern Journal of Law and Social Policy* 274 (2010).

11. See, e.g., Craig v. Masterpiece Cakeshop, Inc., 2015 WL 4760453 (Col. Ct. App.); In re Matter of Klein, Oregon Bureau of Labor and Industries, Case No. 44-14 & 45-14 (2015); State v. Arlene's Flowers, Inc., No. 13-2-00871-5 (Wash. Super. Ct. Feb. 18, 2015); Gifford v. McCarthy, 137 A.D.3d 30 (N.Y. App. Div. 2016).

12. Douglas NeJaime and Elizabeth Sepper have also contended that the scope of religious exemptions from LGBT equality measures should be determined from within the purview of antidiscrimination law. See Douglas NeJaime, "Marriage Inequality: Same-Sex Relationships, Religious Exemptions, and the Production of Sexual Orientation Discrimination," 100 *California Law Review* 1169 (2012); Elizabeth Sepper, "Doctoring Discrimination in the Same-Sex Marriage Debates," 89 *Indiana Law Journal* 703 (2014).

13. Employment Division v. Smith, 494 U.S. 872 (1990). It bears noting that the Court, in the decades before *Smith*, held that the Free Exercise Clause required exemptions for religious actors in some circumstances. See Wisconsin v. Yoder, 406 U.S. 205 (1972) (requiring exemption for the Amish from a compulsory education law); Sherbert v. Verner, 374 U.S. 398 (1963) (requiring exemption from denial of unemployment benefits to Seventh Day Adventist after she was fired for refusing to work on Saturdays, her faith's Sabath Day).

14. *Smith*, 494 U.S. at 878, 885.

15. Ibid., 889, 888.

16. Ibid., 890.

17. See, e.g., United States v. O'Brien, 391 U.S. 367, 376 (1968).

18. Religious Freedom Restoration Act of 1993, 42 U.S.C. §§ 2000bb–2000b-4.

19. City of Boerne v. Flores, 521 U.S. 507 (1997).

20. Religious Freedom Restoration Act of 1993, Judiciary Committee, H.R. Rep. 103-88, 103rd Cong., 1st Sess. (May 11, 1993), 9; Religious Freedom Restoration Act of 1993, Judiciary Committee, S. Rep. 103-11, 103rd Cong., 1st Sess. (July 27, 1993), 13.

21. 139 Congressional Record H2356 (1993); 139 Congressional Record S14350 (1993).

22. Alex J. Luchenitser, "A New Era of Inequality? *Hobby Lobby* and Religious Exemptions from Discrimination," 9 *Harvard Law and Policy Review* 63, 84 (2015). There is a disagreement among judges and commentators over whether RFRA can be used as a defense in litigation between private parties, such as in discrimination claims brought by private-sector employees

against their employers. For the argument that RFRA applies to private claims, see Shruti Chaganti, "Why the Religious Freedom Restoration Act Provides a Defense in Suits by Private Plaintiffs," 99 *Virginia Law Review* 343 (2013). For the opposite contention, see James M. Oleske Jr., "Obamacare, RFRA, and the Perils of Legislative History," 67 *Vanderbilt Law Review En Banc* 77 (2014).

23. Baehr v. Lewin, 852 P.2d 44 (Ha. 1993).

24. Romer v. Evans, 517 U.S. 620 (1996).

25. Thomas v. Anchorage Equal Rights Commission, 165 F.3d 692 (9th Cir. 1999), reversed on other grounds by 220 F.3d 1134 (9th Cir. 2000) (en banc). Around this time, other courts entertained, but ultimately rejected, similar claims on behalf of religious landlords. See, e.g., Swanner v. Anchorage Equal Rights Commission, 874 P.2d 274 (Alaska 1994); Smith v. Fair Employment and Housing Commission, 913 P.2d 909 (Ca. 1996); Attorney General v. Desilets, 636 N.E.2d 233 (Mass. 1994). Although these cases involved questions of marital-status discrimination against heterosexual cohabiting couples, it was widely understood that if religious landlords prevailed in such cases, they would also likely prevail in discrimination cases brought by lesbian, gay, and bisexual tenants.

26. See Religious Liberty Protection Act: Hearings on H.R. 1691 before the Subcommittee on the Constitution of the House Comm. on the Judiciary, 106th Congress (May 12, 1999) (statement of Christopher E. Anders, Legislative Counsel to the American Civil Liberties Union); ACLU, Effect of the Religious Liberty Protection Act on State and Local Civil Rights Laws (January 25, 1999), available at http://www.aclu.org/religion-belief/ effect-religious-liberty-protection-act-state-and-local-civil-rights-laws.

27. Patricia Salkin and Amy Lavine, "The Genesis of RLUIPA and Federalism," 40 *Urban Lawyer* 195, 206 (2008). The scope of the Religious Liberty Protection Act was later narrowed to apply only to land use and prison regulations. The narrower measure became the Religious Land Uses and Institutionalized Persons Act of 2000.

28. For an exploration of the same-sex marriage cases brought in the early 1970s, see Michael Boucai, "Glorious Precedents: When Gay Marriage Was Radical," 27 *Yale Journal of Law and Humanities* 1 (2015). For a discussion of the ways in which the LGBT movement's priorities have shifted through the decades, see Carlos A. Ball, "A New Stage for the LGBT Movement: Protecting Gender and Sexual Multiplicities," in *After Marriage Equality: The Future of LGBT Rights*, Carlos A. Ball, ed. (New York: New York University Press, 2016), 157.

29. Carlos A. Ball, *From the Closet to the Courtroom: Five LGBT Cases that Have Changed Our Nation* (Boston: Beacon Press, 2010), 165–166.

30. *Baehr*, 852 P.2d 44.

31. Baker v. State, 744 A.2d 864 (Vt. 1999).

32. Goodridge v. Department of Public Health, 798 N.E.2d 941 (Mass. 2003).

33. In re Marriage Cases, 183 P.3d 384 (Ca. 2008); Kerrigan v. Commissioner of Public Health, 957 A.2d 407 (Conn. 2008); Varnum v. Brien, 763 N.W.2d 862 (Iowa 2009).

34. Conaway v. Deane, 932 A.2d 571 (Md. 2007); Hernandez v. Robles, 855 N.E.2d 1 (NY 2006); Andersen v. King County, 138 P.3d 963 (Wash. 2006).

35. Abby Godnough, "New Hampshire Legalizes Same-Sex Marriage," *New York Times*, June 3, 2009; Michael J. Klarman, *From the Closet to the Altar: Courts, Backlash, and the Struggle for Same-Sex Marriage* (New York: Oxford University Press, 2013), 129.

36. New Hampshire House Bill 73 (2009); New Hampshire House Bill 436 (2009).

37. Godnough, *New Hampshire Legalizes Same-Sex Marriage.*

38. Connecticut General Statues Annotated, §46b–35a; Vt. Stat. Ann. tit. 8, §4501(b), tit. 9, §4502(l); D.C. Code §46-406(e). The Connecticut and New Hampshire statutes also contained exemptions for fraternal organizations associated with religious entities. The exemptions allowed those groups to determine membership criteria, and to deny insurance benefits, according to their religious views.

39. Jeremy W. Peters, "New York State Senate Turns Back Bill on Gay Marriage," *New York Times*, December 3, 2009.

40. Danny Hakim, "Exemption Were Key to Vote on Gay Marriage," *New York Times*, June 26, 2011. For the religious exemptions to New York's marriage law, see N.Y. Dom. Rel. Law §10-b.

41. See, e.g., Letter from Robin Fretwell Wilson et al. to Governor Pat Quinn, Illinois (December 18, 2012), available at http://mirrorofjustice.blogs.com/files/ill-letter-12-2012.pdf; Letter from Douglas Laycock et al. to Lisa Brown, Senate Majority Leader, Washington State Senate (January 28, 2012), available at http://mirrorofjustice.blogs.com/files/washington2012-me-too-brown.pdf.

42. Robin Fretwell Wilson, "Marriage of Necessity: Same-Sex Marriage and Religious Liberty Protections," 64 *Case Western Reserve Law Review* 1161, 1193 (2014).

43. Letter from Robin Fretwell Wilson et al. to Governor Pat Quinn, Illinois, 1.

44. Haw. Rev. Stat. §§572-E, 572B-9.5; Md. Code Ann., Fam. Law §2-202; Minn. Stat. §517.201(1); R.I. Gen. Laws §15-3-6.1(a), (c)(2), (d), (e) (2013); Wash. Rev. Code §§ 26.04.010(5), (6), (7), 26.04.900.

45. The Illinois exemption applies only to religious organizations in their operation of "facilities." See 750 Ill. Comp. Stat. 5/209 (a-10). The Maine statute exempts the performing or hosting of marriages by religious organizations. See Maine Revised Statutes 19-A, §655(3).

46. Del. Code Ann. tit. 13, §106.

47. Hollingsworth v. Perry, 133 S. Ct. 2652 (2013).

48. United States v. Windsor, 133 S. Ct. 2675 (2013).

49. Arizona Statute §41-1493.01.

50. Arizona Senate Bill 1062 (2014).

51. Fernanda Santos, "Arizona Governor Vetoes Bill on Refusal of Service to Gays," *New York Times*, February 26, 2014.

52. Reid Wilson, "Mississippi Passes Arizona-Style Religious Freedom Bill," *Washington Post*, April 1, 2014.

53. Indiana SB 101 (2015); Arkansas HB 1228 (2015).

54. Baskin v. Bogan, 766 F.3d 648 (7th Cir. 2014); Jernigan v. Crane, 64 F. Supp.3d 1260 (E.D. Ark. 2014).

55. Michael Barbaro and Erik Eckholm, "Indiana Law Denounced as Invitation to Discriminate Against Gays," *New York Times*, March 27, 2015.

56. Monica Davey, Campbell Robertson, and Richard Perez-Peña, "Indiana and Arkansas Revise Rights Bills, Seeking to Remove Divisive Parts," *New York Times*, April 2, 2015. For the replacement provision enacted into law, see Indiana Senate Bill 50 (2015).

57. Campbell Robertson, "Arkansas Moves to Revise Legislation as Concerns of Religion and Gay Rights Intensify," *New York Times*, April 1, 2015.

58. Davey et al., *Indiana and Arkansas Revise Rights Bill*; Arkansas Senate Bill 975 (2015).

59. Richard Fausset and Alan Blinder, "States Renew Fight to Stop Same-Sex Marriage," *New York Times*, January 28, 2015.

60. Ibid.

61. Alan Blinder, "Alabama Judge Defies Gay Marriage Law," *New York Times*, February 9, 2015.

62. Associated Press, "Confusion Reigns over Same-Sex Marriage in Alabama," February 11, 2015.

63. Campbell Robertson, "Alabama Court Orders a Halt to Same-Sex Marriage Licenses," *New York Times*, March 3, 2015.

64. Richard Fausset, "Federal Court in Alabama Is Asked to Clear Way for Same-Sex Marriages," *New York Times*, March 6, 2015.

65. Associated Press, "9 Alabama Counties Still Not Issuing Gay Marriage Licenses," July 22, 2015. In 2016, Roy Moore, the chief justice of the Alabama Supreme Court, issued an administrative order prohibiting probate judges from granting marriage licenses to same-sex couples. Alan Blinder, "Top Alabama Judge Orders Halt to Same-Sex Marriage Licenses," *New York Times*, January 6, 2016. Several months later, the state's Court of the Judiciary suspended the chief justice for the remainder of his term on the ground that he had violated the state's canon of judicial ethics by instructing probate judges to defy federal law. Campbell Robertson, "Roy Moore, Alabama Chief Justice, Suspended over Gay Marriage Order," *New York Times*, September 30, 2016.

66. The First Amendment Defense Act, H.R. 2802, S. 1598, Sec. 3(a), 114th Cong. (2015).

67. After the original FADA bill was introduced, some conservative legislators proposed a modified version. Although somewhat narrower than the

original, the modified version would still preclude the federal government from denying a job, grant, contract, or benefit to persons who treat sexual minorities (or heterosexuals who have sex outside of marriages) differently as long as the reasons for doing so are grounded in religious or moral doctrine.

68. "Memorandum on the First Amendment Defense Act," Public Rights/Private Conscience Project, Columbia Law School, July 11, 2016.

69. North Carolina General Statutes Annotated §51-5.5.

70. Utah Code Annotated § 17-20-4.

71. Sheryl Gay Stolberg, "Kentucky Clerk's Defiance Tests Boundaries of Gay Marriage Ruling," *New York Times*, August 14, 2015.

72. Alan Blinder and Tamar Lewin, "Clerk in Kentucky Chooses Jail over Deal on Same-Sex Marriage," *New York Times*, September 3, 2015.

73. Alan Blinder, "Kentucky Clerk Allows Same-Sex Licenses, but Questions Legality," *New York Times*, September 15, 2015.

74. Kentucky Senate Bill 216 (2016).

75. Alan Blinder and Richard Perez-Peña, "Georgia Governor Rejects Shielding Critics of Same-Sex Marriage," *New York Times*, March 29, 2016.

76. Mississippi House Bill 1523 (2016).

77. The state of Mississippi has never enacted a provision rendering discrimination against LGBT people illegal. A tiny number of local regulations in the state may protect LGBT individuals from discrimination by places of public accommodation. "Mississippi H.B. 1523 and the Establishment Clause," Public Rights/Private Conscience Project, Columbia Law School, April 5, 2016, 3, available at http://web.law.columbia.edu/sites/default/files/microsites/gender-sexuality/files/memo_regarding_ms_hb1523.pdf.

78. The day before the Mississippi law was to go into effect, a federal district court struck it down as unconstitutional under the Establishment Clause and the Equal Protection Clause. See Barber v. Bryant, 2016 WL 3562647 (S.D. Miss).

79. On ENDA's legislative history regarding religious exemptions, see Steven H. Aden and Stanley W. Carlson-Theis, "Catch or Release? The Employment Non-Discrimination Act's Exemption for Religious Organizations," 11 *Engage: Federalist Society Practice Groups* 4 (2010); Julie Dabrowski, "The Exception that Doesn't Prove the Rule: Why Congress Should Narrow ENDA's Religious Exemption to Protect the Rights of LGBT Employees," 63 *American University Law Review* 1957 (2014).

80. Michelle Boorstein, "Faith Leaders: Exempt Religious Groups from Order Barring LGBT Bias in Hiring," *Washington Post*, July 2, 2014. In his executive order, President Obama did not include an exemption allowing federal contractors to discriminate on the basis of sexual orientation or gender identity on religious grounds. See Executive Order No. 13672 (2014).

81. Equality Act, U.S. Senate Bill 1858 (2015).

82. Burwell v. Hobby Lobby Stores, Inc., 134 S. Ct. 2751 (2014).

83. United States v. Lee, 455 U.S. 252, 261 (1982). For a thoughtful and thorough exploration of the likely impact of *Hobby Lobby* on questions related to religious exemptions, see Ira C. Lupu, "*Hobby Lobby* and the Dubious Enterprise of Religious Exemptions," 38 *Harvard Journal of Law & Gender* 35 (2015).

84. *Hobby Lobby*, 134 S. Ct. at 2784.

85. Ibid., 2804–2805.

86. It is worth noting that, as explained in Chapter 5, the Court has rejected the notion that for-profit entities have a First Amendment right to discriminate on the basis of gender, as an all-male law firm partnership argued in the 1980s. See Hishon v. King & Spalding, 467 U.S. 69, 78 (1984).

87. *Romer*, 517 U.S. 620.

88. Lawrence v. Texas, 539 U.S. 620 (2003).

89. *Windsor*, 133 S. Ct. 2675.

90. *Obergefell*, 135 S. Ct. 2584.

91. Fay Botham, *Almighty God Created the Races: Christianity, Interracial Marriage, and American Law* (Chapel Hill: University of North Carolina Press, 2009); James M. Oleske Jr., "The Evolution of Accommodation: Comparing the Unequal Treatment of Religious Objections to Interracial and Same-Sex Marriages," 50 *Harvard Civil Rights-Civil Liberties Review* 99 (2015).

92. Brief of Douglas Laycock et al., as Amici Curiae in Support of Petitioners, Obergefell v. Hodges, 135 S. Ct. 2584 (2015), 2–3.

93. *Obergefell*, 135 S. Ct. at 2602.

94. Ibid., 2607.

95. Ibid., 2637.

96. Ibid., 2625.

97. Ibid., 2625–2626.

98. The Supreme Court upheld the constitutionality, under the Establishment Clause, of Title VII's principal religious exemption in *Corporation of the Presiding Bishop v. Amos*, 483 U.S. 327 (1987). In doing so, the justices explained that the type of case-by-case analysis required by an exemption scheme that only covers the religious activities of religious organizations may lead to problematic levels of governmental intrusiveness in the internal affairs of those organizations and to self-imposed restraints on how they go about pursuing their spiritual missions. See *Amos*, 483 U.S. at 336 (majority opinion); 343–344 (Brennan, J., concurring).

99. See, e.g., Florida Statutes Annotated §760.10(9) (employment and public accommodations); N.Y. Exec. Law § 296(11) (employment and housing).

100. See, e.g., Rayburn v. General Conference of Seventh-Day Adventists, 772 F.2d 1164, 1166 (4th Cir. 1985).

101. See, e.g., New Jersey Statutes Annotated §10:5-12; Oregon Statutes §659A.006. Utah appears to be anomalous in that it categorically exempts religious organizations from the state's employment antidiscrimination law, allowing such organizations to make all employment distinctions on any basis, including race, national origin, and sex. See Utah Code Annotated

§34A-5-102(h)(ii). The religious exemption that is part of Title IX of the Education Amendments of 1972 is also unusually broad in that it exempts educational institutions that receive federal funds from the statute's prohibition of sex discrimination when such a prohibition "would not be consistent with the religious tenets of such organization." 20 U.S.C. § 1681(a)(3). For a detailed analysis of Title IX's religious exemption, see Kif Augustine-Adams, "Religious Exemptions to Title IX," 65 *University of Kansas Law Review* (forthcoming, 2017).

102. Executive Order No. 13,279 (2002).

103. For this reason, it is unfortunate that the Employment Non-Discrimination Act (ENDA), as introduced in Congress several times between 1994 and 2014, included a religious exemption that was much broader than that contained in Title VII—it categorically exempted religious organizations from any obligation not to discriminate in employment matters on the basis of sexual orientation and gender identity. It is simply not the case, as some supporters of religious exemptions from antidiscrimination obligations have claimed, that the ENDA exemption essentially tracked the one contained in Title VII. For an example of such a claim, see Robin Fretwell Wilson, "Bargaining for Religious Accommodations: Same-Sex Marriage and LGBT Rights after *Hobby Lobby*," in *The Rise of Corporate Religious Liberty*, Micah Schwartzman, Chad Flanders, and Zoë Robinson, eds. (New York: Oxford University Press, 2016), 257, 258.

104. *Craig*, 2015 WL 4760453 at *7n8.

105. Ira Lupu, "Moving Targets: *Obergefell*, *Hobby Lobby*, and the Future of LGBT Rights," 7 *Alabama Civil Rights & Civil Liberties Law Review* 1 (2015).

106. This point was recognized by the Department of Justice during the presidency of George W. Bush. See Memorandum for William P. Marshall, Deputy Counsel to the President, Office of Legal Counsel, Department of Justice, October 12, 2000, 2 (concluding that the Title VII religious exemption "does not permit an employer to escape Title VII proscriptions against race and sex discrimination, even when the employer may be religiously motivated to engage in such forms of discrimination"). A federal appellate court has held that a religious school, which denied health insurance benefits to married women while providing them to married men, violated Title VII and was not entitled to immunity under the statute's religious exemption even though the school's view that only a man can be "head of the household" in a marriage was grounded in religious doctrine. EEOC v. Fremont Christian School, 781 F.2d 1362 (9th Cir 1986).

107. See Herx v. Diocese of Fort Wayne–South Bend, 48 F. Supp.3d 1168 (N.D. Ind. 2014); Herx v. Diocese of Fort Wayne–South Bend, 2015 WL 1013783 (N.D. Ind.).

108. Little v. Wuerl, 929 F.2d 944, 951 (3rd Cir. 1991).

109. See *Fremont Christian School*, 781 F.2d 1362.

110. See, e.g., Rhode Island General Laws §28-5-6(8)(ii); Oregon Statutes

§659A.006(4).

111. EEOC v. Townley Engineering & Manufacturing Co., 859 F.2d 610, 618 (9th Cir. 1988)

112. LeBoon v. Lancaster Jewish Community Center, 503 F.3d 217 (3rd Cir. 2007).

113. N.Y. Dom. Rel. Law §10-b(2).

114. 118 Congressional Record 1976 (1972).

115. Senator Ervin argued "that a small businessman ought to have the liberty to employ a person of his own race instead of a person of another race. I do not think there is any evil or any wickedness or any iniquity in a small businessman enjoying that right." Ibid.

116. Although Title VII excludes small business—those with fewer than fifteen employees—from its coverage, that exclusion is not a religious exemption. Instead, it spares all businesses under a certain size from the legal obligations imposed by the statute.

117. Luchenitser, *A New Era of Inequality?*, 77 (citing *Townley Engineering*).

118. 42 U.S.C. §3607(a).

119. 42 U.S.C. §12113(d)(1). Similarly, Title III of the ADA, which prohibits discrimination by places of public accommodation on the basis of disability, exempts only "religious organizations or entities controlled by religious organizations, including places of worship." 42 U.S.C. §12187.

120. For a discussion of religious exemptions from state laws prohibiting sexual orientation discrimination, see NeJaime, *Marriage Inequality*, 1190–1195.

121. Newman v. Piggie Park Enterprises, 390 U.S. 400, 402n5 (1968).

122. Western Turf Association v. Greenberg, 204 U.S. 359, 363–364 (1904).

123. Heart of Atlanta Motel, Inc. v. United States, 379 U.S. 241, 259 (1964).

124. Runyon v. McReary, 427 U.S. 160, 174–175 (1976); *Hishon*, 467 U.S. at 78.

125. Roberts v. United States Jaycees, 468 U.S. 609, 634–635 (1984). As Dale Carpenter notes, the Court in its freedom of association cases "has implicitly adopted a distinction between expressive associations (generally protected from the application of anti-discrimination law) and primarily commercial associations (not strongly protected)." Dale Carpenter, "Expressive Association and Anti-Discrimination Law after *Dale*: A Tripartite Approach," 85 *Minnesota Law Review* 1515, 1564 (2001). Carpenter defends the distinction, as does Seana Shiffrin in "What Is Really Wrong with Compelled Association?," 99 *Northwestern University Law Review* 839 (2005). For the argument that the freedom of association should prohibit, in the absence of monopoly power, the application of antidiscrimination laws in cases involving commercial associations, see Richard A. Epstein, "Public Accommodations Under the Civil Rights Act of 1964: Why Freedom of Association Counts as a Human Right," 66 *Stanford Law Review* 1241 (2014). Others have criticized the use of the commercial versus noncommercial distinction in determining the scope of First Amendment immunity from the application of antidiscrimination laws. See, e.g., John D. Inazu, "The Unsettling 'Well-Settled' Law of Freedom of Association," 43 *Connecticut Law Review* 149, 188 (2010).

126. Citizens United v. Federal Elections Commission, 558 U.S. 310 (2010).

127. For a volume of essays generally discussing this topic, see Schwartzman et al., *The Rise of Corporate Religious Liberty*. It bears noting that the Court in *Hobby Lobby* could muster only one example of a religious exemption that covers for-profit entities. *Hobby Lobby*, 134 S. Ct. at 2773 (citing 42 U.S.C. §300(a)-7(b)(2)) (prohibiting the government from requiring an entity that receives federal funds from making its facilities available for sterilization and abortion procedures).

128. *Hobby Lobby*, 134 S. Ct. at 2760.

129. Ibid., at 2787.

130. See, e.g., Nelson Tebbe, *Religious Freedom in an Egalitarian Age* (Cambridge, MA: Harvard University Press, 2017), 55.

131. 42 U.S.C. §2000e(j). In interpreting this provision, the Supreme Court has held that Title VII does not require an accommodation that imposes more than a de minimis burden on others. See Trans World Airline, Inc. v. Hardison, 432 U.S. 63, 84 (1977). It should be noted that Title VII does not apply to elected officials.

132. See, e.g., Endres v. Indiana State Police, 349 F.3d 922, 925 (7th Cir. 2003); Rodriguez v. City of Chicago, 156 F.3d 771, 778 (7th Cir. 1998) (Posner, J., concurring).

133. My argument is not that religious government employees should never be granted accommodations under Title VII. Such accommodations may be appropriate in some contexts. See, e.g., American Postal Workers Union v. Postmaster General, 781 F.2d 772 (9th Cir. 1986) (concluding that Title VII might require accommodating postal workers who have religious objections to processing draft registration forms). My point is instead that Title VII should not be understood to require public employers to accommodate religious employees when they refuse to serve particular classes of individuals protected by antidiscrimination laws.

134. See Miller v. Davis, 123 F. Supp.3d 924, 943 (D. Ky. 2015).

135. This was the conclusion of a federal district judge who issued a preliminary injunction prohibiting the enforcement of the Mississippi law. See Barber v. Bryant, 2016 WL 3562647 (S.D. Miss).

136. For a detailed discussion of the legal issues raised by the Kentucky county clerk case, see Ruth Colker, "Religious Accommodations for County Clerks?," 76 *Ohio State Law Journal Furthermore* 87 (2015). The Vermont Supreme Court has deemed "highly questionable the proposition that a public official—here a town clerk—can retain public office while refusing to perform a generally applicable duty of that office on religious grounds." Brady v. Dean, 790 A.2d 428, 434 (Vt. 2001). For its part, the Rhode Island Supreme Court has rejected the contention that requiring firefighters who object to same-sex sexual conduct on religious grounds to drive a fire truck as part of a gay pride parade violated their freedom of speech or of religion under the First Amendment. Farbrizio v. City of Providence, 104 A.3d 1289

(R.I. 2014).

137. It is worth noting that accommodating religious government clerks by removing their names, but not their official titles, from the marriage licenses (as Kentucky has done) may be appropriate. This type of limited accommodation may be acceptable because it is less likely to engender the status of second-class citizenship that would accompany a more expansive exemption allowing public officials to cease issuing marriage licenses altogether because of their religious objections to same-sex marriages.

138. Nelson Tebbe points out that judges who oppose the death penalty are allowed to recuse themselves from death penalty cases and that judges who oppose abortion are able to recuse themselves from so-called judicial bypass proceedings that allow minors to choose an abortion without parental consent. Tebbe, *Religious Freedom in an Egalitarian Age*, Ch. 9.

139. It has been suggested that religious organizations that discriminate against LGBT people should lose their tax-exempt status. See, e.g.. Austin Caster, "'Charitable Discrimination': Why Taxpayers Should Not Have to Fund 501(c)(3) Organizations that Discriminate Against LGBT Employees," 24 *Regent University Law Review* 403 (2012); Felix Salmon, "Does Your Church Ban Gay Marriage? Then It Should Start Paying Taxes," Fusion, June 29, 2015, available at http://fusion.net/story/158096/does-your-church-ban-gay-marriage-then-it-should-start-paying-taxes/. It is true that the Supreme Court has held, in the context of educational institutions that discriminate on the basis of race (as discussed in Chapter 6), that such revocations are constitutional. Bob Jones University v. United States, 461 U.S. 574 (1983). Nonetheless, the government's revocations of religious organizations' tax-exempt status in order to advance antidiscrimination objectives have been extremely rare. As a result, I do not believe it would be appropriate for the government to take away the tax-exempt status of religious organizations on the ground that they discriminate against LGBT people.

140. Alan Brownstein, "Gays, Jews, and Other Strangers in a Strange Land: The Case for Reciprocal Accommodation of Religious Liberty and the Right of Same-Sex Couples to Marry," 45 *University of San Francisco Law Review* 389, 409–410 (2010).

141. It bears noting that some academic supporters of broad religious exemptions have called for exemptions that would allow religious organizations to deny goods, services, and facilities to married same-sex couples *at any time*, not just during the solemnization or celebration of their marriages. See, e.g., Letter from Robin Fretwell Wilson et al. to Governor Pat Quinn, Illinois, 2.

142. For a detailed analysis of exemptions from public accommodation laws, including the limited number of such laws that contain religious exemptions, see Elizabeth Sepper, "The Role of Religion in State Public Accommodation Laws," 61 *St. Louis University Law Journal* (forthcoming, 2017).

143. Sepper, *The Role of Religion in State Public Accommodation Laws*.

144. It is important to keep in mind that in order for a state antidiscrimination

law to apply in this context, *the religious organization must operate a place of public accommodation.* This means, as a general matter, that the organization must make its goods, services, or facilities available to the general public. As a result, for example, a meeting hall owned by a Catholic organization used for the celebration of only Catholic weddings would not be subject to antidiscrimination laws because the organization does not make it available to the general public. In contrast, if the same organization makes its hall available for weddings regardless of their religious content, then the facility may qualify as a place of accommodation within the meaning of antidiscrimination laws.

If the rate of litigation over these matters is any indication, it is rare for a public accommodation antidiscrimination law to be applied to the provision of wedding-related goods, services, or facilities made available to the general public by religious organizations. In fact, in the context of LGBT issues, the only such litigated case I am aware of is a New Jersey dispute from the early 2000s in which a state agency determined that a Methodist association, which rented out its beachfront boardwalk pavilion to members of the public for many different kinds of events and celebrations including marriages but refused to permit a same-sex couple to celebrate their civil union at its facility, had violated New Jersey's law against discrimination on the basis of sexual orientation. See *Bernstein,* New Jersey Division of Civil Rights Docket PN34XB-03008 (2012). Most of the disputes involving the provision of goods, services, or facilities for the celebration of same-sex unions have arisen not in the context of religious organizations, but in that of for-profit entities that make no claim to be religious organizations (though the owners profess to religious beliefs that are inconsistent with LGBT equality). This litigation pattern makes sense because the vast majority of places of public accommodation that provide goods, services, or facilities for wedding celebrations are for-profit enterprises that have no religious affiliations.

145. See Nelson Tebbe, "Religion and Marriage Equality Statutes," 9 *Harvard Law & Policy Review* 25 (2015).

146. Andrew Koppelman, *Antidiscrimination Law and Social Equality* (New Haven, CT: Yale University Press, 1996).

147. Douglas Laycock, Afterword to *Same-Sex Marriage and Religious Liberty: Emerging Conflicts,* Douglas Laycock, Anthony R. Picarello Jr., and Robin Fretwell Wilson, eds. (Lanham, MD: Rowman & Littlefield, 2008), 198.

148. Thomas C. Berg, "What Same-Sex-Marriage and Religious-Liberty Claims Have in Common," 5 *Northwestern Journal of Law & Social Policy* 206, 229 (2010).

149. See, e.g., Andrew Koppelman, "Gay Rights, Religious Accommodations, and the Purposes of Antidiscrimination Law," 88 *Southern California Law Review* 619, 643–644 (2015). Elizabeth Sepper has questioned the claim that such requests are or will become rare. Elizabeth Sepper, "Gays in the Moralized Marketplace," 7 *Alabama Civil Rights & Civil Liberties Law Review* 129, 162–165 (2015).

150. Exemption supporters also minimize the difficulties of implementing legislative exemption schemes that would require judges to assess market conditions to determine when there are sufficient alternative providers willing to serve LGBT people so as to trigger the applicability of the exemption. It is unclear, for example, at what point same-sex couples would be permitted to stop searching for businesses willing to serve them. Would sexual minorities be entitled to sue for discrimination after they are turned down by two businesses, or would they have to wait until they are turned down by five or ten? For other practical questions and concerns about proposals aimed at exempting for-profit businesses from LGBT equality measures, see Mary Anne Case, "Why 'Live-and-Let-Live' is not a Viable Solution to the Difficult Problems of Religious Accommodations in the Age of Sexual Civil Rights," 88 *Southern California Law Review* 463, 470n28 (2015); Sepper, *Gays in the Moralized Marketplace*, 156–157.

151. Chai R. Feldblum, "Moral Conflict and Conflicting Liberties," in *Same-Sex Marriage and Religious Liberty*, Laycock et al., eds., 153.

152. Deborah Hellman, *When Is Discrimination Wrong?* (Cambridge, MA: Harvard University Press, 2008), 28.

153. NeJaime and Siegel, *Conscience Wars*, 2577.

154. Ibid., 2577–2578.

155. Civil Rights Act of 1964, S. Rep. 88-872, 88th Cong., 2d Sess. 1964, 16.

156. Ibid.

157. *Roberts*, 468 U.S. at 625.

158. This point has been made by other commentators. See, e.g., NeJaime and Siegel, *Conscience Wars*, 2526 (discussing *Wisconsin v. Yoder* and *Sherbert v. Verner*). The granting of exemptions that generate significant third-party harms raises questions under the Establishment Clause. See Estate of Thornton v. Caldor, Inc, 472 U.S. 703, 709 (1985); Cutter v. Wilkinson, 544 U.S. 709, 720 (2005). For discussions of Establishment Clause limits to the scope of religious exemptions based on harms to third parties, see Frederick Mark Gedicks and Andrew Koppelman, "Is *Hobby Lobby* Worse for Religious Freedom than *Smith*?," 10 *University of St. Thomas Journal of Law and Public Policy* (forthcoming, 2017); Frederick Mark Gedicks and Rebecca G. Van Tassell, "Of Burdens and Baselines: *Hobby Lobby*'s Puzzling Footnote 37," in Schwartzman et al., *The Rise of Corporate Religious Liberty*, 323. For an extensive discussion of the role that avoiding harms to others should play in determining the scope and applicability of religious exemptions from antidiscrimination laws, see Tebbe, *Religious Freedom in an Egalitarian Age*, Ch. 3.

159. Douglas Laycock and Thomas Berg, "Protecting Same-Sex Marriage and Religious Liberty," 99 *Virginia Law Review In Brief* 1, 3–5 (2013).

160. Thomas C. Berg, "Religious Accommodation and the Welfare State," 38 *Harvard Journal of Law & Gender* 103, 115 (2015).

161. Laycock, Afterword, 195.

162. Berg, *What Same-Sex-Marriage and Religious-Liberty Claims Have in Common*, 235.

163. Wilson, "Matters of Conscience: Lessons for Same-Sex Marriage from the Healthcare Context," in *Same-Sex Marriage and Religious Liberty*, Laycock, et al., eds., 101.

164. There is an extensive literature on the ways in which some religious denominations relied on religious claims to defend racial inequality in the United States from before the Civil War through the civil rights era. See, e.g., Botham, *Almighty God Created the Races*; Jane Dailey, "Sex, Segregation, and the Sacred after *Brown*," 91 *Journal of American* History 119 (2004); William N. Eskridge Jr., "Noah's Curse: How Religion Often Conflates Status, Belief, and Conduct to Resist Antidiscrimination Norms," 45 *Georgia Law Review* 657 (2011).

165. For example, although the Supreme Court in *Bob Jones University* rejected the university's contention that its religious-based understandings of racial equality precluded the government from withdrawing tax benefits because of the institution's race-based policies, it accepted the proposition that the university had "a genuine belief that the Bible forbids interracial dating and marriage." *Bob Jones University*, 461 U.S. at 602n28. See also Ira C. Lupu, "Where Rights Begin: The Problem of Burdens on the Free Exercise of Religion," 102 *Harvard Law Review* 933, 954 (1989) ("the inquiry into sincerity cannot completely escape the distinctly bad aroma of an inquisition. The decisionmaker can rarely be morally certain that the claimant is not sincere in his professed religious commitments."); United States v. Ballard, 322 U.S. 78, 87 (1944) ("The religious views espoused by respondents might seem incredible, if not preposterous, to most people. But if those doctrines are subject to trial before a jury charged with finding their truth or falsity, then the same can be done with the religious beliefs of any sect. When the triers of fact undertake that task, they enter a forbidden domain.").

Conclusion

1. See, e.g., Leslie C. Griffin, "A Word of Warning from a Woman: Arbitrary, Categorical, and Hidden Religious Exemptions Threaten LGBT Rights," 7 *Alabama Civil Rights & Civil Liberties Law Review* 97 (2015).

2. Douglas Laycock and Thomas Berg, "Protecting Same-Sex Marriage and Religious Liberty," 99 *Virginia Law Review In Brief* 1, 3 (2013).

Acknowledgments

The generosity and support of many individuals contributed in crucial ways to the writing of this book. Andy Koppelman and Nelson Tebbe read earlier versions of the entire manuscript. Both Andy and Nelson have thought long and hard about many of the issues explored here, and they provided me with extremely helpful guidance and suggestions. I am also deeply appreciative of colleagues who read sections of the manuscript at different points in its development and gave me thoughtful comments and suggestions for improvement: Erez Aloni, Mary Bernstein, Dale Carpenter, Donna Dennis, Carlos Gonzalez, Doug NeJaime, Elizabeth Sepper, Brian Soucek, and Timothy Zick. I also thank the peer reviewers used by Harvard University Press for engaging with the manuscript so thoroughly and for their extensive comments and insights.

I presented sections of the manuscript at the 2016 annual meetings of the Association of American Law Schools (New York City) and of the Law and Society Association (New Orleans), at a book symposium at St. John's University School of Law on religious exemptions, as well as at faculty workshops on the Camden and Newark campuses of the Rutgers Law School. Many thanks to those who attended these events for their participation, questions, and suggestions. Thank you as well to the Lesbian Herstory Archives in Brooklyn, New York, for making its extensive collection available to researchers like me. And thank you to my research assistant Blan Jarkasi for spending countless hours studying the legislative history of the Civil Rights Act of 1964.

Two editors were instrumental in the publication of this book. At the beginning, Brian Distelberg saw the project's potential and helped me distill some of its major themes. More recently, the project has benefited immensely from Thomas LeBien's considerable editorial expertise and good judgment.

Large portions of this book were written while on sabbatical in Barcelona, Spain, in the company of my beloved husband, Richard Storrow, and our beautiful sons, Sebastian and Emmanuel. Those precious months in Barcelona confirmed to me how incredibly fortunate I am both to cherish what I do for a living and to be able to do it while nourished and strengthened by their love.

Finally, this book is dedicated to four very special individuals in my life whose love, friendship, and guidance since I was a child have helped make me the person who I am.

Index

9 780674 972193